HARD BROKE

HARD BROKE

Asymmetric Warfare, Great Power Competition, and Institutional Paralysis

COLONEL M. D. MATTER, U.S. ARMY (RET.)

Pennsylvania & Yorkshire

Published in the United States of America and Great Britain in 2025 by
CASEMATE PUBLISHERS
1950 Lawrence Road, Havertown, PA 19083, USA
and
47 Church Street, Barnsley, S70 2AS, UK

Copyright © 2025 Colonel M. D. Matter, U.S. Army (Ret.)

Hardcover Edition: ISBN 978-1-63624-443-3
Digital Edition: ISBN 978-1-63624-444-0

A CIP record for this book is available from the British Library

All rights reserved. No part of this book may be reproduced or transmitted in any form or by any means, electronic or mechanical including photocopying, recording or by any information storage and retrieval system, without permission from the publisher in writing.

Printed and bound in the United Kingdom by CPI Group (UK) Ltd, Croydon, CR0 4YY
Typeset in India by DiTech Publishing Services

For a complete list of Casemate titles, please contact:

CASEMATE PUBLISHERS (US)
Telephone (610) 853-9131
Fax (610) 853-9146
Email: casemate@casematepublishers.com
www.casematepublishers.com

CASEMATE PUBLISHERS (UK)
Telephone (0)1226 734350
Email: casemate@casemateuk.com
www.casemateuk.com

The views expressed in this publication are those of the author and do not necessarily reflect the official policy or position of the Department of Defense or the U.S. government.

Cover images: (Top left) United States capitol. (Wikimedia Commons); (top middle) The Pentagon in April 2002. (Wikipedia); (top right) U.S Marine Corps scout snipers assigned to Lima company. (Itoldya420); (center right) U.S. Marines and sailors carry a casket inside a U.S. Air Force C-17 Globemaster III at Marine Corps Air Station Miramar, California, August 12, 2020. (Marine Corps photograph by LCpl Brendan Mullins); (bottom left) A Cougar undergoing an explosives test (Wikipedia); (bottom middle) DOD seal (Lisa Ferdinando, Department of Defense); (bottom right) IEDs captured in a police raid in Baghdad, 2005. (Wikimedia Commons/Department of Defense)

The Publisher's authorised representative in the EU for product safety is Authorised Rep Compliance Ltd., Ground Floor, 71 Lower Baggot Street, Dublin D02 P593, Ireland.
www.arccompliance.com

Contents

Preface   vii
Introduction   ix

Part I: IEDs and Irregular Warfare   1

1. IEDs: Asymmetric Warfare or a Condition on the Battlefield?   3
2. Death by a Thousand Cuts: The IED and the Asymmetric Challenge   10
3. Switched Off: The Government's Inability to Understand the IED   29
4. Seven Simple Lessons of Counterinsurgency   62
5. The Principles of War for IEDs and UAS Platforms   70
6. Playing Hardball: Getting After the Network   94
7. The Counter-IED Playbook: Break out the Sledgehammer   105

Part II: Institutional Paralysis   141

8. Organizational Change: IEDs and Unmanned Systems   143
9. Unmanned Systems   156
10. 21st-Century Blitzkrieg: Fires and Effects Integration Prisms   177
11. Great Power Competition: Relevant Lessons from the Past   199
12. End-to-End Kill-Chain Convergence   205

Conclusion   221

Appendix A: C-IED White Paper   227
Appendix B: Optimized Fires Brigade   237
Endnotes   241
Bibliography   249

Preface

This book was originally born as an attempt to get our arms around the IED problem in Iraq for nearly 20 years. Through its development I changed the title of this book several times, always keeping the moniker of "hard broke." Some might ask why that is and my response would be it's a slang term in the environment that I served in when someone or something is so off track that the amount of effort required to get that person or concept back on track is exponential, and consequently, referred to as "hard broke." The book grew from one chapter to roughly 180 pages that were originally classified and had to be redacted multiple times over a series of years to get to the point that it is currently.

Throughout the development of this book, I do not know how many times I have been asked why I chose to write about these problems but, to put it mildly, it was significant. Several senior officers along the way told me I needed to get this on the street for all kinds of reasons. It took almost five years of effort to get the first portion of this book, the original "Counter-IED Playbook," the chapter now renamed "Playing Hardball: Getting After the Network," to an unclassified level. This book first and foremost is about IEDs and IED-enabled asymmetric warfare. At a minimum, there are probably 10 years of my life and over 100 months of combat operations and experiences encapsulated in this work. In a sense it might be a personal-experience monograph at a macro level for the problem sets that I worked on while on active duty in the army, which were predominantly fires, effects, IEDs, close target reconnaissance, tracking-tagging-locating (TTL), and information operations, which I have always said, is primarily fires. This book is about a personal journey through some of the most complicated problems inside of the Department of Defense, and the army. My earnest desire is to see two primary problems discussed in this book resolved. The first is how we are organized to deal with the problem of IEDs, and more specifically, how the government is organized, manned, equipped, and trained to deal with that problem. The second is how the army is doctrinally organized to deal with an emerging revolution of military affairs, the challenge of 21st-century fires and effects. There are elements of this book that date to the initial stages of both Operation *Enduring Freedom* and Operation *Iraqi Freedom*, and a small amount from previous experiences in the Persian Gulf. Many of the chapters were written in combat and were either meant to address ongoing or emerging problems. This book is not meant to be an end all, but simply an opening salvo in an ongoing discussion on how to deal with these problems. The final category that I wanted to address was the concept of "institutional paralysis." Although there have certainly been times where I felt that some of what I witnessed was professional incompetence, sheer ignorance, or actions consistent with being an idiot, I felt it all fell under "institutional paralysis." The truth is that all the above and this book led to the realization that the institution is just incapable of changing by itself, that it requires additional outside intervention to do so.

Colonel M. D. Matter, U.S. Army (Ret.)

Introduction

The American incursion into Iraq revealed significant shortcomings in how the U.S. understood asymmetric warfare and dealt with an enemy using unconventional tactics. This should be no major surprise given our history in Vietnam, Lebanon, and Somalia. This central feature of American warfare is typical of our culture. Our approach brought American firepower and military dominance to the brink of failure. We seek complete victory not necessarily understanding subtle differentiation fighting conflicts on the edges or periphery. Consequently, the U.S. had a limited understanding about how to deal with the improvised explosive as both a device and a concept and tactic. Despite American military power and technological advantages, we were brought to the brink of failure in Iraq because we did not understand how the adversary utilized IEDs as the primary weapon to attack our "center of gravity." This book postulates that IEDs, coupled with UAS/UAVs, are the latest approach in asymmetric warfare and the U.S. must develop tactics, techniques, and procedures (TTPs) to counter IEDs or risk failure in future asymmetric warfare. Second- and third-order impacts of failure increase potential proliferation of these techniques to other areas. The most concerning, unintended consequence of this problem infers increased IED and UAS/UAV utilization by asymmetric actors such as terrorists and guerillas, potentially enabling weaker actors to engage superior actors and win. That was always the danger in not truly defeating this approach.

***

The first eight chapters of this book are devoted to counter-IED concepts. Over time as this problem emerged in Iraq, we had to learn how to cope with IED-focused asymmetric warfare. Because of this fact, we had to learn to defend against this threat and then ultimately defeat that threat. This book was designed to ultimately defeat that threat. Many of the concepts, although watered down for obvious classification reasons, have still not been actioned. As an example, I was always an advocate of creating multiple mobile C-IED strike force units, creating expertise. Lessons from previous conflicts show that most successful counterinsurgency operations require adjusting formations to adaptations the enemy makes. In simple terms, adjusting your units and their attributes to the threat they face. We still push C-IED capabilities into our tried and tested company, battalion, brigade, and division formations. If you sense a hint of sarcasm, it is warranted. If you destroy IED networks faster than they can regenerate because you develop expertise and utilize the "inkblot" method, this approach enables reducing networks faster than they can regenerate. You win and the enemy loses. Since we never put that into action, and simply attempted to jam C-IED capabilities into traditional formations, we had limited success. I suspect had we approached it differently we could have defeated this concept in detail. The chapters in the second part of this book about UAS (unmanned aerial systems) operations and the approach recommended break paradigms and, in that capacity, would require the DOD writ large to stop worrying about rice-bowl mentality.

***

The first chapter of Part I was first drafted when I was the 101st Airborne Division (AASLT) G7 during OIF 05-07 during a one-year tour in Iraq from September 2005 through September 2006. A simple list of techniques to accomplish the mission is akin to providing a man a fish rather than teaching the man to fish for himself. The "C-IED White Paper" (Appendix A) addressed how to effectively conduct brigade- and division-level counter-IED operations and the inherent competition existing between the two levels. The document was written in January of 2006 during an intense debate in the 101st Airborne Division over where the primary responsibility resided. Specifically, the debate focused on whether the division was better off running counter-IED operations at the division level or pushing assets down to the brigade level. The second chapter, "Death by a Thousand Cuts: The IED and the Asymmetric Challenge" was initially written in 2007 to provide the reader with a better understanding of asymmetric warfare and how the IED was merely an extension of an asymmetric process. The chapter provides several references to asymmetric tactics while expanding on the requirements, logic, and consequences of adapting to the current manifestation of IED-centric warfare. Additionally, the chapter provides a basis for understanding what the enemy was attempting to accomplish in relation to the U.S. presence in Iraq. Finally, the document discusses several historical examples of asymmetric warfare, the relevant factors affecting those conflicts, and recommendations to avoid past failures.

Chapter 3, "Switched Off: The Government's Inability to Understand the IED," was first written in 2007. I have left most of this chapter unchanged from its original structure, except to add in some material on Algeria from a piece written in May 2007. Where applicable I made some administrative changes but nothing substantive. This chapter focuses on the threat we were facing and what the enemy was attempting to do so that we could have a better understanding of exactly how to achieve victory. This chapter is a critical document because it focuses so much else of what I was attempting to do in understanding this threat. Our entire approach in Iraq revealed multiple shortcomings in how the U.S. understood asymmetric warfare with an enemy using unconventional tactics. I pointed out that this was not the first time we had faced this type of approach although the IED threat in sum was significantly different. Although some prominent leaders felt that it was simply a condition on the battlefield, I felt that their understanding of this fell short; in essence, the IED had become THE BATTLEFIELD. Some units were fairly proficient at dealing with this threat while others were simply miserable. We value complete victory, and this threat does not potentially lend itself to that approach; instead of using the task of defeat, it may in fact become necessary to use the task of degrade and in doing so you achieve irreversible momentum which ultimately leads to defeat (of the enemy) but requires a different way of thinking. My final point and biggest fear were that the implications of not getting this right had massive second- and third-order consequences for the traditional nation-state system unless we learned how to defeat this type of approach.

Chapter 4, "Seven Simple Lessons of Counterinsurgency" is an examination of the principles which assist in defeating insurgencies and how to organize efforts to enable a successful outcome when dealing with counterinsurgency operations. This chapter details other nations' experiences in previous small wars and insurgencies offering prospective students of warfare the opportunity to garner what works and what does not work in similar environments. All insurgencies are different. What works in one place may or may not work in another location. There are no cookie-cutter approaches in this business. Conversely, a prudent student of warfare ensures that he is aware of those same lessons and acknowledges their application, where appropriate.

Chapter 5, "The Principles of War for IEDs and UAS Platforms" addresses several critical issues that were continually forgotten in this fight, namely Islam, the principles of war, and the root causes of resistance in the Middle East and Central Asia. This chapter was an attempt at tackling some really tough subjects that few people or organizations want to approach. I honestly believe that this was the first attempt of taking a broad overview of the principles of war and how they impact the IED fight. In this case, I went a little further because, just like I did in 2003 through 2007, I saw this coming. As such, I also looked at UAS platforms and how they might impact this emerging discussion and problem frame. Additionally, understanding critical lessons with insurgency and asymmetric warfare campaigns continues to be noticeably absent in many of our ongoing approaches to solving issues in conflict zones. This chapter was written to suggest approaches that attack these types of problems.

Chapter 6 is entitled "Playing Hardball: Getting After the Network" and is designed to provide an initial methodology to degrade the IED network. It is a combination of a concept to attack the IED network as well as an abbreviated center-of-gravity study on the redefined IED network. In doing the research for this, it became obvious that despite volumes of material about IEDs, no one had ever really tried to define the IED network. This chapter offers a definition of the IED network and then utilizes a center-of-gravity approach, developed by Dr. Joe Strange of the Marine War College, to attack the network. The remainder of the chapter is centered on defining the critical capabilities, critical requirements, and the critical vulnerabilities associated with the IED network. Having finally defined the network and arriving at each of the critical vulnerabilities, there are initial recommendations on how to attack these vulnerabilities. In simple terms, vulnerabilities equate to targets.

Chapter 7, "The Counter-IED Playbook: Break out the Sledgehammer," is the cornerstone of this effort. It is an attempt to characterize, to date, what remains undefined. The chapter focuses on counter-IED tactics, techniques, and procedures (TTPs). This design provides the warfighter with a better understanding of the fight they are in, how the enemy choose to engage our forces, and how we can destroy/degrade the IED network. I provide a structural framework and visualization of the IED early warning network. I also provide a generic discussion of the forward operating base (FOB) and how to visualize a concentric-circles approach to define any operating environment. The TTP discussion provides over 35 different vignettes and approaches detailing how to attack the IED network, utilizing a diverse range of capabilities, methods, and equipment. It also discusses how to defeat or mitigate specific special-category IEDs. The categories are broken down into large buried IEDs, explosively formed penetrators (EFPs), vehicle-borne IEDs (VBIEDs), and suicide vehicle-borne IEDs (SVBIEDs). A short summary of each and the techniques designed to degrade, defeat, or destroy these types of weapons and the networks supporting them is provided in both effects methodology and the find, fix, finish, exploit (F3EA) approach. This was the original IED playbook. It has been completely revamped and condensed to make it easier to understand and utilize to attack IED networks, emplacers, and how to think about the overall problem set. It was never meant to be the authority but simply a way of getting after the enemy. Ideally, people should take what is provided here and expand on it, and then publish additional techniques among those who use this information to attack the enemy. It is a start point and will constantly evolve. Initially completed during the Iraqi surge, its purpose was to help units attack the network and kill IED-placement teams. It is not exhaustive and will always evolve with additional equipment and capabilities as technology and tactics, techniques, and procedures (TTPs) evolve. The last part of this chapter rolls up individual issues which do not fit neatly into any of the other chapters and aims to inculcate the counter-IED methodology mindset through training, simulations, organization, or methodology. It is designed to achieve efficiencies through training and integrating relevant data into the training base. Finally, there are recommendations for changes in current force structure for organizations in combat.

**

As a 30-year man who has spent pretty much his entire adult life as a military officer or now as civilian GS chief of staff for a military organization, I am amazed by our inability to adapt. The places I grew up in that prided themselves in the organization's ability to improvise, overcome, and adapt have become stagnant. I once had a conversation downrange with a SEAL flag officer and his comment to me was that even some of the most elite army special operations units have lost their ability to think outside the box, and that we have become executors not innovators. I don't know if I totally agreed with him, and I pointed out in that conversation that it wasn't black and white. There is a lot of truth to what he said but it wasn't completely accurate and there are reasons that I can't allude to in this medium that we probably got there but it wasn't 100 percent accurate either. As I sit writing this, and think about that conversation, and how I am writing on this subject, that observation extends to a lot of this and had I thought about it at the time my comments would be focused on the bigger takeaway, namely, it's institutional paralysis that doesn't allow us to change.

Part II focuses on institutional paralysis in IEDs, UAVs and fires. Chapter 9 examines the threats associated with IEDs, UAS platforms, and the asymmetric threats they pose. Within that problem frame, the chapter focuses analysis on the organizational framework of how the U.S. government has organized to attack this problem. Is the way the U.S. has approached the problem the best way or are there potentially better methods to attack these issues? Significant problems exist within the current approach and this book will suggest recommendations aimed at providing better alignment to achieve greater impacts against these threats. The Department of Defense has never truly broken the code on this in large part because the system is reactionary and is incapable of doing so because of the very nature of this problem. This chapter also examines establishing future C-IED and asymmetric warfare warfighting requirements. At various times throughout this war, there have been attempts to figure out how to reduce the effectiveness of the adversary's IED campaign. There is ample evidence that the amount of effort, resources, and money spent attempting to reduce IEDs when juxtaposed against the results defies any degree of logic given the lack of substantive results attained, to date.

Chapter 10 attempts to approach the IED and IED-enabled asymmetric warfare through going airborne 24/7 and making it extremely difficult for our adversaries to use IEDs against our forces by imposing an excessive cost on attempting to continue to place IEDs on our lines of communication and transportation arteries. This approach is both cheaper in the long run and reduces the enemy's freedom of maneuver. This chapter offers some insights into the potential approaches and varying payloads that might provide a better way to approach C-IED operations and discusses the potential threats associated with UAS systems potentially driving C-UAS approaches that will undoubtedly emerge as a future threat if we don't act soon. This chapter also examines how airline crews do their job and apply it to crew-served approaches to IED-enabled asymmetric warfare. To be clear, throughout this book, I have always advocated going after the enemy before the IED is emplaced, what has been referred to as "getting left of boom." While there is unquestionable value in attacking the network throughout its breadth and depth and doing things like restricting or corrupting the supply chain, not a lot of work has been done on approaching the problem from a teamwork construct. The final part of this chapter focuses on the requirements necessary to build UAS platforms for a C-IED strike and reconnaissance payloads. These focus on what types of weapons and payloads would provide the best advantages to attack an enemy that uses asymmetric techniques like IEDs to engage our forces. This also extends to reconnaissance payloads and how to maximize their efforts in this fight. This chapter also revisits the force structure discussion to further define how to arrive at a potential airborne 24/7 basis of issue for units realizing that in most cases it may in fact be dictated by the terrain.

Chapter 10 is my attempt to tell the army that there is a better way to do what they are doing about fires and information operations. It has always amazed me that a lot of what we did was glossed over and ignored. Four separate joint exercises in two different combatant commands and each and every time the exercise evaluators designated what we were doing with combining all kinetic and non-kinetic fires under one director/commander as best practice. The army can do this better with less people and turn faster, and yet even in this zero-growth environment they just do not want to change. A senior Army general officer actually agreed with my assessment and sent a note to another general officer who contacted me but nothing ever came of it, which reinforces that the organization is resistant to change, assuming that what I have offered in my recommendations is something of substance. In any case, it talks about the construct of what right might actually look like in the world of integrating fires and information operations (non-lethal fires) and a way ahead. In this case, it's an idea that is worthy of examination and ultimately provides military advantage because it allows our forces to turn faster than our adversaries.

Chapter 11 is an attempt to refocus on lessons of the past as they relate to emerging requirements for all-domain fires and great power competition against peer threats like China and Russia. This chapter focuses on three lines of effort, creating multiple dilemmas for our adversaries, logistical requirements, and provides recommendations to get us back on track toward providing a way ahead to win wherever we are called to fight.

Chapter 12 is an attempt to create a decisive military advantage by compressing the end to end kill chain/web requirements to prosecute targets. This is a breakthrough in streamlining the process of finding, fixing and then finishing potential targets enabling speed, mass, simplicity and unity of effort. Great power competition and the advancement of A2AD/C2D2E adversary capabilities forces professional military leaders to rethink existing paradigms. Traditional models create episodic success at best. The recommended model guarantees significant advancement toward continuous excellence.

PART I

IEDs and Irregular Warfare

CHAPTER I

IEDs: Asymmetric Warfare or a Condition on the Battlefield?

At the beginning of the Iraq War, I remember distinctly being surprised by the choices we made. The first was "DeBa'athification." While we weren't popular in Iraq, I would hazard a guess that most Iraqis and even most Sunni were happy to be rid of Saddam. The decision to DeBa'athify was in my estimation one of the more consequential unforced errors in Iraq right up there with the Abu Ghraib stupidity. There were three converging issues that made IEDs a huge problem in Iraq. The first was we didn't have enough troops, and that was the often-forgotten comment made by General Eric Shinseki as the Army Chief of Staff where he said we needed more troops for constabulary operations. To be fair, we could have used Iraqi forces right up until the point that our leadership (the Coalition Provisional Authority) decided to DeBa'athify, at which point that no longer was an option. The second factor was that Iraq was a gigantic ammo dump with ordnance all over the place and when we decided to get rid of the constabulary force, we made it almost impossible to keep a lid on that problem. Finally, with Abu Ghraib, no weapons of mass destruction (WMD), not enough forces on the ground to conduct effective constabulary operations, and a readymade propaganda platform of we were there to steal the oil, it's no surprise that there was a readymade insurgency/resistance movement at the end of that equation. That's really where the asymmetric warfare and IED-enabled asymmetric warfare problem started to emerge. The resistance wasn't going to take us on in maneuver warfare because they would lose so they did what any rational actor would do—they used asymmetric warfare to create casualties and make the Iraq operation a cost-imposing, long-term affair.

IEDs were emerging and starting to kick our collective asses. We weren't equipped for that fight, and the proof of that was in what a lot of us called "hillbilly armor"—units started welding iron plates on to HMMMVs and our vehicles. I used to move around in an Iraqi vehicle and had Kevlar blankets inside the vehicle to protect us against potential IEDs. As this problem began to emerge, there were pockets of success, but most units out there were not faring well in the fight.

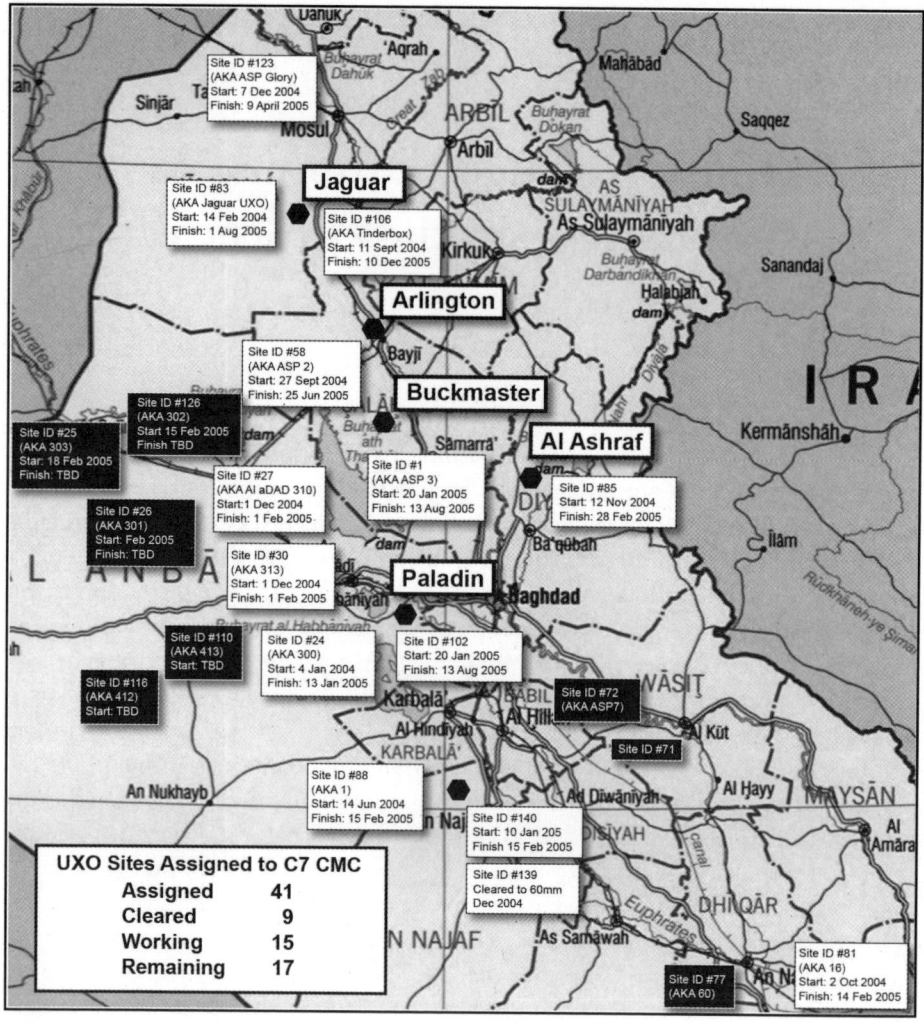

An IED perfect storm. (Edward Salo and Patricia Stallings, 2013, "There Is More Ammunition In Iraq Than Any Place I've Ever Been In My Life, And It Is Not All Securable," The U.S. Army Engineering And Support Center, Huntsville Captured Enemy Ammunition And Coalition Munitions Clearance Mission, 2003–2008)

I started writing about this in January 2006. I was almost four months into a yearlong deployment into Multi-National Division–North and had already had multiple deployments in special mission units and special operations task forces. What I witnessed scared the hell out of me, because we didn't get it. We didn't understand this fight. At various times in this deployment, I witnessed multiple what I refer to as "you can't make this shit up" moments.

I watched another LTC tell the effects working group that "Crystal Software" predicted that IEDs would go off between approximately 0700 and 1000 and that we should avoid the roads at those times because the software program we had purchased from some vendor analyzed various data sources and told us to stay off the roads during that time frame. The concept that the enemy makes an appointment to kill you is not only bizarre, but it also borders on complete ignorance. I almost exploded out of my seat. I said, "That is the stupidest thing I have ever heard" and that IEDs going off weren't because some ridiculous analytical program predicted it, but instead because the enemy had adjusted to our operational patterns. We sent out route clearance teams between 0500 and roughly 0700 and cleared the routes of any IEDs that had been placed overnight, then declared the routes open and cleared. The enemy having figured this out, ultimately would immediately reseed the routes as the route-clearance teams left, and then the first convoys out would predictably get hit by IEDs. A smarter approach would have ensured there was some kind of kinetic interdiction after the route-clearance teams left, hammering the returning IED emplacement teams, using snipers, aerial weapons teams, CAS, or some strike asset to deter the enemy from reseeding the roads.

When the Commanding General of Multi-National Force-Iraq flew up to FOB Speicher and gave us some kind of pep talk at our headquarters, he told us that success in Iraq was training the Iraqi Army and that was our exit strategy. At that point, like every other O5 in there, I think I realized we didn't care about conditions on the ground nor protecting the population (typically key to rooting out insurgents in most counterinsurgency fights). I kept my mouth shut and just acknowledged that we had no idea what the hell we were doing. Damn the conditions on the battlefield: if the Iraqi Army was trained, that's success and we could leave. Days like that were hard to stomach. As I said, you can't make this shit up … it actually happened.

Then there was the response to recurring problems with escalation-of-force incidents where we would end up shooting up Iraqis on the military supply routes (MSRs) because they got too close to our vehicles during operations or when we were moving convoys along the MSR. The intermixing of local Iraqi vehicles and our military convoys either conducting resupply, movement, or operations wasn't an easy task to deconflict. At one point earlier in the war, I came very close to getting killed by our own troops when I was operating in a local Iraqi vehicle and I tried to merge into a convoy, and they couldn't see the flag on my dashboard. I had to break my window with a pistol to show then that I was an American and not some Iraqi trying to infiltrate their convoy. There is no easy solution for this; the right answer is probably some type of massive public information campaign that makes every Iraqi understand that you can get killed if you get too close to a Coalition vehicle convoy. Yes, shooting up Iraqi vehicles in an escalation of force to prevent what appears to be a potential attack can create frustration and encourage locals to join the insurgency, but the alternative was far worse. Multi-National Force-Iraq chose to put out a curfew where Iraqis were not allowed on the road after 2000, and that all Coalition vehicles would use the roads after 2000. This would eliminate escalation-of-force incidents. Yep, that is idiotic. After 2000, every vehicle on the road is a legitimate target in a free fire zone and a target-rich environment for the enemy, almost a carnival "shoot 'em up arcade." Unsurprisingly, escalation-of-force incidents went down and IED strikes and ambushes went up significantly.

In 2005/6 in our sector, in MND-North, the two worst targeted areas of interest (TAIs) in Iraq were TAI Connecticut and Massachusetts, along the MSR just outside of Balad and FOB Anaconda. Both these TAIs were in our sector. We owned the battlespace. We had more IEDs going off per week than any other location in Iraq in these two TAIs. Having recently left a special mission unit, I made a trip down to Balad to talk to my old friends and asked for a favor, that when the AC-130 wasn't flying for them, could it drop in on whatever designated TAIs or locations we asked them to provide overwatch on. This is not an easy task, because it is an asset in high demand and clearly capable of delivering a significant punch on targets like insurgents putting IEDs in on the MSRs. I was able to get their help and wrote a concept of operations (CONOP) called "Zeus." The primary aim of that CONOP was to kill IED emplacers. This causes a second-order effect of increasing the price of paying emplacers to put IEDs out and consequently reduces the total number of IEDs. This of course assumes all other things being equal and Al-Qaeda and resistance forces not having an unlimited supply of cash to continue paying these people to put in IEDs. I and one of my deputies flew separately multiple times on a platform called AIRSCAN which is an unarmed ISR platform to assist while the AC-130 was up and in our sector. Ultimately, after about a month of doing this, we came close to killing some emplacers, but we couldn't get positive identification (PID). Interestingly, as we were going through the weekly effects meeting, the statistic that became obvious was that IEDs in those two TAIs had dropped to zero. Yes, you heard that right, the IEDs per two-week cycle had dropped to zero. I had to take a step back for a second and asked myself what we were trying to do. Clearly, I wanted to kill emplacers putting IEDs in because it has a twofold effect of taking insurgents off the battlefield but also causing the price of IED emplacement to increase.

The law of unintended consequences was alive and well, and in this case, working for us. The insurgents were hearing the gunships when they were at 8,000–10,000 feet and were not coming out because they knew what happened when they ran into an AC-130 while doing bad things. So, while I was mildly entertained by the thought of having them go up to a higher altitude, I thought to myself, wow, if they hear an AC-130 which sounds just like every other C-130 in the middle of the night, then I need to use that. They will either stay away and stop emplacing IEDs or they will come out when they shouldn't, and they will get hammered. The rare win-win. If they do not come out that's awesome—fewer IEDs and fewer casualties. If they do come out, well then, they are going to get whacked and then the price of IEDs is going to go up. Additionally, resources available to the insurgents will go down, and their ability to recruit becomes more difficult. There is always a better alternative to being an insurgent when the price starts to get too high. So, me, being me, I said, you know we set out to reduce the number of IEDs going off along the MSR on Tampa and in TAI Connecticut and Massachusetts while also increasing the price for Al-Qaeda to pay for the emplacement of IEDs. At that point, after reviewing the numbers that had come out for that assessment cycle, I immediately said go get the Air Liaison Officer (ALO). He came down to the meeting and I said, "I want every C-130 coming through our airspace in the middle of the night to do three turns around whatever TAI we tell them to whether it's a vanilla C-130 or an AC-130." He called the Combined Air Operations Center (CAOC) and requested exactly that. The answer he got back dumbfounded me and still does, to this day. They actually said no. I don't know when I eventually told General Petraeus about this, but I think it was during the middle of the surge, on email, and he said something like, "You're shitting me" ... and I sent back, "No, sir, we missed the boat on this one." Another missed opportunity to roll back the enemy's ability to think they could operate with any degree of freedom of action and maneuver by using military deception and close air support.

The recurring theme in this discussion is that maybe the problem was us. This was the backdrop, for the initial C-IED White Paper (Appendix A), which was an attempt to redefine the problem and how we attacked it. Ultimately, I wrote it to change the minds of my superiors on how we task-organized for the fight as well as modifying our approach to attacking the IED network. It wasn't just a condition on the battlefield that we had to deal with, it was a fundamental shift in how irregular forces engaged stronger forces.

This is a thinking man's game. During World War II, had I told subordinates that the enemy was going to show up at some point on a stretch of road of X distance and at Y location in the next 24 hours, and place bombs that would later blow up friendly forces in a desert environment, those same leaders would have figured out how to kill or capture the enemy. Drop off patrols, snipers, aerial weapons teams, CAS, and ambushes are all different ways to achieve the net effect of hammering the emplacement arm of that equation: yet in Iraq, we were waiting for someone to tell us it was okay to do that.

IEDs aren't a condition on the battlefield, it's how the enemy is engaging you. We must take their ability to use these capabilities away from them. We don't have to go back to the FOB. Almost universally, if you are off the FOB for anywhere from two to six hours a day doing your patrols or mission, that is not enough to protect the population from enemy insurgents if you aren't there for the next 18 hours. This isn't an easy business; you can't live on the FOB all the time and expect to achieve anything. The FOB should be where you go to rearm, refit, and get occasional rest. Eventually, this reality set in during the surge when we started finally setting up combat outposts. We put up cameras covering areas in Mosul and covered them with snipers, and amazingly, the insurgents didn't like that. It worked.

Economy of Scale

When IEDs emerged as a threat in Iraq, certain observations surfaced immediately. Rumsfeld was right about the fact that you go to war with the army you have, not the one you want.[1] Building "hillbilly armor" to protect vehicles is an example. That of course leads to the revelation that all we were doing was continuing a losing strategy, namely, building better mousetraps to overcome the effects of some bomb placed by an enemy instead of destroying the network that allowed the bomb to be placed there in the first place. To a degree, that concept has been called many things, primarily "getting left of boom." It is an analogy to move left on the timeline where the bomb never goes off. The problem with the "left of boom" approach is that it was never really applied. I can personally attest to multiple organizations at the tactical level, all the way to the strategic level, not exhibiting any 'tactical patience" in going after the network. Too many times, I witnessed organizations attempting to justify their own existence and going after some kind of worthless public relations victory instead of making true impact on the network. I personally witnessed JIEDDO (Joint Improvised Explosive Device Defeat Organization), now JIDA (Joint Improvised Threat Defeat Agency) worrying more about saying they took some action, as an example, getting a person of interest and key element inside a network on a State Department 13224 designation.[2] This is almost meaningless in having any impact on a network downrange but enabled them to say they did it. Operators forward requested not to take that action because it would alert the target to the fact that they were being surveilled, thus changing their pattern of life. I saw this type of idiotic action happen more times than I care to remember. Result: loss of pattern of life, loss of intelligence on a target that might have with—some tactical patience—enabled U.S. or host nation forces the ability to completely take down a network.

It is important to note the "why" in this discussion. In World War II we lost thousands of people in one day, so why does 127 KIA per month create an issue. It's simple: World War II was a war of national survival, Iraq isn't. You can make an argument that Iraq was in our "national interest," but equally, no reasonable person would argue that winning or losing, succeeding or failing in Iraq, amounted to the same level of national survival juxtaposed against World War II. Add into this equation the politicization of the war during the 2004 and 2008 elections and you have one hell of an equation for not being able to support 127 KIA per month—it was important to get that number down. Consequently, this was a significant issue that we had to solve or run the risk of creating greater instability throughout the world. Our adversaries were capitalizing on this approach, and we had to learn how to defeat it. Thus, once that rationale was arrived at, most of the other courses of action available to the nation weren't feasible or acceptable because they didn't solve the problem. Leaving was clearly not an option without some greater effort at establishing stability in the region in one capacity or another. Sending more troops was likely also not an option so essentially, we had to learn to deal with this problem by becoming more efficient with our resources, ideally reducing casualties, and finally learning to defeat the current strategy being utilized by the enemy. We didn't defeat this strategy, and only ever succeeded at degrading the enemy's efforts but it cost billions of dollars, which in and of itself is a defeatist, cost-prohibitive strategy.

We spent inordinate amounts of money on developing vehicles and capabilities that could survive IED blasts, and eventually, because we did not effectively attack the network emplacing the IED, the enemy just put bigger bombs out there so that they achieved the same effect. I am not sure what that economic equation is but I am almost 100 percent sure that we were losing that fight because we were spending a hell of a lot more money than the enemy. In fact, that was maybe exactly the battle the enemy wanted us to participate in—ultimately causing us to go broke.

Changing the approach would not have required anywhere near the resources we were spending. I operated up and down the most dangerous road in the world for years with upward of 250 round trips on what used to be "Route Irish" in Baghdad, and I am still here, and so are all my people because I refused to play by the same rules that everyone else played by. I changed my times, I operated with different vehicles, I was armed to the teeth, I even operated completely blacked out in the middle of the night.

IEDs, irregular and asymmetric warfare are not going to go away as a strategy to resist a stronger actor and this problem set will only get worse unless we learn how to defeat it. IEDs are dangerous because they are cost intensive. It is a fundamental shift change in the threats traditional nation-states face and will create ungoverned space, leading to things like 9/11. We must defeat this type of warfare, we can get there, but the biggest obstacle we face is our own institutions' inability to adjust to the fight we are in, what I have coined as "institutional paralysis."

CHAPTER 2

Death by a Thousand Cuts: The IED and the Asymmetric Challenge

As the United States military entered its fourth year of war in Operation *Iraqi Freedom*, the concept of asymmetric warfare and how to defeat the insurgency was at the forefront of professional discussion in the military and intelligence communities. With the fall of the Soviet Union in 1991, and the ascendancy of the United States to the world's only superpower, challengers to United States' interests have sought to check American advantages in conventional firepower and technology. Like the biblical figure David and his battle against Goliath, the IED represents a modern parallel.

To understand the IED, we must first understand the model of asymmetric warfare. The concept of "asymmetric warfare" is not new. In fact, Sun Tzu promulgated the concept in his timeless work, *The Art of War*: "If he [the enemy] is superior in strength, evade him. If his forces are united, separate them. Attack him where unprepared; appear where you are not expected."[1]

Giving a common definition of "asymmetric warfare" is exceptionally difficult given the proliferation of viewpoints and definitions. In the interest of brevity, a modification of LTC Kenneth F. McKenzie's definition from *The Revenge of the Melians: Asymmetric Threats & the Next QDR* provides the greatest opportunity for practitioners to develop a common departure point:

> Leveraging inferior tactical or operational strength against American vulnerabilities to achieve disproportionate effect with the aim of undermining American will in order to achieve the asymmetric actor's strategic objectives.[2]

By removing the "American" aspect of this definition and replacing it with a generic "stronger actor" phrase, we can arrive at a definition that works beyond the American experience. Using this as a departure point, the improved definition of asymmetric warfare would look like this:

> Leveraging inferior tactical or operational strength against a stronger actor's vulnerabilities to achieve disproportionate effects with the aim of undermining the stronger actor's will in order to achieve the asymmetric actor's strategic objectives.

This definition allows a better transition toward understanding the principal problem set involved in this discussion. A quick analysis of selected conflicts that involved some form of asymmetric warfare provides a solid base for setting the stage for the situation faced in Iraq.

The Revolutionary War

The first conflict, which provides an excellent example of asymmetric warfare, is the Revolutionary War between the United States and Great Britain. The United States for all intents and purposes popularized guerilla warfare. The United States used previously unheard-of techniques, which included major deviations from established and accepted tactics of the day. These techniques, as an example, included firing at officers. At the time, it was both unheard of and actually a departure from the existing laws of war. Additionally, American military forces used cover (walls, trees, any object that prevented bullets from hitting you) to fire from, which at the time was considered unmanly and an unheard-of tactic. Attacks along British supply lines by leaders of military and paramilitary guerilla forces like Francis Marion, Andrew Pickens, and Thomas Sumter were deviant departures from the tactics of the day. These tactics, at the time wholly unheard of, were essentially asymmetric in nature and enabled American forces to shape the battlefield. Consequently, over an extended period, the Continental Army was able to gain the upper hand in resources and, with assistance from the French Navy, defeat the British at Yorktown, and ultimately achieve American independence. Without the use of asymmetric tactics, the American military would never have had the time nor the resources to mature to the point where it could defeat the British. This example exemplifies the nature of understanding the vulnerabilities of your enemy. The nature of the warfare was asymmetric in character, but the strategy was not. The British were thousands of miles away from their support base and had a finite number of troops to prosecute the fight, which over time were interdicted, delayed, and frustrated until finally there was a competent and capable colonial force proficient enough to defeat them.

Vietnam

The next example of asymmetric warfare worthy of examination is the Vietnam War. Although the United States never lost a major battle in Vietnam, the United States was unsuccessful in defeating the North Vietnamese aim of unifying Vietnam under a communist regime run and led from Hanoi. The failure of Vietnam was one of the most discussed subjects for years following the pullout of South Vietnam. Generations of American military officers have studied the lessons learned from the Vietnam War. Much has been made of the fact that we "took council of our fears" and failed to correctly apply the principles of war toward reducing the primary belligerent vice fighting the effect (Viet Cong) and not the cause (North Vietnam).[3] Illustrating this point is the often-quoted exchange between American Colonel Harry Summers and an unknown Vietnamese colonel:

"You know you never defeated us in the field."

"That may be true, but it is also irrelevant."

Winning the battles was not enough in Vietnam. Our adversaries manipulated events and used our own press to erode the "national will" to continue the fight. We did not anticipate that these events would have the effect that they did back in the United States and, over time, our national resolve faded. To truly understand the radical departure from traditional military theory, had one polled major military theorists of the day, not one would have agreed with a statement that any victory could be attained without achieving some limited success on the battlefield. From an asymmetric perspective, this concept was unheard of. The Tet Offensive was a tactical failure but a resounding strategic success. In today's terms, it was a decisive information operations victory. The concept of tactical or even operational defeat resulting in a corresponding strategic victory in modern combat is unparalleled.

An analytical examination of the situation provides an exceptional example of capitalizing on an initially unforecast weakness. There is little doubt that American military planners could have accurately predicted the type of reaction that occurred over time regarding resistance to the Vietnam War. As time went on, and a growing resistance within the United States materialized, the government inadequately addressed perception and strategic communications efforts to minimize the effects of the peace movement. As a result, when the Tet Offensive took place, leaders had positioned the war as being nearly over, but Tet ran counter to everything that was being presented. As mainstream America saw the offensive unfold, which received significant airtime, their collective feelings about the war came into doubt. The public started to question the accuracy of the reports that they were being given by the government. Nearly everything they saw ran counter to what the government had provided, ultimately creating significant misgivings throughout mainstream America about the validity of the mission. This was the turning point in the Vietnam War. We never recovered from the change in momentum despite having soundly defeated both the Viet Cong and the NVA on the battlefield.

How is all this relevant? The significance of this adaptation is that this is just another form of asymmetrical warfare. Specifically, the United States failed to recognize the importance of what would amount to a strategic communications fight or information operations campaign directed at one of America's unrecognized centers of gravity (American national will). As a result of the Vietnamese strategic communications plan, the United States did not achieve its objectives in Vietnam while never losing on the battlefield.

The takeaway from this should remind every soldier that we can win the tactical fight but lose the strategic battle. There is obviously no cookie-cutter approach to this business, and it seems fairly apparent that each situation must be judged on its own merits to arrive at what makes any given actor vulnerable. In this case, the United States was vulnerable to an unforeseen chink in its armor, all the while not understanding that it was vulnerable, given the fact that at that point, the events that were unfolding were truly uncharted territory. The takeaway from this is that we need to get on the other side of the problem and not be caught repetitively with our pants down but get ahead of this phenomenon.

Algeria

The Algerian War presents an interesting case study. There are divergent opinions on whether the French or the Front de Libération Nationale (FLN) won this conflict. From all accounts, it is apparent that the French military was successful in achieving victory on the battlefield, yet the war became increasingly unpopular in France. This is one of those lost observations that create the classic dilemma (question) of how hard the government should push to retain the status quo and what are the potential second- and third-order consequences of taking these actions? Initially the French government was completely committed to the retention of Algeria and maintaining it as part of the republic. This attitude prevailed over most of the conflict but changed drastically over the last two years of it, during 1960 and 1961.[4]

It is important to draw the contrast about what was going on the ground and where the general national will sat at the time of the discussion. Despite the situation on the ground, where between 1958 and 1959, the French Army had established military control in Algeria, the war had become extremely unpopular, which like many of these conflicts appears a contradiction.[5] The war started on November 1, 1954 and eventually required over 400,000 soldiers and tied up in Algeria roughly a third of the French Army.[6] An understanding of previous events and various perspectives of French national conscience shape the context of their dilemma.

France had suffered a devastating defeat at Dien Bien Phu, by its former colony Vietnam and was subsequently defeated in Vietnam and then evicted, by of all things, an Asian army. While the Russo-Japanese War of 1905 provided an earlier instance of a European force being defeated by an Asian force, the level of French defeat in Vietnam was a significant blow to French national pride. It is true that an Asian force had already defeated a European navy previously when the Japanese had defeated the Russians, but it was in a single naval battle, not a prolonged campaign. Consequently, at the time the Algerian War commenced, the French national conscience, already suffering from a decisive psychological blow, was now forced to deal with the Algerian rebellion, exacerbating a festering wound. On November 1, 1954, responding to the FLN broadcast calling on all Muslims to join in a national struggle, François Mitterrand, the socialist French minister of the interior responded: "The only possible negotiation is war."[7] This sets the stage for a war where the French were already suffering a significant blow to their national pride, and consequently made them dig in even deeper to maintain their rightful empire. This was France's entry into the Algerian War. The French entered the conflict with assumptions that were no longer valid as well as a national will resembling a collective form of desperation.

The French–Algerian War was exceptionally brutal on both sides. The FLN used extremely brutal tactics often directed at the civilian population, the French, and those whom they viewed as collaborators. Because of this type of brutality, terrorism emerged as a valid tactic for several reasons: (1) The FLN was incapable of symmetrically defeating the French in a force-on-force battle, (2) The French were willing to send enough troops to gain basic control of the countryside and had 400,000 troops involved in the counterinsurgency effort, (3) The French Foreign Legion, one of the world's elite fighting forces, was used almost exclusively to combat the guerilla forces and had extensive experience in counterguerrilla operations from their previous experiences in Vietnam.[8]

Given the situation they were facing, the FLN had but one real choice in trying to achieve their objectives. It chose terrorism tactics as their primary approach to resist French military power and counterinsurgency tactics. By 1959, the French were successful in pacifying the Algerian countryside through exceptionally brutal measures. Unfortunately, they alienated the very people they needed support from to maintain Algeria as part of the republic. Clearly, the French response was simply a direct response to the brutality and vicious conduct of the FLN. Consequently, the result of this brutality resulted in a polarization of the population, creating significantly greater challenges to maintaining popular support for French objectives. When the conflict began, most Algerians favored some sort of inclusion into the greater French republic, rather than independence.[9] Over time, this feeling eroded, in large part because of the brutality of the French counterinsurgency approach to the conflict. It is interesting to note that it may in fact be the heavy handedness of the French that eventually drove a significant majority of the people to become less enthusiastic about French governance. Eventually, this led to wholesale opposition for supporting anything other than independence.

By the time Charles de Gaulle returned to power in 1958, the situation had completely reversed itself, creating an environment where most of the French population, as well as the Algerian population, tired of the war, were ready for independence.[10] Attitudes had shifted drastically since the beginning of the war, creating significant barriers to reconciliation. How did this occur? First, the measures that the French Army took in response to terrorism by the FLN had drastically eroded any popular support and possible reconciliation. Second, the war's popularity waned over time. That was likely a function of the 400,000 soldiers assigned across Algeria, representing over one-third of the French Army. In a very simple sense, the vast numbers of French soldiers, through personal connections and family ensured that the French population was exposed to the horror of an insurgency as well as the unfortunate brutality associated with the Algerian War.[11] Additionally, the French Army was never guilt free and bore a great burden of the responsibility in creating an environment that polarized both sides.

De Gaulle attempted reconciliation when he made his famous comment, "*Je vous ai compris*" (I have understood you).[12] His effort was characterized by sweeping changes. He proposed economic, social, and political reforms to remove the conditions which were causing many of the Muslim population to support the insurgency, and recognize French Algeria as part of the greater republic, instead of a French territory (or colony, which comes with an extremely negative connotation).[13] These efforts were valiant but eventually failed, causing De Gaulle to accede to Algerian self-determination.

The French won militarily but failed to ensure that the population in Algeria continued to view them as a viable alternative to a new or different form of government. In doing so, they fell into the trap of overreacting to acts of terrorism that were probably undertaken for that sole purpose. As a result of their heavy-handed brutality, the French ultimately failed in their quest to retain Algeria as part of France. In doing so, they assisted in validating the belief on the "Arab Street" that terrorism was a valid asymmetric approach that influenced generations of modern terrorists, especially Arab terrorists/jihadists. Although the West and the "developed world" views terrorism as a crime, terrorism is now considered a valid concept in asymmetric warfare and provides many disaffected groups an avenue to level the playing field. Given the nature of this trend, it would be wise for many nation-states to invest in understanding the root causes of rebellion as well as learning to respond in a calculated measured manner rather than being perceived as too aggressive. Addressing the root causes of rebellions and providing measures to reconcile those differences is a far better strategy in counterinsurgency than a simple brute-force approach.

Once De Gaulle and France moved toward self-determination for Algeria, the die was cast. The army and the European minority (European Algerian *colon* extremists[*]) in Algeria felt as though they had been betrayed and attempted an insurrection in January 1960.[14] The coup failed and many of the leaders were either imprisoned or transferred to areas where they were no longer a danger. Unfortunately, events at this point were really past the point of no return. Extremists on both sides were so committed to their cause that there was no way that either party was going to make any attempt to settle their differences peacefully or attempt to alleviate the problems that faced Algeria. One more coup was attempted in April of 1961 called the "The General's Putsch."[15] It involved the French Foreign Legion as well as elements of *colons* and was intended to cause the downfall of the De Gaulle government.[16]

---

[*] *Colons* or colonists—also knowns as *pied-noirs*—were mainly French people born in Algeria during French colonial rule from 1830–1962.

This coup would fail too, but the cost this time would be a three-month civil war between the *colon* extremists and the FLN, which would see 1.4 million Jews and most of the moderate European Algerians return to France. The consequences of all this violence and upheaval created an environment that was the final setting for the Algerian referendum. On July 1, 1962, six million Algerians cast their votes in a referendum on independence, and the vote was nearly unanimous in favor of independence. On July 3, 1962, De Gaulle declared Algeria an independent country.

Causes and Applications

Returning to the original purpose of this chapter, the goal of this research was to determine the relationship between the Algerian War (1954–61) and the concept of asymmetric warfare and how it relates to terrorism. An additional goal was to characterize and account for any lessons learned in this process which might be helpful given the current conflicts we were facing. Most scenarios that pit a symmetrically dominant actor against a symmetrically inferior actor usually result in some form of asymmetric warfare. Although not a given, most asymmetric actors will employ some form of asymmetric warfare approach to achieve their goals. This only makes sense given the fact that to do otherwise is illogical and not in one's self-interest. Examples of asymmetric approaches include but are not limited to the following: (1) Terrorism and or some associated form of criminal behavior, (2) Guerilla warfare with an associated movement toward a conventional defeat of the symmetrically dominant military forces at a point when the guerilla forces are capable of rising and defeating the dominant actor, and (3) Peaceful resistance and change from in the established system (Gandhi model).

The Algerian resistance movement, primarily through the FLN, chose to conduct a campaign of terrorism. Given the historical context of the time, that might have been a deviation from what would have been considered the norm. Mao's movement in China, Ho Chi Minh's movement in Vietnam, and Castro's guerilla war in Cuba are all examples of the more classical resistance movements of the day, which were romanticized and successful. In comparison, those movements that used terror only to achieve their goals appear at the outset to have been less successful. The Irish resistance movement provides an example of a resistance movement, which tended to be more along the lines of the militant resistance exhibited by the Algerian War. Thus, the classic question which a student of warfare is forced to ask is, what is the difference and why did the Algerian movement succeed? Simplified even more, why did the French fail and what contributed to that failure? Militarily, the French eventually were able to establish control over the countryside and deny sanctuary to the insurgents, depriving them of a stable base of operations. The FLN was unable to establish a solid base of operations, yet the French failed to achieve their ultimate objective of maintenance of a colonial Algeria in one form or another.

Was this an anomaly or a failure in strategy of the French? Terrorism is a calculated risk. It does not always work. In fact, throughout history, a directed terror campaign has been less likely to succeed than a guerilla movement. Clearly, there are multiple examples of guerilla-type wars, which have been fought and won throughout recent history. There are fewer examples of campaigns of terror that take on characteristics consistent with terrorism, which succeed. The Algerian conflict more closely resembles a campaign displaying characteristics closer to terrorism than to a traditional guerilla campaign. As such, it compels the professional "warfighter" to question the application of assets, the strategy, and ultimately the causes and applications of this strategy. What can be learned from this war and why did it succeed when other movements did not?

The French may have fallen into the classic trap of overreacting to the acts of terrorism, ultimately influencing the average Algerian to arrive at a general conclusion that independence was better than the other alternative of remaining in the republic. It also seems clear that although the French succeeded militarily, they chose not to continue the fight given their internal population's unwillingness to support an increasingly unpopular war. Additionally, given the instability of the Algerian state and the intransigence of each side in the greater conflict, it is probably logical that the French chose to extricate the army from the quagmire they were in. On the other hand, a case could have been made that they "stole defeat from victory" when it was in their very hands.

Lessons Learned

A greater understanding of the indigenous population goes a long way in helping to assist in removing the root causes of rebellion. Caught early enough while there was still a relative middle position, and a non-polarization of the population, it is likely that reform could have made a difference in quelling the rebellion. Simply put, early identification of the grievances of various parties could have avoided outright open rebellion and served to provide a base to build for future reconciliation. Additionally, the principle of inclusion vice exclusion tends to eradicate conflicts as opposed to starting them. Heavy-handed reprisals usually result in increasing the numbers of the insurgents and reduces the legitimacy of the government's position. The response of the stronger actor vis-à-vis what the response of the asymmetric actor is as it relates to terrorism tends to be exponential. In simple terms, the asymmetric actor or terrorist can often get away with behavior that the government simply cannot. The very nature of the government and its responsible-actor label suggests that a directly proportional response only serves to increase the animosity toward the government and swell the ranks of the insurgent or asymmetric actor. The French displayed a failure to understand the need for tactical patience and measured response, ultimately resulting in alienating the general population which is a classic blunder in counterinsurgency operations. You win the battle but lose the war. The critical task seems more likely to have been a solid cultural understanding of what is acceptable, vice what is not acceptable in the given construct.

This very conflict may have assisted significantly in motivating the modern terrorist/insurgent attempting to change the status quo. One of the byproducts of this war in the Arab world is that terrorism ultimately emerged as a valid tactic that, from their vantage point, was successful. Another example is the Golden Mosque in Samarra as a watershed event that created lasting animosity between the Shia and Sunni in Iraq since it was perceived that the Sunni destroyed a significant Shia holy site. This created long-lasting animosity and fuels persistent conflict. More appropriately, symmetrically dominant actors must exercise restraint and show patience in quelling insurgents. The French did not do this.

What are the lessons that applied to Iraq and what can we learn from the mistakes that occurred in Algeria? First and foremost, we should have allowed disaffected groups to air their grievances without reprisal, determining the sources of conflict in the various areas of resistance inside of Iraq and finding a way to either resolve those problems or address them. We should have ensured that we did not lose sight of the fact that we should have maintained a greater degree of civility than the enemy. While it is easy to match violence with violence, that is a short-lived victory, for in the end, the population will reject our aims and objectives just as much as they reject the jihadists and former regime loyalists. It was critical to offer an alternative that was attainable and desirable as well as finding the proper balance between the stick and the carrot. Failure to do this resulted in the society rejecting a movement toward the ideals of a modern Iraqi democracy. Education, women's rights, and religious tolerance should have been at the top of our priorities. These concepts are critical weapons in the fight against jihadists, reactionaries, and Islamic fundamentalists. Failure to utilize these concepts does nothing to ameliorate the conditions, which allow the roots of radical, fundamentalist Islam to prosper.

Sri Lanka

Another noteworthy example of asymmetric warfare was the conflict in Sri Lanka between the Sinhalese and the Tamils. The Liberation Tigers of Tamil Eelam, or Tamil Tigers, and a suicide wing in this organization known as the Black Tigers, were exceptionally effective at achieving disproportionate results in their campaign against the Sri Lankan Army.[17] The suicide bomber campaign by the Black Tigers successfully assassinated Indian Prime Minister Gandhi in 1991.[18] Although they represented less than 20 percent of the population, the Tamil Tigers essentially created a separate government on Sri Lanka while simultaneously successfully intimidating the Sri Lankan government to stay out of Jaffna, the Tamil base of operations in the northwest of the island. The most effective tactic in this conflict was the suicide bomber and their ability to create disproportionate effects. This tactic created a situation favorable to their long-term strategic goals and undermined the general will of the Sri Lankan population to achieve a full reunification through force. The consensus was that the price was too high to pay. However, the Tamil Tigers were ultimately destroyed by the Sri Lankan Army who brutally devastated the Jaffna peninsula

The Middle East

Contrast this with the use of suicide bombers in Israel and how Israel has dealt with similar demands from the Palestinians. Israel will likely never capitulate to these types of demands despite the use of suicide bombers and endless attacks against Israelis. Interestingly enough, Israel itself is a potential victim of an asymmetric campaign by Hezbollah.

Hezbollah in Lebanon presents a fourth and final case of asymmetric warfare that is worth examining. The 2006 conflict between Israel and Hezbollah presents an excellent opportunity to study a set of data, which directly correlates to a recent asymmetric set of events. This case provides a solid example of what appears to be an attempt at asymmetric warfare that was, in fact, be particularly effective. Clearly, Israel is the preeminent military power in the Middle East while Hezbollah is not even a nation-state that occupies a small portion of Lebanon. Despite being at a severe disadvantage militarily, Hezbollah's operations in that conflict provoked Israel into exactly the response that Hezbollah wanted. In sustaining combat operations, every organization must be able to attract recruits or it will eventually fade away and die. Of course, any discussion on this subject has two sides. One side of the coin suggests that by taking action and reacting to Hezbollah's operations, the Israelis fell into the trap and did exactly what Hezbollah wanted them to do. This reasoning centers along the belief that by trying to destroy Hezbollah they actually created more recruits than had they just left things alone. Unfortunately, there is a counterinterpretation that says that by doing nothing they increase the prestige of Hezbollah and reinforce their strength, which plays well into Arab culture, also attracting recruits.

Finally, the current conflict in Israel may signal a new shift to Arab- and Iranian-funded opposition. It appears from a distance that the October 7, 2023 attacks were so grotesque that the purpose was intended to draw the Israelis into another conflict because they would have no other choice than to level the opposition. That has led to a current situation of a much wider Middle East conflict that could be by design. A student of warfare, remembering that war in a Clausewitzian context is simply an extension of politics by other means demands further examination of what exactly the affected parties are attempting to achieve. Is this meant to draw Israel into a conflict or not? At this point, they are, and the initial acts of terror were so over the top that one is forced to consider that those involved had to know that this would be the current response. Where this is concerning from an American perspective is that we may be at open conflict between the Israelis and the Iranians and not just their proxies. It's also concerning when you view these events from a greater distance and potentially ask yourself if this isn't designed to strip away strategic assets like carrier strike groups that might otherwise be utilized in places like the Pacific. Ongoing wars in the Ukraine, Syria, the Red Sea and now the emerging Israel–Iran/Lebanon flareup, create conditions where the U.S. deploys forces. If you view this as a potential alliance between China, Russia, and Iran, it forces one to consider whether Taiwan is just over the horizon. When viewed from that prism, all these seemingly independent actions start to make sense but that's always a gamble because it assumes that there must be some underlying purpose rather than assessing incompetence because we make the assumption that they are all rational actors, when in fact, they may not be.

An alternative interpretation is that Israel may have in fact taken all the above into account and decided to use the attacks as an opportunity to significantly reduce the combat power of Hezbollah in a type of spoiling attack. In essence, the Israelis went into that conflict knowing that they were going to create a "propaganda win" for Hezbollah but primarily aimed at degrading their military arsenal and future operations capability.[19] Ultimately, it is all speculation, but what is relevant to the context of this problem set is that the Israelis possess one thing that may make them different from nearly all the other actors filling the role as the symmetrically dominant power: their national will may be based more on a perceived national will to survive rather than a will to simply engage in a given conflict. Other nation-states involved in asymmetric conflicts do not usually possess perceptions that they are in a fight for national survival and are less willing to pay high costs to achieve a given objective. As a result of this, it is advantageous to appreciate the potential value of the commitment of any given potential symmetrically dominant power for any given set of circumstances. This is the critical question that applies to what the United States did in Iraq.

***

The security environment in Iraq in 2007 was characterized by a recurring and systemic use of IEDs. The IED was single-handedly killing more American soldiers than all other approaches combined. Philosophically, an IED is designed to be a standoff engagement system, initiated through some type of remote control, command wire, or self-initiated as a booby trap, which allows the opposing force to disengage rapidly and escape detection by friendly forces. This type of attack allows the enemy to asymmetrically overcome firepower and the disadvantages inherent to an insurgent force. The insurgent does not want to become decisively engaged. If the insurgent gets decisively engaged, they almost universally get killed or captured.

An IED in a live fire demonstration. (Wikimedia Commons/United States Navy ID 090226-N-7090S-115)

IEDs served an additional purpose by decreasing Coalition forces' freedom of action and increasing the insurgents' ability to move around the battlefield at significantly lower risk of detection or interdiction.

The key to defeating or disrupting the concept of the IED is understanding the development cycle, employment cycle, and vulnerabilities that are intrinsic in the IED system.

What is the IED really designed to do? There are many that believe that the IED is simply a condition of the battlefield.[20] Far from it, the IED in Iraq had multiple purposes but none greater than simply slowly eroding the national will of the American population through attrition, killing soldiers here and there, a few at a time, little by little. Is this so hard to fathom? This policy was successful in Vietnam and Lebanon. In each of these conflicts, the United States left having failed to achieve the objectives originally set forth. The lowest common denominator in those equations suggests that if the asymmetric adversary desires success against the United States, then undertake a campaign to slowly "bleed" the United States until the United States loses interest because costs are too high. As discussed, the United States left Vietnam when the country no longer supported the effort. We left Beirut and Somalia because we achieved single-day casualty rates greater than we were willing to pay. That policy sends a clear message: if you can kill enough American soldiers, then eventually the United States will pack up and leave. What are the consequences of that kind of policy? Surely, they are not favorable. Is it any surprise that opposition groups anywhere, or for that matter in Iraq, would use this tactic in trying to defeat United States objectives? This situation creates an interesting paradox for our military planners. On one hand, the United States possesses the most dominant military in recent history yet lacks the long-term will to carry out protracted operations of lower intensity. It is almost like that old golf analogy, that says, "you drive for show but you putt for dough." In a very similar sense, we have mastered the drive by being able to lethally destroy any major competitor on the battlefield but lack the sophistication to putt well and conduct counterinsurgency operations to complete the task.

In Iraq, the use of the IED by insurgent forces was no different conceptually than American colonial forces using walls and trees to fire from. The insurgent is at a distinct disadvantage if they become engaged directly by forces with superior firepower and maneuver. In a similar sense, the Iraqi insurgent was forced to fight asymmetrically or run the risk of being killed or captured. During the Revolutionary War, this is the exact tactic that we used to succeed. A war of attrition was what Washington sought as illustrated by the quote below from Russell Weigley's work, *The American War of War*:

> The most familiar visual depiction of Washington as a general is probably Emanuel Leutze's version of him, wrapped in muffler against freezing December as he crosses the Delaware on Christmas Day, 1776. Whatever documentary or esthetic misgivings the painting may occasion, its popularity is appropriate enough, for it suggests the essence of Washington's way of war, a strategy of attrition. The passage over the Delaware to raid the Hessian barracks at Trenton was the most successful single example of his chief stock in trade of active war, the erosion of the enemy's strength by means of hit-and-run strikes against his outposts.[21]

Continuing the Revolutionary War example, the British should have developed tactics that were consistent with defeating forces that refused to engage them directly. The British did not adjust to colonial tactics, eventually failing. An interesting point of note is that one can make the argument that British interests were threatened more by French capabilities than their temporary setback in the colonies. There was a false assumption that they could always return and solve it at a later date. In a sense, the British lost the political will to continue the fight in the same way the United States would lose the will to continue to prosecute Vietnam, Lebanon, and Somalia.

If there is a lesson learned here, it lies in the fact that as a country and military, the United States must develop tactics, techniques, and procedures to enable our forces to succeed in IED asymmetric fights. This prevents political tipping points where costs are no longer worth the perceived expense. There is clearly a case for how asymmetric warfare has successfully been used in the past to defeat symmetrically stronger opponents. Additionally, the discussion focused on how the United States has had a recent history of leaving at the first sign of difficulty (Somalia, Lebanon). Given that history, American military professionals must learn to overcome these tactics of asymmetric warfare. That requires learning how to defeat the IED and its components, and how our adversaries use it against us.

What is an IED? It is multiple things. It is a weapon of attrition and a weapon that requires minimum force at the point of execution. It helps the enemy to fix and frustrate Coalition forces. It serves as an early warning device: when a Coalition patrol was hit by an IED, they stopped whatever their intended mission was and reacted to the IED. Failure to address how the IED was placed there in the first

A Cougar hit by an IED in Al Anbar, Iraq, 2007. (Wikimedia Commons/U.S. Military)

place is the moral equivalent of ceding the offensive to the enemy. The necessary question is how do I prevent the IED from getting there in the first place? Creating better armored vehicles and creating devices that cause the device not to function properly does nothing more than mitigate the problem. An offensive strategy is essential to defeat the IED as a system to defeat its use as an asymmetric concept.

Actions to Defeat the IED System

Defeating the IED system requires understanding its components. Logically, the IED can be broken down into several subsystems:

1. A supply or logistics system that provides access to or replenishes insurgents with IEDs or components to make IEDs.
2. A delivery system, requiring manpower and transport capability, to emplace them in their attack sites.
3. Money.
4. A form of command and control for the network.
5. Effective leadership able to prioritize resources and focus assets at the right time and place.

6. A way to incorporate lessons learned.
7. The support of the local population.

These elements represent systems that the traditional symmetric actor must target or establish effects against (disrupt, degrade, destroy, etc.) to reduce the IED system. The next step is to develop a plan of action to interdict the systems that provide the enemy his capability to wage war asymmetrically.

One of the most basic concepts of modern warfare is that units must be replenished with supplies and ammunition, or they become combat ineffective. In an extremely basic sense, the IED system is the same. If one can limit or disrupt the ability of the enemy to sustain his throughput of IEDs, then there will be a corresponding decrease in attacks and casualties. Tactics, prioritization, and technology can effectively reduce any potential resupply of insurgents. Over time, the insurgents will shoot their basic load and ultimately become combat ineffective because they cannot sustain the fight.

Insurgents must develop a system to effectively place IEDs in areas where the enemy will travel along. Like any normal organization, that system must have a command-and-control node and an element that is a reconnaissance or early warning element to effectively achieve this goal. "Rolling back" the early warning network and degrading the insurgent command and control using offensive tactics,

Items such as pressure cookers, homemade pressure plates and other common materials are often used by enemy forces to make improvised explosive devices. (Wikimedia Commons/United States Marine Corps ID 101117-M-5889H-008)

IEDs captured in a police raid in Baghdad, 2005. (Wikimedia Commons/Department of Defense)

technology, and actions will provide more freedom of movement and simultaneously reduce the insurgent's freedom of action. The second-order effect of this action is that the enemy is less capable of placing IEDs without being interdicted, resulting in a corresponding drop in both IED numbers and effectiveness. This reduces deaths and casualties. By degrading the command and control of the insurgent, we reduce the enemy's ability to provide prioritization, massing of resources, and the sharing of information to improve their operations (lessons learned).

Money is the lifeblood of the IED system. Like any other organization or system, the IED system requires money. Money buys IED components as well as paying for personnel to place IEDs. Interestingly enough, the absence of any significant economy in most of the areas of Iraq where IEDs were a recurring problem suggested that the money was coming from outside the area if not outside of Iraq. Degrading the ability of the insurgent to transfer money with limited visibility reduces the capacity of the enemy to purchase components, placement teams, early warning members, and supplies that assist in the overall production and delivery of any given network.

Degrading the command and control of the manpower recruitment system has a corresponding effect by reducing the number of potential recruits. Fewer recruits over a significant period can have devastating impact on an organization if the loss of personnel is higher than the recruitment pipeline can replace. The second-order effect of this is that with fewer soldiers, there is corresponding drop in IEDs and network efficiency.

All organizations require some degree of effective leadership. The less effective the leadership, the less effective organization is. Active targeting of leaders assists in decreasing the overall effectiveness of the organization. Since all cellular organizations have a pattern of relying on specialists that know only one or two components of a particular network, then any interdiction of a major leader can have a cascading impact on that organization. As insurgents and our enemies use the internet to communicate, it only makes sense to employ some capability to degrade the enemy's ability to utilize that medium with confidence. This objective seems fairly straightforward and would have a significant impact on limiting communications, sharing lessons learned, or coordinating insurgent/IED operations.

The often-overlooked aspect of an insurgency is defining what the roots of political resistance are. By defining what the political roots of resistance are, the symmetrically superior actor can offer a method to the insurgent/asymmetric actor to resolve most if not all the major differences causing armed resistance. In Iraq, that could have ranged from economic incentives to simply engaging the tribal and religious leaders in a community on a routine basis. Of note, continual one-year rotations of units to Iraq were not the most effective course of action to achieve building long-term relationships with tribal, religious, and community leaders. If, in fact, we live in an age where one-year rotations are the norm, and we are incapable of sending a unit to combat till the job is done then there are better ways to accomplish the building of relationships. For example, rather than simply rotating a unit in arbitrarily, the more effective course of action would have been to always send the same unit back to the same geographical location ensuring that the unit was both familiar with the territory as well as the local leaders that inhabited the general area. It is interesting to note that as other aspects of the security situation improve there is usually a corresponding increase in effectiveness with "face-to-face" engagements. The goal of any operation, kinetic or non-kinetic, should be to reduce the underlying roots of resistance. Over time, by offering a method to alleviate the perceptions and concerns of the insurgent/asymmetric actor, the symmetrically dominant actor can reduce the causes of the insurgency. The key to all these actions is balance. Heavy-handed kinetics can result in providing a reason to join the insurgency, while not doing enough can limit the effectiveness of non-kinetic approaches. In Iraq, the United States as the symmetrically dominant actor had to work harder at defining the roots of political resistance while simultaneously increasing the overall effectiveness against IEDs.

***

As I started to reflect on some of the biggest challenges we faced, the first thing that stuck out to me were the comments on the "strategic communications" fight. We continually appeared to struggle with this. The observation that we lost Vietnam not because of anything on the battlefield, but because we failed to either accurately describe the challenges we were facing, and/or an inability to maintain the support of the population (the national will), stands out as something that we came very close to repeating in the middle of the Iraqi surge. There was a point when we simply realized that we could not sustain 127 KIA per month, that the American public would not support it, so we had to change what we were doing. To some degree, simply getting off the forward operating base (FOB) was the first thing that we had to do to protect the population (a critical element in any counterinsurgency operation).

The second issue that I do not think we did really well, but we came up with a compromise, more by luck than anything else, was to essentially remove the root cause of the problem, which was the support of the Sunni tribes in Iraq for the insurgents and Al-Qaeda in Iraq. We achieved this by developing what was called the Sons of Iraq, which I actually saw before it was the Sons of Iraq when I was down in Baghdad in 2006, and some folks from SOCOM asked me what I thought of an idea called the "Desert Protectors." It was a good idea, and I think that when General Petraeus came back in 2007 as the MNF-I commander, he jumped on that idea, which up to that point had really been an isolated effort out near Al Qaim. The idea, which appealed to the Sunni tribes, and amounted to buying them off to provide local security services, took away the insurgent support from local tribes while also employing them as a local militia, a technique that probably saved lives and money delayed the eventual outcome of what we were trying to achieve.

Part of my original intent, when I started writing about these issues, was to address what I saw as a continual problem, which was that in multiple venues, we were continually ceding the initiative to the enemy. We stayed on FOBs, we did not use Islam or religion as a tool to address the root causes of the fight, we did not take prudent risk, we did not make a major effort to interdict and disrupt the supply chains along the borders of Iraq or Afghanistan; the list can go on and on.

The IED network needs resources, and the Hawala system moves money clandestinely, to say outside various international law enforcement agencies' ability to track and monitor those systems. In that sense the ability to tag and track money or anything inside the IED supply chain enhances friendly forces' ability to degrade or disrupt the logistical supply chains of adversary networks. This same principle applies to any part of the network you are attacking. Networks require resources, manpower, weapons, supplies, training areas, sanctuary, bomb-building expertise (IED networks), command and control, and a central belief or because that motivates its members. If you can gain knowledge of these networks, insert tracking devices (tags) in, or corrupt those supply systems, then you can severely impact those networks.

Illuminating critical entities inside IED networks while exercising tactical patience would surely have enabled our forces to deal crushing blows to any network. As an example, the enemy learned to deal with us taking out their leadership; they simply picked up the gun and continued to fight. There is absolutely an effect on the network when you take out critical leadership, but they learned to deal with it, and it was not the critical blow it once was. My observation was that you get more bang for your buck by eliminating or capturing single points of failure. Disabling critical components or resources are the key to dealing a decisive blow to any network. I have personally witnessed the Washington, D.C. targeting cycle focus more on political approaches instead of actually focusing on taking out critical elements of any network because "it briefs well."

Homemade explosives (HME) in Pakistan were usually made from calcium ammonium nitrate (CAN-26) and we proved on multiple occasions that it was a parabolic curve on return. Simply put, you can continue to remove HME, but it will not have any effect on the total numbers of IEDs. Conversely, critical components to any explosive kill chain like the blasting cap or the bomb maker have disproportionate effects. Yes, that also falls into the "you can't make this shit up" category. It took me almost 18 months downrange to finally change the way Joint Improvised Explosive Device Defeat Organization (JIEDDO) viewed that problem, at the expense of probably pissing off everyone important in that organization because, for the most part, they just did not get it. HME did not matter, nor did beating up the Pakistanis when they were taking more casualties than us because of IEDs. Figure out how to disable the network and you make everyone a winner rather than worrying about pointing fingers at others. As I left Pakistan, I was finally able to get JIEDDO to send people forward to support our targeting cycle and let that drive what we were doing in D.C., not the other way around.

Asymmetric Warfare and our Adversaries

One should identify the root causes of any problem and then start to "peel off" portions of the insurgency or cause. We were not doing that, and if we were, then we were not being honest with our assessment of how we were doing. IEDs were a serious problem, and they would continue to be until we developed TTPs, strategies, and strategic communications plans that addressed the issues from the tactical to the strategic levels of the conflict. We also must be cognizant of how our adversaries position themselves toward their longer strategic goals. View this problem from their perspective, and what they are after, and not a mirror imaging approach. If we are tied up everywhere else but the Pacific Rim, then the Chinese are gaining from that expenditure of resources. They get stronger relative to the total amount of resources we can spend on Chinese ventures in the Pacific. At a macro level on a strategic scale, death by a thousand cuts occurs by forcing the United States to focus resources everywhere but where the Chinese are building up their forces. Do we have enough for both—probably—but at some point, over time, that becomes a losing equation where we should prioritize our resources on larger problem sets like Taiwan. If we were more successful in dealing with this IED problem, we would spend less time, money, human capital, and consequently devote more of our time, energy, and money on the Pacific Rim.

CHAPTER 3

Switched Off: The Government's Inability to Understand the IED[1]

What is an IED?

Rick Atkinson, in his article, "The single most effective weapon against our deployed forces," suggests IEDs emerged as the signature weapon of the Iraq conflict.[2] In writing his article, he interviewed General (Retd.) Montgomery Meigs. Meigs, the director of Joint Improvised Explosive Device Defeat Organization (JIEDDO), suggested that IEDs were the enemy's artillery system including vehicle-borne IEDs, as well as suicide bombers.[3] One should always attempt to view this through the prism of what the enemy is attempting to do to you, to understand the purpose and intent of their efforts. Interestingly, I had already suggested that the IED represented the enemy's primary engagement system and that varying types of IEDs epitomized traditional equivalent artillery weapons systems. In that capacity, specific types of IEDs replicated differing types of conventional fire support systems. Thus, a simple roadside bomb could equate to a 60mm or 81mm mortar system while a large buried IED or explosively formed penetrator (EFP) could equate to precision-guided munitions. Again, I don't think the enemy was developing an artillery system, but they used IEDs for specific purposes. Suicide bombers and vehicle-borne IEDs correlate to larger-caliber weapons systems designed primarily to maximize damage and cause as much death and destruction as possible. There were even some crude attempts at combining large IEDs and chemicals (chlorine), ultimately displaying innovation and imagination of an adaptive adversary. Short of the suicide versions of IEDs (vehicle-borne improvised explosive device and suicide vest), the enemy's apparent primary purpose was to inflict as much damage against American/Coalition troops while simultaneously avoiding decisive engagement. This makes sense given American history and the propensity to depart when taking significant casualties. This is the adage of maintaining the "national will" and when folks at home see body bags coming home or hear about high numbers of casualties on the news, then average Americans start to ask why we're there. Generally, one of the observations I made was there was ample evidence suggesting that the killing or injuring of troops was almost secondary to doing so on video or ensuring the event was recorded on some form of media. To be clear, I am not suggesting that the recorded event is more important than the action itself but instead suggesting that the enemy used these events to attract recruits and financing. The two go hand in hand. The recorded event could then be sent to friendly media conduits or released on the internet. Within that specific propaganda observation was a communications strategy aimed apparently toward their perception of the U.S. center of gravity, namely the will to continue to prosecute the fight amid mounting casualties.[4]

This is the damage that an EFP can do to a tank and in that creating spall and overpressure likely killing or severely wounding most, if not all, of the crew. (Wikimedia Commons)

What are IED Characteristics?

Why are IED characteristics important? They are important because they add to the general understanding of what the enemy is trying to accomplish. In very simple terms, understanding IED characteristics contributes insight into the greater motivation of the enemy, their TTPs. Minimal literature exists on IED characteristics. Having worked on this problem almost from the outset, I concluded that IEDs exhibited multiple purposes. In some cases, they were designed primarily to inflict casualties on American or Coalition forces while in other cases they were used as obstacles or early warning devices. Additionally, they were used to complement traditional ambushes or raids. All this created significant confusion. It takes familiarity with the terrain, pattern analysis, and intelligence to properly ascertain what the true purpose of each IED is. Not all IEDs have the same purpose or intent. IEDs are multipurpose weapons, allowing adversaries to inflict casualties, deny terrain, or provide early warning in support of their military or political objectives. My Counter-IED Playbook noted that IEDs were typically placed along highly trafficked areas with certain criteria (see Appendix A).

Noah Shachtman discussed forensics associated with IEDs and how Coalition forces were using those "fingerprints" to identify and then catch IED engineers.[4] This created a significant debate in this community, namely, how we approached this problem. Was this an evidence-gathering approach akin to police work or were we attempting to destroy or degrade the network? My answer always focused on the latter while still providing enough support to the forensic approach to assist in network identification and target development. The three Ds commonly referred to as destroy, degrade and disrupt are all tactical tasks that should have driven our approach. Dedicating overwhelming resources toward post-blast analysis is passive. Personally, I found this approach to be weak and inconsistent for two primary reasons. The first obvious one is that it is reactive and time- and resource-intensive. The second observation is more concerning that even when we identified critical nodes in the network, we showed no tactical patience to take down the entire network simultaneously, thereby crippling it. Instead, we went after the first lead and the low-hanging fruit, invalidating the entire premise of that approach. Ostensibly, if you're going to spend the time doing forensics you ought to have the tactical patience to take down the entire network rather than one element at a time and this was far too often what we did. Forensic capabilities speak less to the actual characteristics of how IEDs were being used and more to how IED signatures were utilized to capture the bomb builders and destroy the networks supporting assembly and distribution of IEDs. James Dunnigan published an article describing IED characteristics in 2005. He contended most IEDs occurred in Sunni-controlled areas and additionally asserted most IEDs were employed between 0900 and 1200.[5] I wrote as far back as 2005 and early 2006 this idea was idiotic. Additional writings in 2007 reemphasized this idea, stating that avoiding a specific time block is ludicrous because the enemy engaged friendly forces based on our own friendly pattern vulnerabilities, not some predetermined attack time. This logic suggested that if I simply avoided going out on the roads at those times, the entire enemy's IED campaign would be rendered useless. That is laughable. Instead, the enemy engaged American or Coalition forces through an early warning network and utilized cellular and radio communications to do so. Those engagements were based on friendly patterns, not some arbitrary time that the enemy decided to engage. When the IED went off was more a function of when our forces operated and how they operated, not the enemy operating on some predetermined time schedule. The enemy engaged targets based on the target behavior, not the desire of the enemy to engage targets primarily between 0900 and 1200. Typically, the enemy engaged weakness through repetitive patterns vulnerabilities where he could inflict damage and escape without losses. The harder you make it for the enemy, the less predictable you are, and the more likely the enemy is to be decisively engaged, the more likely it is that the enemy will avoid contact.

Other sources of literature are limited but provide various ancillary data about IEDs. Michael Carden's article about IED classes provided information about the army's efforts at educating soldiers in recognizing IED signs and tipoffs prior to the IED exploding. His article explained, at the tactical level, what the army was doing to provide education to the average soldier. He also discussed how various systems were being incorporated into the fight and how those systems assisted tactical units in their day-to-day operations. My own observations are the army can do this better, and I am sure that throughout this book I have provided an observation that the army force-generation cycle is monumentally stupid. One of the most critical factors in reducing casualties is familiarity with the terrain and situational awareness regarding culture, leaders, and tribal considerations. If you frame this problem with a general context of two extremes, then the logical solution becomes apparent.

What do I mean by this? If we go back to World War II and examine the approach we took, then you realize it was basically go until the job is done and the sooner you finish, the sooner you get home. World War II was a war of national survival; I don't think recent conflicts rose to that level. Therefore, we cannot simply deploy our forces and say, "stay there until the job is done;" that just won't work today. Conversely, if one examines the Vietnam conflict, what we had were 12 individual one-year experiences resulting in chaos, no vision for victory, and 12 one-year wars. That approach doesn't work either as evidenced by the outcome. A smart guy finds something in between. The analogy I used to make in all this, in the beginning of the war: 3rd Brigade of the 101st deployed four separate times in almost the first five years and in each case, they deployed to a different location. That's looking a lot like 12 one-year wars. Instead, the army should have given the 101st a sector for the next 10 years and then resourced them four deep at every position to rotate people in and out, always maintaining continuity. If you were trying to approach the Iraq War through a traditional, conventional mindset, you got 12 one-year experiences but if you adapted your formations to the fight you were in, you made changes that ensured people were familiar with the ground they were fighting on. One can only contemplate how many lives might have been saved by taking this type of approach rather than the one we did.

Port side view showing the damage sustained by the Arleigh Burke-class guided missile destroyer USS *Cole* (DDG 67) on October 12, 2000. (Wikimedia Commons/United States Navy ID 001012-N-0000N-001)

Utilizing simulation and intelligence fusion can also reduce unfamiliarity for those who haven't ever deployed to a particular area. I have always felt that using gaming to facilitate this type of learning provides another option to increase situational awareness, but we haven't done that either. To be clear, there are gaming applications out there that the army uses. These aren't what I am suggesting. Take existing topographical data and simulation and merge IED strikes into a three-dimensional gaming scenario that is constantly updated so that units can go over these scenarios prior to deployment. Again, my premise here was anything you do to decrease the first 90 days of unfamiliarity in combat saves lives.[6]

An article in *Global Security* provides an excellent overview of common components of IEDs, offering insight into the poor enemy success ratio regarding inflicting casualties on friendly soldiers.[7] It also provides a terrible comparison of soldierly qualities of Arabs vice Vietnamese. The author who is unknown provides a specious argument articulating that Arabs are poor soldiers comparatively speaking to Vietnamese. In this premise, the author points out that the Vietnamese were more successful in inflicting casualties in Vietnam with similar devices. I disagree with this comparison that Arabs are poor soldiers. It is difficult to compare the two conflicts and their participants. The terrain is significantly different, and the Vietnamese were at war for much longer than the Arabs in Iraq were.[8] Thus, making inferences based solely on successful casualty-producing events without considering the terrain, the experience, and technology is a recipe for flawed conclusions. As this

View of the USS *Cole* showing suicide boat IED damage. (Wikimedia Commons/U.S. Navy photo by PH2 Leland Comer)

chapter progresses, it is important to focus on understanding the greater context of any conflict. The next portion of this chapter attempts to understand that through what is referred to as a center-of-gravity approach.

Strategic Center of Gravity (COG) Concept

The next work examined in this analysis is the theory of Dr. Joe Strange's "Centers of Gravity & Critical Vulnerabilities: Building on the Clausewitzian Foundation So That We Can All Speak the Same Language."[9] Dr. Strange postulates:

> We should retain the current concept of critical vulnerabilities but should return to the original Clausewitzian concept of centers of gravity, and that Joint Pub 3-0 should be revised accordingly. It also indicates two new conceptual terms, "critical capabilities" and "critical requirements." These later terms bridge the gap and explain the relationship between centers of gravity and critical vulnerabilities and provide Service and Joint planners a logical and useful aid in designing OPLANS to protect friendly sources of power while facilitating the defeat of the enemy's sources of strength.

Building upon the traditional Clausewitzian concept of centers of gravity, Dr. Strange clarifies the concept and relationship between centers of gravity and critical vulnerabilities. He does so without corrupting the genuine good sense and wisdom found in each of the current Joint and Service manuals regarding defeating the enemy at the strategic, operational, and tactical levels of war. His clear and compelling discussion of the critical concept merits serious consideration by those responsible for clarity of thought as well as unity of effort in the development and execution of war plans.

Dr. Strange's work is qualitative analysis and utilizes various historical records of warfare and selected major conflicts involving American military forces since the Revolutionary War. The variables in this study are essentially qualitative and provide greater clarity by exposing adversarial vulnerabilities in a more precise and logical manner than previous efforts at describing warfighting doctrine. The study populations for this concept are conflicts and warfare the United States of America participated in since the inception of our armed forces. The study found that United States military warfighting doctrine did not adequately address the process of determining adversary critical vulnerabilities in evaluating previous adversaries. Dr. Strange suggests we need to go back to the original concepts of Clausewitz and expand on this methodology while adding systemic logical processes to determine enemy critical vulnerabilities focusing our strategic efforts.

Dr. Strange concluded the incorporation of this approach to conducting analysis of enemy centers of gravity and corresponding vulnerabilities improved existing warfighting doctrine. He also postulated commanders and their staffs were provided with more effective processes to attack the enemy while preserving friendly centers of gravity. Dr. Strange's work is exceptional but does not address political-military factors of potential adversaries. Although his theory provides an effective means of determining adversary vulnerabilities, the theory fails to address critical components of society and culture, which can influence conflicts outcome. In essence, the theory is valuable along first-order effects but potentially breaks down as we approach second- and third-order linkages in any given society.

Understanding this concept and determining a reverse "center of gravity" analysis is critical to protecting one's own internal centers of gravity. This is all too inconsistent in determining our own internal weaknesses. This has been a critical observation throughout a significant number of conflicts. As a matter of record, one of the constant themes throughout the American military experience, over the last 30 years, has been a strategic lack of patience. A prime example was the mission in Somalia in 1993. Loss of 18 soldiers during a heated battle in Mogadishu expedited our departure. Historically, the collective patience level of the American public is minimal at best. This factors into these types of conflicts and the calculus to undertake them. Again, it bears repeating that IEDs are weapons that appear primarily focused on attacking the American national will while simultaneously disrupting our freedom of action.

The next resource evaluated is a handbook produced by the John F. Kennedy Special Warfare Center (JFKSWC) titled *Special Operations and International Studies Political Military Analysis Handbook*. The basic premise of this study is the following:

> This handbook has been prepared by the faculty of the "Regional Studies Course" to support a program of study that prepares Army officers for Special Forces, Civil Affairs and Psychological Operations assignments abroad. In the course, students survey five world "regions"—Africa, Asia, Europe, Latin America, and the Middle East—and study one of them in some depth. The faculty uses the sixteen discrete "Political-Military Factors discussed herein as common reference pints for teaching the course's five regionally focused seminars. More important, they are introduced to the students as a reliable framework for analysis that, when applied judiciously, will lead to a sophisticated understanding of the dynamics within the foreign country or region of their assignment. Furthermore, the framework provides a start point for specific analyses of associated operational issues, questions, and problems.[10]

Essentially, the nature of this approach is to define the operating environment first rather than going straight to the adversary. It is an attempt to understand how the overarching environment impacts the mission you are conducting. It is important to note the U.S. Army designates only one center of gravity, although recently there has been significant debate regarding this paradigm. I have witnessed units designate multiple centers of gravity and that always confused me because these approaches don't always align under the mission and run the risk of corrupting any guidance provided in commander's intent. Thus, the context of this work provides for developing an initial understanding of the operating environment through the study of the specified 16 political-military factors that assist units in understanding their area of operations. A rigorous analysis of the political-military factors provides the basis for exposing critical vulnerabilities and serves essentially as a quasi-full-spectrum intelligence preparation of the battlefield. The fusion of this information ultimately allows the commander and his staff to determine the enemy's center of gravity and attack the vulnerabilities ascertained.

The construct of this work is qualitative and provides examples of the relevance of each of the political-military factors through various vignettes. A potential shortcoming in the study is not utilizing a specific set of data points. To maintain consistency, the study should examine all wars of a given nation-state and apply the political-military factors accordingly. The variables of this study are essentially qualitative and provide commanders and their staffs with a conceptual and cognitive framework to break down geographic areas where friendly forces might conduct operations. This approach is certainly not quantitative and lacks consistent analysis to be truly effective as a qualitative study. The overall effort is positive and provides an approach to exposing adversary vulnerabilities or understanding greater personalities involved in the framework of where a given unit is operating. The study populations for this concept are conflicts and warfare. The study is a core text for U.S. Army civil affairs, special forces, and psychological operations officers, providing doctrine on how to conduct systemic analysis on a geographic area to assess probable behavior and vulnerabilities of potential adversaries. It is a doctrinal cornerstone of how special operations forces conduct area studies and develop courses of action for military operations.

The text provides a construct, allowing a complete political and military analysis of a potential area of operations. This prepares U.S. special operations forces for any type of potential operation. Contextually, the study provides a theoretical framework supporting current army doctrine. It represents an intangible in that there is minimal quantitative evidence offered other than the logical assertions. It provides an excellent model to conduct traditional analysis for conduct of military or peacekeeping operations in a given geographic area. The method proscribed in *Political Military Analysis Handbook* provides all the tools necessary to assess the thoughts, mindset, and feelings of an indigenous population or set of populations. This essence of what lies between the "gray matter" of local populations, in a given geographic area, is what is missing from Dr. Strange's centers-of-gravity approach. The incorporation of political military factors would presumably allow for broader understanding of potential operating environments incorporating emotional and native knowledge presently unaccounted for.

Although there are no sources that directly address a hybrid theory of both studies, there are several short works or papers that address Dr. Strange's COG concepts. Most notably are the works of LTC Antulio Echevarria. Echevarria wrote a paper in 2002 addressing Dr. Strange's COG concepts, *Clausewitz's Center of Gravity: Changing our Warfighting Doctrine Again.*[11] While he agrees in principle with Dr. Strange's methodology, he disagrees with the premise that there can be more than one COG. Although he does not directly come out and say it, he does as much when he advocates a change of Dr. Strange's COG to a critical capability. Additionally, he contends that the following caveats should be added to the COG concept:

> However, getting the definition of a CoG correct is only half the battle. War planners need a practical method for determining what a specific adversary's CoG is. Such as:
> Step 1: Determine whether identifying and attacking a CoG is appropriate for the type of war we are going to wage.
> Step 2: Determine whether the adversary's whole structure or system is sufficiently connected to be treated as a single body.
> Additional Recommendations:
> Redefine CoG as follows: Centers of Gravity are focal points that serve to hold a combatant's entire system or structure together and that draw power from a variety of sources and provide it with purpose and direction.
> Resist "salami-slicing" the adversary into tactical, operational, and strategic CoGs. The bulk of our efforts and intermediate objectives should focus on destroying the CoG.

Echevarria's analysis provides an interesting critique of Dr. Strange's work and adds to that work by suggesting that we may need to go back to the original context of Clausewitz, or at least his personal interpretation of what Clausewitz was trying to say. The central focus of his study is war and the theories of Clausewitz. The study is qualitative and provides vignettes where the author feels a need to address an appropriate issue. Overall, the work is thought-provoking and provides valuable insight into an army-centric perspective on Clausewitz's theory presented in *On War*.[12] As it relates to this book, it is another take on how we should be framing these problems rather than simply a debate over what Clausewitz was attempting to say.

I have always tried to look at the context of the fight I am in because, depending on the effect you are trying to achieve, it may dictate different considerations attacking an alternative center of gravity. So, in Iraq, was I attempting to defeat the Sunni or the Shia, or was I attempting to empower one or the other? That question will dictate almost certainly a different tactical and operational center of gravity to say the least. As stated throughout this book, I always questioned the rationale of what we appeared to be doing. To further examine this construct, if we were hell bent on establishing a democracy in Iraq then we should have acted like it. I am fairly sure we weren't, but that seemed to be the direction we were headed for most of the last 20 years. What exactly were we trying to do? If we were attempting to further democracy, then the Shia were going to be in charge in Iraq and that meant that Iran would become the dominant actor in the region. I am sure that's not what we set out to do, but that is the path that occurred. As a result, where that center of gravity lay depended on what exactly we were attempting to do in Iraq. Ultimately, the debate about what constitutes a center of gravity and how that concept is defined is a necessary discussion contributing to greater understanding of what role IEDs plays in current warfare. It also potentially applies to asymmetric warfare.

Asymmetric Warfare Foundations

The fourth category of literature are works that fit under the greater umbrella of asymmetric warfare. These provide philosophical arguments supporting the assertion consistent with the premise contained in this chapter. The primary question in this debate is whether guerrilla warfare falls into the greater context of asymmetric warfare or not. Rick Atkinson suggested that the IED provided a method to engage the United States unconventionally and focused on our strategic center of gravity, which was the number of U.S. casualties.[13] It goes without saying this approach falls into an asymmetric category but some of these problems were created by bad choices not a sinister design by some informed resistance plan. We got here on our own account, not by some dastardly plan of the resistance. When we chose to "Deba'athify, we basically started a resistance movement with people who were potentially on our side and then we rubbed salt in the wound when we went down the path of democracy, almost guaranteeing Sunni resistance.

Tony Capaccio argues the conventional thought process of building better armor does not overcome an enemy who builds bigger bombs. He believes it was simply a cat and mouse game, which the enemy adjusted to through building larger bombs.[14] This was also the argument that several of us made over time, as it applied to an "economy of scale" failure because the amount of money we spent was inordinately high compared to the amount of money the enemy spent to counter our protective technology. That was a losing approach. We go bankrupt over time because we don't attack the problem, instead dealing with the symptom (roadside bombs). A better approach attacked the network while simultaneously addressing why the population resisted our efforts. Of course, if we managed to make an enemy of the Sunni because of the path we took, then no approach other than victory in this battle would dislodge them from their approach. John Poole argues that Islamic armies are 0 and 7 when fighting conventionally and 5-0-1 when fighting unconventionally or asymmetrically.[15] This observation is critical to this chapter and the premise discussed previously about how the enemy engaged us and how they approached their efforts to dislodge us from Iraq. An observation throughout this, is that we were still running the equivalent of the "fullback dive" in football, simply attempting to run the same play. We did not adjust our formations, we did not adjust our deployment preparation cycle, and we did not effectively attack the network. In a similar construct, Robert Steele, provided a monograph stating that the threat abided by no established set of rules as traditional nation-states do and consequently required entirely new strategies to deal with.[16] I pointed this out throughout the fight and continued to champion moving away from attempting the time-tested approach of trying to drive a round peg into a square hole. This fight required different thinking and different people than the army traditionally produces. A similar observation was provided by the late Congressman Ike Skelton who stated that to adjust to the tactics of our adversaries we needed to learn from the past.[17] Personally, I would be all for this since one of our shortcomings continues to be not considering the lessons of the past. This book discusses many of the problems I personally witnessed. It never hurts to keep a historical perspective and consider lessons learned from the past regarding asymmetric strategies. While not all inclusive it is always better to understand what lessons from the past are before departing on a different approach. Put another way, if you are blindly going down some misinformed strategy, then you are a fool. A lot of the choices we made in this fight bordered on incompetence, and I discuss them throughout this book. Understanding these types of conflicts will assist us in our future endeavors and is the key to developing strategies for tomorrow's conflicts.

DK Matai argues there are five dimensions of asymmetric warfare and that traditional nation-states are ill-prepared to conduct warfare in this paradigm.[18] He focuses on cyber warfare as a trend that will characterize the future, but also points out what we in the DOD would characterize as domains, making specific mention of land, air, sea, and space. This is not a blinding flash of the obvious for those that have been professional military officers as we have also task-organized forces and doctrine to work in these domains. What changed was how our enemies attacked us and later in this book there will be significant discussion on technology and unmanned systems as threats and opportunities. Unfortunately, I have minimal confidence in our government's ability to address this because we appeared to have missed the changes in how these systems presented serious threats. My personal study of unmanned aviation systems, and how little the FAA has done to address these threats should create significant concerns for any student of asymmetric warfare.

Heller and Stofft in *America's First Battles* state America's ability to predict a future war has been abysmal and we must learn from our past mistakes to adjust to the unpredictable nature of modern warfare.[19] As this book is being finished, we have been at war for nearly 20 years in the Middle East and Southwest Asia and from my own personal perspective I don't believe we are any closer to achieving what we set out to achieve than when we started this mess. This always goes back to the question: What exactly are we attempting to achieve? As you will hear me say time and time again, were we attempting to empower the Sunni, Shia, or sit on the fence? First, sitting on the fence doesn't appear to work very well in that part of the world and almost inevitably upsets both sides and puts our military forces at risk. I am relatively confident we weren't attempting to further Iranian hegemony in the Persian Gulf so that only left one choice left, and that was to theoretically empower some secular Sunni government in Iraq which served as a counterbalance to Iran. That was always the concern with all this and drove my own personal observations about how we approached this war. This cannot be overstated: What exactly were we trying to achieve? From that recognition, flows a center-of-gravity analysis. This should then have driven our targeting and operational efforts. This also becomes apparent later as I discuss technology and how it is potentially a game changer in this type of warfare. Finally, when examining this problem set, we need to do so with an eye on potential major combat operations against a rising threat in the Pacific from China. As I will continue to state throughout this book, every dollar I spend on the fight in the Middle East and Southwest Asia is a dollar I am not creating potential future capability against a peer/near-peer adversary. Bernard Fall in *Street Without Joy* suggests in 1964 that the concept of "revolutionary warfare" was as misunderstood then as I suggest that asymmetric warfare is misunderstood today.[20] Isn't that the truth. It is amazing that all this literature and previous experiences point to many of the solutions that ought to guide our approach to this problem. Do not hold your breath in expectation of any emergent epiphany.

The Department of the Army study on anti-guerrilla warfare (1954) reinforces that many of the lessons of counterinsurgency and irregular warfare remain timeless.[21] This is discussed in a later chapter that makes many of the same observations, yet we often repeat the same mistakes time and time again. It clearly never hurts to look back at the core elements of revolution and Mao in 1937 argues that the purpose of all engagements is to provide the background for the propaganda war.[22] Despite these observations we continue to ignore this core precept. Mao goes further to state that in an unconventional construct, everything is propaganda. Personally, I differ somewhat on this because all the creative propaganda in the world doesn't replace victory on the battlefield. Most wars are won by destroying your opponent's will to wage war and this is done by removing the critical components that allow the adversary to conduct warfare. Make no mistake, the will to continue the fight was critical but it did not replace an ineffective campaign on the ground. The goal in all this should have been to find balance and it was my observation that we actually missed the boat on both these fronts. All this created an interesting debate given the trend of Islamic extremists' actions. Reinforcing these observations is T. E. Lawrence's classic work, which provides examples of what an Arab unconventional approach can accomplish with minimal resources.[23] Given our lack of planning in the initial stages of this war, and the fact that both Iraq and Afghanistan were gigantic weapons caches, was it any wonder that we found ourselves in the predicaments we were in? It shouldn't have been and instead of attacking the network, for most of this war we were risk adverse, choosing to remain on the FOB rather than getting out among the people. This was a critical mistake in dealing with these threats. All these works suggest that the purpose of guerrilla warfare allows an inferior actor to engage superior actors and defeat them. While each author may approach the argument in their own way, they arrive at similar conclusions. Authors who either through outright dismissal of the concepts of guerrilla warfare, or failure to address these concepts, impart valuable insight into conventional thought and reluctance to engage in new warfare paradigms. I personally find this indicative of where the vast majority of army is and is one of the primary reasons I wrote this book, attempting to change the way our leadership and officers think about this war. There is ample evidence that authors like Rosen (*Innovation and the Modern Military: Winning the Next War*, 1991) and Liddell Hart (*Strategy*, 1954) never really understood the impacts of asymmetry and devoted little energy toward addressing the concept, being more content to address the traditional aspects of warfare. This is the classic example of traditionalists versus out-of-the-box thinkers.

Religious Terrorism

The next discussion applicable to this subject is the question of whether "religious terrorism" and jihad are a greater part of asymmetric warfare. Jonathan White devoted an entire chapter to "religious terrorism" in *Terrorism and Homeland Security*. White summarizes the different arguments, by various experts, regarding the differences and motivations associated with the concept of religious terrorism. White's work provides an excellent reference document and provides linkages to other scholarly works on the subject of religious terrorism.[24] Poole argues in *Tactics of the Crescent Moon* that Al-Qaeda in Iraq's motivation was to expel the United States from Iraq and form an Islamic caliphate.[25] In doing so, the tactics they chose were central to the idea that the IED supported religious terrorism as a subset of asymmetric warfare. The IED and suicide bombers were primary major weapon systems of Al-Qaeda in Iraq.

Ahmed Hashim provided a discussion on the nature of the insurgency in Iraq. Within this insurgency, Hashim, points out that there were multiple fragmented religious movements resisting the United States and Coalition objectives due to the perception of many Muslims that westerners were in Iraq to seize their resources. Additionally, Hashim saw a religious overtone where clerics were reviving the concept of jihad and the need to expel infidels from Muslim lands.[26] Sandra Mackey contributed insight into the state of Iraq just prior to the invasion and the complexities associated with a potential American intervention into the fabric of Middle Eastern society. She expanded on this concept by exposing the potential flaws with prospective United States offensive actions in a post-9/11 world.[27] Esposito in *What Everyone Needs to Know about Islam* argued that the Sunni developed a model that marginalized opposition and manifested a culture of violence. Esposito also pointed out that the normal form of opposition expressed itself in various coups, violent overthrows, or religious wars of one form or another.[28] All of these concepts were supported by the belief that their cause was both pure and true, ultimately nesting it under a form of jihad. Given the nature of upheaval in Iraq and the Middle East, it was no surprise that this data was applicable to the situation the U.S. faced. Rohan Gunaratna in *Inside Al Qaeda* and "Suicide Terrorism: A Global Threat" provided a solid argument that Al-Qaeda was not just fighting in Iraq or Afghanistan but was instead waging a "universal jihad" and was far from defeated. Gunaratna provided an additional argument that the conflict was not necessarily a clash of civilizations but instead a clash within the civilization of Islam. He pointed out that only a minimal percentage of Muslims supported terrorism. This debate is critical to understanding why the voices of moderate Islam have been suppressed for so long and why we should focus our efforts to assist in a counter narrative.[29] Ahmed Rashid in his work *Taliban: Militant Islam, Oil, and Fundamentalism in Central Asia* contributed an excellent chapter on what he considered to be the "New Great Game." This referred to the competition between Russia and the United States (replacing Great Britain) for influence and control over Central Asia and the resources that accompanied that control.[30] This information allows the reader to understand the force of the perceptions at work in this region and the greater Middle East. Although not directly related to the current construct of this chapter, the information provided background data indirectly into the greater perceptions of Muslims throughout the region. The extension of that argument was itself a critical debate. Was this a war against specific actors (primarily nontraditional) in the Middle East or was this a war of ideas? If this was a war of ideas, then what actions were traditional nation-states, to include the U.S., taking to promote moderate interpretations of Islam vis-à-vis extremist approaches? What role did the IED play in all this? There are ample resources on the subjects of asymmetric warfare, religious terrorism (including jihad), and guerrilla warfare but there is absolutely no scholarly data on what role the IED plays in these asymmetric strategies.* In searching to define the concept of asymmetric warfare, three is a plethora of definitions that exist and the easiest approach in attempting to define this is to use a common definition. Dictionary.com defines the concept as:

> Warfare in which opposing groups or nations have unequal military resources, and the weaker opponent uses unconventional weapons and tactics, as terrorism, to exploit the vulnerabilities of the enemy.[31]

Contrast the above definition with LTC Kenneth F. Mckenzie's definition of asymmetric warfare from *The Revenge of the Melians: Asymmetric Threats & the Next QDR* provided to assist in defining this problem:

> Leveraging inferior tactical or operational strength against a stronger actor's vulnerabilities to achieve disproportionate effects with the aim of undermining the stronger actor's will in order to achieve the asymmetric actor's strategic objectives.[32]

This definition synthesizes how IEDs potentially related to the concept of asymmetric warfare. In very simple terms, a weaker actor despite being outgunned and outmatched technologically can inflict significant damage upon the stronger actor through a series of engagements that amount to nothing more than small hit-and-run

---

* This is one of those epiphanies that happen to you in combat when you realize that we are potentially going about this the wrong way. While not the only realization I came to (there were many), this one hit me somewhere between 2003 and 2004 when I was a member of a Special Mission Unit and I was tasked with dealing with the emerging threat of IEDs.

missions. The key to this concept is disproportionate effect, not the relationships. Over time, this enables the weaker actor to inflict constant damage to the stronger actor. One of the primary lessons learned from the Vietnam War was that any war that the United States undertook required the support of the greater population. In an open and frank discussion of internal shortcomings, the United States revealed what amounts to a strategic center-of-gravity vulnerability. The United States when conducting a lengthy war effort must gain and maintain the support of the population. U.S. adversaries have learned this and are under the belief that if you kill a few Americans constantly, eventually the United States population, and by extension the government, will lose the will to continue the fight.

The next definition, which requires examination, is guerrilla warfare. John Nagl in his work *Counterinsurgency Lessons from Malaya and Vietnam: Learning to Eat Soup with a Knife* contributes to the discussion with the following definitions:

> The essential features of guerrilla warfare are avoiding the enemy's strength—his main fighting forces—while striking at outposts and logistical support from unexpected directions. This principle is now often described as "asymmetric" but is as old as the word "**guerrilla**" itself.

and

> The essential features of guerrilla warfare—the tactics of applying weakness against strength and the clever use of terrain to conceal guerrilla forces from the enemy's main body—have barely changed since the days of the Romans and the Persians. What has changed and made guerrilla warfare an altogether more potent form of conflict for the accomplishment of political goals, is the addition or revolutionary politics to the mix.[33]

From the definitions above it is easy to see how the concept of guerilla warfare related to the use of IEDs in Iraq. An application of the use of IEDs is consistent with the spectrum of guerilla warfare involving small-scale attacks and ambushes. This enables the insurgent to avoid becoming decisively engaged. In very simple terms, the use of IEDs fits well into the guerilla warfare construct. Having established definitions for both asymmetric warfare and guerrilla warfare, we will move on to establishing definitions for terrorism, religious terrorism and jihad.

Religious terrorism and jihad are not terms that are interchangeable but often their meanings are often interpreted to be the same. The term that is easiest to define is jihad, defined by John Esposito in his work on Islam as follows:

> Jihad (to strive or struggle) is sometimes referred to as the Sixth Pillar of Islam. The importance of jihad is rooted in the Quran's command to struggle (the literal meaning of the word jihad) in the path of God and in the example of the Prophet Muhammad and his early companions.[34]

and

> The history of the Muslim community from Muhammad to the present can be read within the framework of what the Quran teaches about jihad. These Quranic teachings have been of essential significance to Muslim self-understanding, piety, mobilization, expansion, and defense.

> Jihad as struggle pertains to the difficulty and complexity of living a good life: struggling against the evil in oneself—to be virtuous and moral, making a serious effort to do good works and help to reform society. Depending on the circumstances in which one lives, it also can mean fighting injustice and oppression, spreading and defending Islam, and creating a just society through preaching, teaching, and, if necessary, armed struggle or holy war.[35]

In exploring the above definitions, both citations easily incorporate the use of IEDs into a greater interpretation of jihad. If the Iraq conflict was interpreted as a form of resistance to the perceived occupation of Muslim lands requiring expulsion of infidels from Muslim territories, it fits well. Additionally, these definitions are often manipulated for the benefit of extremist Islamic movements to justify violence in support of their specific cause. Referring to the definitions of asymmetric warfare and guerrilla warfare, it also becomes apparent that both guerrilla warfare and jihad are more likely forms of asymmetric warfare than potentially the other way around. It is easier to fuse the concepts of guerrilla warfare and jihad into asymmetric warfare than attempting to approach the concept from the alternative explanation in which asymmetric warfare is potentially a subset of guerrilla warfare or jihad.

The more difficult concept to deal with is "religious terrorism." In dissecting the meaning of this term, it becomes necessary to define terrorism and then add in the meaning of religious. Jonathan White defined terrorism in *Terrorism and Homeland Security* as the following:

> Terrorism is an anxiety-inspiring method of repeated violent action, employed by (semi-) clandestine individual, group, or state actors, for idiosyncratic, criminal, or political reasons, where-by –in contrast to assassination—the direct targets of violence are not the main targets. The immediate human victims of violence are generally chosen randomly (targets of opportunity) or selectively (representative or symbolic targets) from a target population and serve as message generators. Threat-and violence-based communication processes between terrorist (organization), (imperiled) victims, and main targets are used to manipulate the main target (audience (s)), turning it into a target of terror, a target of demands, or a target of attention, depending on whether intimidation, coercion, or propaganda is primarily sought.[36]

Religious terrorism is another subject altogether and in looking up a suitable definition for this term, there were several definitions available, but Bruce Hoffman in *Holy Terror: The Implications of Religious Terrorism* provided ideally the most useful application of a definition for that concept. That definition is:

> The volatile combination of religion and terrorism has been cited as one of the main reasons for terrorism's increased lethality. The fact that for the religious terrorist violence inevitably assumes a transcendent purpose and therefore becomes a sacramental or divine duty [that] arguably results in a significant loosening of the constraints on the commission of mass murder. Religion, moreover, functions as a legitimizing force, sanction[ing] if not encouraging wide scale violence against an almost open-ended category of opponents. Thus, religious terrorist violence becomes almost an end in itself—a morally justified, divinely instigated expedient toward the attainment of the terrorists' ultimate ends. This is a direct reflection

of the fact that terrorists motivated by a religious imperative do not seek to appeal to any constituency but themselves and the changes they seek are not for any utilitarian purpose but are only to benefit themselves. The religious terrorist moreover sees himself as an outsider from the society that he both abhors and rejects, and this sense of alienation enables him to contemplate—and undertake—far more destructive and bloodier types of terrorist operations than his secular counterpart.[37]

The examination of these two definitions provides the foundation for incorporating religious terrorism under the greater umbrella of asymmetric warfare. Terrorism or religious terrorism is a tenet and subset of asymmetric warfare that applies to how the concept, tactic, or weapons known as IEDs were being utilized in an asymmetric approach primarily in Iraq. Within this specific branch is a belief that religious terrorism drives terrorists who are driven by religious beliefs to wage war against a superior actor (primarily the United States) in the hopes of recruiting new members and furthering their cause. IEDs and suicide bombers merely represent a set of tools that the religious terrorists use to further their aims.

While inquiring into the concepts of jihad and religious terrorism, a prudent scholar is forced to evaluate the differences between the two concepts. From the definitions provided above and an extension of common sense, it seems fairly obvious that although the two concepts are similar, they are in fact different. Jihad is meant to be pure. It is why nearly all extremist Islamic movements seek to declare some form of jihad through a recognized *fatwa* or use of a significant religious cleric, thereby giving them a form of legitimacy. On the other hand, the concept of religious terrorism is aligned more closely with being an extreme position taken by a fringe sect. Thus, there is obviously a difference that is often overlooked between these terms that often becomes interchangeable to the misinformed.

One of the aims of this chapter of is to provide an approach that represents a significant move forward in the study of this phenomenon because there is no significant literature that addresses the use of the IED as an emerging tactic in asymmetric warfare. As a result of the shortage of material associated with this discussion it was necessary to merge several related concepts into an overarching paradigm which addresses the potential divergent motivations of various groups. The integration of the concepts of guerrilla warfare, jihad, terrorism, and religious terrorism under the umbrella of asymmetric warfare provides a hypothesis that comprises all the potential motivations of current and future adversaries. There is a relative if not complete absence of information regarding this subject and is why this book provides value to the ongoing debate. The significance to the Department of Defense and capacity to promote American national interests should be invaluable. Failure to address these information gaps and provide recommendations could result in grave consequences. At the very least, the U.S. and other Western democracies will continue to see a rise in this type of warfare unless we learn to defeat it.

Notable Statistics on IEDS and Asymmetric Conflict: Strategies Existing for Dealing with IEDs and Asymmetric Conflicts

Rick Atkinson in his work discussed the rise in numbers of IEDs in both Iraq and Afghanistan over the last few years.[38] A greater question emerged from this data, namely was this trend limited to Iraq and Afghanistan or was this indicative of a future trend? To date, there are no known works associated with the concept of incorporating IEDs countermeasures with asymmetric conflicts. Not surprisingly there are many materials and approaches, which deal with how to mitigate the consequences of an IED, reducing the effects of IEDs, how to spot them, and how to react once they go off. What is missing and has been missing in this discussion is how to combat the use of IEDs. How do you defeat the entire concept? How do we engage asymmetric actors and their actors emplacing IEDs before the explosion? How do we defeat their networks?

The Problem

The improvised explosive device (IED) was the latest concept or weapon that empowered the advancement of asymmetric warfare. Unless countered, this trend in warfare would allow weaker actors to engage superior actors and win.

The fire ship is conceptually the same as a kamikaze attack in WWII and the 9/11 bombers using commerical planes as suicide airborne IEDs designed to create mass casualties in the Pentagon, the World Trade Center, and White House. It's also conceptually no different than a suicide VBIED, which is what was used in Lebanon (1983), and multiple events in Iraq and Afghanistan. (Wikimedia Commons/*The Royal Navy*, 1907, A. London and C. Black)

Opposing Arguments: Centers of Gravity

The primary requirement for any asymmetric approach to succeed is the availability of an exploitable vulnerability. Without that vulnerability, there is no asymmetric advantage. The theory provided above requires the United States possess a critical vulnerability that opponents can attack. Dr. Joe Strange's center of gravity (COG) work provides the framework for arriving at U.S. internal critical vulnerabilities. That process arrives logically at a friendly center of gravity, which centers on the national will of the United States. American adversaries in Iraq were incapable of defeating United States military forces on the field of battle. Unfortunately, not all battles are won or lost on the battlefield.

The Vietnam War provides an excellent example of how a nation's military can win nearly every major battle on the battlefield but fail strategically—specifically, failure to protect a critical vulnerability linked to a strategic center of gravity. The United States' perceived reluctance to accept casualties is a significant vulnerability that American adversaries seek to exploit. Dr. Strange advocates the use of the center-of-gravity concept to assist in solving these types of strategic discussions. There are two primary alternative methods for defining the operating environment the military conducts operations in. The first alternative method of defining an operating environment is the JFKSWC political-military factors analysis handbook approach.

If the Dr. Strange center of gravity is a top-down logic-centric approach, then the JFKSWC model is the "bottom up" methodology. The 16 political and military factors that the JFKSWC model suggests are the rough equivalent of being told to "understand the environment" that you operate in. To arrive at a conclusion that assists in resolving whatever problem one is forced to deal with, one must understand the environment that they operate in. While Strange is logic driven, the JFKSWC approach is diametrically different and suggests that to solve any given problem an organization faces, the members must be intimately familiar with the political, religious, ethnic, and cultural aspects of the region where they aim to conduct operations. There is legitimate wisdom in this line of thinking. The primary problem with this theory is that it does not account for any internal centers of gravity. It is purely outwardly focused. There is value in applying this methodology to Dr. Strange's approach but not as much value in applying the center-of-gravity approach to the JFKSWC model. Strange accounts for both internal and external centers of gravity while the JFKSWC model accounts for only the external area of operations. In contrast, LTC Echevarria attempts to expand on the Clauswitzian model in his work *Clausewitz's Center of Gravity: Changing our Warfighting Doctrine Again* but differs from Dr. Strange in several key factors.

LTC Echevarria's central theme differs from Dr. Strange because he suggests there is primarily one center of gravity.[†] In essence, Dr. Strange's COG work suggests there can be multiple centers of gravity at multiple levels of war while LTC Echevarria suggests that in sum there is only one primary COG. The experience in Iraq suggested that LTC Echevarria was wrong and Dr. Strange correct. There were multiple organizations or factions resisting the Coalition and Government of Iraq (GOI). To suggest that there was one center of gravity for every organization, faction, criminal enterprise, or tribal entity resisting the establishment defies logic and all common sense. A rudimentary examination along the simple ethnic divisions in Iraq suggested that at the lowest common denominator there were different centers of gravity for either the Shia or the Sunni. Shia support typically came from Iran while Sunni support came from Saudi Arabia, Kuwait, Egypt, and Yemen. Exacerbating this phenomenon was the tribal nature of politics in Iraq and the fact that tribes were not simply aligned along sectarian lines. Tribal confederations are very complex and can involve many different intricacies. LTC Echevarria's examination appears to be more relevant to large, armored battles envisioned on the plains of Europe fought by professional or large standing armies than the nature of conflict the United States faced recently. Given all the above, Dr. Strange's work stands the test of practical application. It is the most flexible of the theories and allows for an easier assimilation of other techniques than the other two primary theories that allow for the inclusion of alternative principles.

Dr. Strange's methodology provides the most comprehensive application of current warfighting doctrine. In that capacity, a good student of Dr. Strange is forced to conduct an internal examination of the United States' potential centers of gravity. It is no secret that in recent campaigns, the United States has either disengaged or failed to achieve its publicly stated objectives—in Vietnam, Lebanon, and Somalia. The common factor in all three conflicts was the reluctance to take casualties or the perception that the war was no longer worth the cost. In Vietnam, in 1968, the Tet Offensive provided the catalyst for the eventual withdrawal from

---

[†] Antulio Echevarria, *Clausewitz's Center of Gravity: Changing our Warfighting Doctrine Again*. PA: Strategic Studies Institute, 2002. As I have said throughout this work the optimal approach to using these models is a hybrid approach. I had thought about conducting a doctoral study with combining those into some greater hybrid theory that I had postulated might be called theory that I had coined POL-MIL-COG. I am still convinced that combining both approaches provides a better predictive model than using each individually. That goes as far back as 1998. Once the GWOT started, I was decisively engaged for the next 14 years. I don't agree with LTC Echevarria's point that there is only one true center of gravity. I think the move toward complex adaptive problem models makes that construct problematic as planners too often attempt to identify one center of gravity. In the end, it's a movement to contact, and the C-plus plan rehearsed seven times is infinitely better than the A-plus plan never rehearsed. Sometimes it's just better to get after the problem. In all honestly, the enemy will adapt and the problem will change so it's just better to come up with a decent problem frame and then move out.

Vietnam. Despite decisively losing on the battlefield, the North Vietnamese won a strategic victory. The National Command Authority (NCA), the White House, and the military had, over time, combined to create unrealistic expectations of victory or for simplicity, unrealistic expectations. When the American public was confronted with a nationwide offensive by the Vietcong and North Vietnamese during Tet, they lost faith in the war because the actions on the ground didn't coincide with the message leaders were sending. As a result, the war appeared no longer worth the perceived cost in the national conscience, and eventually led to our withdrawal.

Lebanon and Somalia also provide examples to American adversaries that if one kills enough Americans, the United States will simply pick up and leave. In Lebanon, it was a suicide bombing attack at the Marine barracks in 1983 that killed 243 Marines that led to an immediate withdrawal. Similarly, in Somalia in 1993, 18 soldiers died, and the United States picked up and left. If the mission was worth putting lives at risk prior to those events, then it was certainly worth staying to finish the job. If nothing else, it brings into question the decision making at the National Command Authority level regarding commitment and cost. What message does this type of response send to the adversary? How do IEDs fit into all of this? What is the primary purpose of the IED? As stated previously, the IED appears to be a weapon aimed primarily at creating casualties while reducing freedom of movement.

Opposing Arguments to IED Employment

The IED is a multipurpose weapon ultimately limited to the imagination. While employment seemed primarily focused on killing or maiming American soldiers, IED employment is not limited to hit-and-run tactics or potentially as an asymmetric actor's artillery. Far from it, the IED has multiple uses, which are not limited to only asymmetric tactics. There is nothing to prevent IEDs from being utilized as a canalizing device to support a large complex attack. There is risk in this approach when an asymmetric actor risks annihilation while massing his forces to inflict significant damage on a politically sensitive target. The payoff must be worth the risk as in Tet. There is also nothing preventing conventional forces from utilizing IEDs as a supplemental weapon system against the insurgents. There is evidence that the insurgents utilized IEDs as early warning devices, as obstacle belts to degrade friendly forces' freedom of movement, or to create an improvised defense in depth preventing access to critical insurgent strongholds. There is nothing preventing criminals, terrorists, and rogue agents from utilizing IEDs to support whatever their perceived cause and conscience may dictate.

Despite the alternative arguments, the fact remains that the single most effective weapon against American soldiers was the IED. Recent United States historical precedent for departing after limited casualties provides likely encouragement for any potential adversary. Combine that precedent and engagement patterns in Iraq and it became evident that the primary purpose of the IED was to engage and kill or injure as many American soldiers as possible while avoiding decisive engagement.

Even among high-ranking military officers there is heated debate over the purpose of IEDs. Many officers believe that it is simply a condition of the modern battlefield, and a modern adaptive military must learn to deal with these circumstances.[39] Although the IED is a condition of the modern battlefield, the statement in and of itself reveals nothing about the motivation of the attacker or the method which the adversary intends to deliver it. Understanding adversary motivation and employment is one of many steps in defeating the system. The logic associated with the belief that one should simply learn to deal with it is specious at best, and more than likely tactically negligent. "Just deal with it" doesn't help solve the problem.

Others might suggest that the IED is simply a tool of a greater adversary and not the tool of a spontaneous uprising. Sun Tzu's immortal work *The Art of War* would certainly look fondly on the concept that "The enemy of my enemy is my friend."[40] Did Iran benefit from the United States getting bogged down in Iraq fighting Iraqis? Viewed from a purely Iranian perspective, it is hard to imagine how Iran would have privately objected to the American military being tied up in Iraq rather than being free to potentially pursue American Iranian objectives. The Israeli experience in Lebanon dealing with Hezbollah provides ample evidence that many of the deadliest IED concepts were perfected by an Iranian-backed Hezbollah and exported to Shia resistance groups in Iraq.[41] There is merit in disrupting an adversary's alliances and has been the goal of many nation-states throughout history. The world is not simply black and white. For years, the most ardent support for the Irish Republican Army (IRA) came from the United States yet the object of IRA aggression was the defeat of one of the United States' closest allies (Great Britain). Most of the bombers who hijacked and flew the planes into the World Trade Center and the Pentagon on 9/11 were Saudis. Most fanatical Islamic extremists have their roots in Wahhabist interpretations of Islam. These interpretations of Islam emanate primarily out of Saudi Arabia and Yemen, both allies of the United States. As previously mentioned, the world is not black and white. Sometimes, there are elements in a given ally's borders that work against shared objectives. Consequently, it goes without saying that our long-term objectives should not be derailed because most of the 9/11 bombers came from Saudi Arabia and Yemen or that the U.K.–U.S. alliance should be fractured because most of the money to support the IRA originated in the United States. Given all the above, it was more plausible and practical that the United States, the Government of Iraq, and our combined allies faced a conglomeration of independent movements with varying motivations and differing objectives rather than a single unifying cause.

Opposing Arguments Against Success Associated with Asymmetric Warfare

Statistically, most guerrilla movements and terrorist causes do not succeed. White and Nagl suggest that the number of successful engagements utilizing asymmetric tactics fail to support a conclusion that asymmetric actors succeed in their causes.[42] Prior to the mass utilization of IEDs in Iraq, the IED was not a primary tool of the asymmetric actor. In fact, the asymmetric actor preferred to engage along traditional lines utilizing raids and ambushes. Raids and ambushes were typical with an occasional bombing of politically sensitive or militarily significant targets. The IRA did make use of indiscriminate bombings but those were aimed primarily at creating an atmosphere of terror as opposed to creating casualties simply for the sake of creating casualties. It is interesting to note that the British and American people represent two distinctly differing ends of the cultural spectrum. Americans by nature tend to be impatient and want instant gratification while the British are a more patient culture and consequently more willing to accept casualties. In noting the difference between British and American culture, one can start to discern why the IRA chose not to use roadside bombs simply to inflict casualties on British soldiers. It would have likely had little effect on their primary aim. In contrast, due to the characteristics of American impatience, instant gratification, and reluctance to take casualties, it is highly advantageous for the enemy to build bombs for the primary purpose of killing or injuring American soldiers. In Iraq, the primary purpose was simply to kill or injure soldiers. Given previous precedent, the enemy likely had a perception that he could create enough casualties to ultimately erode the patience of the American public.

A disturbing trend in warfare, the IED presents significant challenges. Previously viewed as a weapon of terror, roadside bombs are now an accepted weapon, thanks in large part to operations in Iraq. Society's acceptance of what was previously viewed as an unacceptable technique and the increasing proliferation of the use of IEDs in new locations indicates that this technique will increase the asymmetric actor's ability to engage superior actors and win. At the very least, the cost of defeating the asymmetric actor will increase significantly. This may move closely contested conflicts toward the advantage of the asymmetric actor. Additionally, the IED is a resource that is easy to assemble, flexible to mission needs, and plentiful. Essentially, the asymmetric actor has a new and effective technique to engage traditional nation-states.

An alternative view to asymmetric warfare and resistance movements is the traditional theory of absolute victory. Conventional wisdom dictates battles are fought to destroy an opponent's army or warfighting capability. What does one do when the warfighting capability resides in the population or in the perceived illegitimacy of a particular government? Asymmetric tactics preclude the use of large standing armies due to their vulnerability and lack of firepower. The key to survival and victory lies in the superior actor's inability to distinguish combatants from noncombatants. Picking the time and place of engagements allows the asymmetric actor to overcome traditional disadvantages. The Algerian conflict, where the French defeated the insurgents but alienated the local population, suggests that there is a fine line between winning tactically and achieving strategic victory.[43] The French were successful in ousting insurgents from the countryside, but they implemented measures that alienated the population. Algerians ultimately opted for independence rather than remain in the republic. There is a lesson learned from that process: one must ultimately refrain from measures so harsh that the average citizen views the insurgent and the government with equal disdain. Nagl suggests that the theories of absolute victory (Jomini, Clausewitz) are outdated and unlikely to occur in the future.[44] One can argue effectively that the last war the United States fought for national survival was World War II. Wars are more likely to occur at a level of national interest rather than national survival. For democratic nation-states to justify and effectively prosecute wars of national interest it is incumbent to maintain the support of the people.

U.S. Strategic Center of Gravity

The United States strategic center of gravity was the "national will" to prosecute the Iraq conflict.[45] The critical vulnerability, which attacked the U.S. center of gravity, was casualties. The more casualties that the United States took in Iraq the more debate there was about the value of American involvement in Iraq. This is no different than the debate that occurred in Vietnam after Tet. It is also comparable in nature to the same debate over whether the nation should have been involved in Somalia or Lebanon. While the circumstances are unique in each case, the principles are similar. As the investment went up, the debate shifted to a cost-benefit analysis and whether the war was winnable. As an open society, our military and political journals reflected discussion over this very debate and assisted our adversaries in determining their strategy. In essence, the debate assisted the enemy in conducting a modified form of battle-damage assessment. As discussed previously, a prudent adversary would note that the United States left Somalia and Lebanon due to casualties. In Vietnam, the United States left without achieving its stated objectives because the war was viewed as a quagmire that could not be won after the Tet Offensive. Is it any wonder then that any adversary would focus on eroding the national will of the United States through creating casualties?

Presumptively, if the national will of the United States is the center of gravity, then casualties are the critical vulnerability, which attacks that center of gravity. The use of IEDs skyrocketed since the initial defeat of the Iraqi armed forces in 2003. Rick Atkinson's previously discussed work provided a stark comparison regarding the rise in rates of IEDs over four years (2003–2007). By comparison, the British saw roughly 7,000 IEDs in 35 years of operations in Northern Ireland. For the first time, in the summer of 2007, IEDs in Iraq topped 3,000 in one month. That is an average of over 100 a day. In January 2006 the rate was approximately 50 per day. What was even more alarming was the proliferation of those trends. In Afghanistan, IED attacks totaled 22 in 2002, 83 in 2003, 1,730 in 2006, and over 1,000 in six months in 2007.[46] There was an obvious trend in these numbers, and it was consistent with the concept that the numbers would continue to rise until a solution was achieved. The IED may be a multipurpose device, but it was being used primarily to attack and kill American soldiers to erode the national will of the United States.

The number of killed in action (KIA) in Iraq did not rise concurrently with the number or IEDs. In very simple terms, the numbers of IEDs rose dramatically but the numbers of KIA remained roughly constant. The highest number of KIA in Iraq for any given was 126, while the lowest number was down in the 40 range. IEDs caused 65 percent of all casualties/KIA in Iraq.[47] Of course, the debate over numbers of killed was more a partisan debate than an actual legitimate discussion focused on practicality. There was a vocal minority in America that wanted the United States to exit Iraq no matter what the cost associated with that withdrawal. Given that, and the propensity of the media to report bad news, it was a ready-made argument. A contention but often necessary discussion was the perceived media bias that focuses on the bad news associated with Iraq. Prior to GEN David Petraeus's arrival as the Multi-National Force-Iraq commander, the mission in Iraq was on course to fail. Like Vietnam, the discussion inside the beltway and throughout America had shifted to a need to leave rather than see the mission through. With the mainstream media focused on casualties and the term "quagmire" being tossed around interchangeably with Iraq, the United States had been on the brink of once again departing without having achieved its stated objectives. Under the leadership of GEN Petraeus and nearly six months of "surge operations," the debate in Washington shifted so dramatically that one struggled to find any news coming out on Iraq at all. The old phrase "the silence is deafening" offers a perfect analogy for what happened after the surge. Unfortunately, it must be noted that the IED was the weapon that nearly brought the United States to the brink of failure in Iraq and our adversaries took notice.

Currently, the United States military has no peer. A logical derivative of that fact drives students of warfare to conclude that U.S. adversaries must seek asymmetric alternatives to challenge U.S. interests. The historical precedent established by U.S. actions in Vietnam, Somalia, and Lebanon encourage adversaries to contest American interests through propaganda and information warfare. The national will or conscience of the United States is influenced by the information environment. Mao asserts that in revolutionary struggle, propaganda is everything.[48] The absolutely insane debate over body armor and armored HMMMVs was the epitome of disinformation. At some point, good enough is good enough. If you build better armored HMMMVs, the enemy just builds bigger bombs. Large buried IEDs disproportionately killed more American soldiers than any other IED.‡ Patton once said, "That the best is the enemy of the good."[49] A similar concept applied to building better mousetraps (armor and high-mobility multipurpose wheeled vehicles or HMMWVs). At some level there was a point of diminishing returns. The author's personal body armor weighed over 33 pounds without a combat basic load and was very bulky during his last rotation to Iraq. The primary combat vehicle of the United States military is the HMMWV. It is hard enough to maneuver in a HMMWV with no body armor on. The requirement to conduct immediate fire and maneuver during a close ambush with body armor on and a basic combat load is extremely difficult. Adding more weight and cube-space to the current setup would preclude effective egress and maneuverability during combat operations. Yet despite these factors, this was the very debate that ensued nationally over the individual body armor and survivability of the HMMWV. Building a better mousetrap did not stop the enemy from building more lethal bombs. Better tactics to kill the enemy before he emplaces the IED or severely degrade his ability to utilize the IED ultimately results in less casualties and more enemy KIA. The enemy understood clearly that he could not defeat the United States militarily and his only hope lay in an information war. Utilizing the IED and a massive propaganda effort, the enemy's aim is to erode the will of the American public to support continued operations in Iraq. The war was about propaganda. No U.S. platoon-sized element ever lost a kinetic engagement in Iraq.

In addition to Mao's previously discussed theories on propaganda, the memorable quote which Richard Halloran describes the exchange between Harry Summers, the author of *On Strategy: A Critical Analysis of the Vietnam War* and an unknown North Vietnamese colonel:

> The late Colonel Harry Summers liked to tell a tale familiar to many who served in Vietnam. In April 1975, after the war was over, the Colonel was in a delegation dispatched to Hanoi. In the airport, he got into a conversation with a North Vietnamese Colonel named Tu who spoke some English and, as soldiers do, they began to talk shop. After a while, Colonel Summers said: "You know, you never defeated us on the battlefield." Colonel Tu thought about that for a minute, then replied: "That may be so. But it is also irrelevant."[50]

This exchange epitomizes the very point that Vietnam, and by extension the Iraq conflict was about propaganda or what the United States military called an information war. An IED going off and killing American soldiers was important, but not nearly as important as getting that incident recorded and then disseminated

---

‡ This has been proven over and over again in Iraq and Afghanistan and is an example of why this was an economy-of-scale battle. You go to war with what you have and you learn to use it. This is not to say we shouldn't develop requirements based on emerging needs, but as a soldier you learn to use what you have. If you attack the enemy's network, then the bomb never goes off. More survivability is always good, but it is not a replacement for the spirit of the offensive.

in whatever way possible to the primary target audience, the American population. The IED was the primary means that enabled this information war. This sparked the debate within the American population about the feasibility, viability, and suitability of continued operations in Iraq. The entire process also supported enemy recruitment and finance because it showed donors the value of their contributions while also serving as a recruiting tool for those who wanted to join the resistance. Ultimately, the IED enabled two critical vulnerability attacks by creating casualties and offering endless propaganda opportunities.

Asymmetric Standoff Weapons

The IEDs is basically a standoff weapon system designed as a casualty-inflicting device. The concept is not much different than the Revolutionary War against the British in which significant combat actions were fought using asymmetric techniques.[51] Pesky colonials refused to engage the British Army in proper combat techniques and gentlemanly conduct of warfare, instead choosing to fight behind walls and trees, rather than squaring off with the most efficient and professional army of the day. The American Revolution was an asymmetric conflict. Much of the American Revolution was characterized by guerilla warfare campaigns led by leaders like Francis Marion and Nathaniel Greene. Does this sound familiar? If they were alive today, they would be disappointed in our institutions' current inability to grasp the significance of the conflict we found ourselves in. Insurgents and asymmetric actors in Iraq were philosophically using the exact same concept, to engage Coalition and U.S. forces—insurgent forces that directly engaged the American military in a firefight typically got killed or captured. Therefore, it was incumbent upon those groups to engage the U.S. or Coalition military forces in a manner where they had an advantage and avoided decisive engagement, allowing them to retain their combat power and fight another day. Failure to do that would typically result in loss of combat power, capture, and or death. The IED allowed the insurgent to engage Coalition and U.S. military forces without getting decisively engaged. The following is a rough list of the primary characteristics of an IED:

1. IEDs are not complex bombs. They are easy to assemble and can be made from a variety of materials. They can be constructed from material as easy to get as fertilizer or expended unexploded ordnance. They come in all shapes and sizes. Propane tanks were used as well as trucks full of explosives. It is really limited to imagination and improvisation.
2. The Iraqi insurgent application and use of IEDs focused predominantly on creating casualties made more sense than a field-expedient form of ammunition or modified obstacle, unless that was all that remained. The

crux of why IEDs were so problematic was the fact that an insurgent blends in with the population because they are part of the population. Thus, while a traditional military organization could use IEDs, it makes less sense to do so and is likely to be used in a latent incipient type of warfare rather than mid- to high-intensity conflict.
3. As stated previously, the IED allows the asymmetric actor to engage their enemy in a standoff engagement. Why become decisively engaged when you don't have to? The answer is straightforward common sense. The IED overcomes inherent firepower disadvantages that the adversary faces and provides the ability to inflict as many casualties as possible while ultimately living to fight another day.
4. IEDs can serve as early warning devices and protect insurgent sanctuaries by using the weapon as an obstacle belt or improvised defense in depth. High-value targets require protection. The IED enables the enemy's ability to restrict the movement of combat power into areas they want to protect. The concepts can be as simple as protecting insurgent leadership or as complex as denying access to a series of shops and factories assembling IEDs. For the patient, patterns emerged which provided valuable clues toward the actual disposition and purpose but there was no easy answer to this problem. It required hard work and familiarity with the terrain to discern the subtle differences. As the enemy became more emboldened and confidence grew in their use of IEDs, they graduated to the use of IEDs in support of complex operations, complex raids, and ambushes.
5. Almost all IEDs come with some form of early warning and communications system to assist in their placement and execution. The enemy was more patient than we as Americans were used to being. It was one of their strengths. They waited to exploit vulnerability and weakness.
6. While not universal, the IED also came with some form of media or propaganda recording device. This was an information war. They wanted to record their success. In some respects, this was more important than the actual IED itself. Casualties were just a medium to initiating the debate among the target audience. There was someone watching and recording what was going on and they wanted to get their message out in most cases, but this was not a universal axiom for the simple reason that if the enemy was using IEDs as an obstacle belt they probably were not recording the event.
7. There was a network which supported the assembly, delivery, emplacement, reconnaissance, and procurement of IEDs. While not universal, an increase in IEDs supported the contention that there was in fact a network that differed significantly in each location.

The Enemy's Artillery

While an IED comes in many shapes and sizes and is really limited to the imagination of the builder, there was a method to all this madness. IEDs were utilized for more than just creating casualties. Make no mistake that the primary purpose of the IED was to create casualties and attack the critical vulnerabilities associated with the U.S. center of gravity. On the other hand, there were instances where the IED was used for other purposes (early warning, obstacles, defense in depth) and in doing so, there must also have been a degree of logic in utilization. It would make no sense to use a large buried IED as an obstacle or early warning device since the purpose of that IED was to destroy or kill as many personnel as possible. That would certainly be a waste of firepower on something where the enemy could use a 60mm or 82mm mortar equivalent in a greater fire support system.

In separate efforts, going as far back as early 2007, when called back as a by-name request to serve as the Commander Multi-National Force-Iraq's personal C-IED advisor, I had written the first version of what has turned into this book. General Meigs simultaneously or near simultaneously had stated that the "IEDs are the enemy's equivalent of artillery, and artillery has always been the largest killer on the battlefield." To this day, I don't know who said it first, he or I, and to be honest it's really irrelevant since none of this is about credit, it's about getting after the enemy. A sort of chance meeting, of all places, out in Japan, in May of 2007 might have been the catalyst that connected the two efforts.§ The original version was called the "Counter-IED Playbook" and was approximately 182 pages. I and General (Ret.) Montgomery Meigs, the Director of JIEDDO, came to similar conclusions at roughly the same time, and both proposed in separate works that there were various types of IED calibers. In both approaches there was a methodology that suggested a rough equivalent of a fire support system of progressive lethality. The enemy did this simply

---

§ I had come out of Iraq in October of 2006, after a yearlong tour and had been assigned to the Standing Joint Force Headquarters (SJFHQ) in USPACOM. In the first few months I was called back to support the Iraqi surge as General Petreaus's personal C-IED advisor, but it was unusual in that I had a 'blank check" to get on a plane from Hawaii and get to Iraq any time I needed to but still remained assigned to PACOM. The first iteration of this support took place from February 2007 to May 2007 where I deployed back to Iraq. I did two things primarily during that time which included going out to support every major element in Iraq and more importantly writing the C-IED Playbook, all of this was done on a classified network. When I returned to Hawaii, I had to support an exercise on the USS *Blue Ridge* in Japan, *Talisman Saber 07*, where I served as the Fires director. These exercises had been supported by what was called a "Gray Beard," a retired general, usually an Army or Marine 3 or 4 star. In this case it turned out to be LTG Randy House who was also serving as an advisor to JIEDDO. My boss asked me to show him what I had written and he immediately asked for the entire file. It was my understanding that he started requiring every commander going through NTC and JRTC, to read it. It is very possible that work influenced much of what came out of JIEDDO, but as I said, as far as credit goes, it doesn't and has never mattered to me.

because he aimed to achieve the best bang for his buck. Assuming the enemy builds IEDs for no objective purpose is the epitome of ignorance. Never underestimate an enemy's capacity to develop a cogent strategy and always remember that the enemy gets a vote in this process. A popular saying that was heard in Iraq after about a year into the war was that "we already killed all the stupid ones." Giving credit where it was due, there was a method to their madness above and beyond simply killing Americans. The table below is a rough approximation of what an enemy fire support system utilizing IEDs might look like:

U.S. EQUIVALENT	ENEMY IED
60mm mortar	Hoax/homemade IED
81mm mortar	Rockets on timer/mortars
120mm mortar	IED on MSR w/accelerant
105mm howitzer	Victim-initiated IED
155mm howitzer	2 or 3 122mm/152mm
227mm MLRS	Daisy chain/complex IED
ALCM/LGB	Suicide vest/bomber
TLAM/LGB	VBIED/SBVIED
Precision-guided munitions	EFP array
JDAM	Large buried IED

While not all-inclusive, there was an overarching lack of effort to define IED design, the above approximation serving as a first attempt to clarify IED utilization. Defining a start point assists in discerning their reasoning, structure, and approach to assist in defeating the enemy's IED campaign. Forcing the enemy to move to a different engagement strategy or severely degrading his IED campaign had cascading positive consequences. Conversely, failure to address this trend would have had profound negative consequences in Iraq as well as on other traditional nation-states areas where asymmetric actors are present and willing to use these tactics.

Given the nature of the U.S. strategic center of gravity, the IED provided our adversaries an effective weapon system to engage American interests. Additionally, what happened in Iraq will also have second- and third-order effects throughout the rest of the free world. This kind of warfare will have a far greater effect on democracies or freely elected governments than it will against autocracies or various forms of dictatorships. Free societies require the will of the people to conduct protracted conflicts. Dictatorships and non-democratic governments do not, by nature, require the approval of the public to go to war. As a result, this trend of warfare will only increase the costs associated with neutralizing organized resistance and separatist movements in democratic countries and societies. Simply put, this new trend in warfare benefits terrorists, insurgents, jihadists, and separatists. Ultimately, by extension, this trend of warfare will extend an advantage to any weaker actor wishing to formulate some type of resistance against a traditional nation-state.

Other Applications: IEDs Enable Asymmetric Warfare

What are the implications of how IEDs could potentially enable asymmetric actions? Why is this important? It doesn't take a rocket scientist to figure out that the Iraqi trend in warfare enabled the traditional model of guerrilla warfare. It was a cheap and easy method to attack the traditional institution of the nation-state, was plentiful, and easy to construct. Traditional models of guerrilla warfare will benefit from the concept and tactics of IEDs. Above and beyond that concept, the IED now has mythical "rock star" status. This is the weapon and strategy that brought the world's only superpower to the brink of failure in Iraq. Warfare in general is basically about adjustments and innovation. History is full of examples of failure to adapt to new forms of warfare.

Terrorists, jihadists, and rogue actors will undoubtedly benefit from the proliferation of IED technology and tactics. Terrorists and religious terrorists display traits and tendencies, which indicate a future expanded use of IEDs. Their mental predisposition to violence, "the ends justify the means," and willingness to die makes them one of the more dangerous organizational models who could potentially adapt to new tactics learned from recent successes. The independent nature and remote characteristics of the IED, as a weapon, provide an ideal approach for terrorist campaigns and objectives. Of all the potential proliferation problems associated with IEDs, this potential branch poses one of the greatest threats. The rise in numbers of IEDs foretells future difficulties. Unfortunately, sooner or later this trend will find its way into the world of international terrorism.

Recommendations to Combat the Rising Trend in IEDs

This trend in warfare will not reverse itself unless specific actions are taken to render these tactics and weapons less effective. This requires a dedicated and deliberate effort by the government and leadership to allocate resources toward solving this problem. This problem will not solve itself. To accomplish that, the following broad actions must occur:

1. Dedicate resources and quality personnel to attack this problem. The Manhattan Project provides an excellent example on how to partner industry, government, and the brightest minds to attack a specific problem set.[52]
2. Develop training centers, a professional force to deal solely with this problem, and a dedicated professional cadre to train the force and increase awareness of this alarming trend in warfare.
3. Develop a comprehensive information operations campaign plan to isolate and vilify the users of IEDs to separate them from their traditional support base.
4. Link the tactical to strategic level of information operations strategy (which currently doesn't exist) and synchronize this plan to our foreign policy to

provide a cogent plan of action. This ensures that actions at the tactical level support strategic intent and that our national actions are coordinated. It is the essence of ensuring your actions and deeds coincide with your narrative.

Conclusion

This chapter provided the rationale for, and evidence of, an increasing use of IEDs in support of asymmetric strategies. IEDs enable asymmetric warfare strategies and place an arduous burden on traditional nation-state resources. Over the past 30 years, the United States has shown a recurring trend to disengage from conflicts when it has taken even a low number of casualties. Consequently, our adversaries perceive that the U.S. strategic center of gravity is the "national will" and we are viewed as a "paper tiger." The IED creates casualties and KIA. The IED directly attacks a critical vulnerability linked to the U.S. center of gravity, which is our "national will." Increased casualties and KIA fueled the debate over the value of the Iraqi War in the United States. The IED is the enemy's artillery as well as a multipurpose weapon. Failure to undertake the actions listed in this document will result in an increasing use of IEDs, greater instability in the world, and potential defeat. The IED presents significant challenges to the traditional nation-state and its ability to maintain order in an increasingly unstable world. The IED provides weaker actors the ability to engage superior actors and defeat them, or at the very minimum, make it so costly for them that they disengage from what would otherwise be viewed as a fight which was both necessary and in their best interest. This chapter has shown how the concept of the "national will" and the reluctance to take casualties can endanger the United States' ability to win potential conflicts with actors that use IEDs to attrite U.S. forces. The IED provides adversaries a cheap and effective way to inflict casualties on a stronger actor and defeat them. The general purpose of IEDs and their characteristics were explained throughout this paper. The IED ultimately enhances asymmetric warfare concepts. This chapter provided statistics on the rising trend in IED use, as well as the prediction that unless actions are taken, a continued expansion of IED-centric warfare will contribute toward enabling weaker actors to defeat stronger actors. The IED is the latest weapon or tactic that enables asymmetric actors to engage traditionally superior actors and win, if we do not develop a counterstrategy to defeat this approach.

Lessons learned from history show the most effective counterinsurgency forces are those that adapt their force structure to the fight they are in. Destroying networks faster than they can reconstitute enables success. Creating specialized forces to deal with this problem enables expertise and familiarity, increasing response times rather than letting each unit fend for itself, which is the existing approach. Philosophically, conventional thinkers believe IEDs are simply a condition on the battlefield. When that's the departure point, you typically don't modify your force structure or change formations to deal with these types of enemy attacks (*this is called institutional paralysis*). That's the insanity associated with big organizations not thinking outside the box ultimately resistant to change. The army spends billions of dollars to build better mousetraps (MRAPs, armored HMMMVs, and gadgets to find IEDs) but can't make even the smallest change in organizational structure. Take that in for a second as well as the implications of that type of problem framing. Historically, most successful COIN operations involve modifying force structure to fit the fight you are in. We're still in almost exactly the same formations we were in and leader selection processes that we have used for most of the last 30 years with minimal deviation. Change for the sake of change isn't good but this approach doesn't encourage innovation or for that matter the building of warriors. We build administrators, and most of them don't get it. It is how you arrive at "Crystal Software says that IEDs are going to go off between 0700 and 1000 hours." No, you bozo, it's just a reflection of how we conduct operations and where we currently have vulnerabilities, and the enemy capitalizing on it. If you were to roll back the "early warning network," don't use one entry and exit point at the FOB, become less predictable, don't clear the roads every morning at the same time as the last six months exactly the same way every day; instead, create combat outposts outside the FOB and use the FOB as a rearm, refit, and reconstitution area vice being on the FOB for 22 hours a day and venturing out for two hours a day, and you might find that the entire equation changes.

A recurring theme in this book focuses on our inability to adjust to emerging threats. Our inability to pivot to emerging threats is a root cause of that problem. As I stated earlier, it is what I have coined "institutional paralysis." We are spending more money, killing more of our troops than we should be, and ultimately getting weaker as a country because we haven't learned to deal with these issues. Who or what organization in our government should this fall under? Is this a DOD problem or is it a proliferation problem? Should we have a civilian IED czar in the CIA (proliferation) or is this something that requires a completely different agency? It was JIEDDO, but that is now Joint Improvised-Threat Defeat Organization (JIDA) under Defense Threat Reduction Agency. I always started out with a premise that unless you are in a war zone, there ought to be a civilian-led effort to bring the interagency efforts together under one whole-of-government approach. DOD leading the interagency approach is problematic, it doesn't work; I used to call it "unified purgatory" because it just doesn't work well.

CHAPTER 4

Seven Simple Lessons of Counterinsurgency[1]

The United States's involvement in Afghanistan and Iraq constituted the latest chapter of an ongoing pattern of involvement in small wars, insurgency, and low-intensity conflicts. There is a substantive body of knowledge detailing previous lessons learned. The collective experiences of other nations' involvement in previous small wars and insurgencies offer the prospective student of warfare the opportunity to garner what works and what does not work in similar environments. It is important to stress, upfront, that all insurgencies are different. Simply put, what works in one place may or may not work in another location. There are no "cookie cutter" approaches to this business. Conversely, a prudent student of warfare ensures that he is aware of those same lessons and acknowledges their application, where appropriate. Thus, when a particular lesson may apply, an enlightened planner can extrapolate that information and utilize that tactic, technique, or strategy, when and where it is applicable. The purpose of part 1 of this chapter is to compare and contrast the lessons learned from previous insurgencies and apply those lessons learned to Iraq and Afghanistan. The following, while not all-inclusive, represent a list of the significant lessons learned:

1. All insurgencies are different; there is no cookie-cutter approach.
2. Utilize one centralized intelligence system. Eliminate multiple-organization intelligence-gathering.[2]
3. Counterinsurgency is manpower intensive.
4. Protect the population.
5. Personalities matter.
6. Organize the armed forces to conduct a counterinsurgency.
7. The host nation's forces must fight most of the conflict.

All Insurgencies Are Different

While there is a lengthy list of small wars and insurgencies which we can acquire vast amounts of data from, the overall aim of this chapter is to provide a common departure point from previous lessons learned, ultimately comparing and contrasting the United States' involvement in Iraq and Afghanistan with regard to those lessons previously learned. What are the insurgencies that apply to what we were ostensibly trying to accomplish in both those countries? First and foremost, there was a potential religious undertone, which applied to operations in Iraq or Afghanistan. The United States was operating in an area where Islam was prevalent, and the perception of religiously motivated warfare affected the perceptions of the inhabitants of both these areas. As a result, clearly any analysis must attempt to use similar experiences wherever possible, although, as previously discussed, no insurgency is the same.

The single most important lesson learned is that there is no "cookie cutter" approach because all insurgencies are different. Culture differs from area to area and personalities matter. Dr. Paul Melshen of the Joint Forces Staff College states that insurgency is a "Thinking Man's game."[3] Despite what seems intuitively obvious, the United States Department of Defense leadership attempted to institute a strategy in Iraq, which emulated success in Afghanistan, yet the two situations were significantly different. What worked initially in Afghanistan proved to be a critical downfall in the initial and subsequent approaches to the invasion and occupation of Iraq. General Eric Shinseki, the Army Chief of Staff during the leadup to Iraq, predicted with remarkable accuracy the numbers of troops needed for the occupation of Iraq.[4] Unfortunately, the Secretary of Defense, Donald Rumsfeld, did not subscribe to the same school of thought, nor had he attended the Joint Forces Staff College and opted for the small wars and insurgencies elective taught by Dr. Melshen, a fantastic class and experience.[5] Had Secretary Rumsfeld attended that course, he might have learned the cardinal rule of insurgency and counterinsurgency warfare, namely, that there is no "cookie cutter" approach to insurgency/counterinsurgency and subsequently made a more informed choice about the actions we undertook in Iraq.

As discussed earlier, there is a plethora of lessons learned from many different insurgencies. While no insurgency is the same, there are similarities where a prudent student of warfare might gain some insight into how previous conflicts were waged—where they were waged successfully or, in some cases, where they were waged unsuccessfully and why. The prime focus of this chapter is to draw general observations regarding Iraq and Afghanistan with respect to previous lessons learned. Additionally, the experiences we want to draw from should bear some resemblance to the conflicts we were recently participating in. As a result, the conflicts which most closely parallel what occurred in Iraq and Afghanistan are Malaysia, Kenya, Algeria, and the Philippines. With the ongoing caveat, that no insurgency is the same, there are some similarities that may help. Iraq and Afghanistan both have overwhelmingly Muslim populations although they are not homogeneous. That is to say that Iraq and Afghanistan are each plagued by tribal and religious conflicts that sometimes make perfect sense and other times have no logic to them at all. It was a complex environment that required a thorough understanding of the landscape to operate effectively. Another of the primary lessons learned from the list of previous conflicts was to establish one intelligence agency responsible for the conduct of intelligence operations.[6] Did we do this in Iraq and Afghanistan? The obvious answer is no.

Utilize One Centralized Intelligence System: Eliminate Multiple-Organization Intelligence-Gathering

Experiences in Iraq and Afghanistan demonstrated that there was no centralized intelligence function singularly responsible for coordinating, synchronizing, and production of intelligence products. How can you have a single intelligence function when you don't even have a singular command-and-control function? The first echelon of command at which the United States may actually come closest to achieving that goal is at USCENTCOM. Even that is open for debate given the fact that there were operating forces from SOCOM which throughout the Iraq War answered only to their respective chains of command, instead of the theater commander which created significant challenges to synchronized and coordinated efforts on the battlefield. Thus, while it may be debatable that at various times, the Combatant Commander (USCENTCOM) may or may not have had operational control (OPCON) of those forces, it goes without saying that the actual theater commander, the individual responsible for Afghanistan or Iraq, did not. By extension, there was no singular intelligence organization responsible to the commander. This created significant problems in attempting to achieve unity of effort.

Counterinsurgency is Manpower Intensive

Counterinsurgency is manpower intensive. To the informed, this statement may seem like a blinding flash of the obvious, but it took arriving at near mission failure in Iraq before the United States took the necessary measures to correct an ongoing attempt to do things "on the cheap." Unfortunately, strategy becomes too often embroiled in the political moment. The author had multiple combat tours in Iraq and Afghanistan with both special mission units and conventional forces. I served as a troop commander, fires coordinator, FST chief, J3-IO, G7, J-39, J-35, A/DCG OPS and personal Counter-IED advisor for General Petraeus in Iraq, Afghanistan, the Horn of Africa, Malaysia, and the Philippines, totaling over 100 months of combat after 9/11. In that capacity, I saw nearly the entire spectrum of the conflict since its inception; this included by-name requests from the commander of MNF-I, a cross-service request from the USMC, and service in elite special mission units.

During the OIF 05-07 rotation a continuing trend, for what appeared to be nothing more than political reasons, Multi-National Division-North (MND-N) downsized from six-plus brigades to three brigades' worth of maneuver troops, ultimately going from 31 maneuver battalions down to 16. There was no justification for this reduction other than it was simply part of a flawed strategy to turn over responsibility to the Iraqi Security Forces, which appeared to be politically motivated toward creating the narrative that we were on a glide slope to turn over Iraq to the Iraqis. Training the ISF was the answer to all our problems.* Thus, when sufficient metrics were met for their training, we offramped another U.S. maneuver battalion. There were many people along the way who suggested that instead of that type of approach, the metrics should have been based on protecting the population and insurgent activity, but "we" had a plan and "we" were going to stick to it. To be brutally honest this type of approach just flat out didn't work, and I question the logic of anyone who thought that it would. You cannot live on the FOB 22 hours a day and go out in your sector three hours a day and expect to protect the population—it just doesn't work. When you are not there, the insurgents are. This was a hard lesson learned. An effective counterinsurgency is manpower intensive. Protecting the population requires constant presence and it takes a lot of troops and ideally a strategy to develop recurring familiarity with a particular sector.

Protect the Population

Throughout numerous small wars and insurgencies, successful counterinsurgent forces learned repeatedly that to succeed they needed to protect the population. Conceptually, if one were to apply that concept to Iraq and Afghanistan, the leadership did not learn that until General David Petraeus assumed command in Iraq. After taking command of Multi-National Force-Iraq (MNF-I), General Petraeus brought in more forces, and then pushed them out to combat outposts to secure neighborhoods, and by extension, secure the population. By doing this, he communicated to the population that the United States was committed to the long-term security of Iraq and reducing the tribal and religious violence that was occurring. One of the most critical aspects of this approach was getting off of the

---

* Then LTC Matter was present in MND-N, when the Commanding General of MNF-I told the assembled staff of MND-N in 2006, that the exit strategy was to train the Iraqi Army. That blew me away because it was so far from the truth of what was actually occurring on the ground. Typically, it should have been conditions-based and just as I made mention of the fact that we downsized from 31 maneuver battalions to 16, those moves should have been also based on conditions and that was not the case. Instead, by doing so we ceded the initiative to the enemy and ultimately, in my personal opinion, the Iraqi surge was simply to correct those mistakes. In the most rudimentary simple terms, it was correcting for exiting too much force when the conditions on the ground didn't dictate it. The idea of simply saying we were training the Iraqi Army and that's good enough and it's now their problem is the height of professional incompetence. It just means you are going to have to come back to fix what you didn't fix when you left too early and it wasn't based on achieving the objectives you set out to achieve. That's exactly what happened.

FOB and taking back neighborhoods from the adversary. This was key terrain and ultimately General Petraeus understood clearly that he had to protect the population to eliminate sanctuary. Consequently, over time, MNF-I, through the local commanders gained the trust of the Sunni population who had reluctantly allowed Al-Qaeda to operate in their tribal spheres of influence. Once the "Sunni Awakening" was underway, Al-Qaeda's survival in Iraq was in serious jeopardy and their days were numbered.

While Iraq became the critical fight, Afghanistan was relegated to the forgotten front. In essence, an argument could be made that Afghanistan had been nothing more than a holding action designed to eliminate sanctuary for Al-Qaeda and its local sponsor, the Taliban. Once the situation in Iraq was stabilized Afghanistan became the main effort. Afghanistan was always the wildcard in the greater U.S. post-9/11 strategy. What were we doing there? Was the United States involved in nation-building? Was the United States involved in counter-terrorism? What exactly was the strategy and what exactly are we attempting to achieve? From all appearances, starting at the initial involvement of United States forces in Afghanistan, a strong argument existed that the entire affair was nothing more than a continuing manhunt for Osama bin Laden and his lieutenants.† For all intent and purposes, the United States never developed an effective strategy to do anything but maintain the original status quo gained during the immediate aftermath of events on 9/11. To no surprise, Afghanistan saw little or no progress over 20 years. We needed to define what we were attempting to achieve there. That would clearly have been in our national best interest. The problem became one of ensuring that we did not allow Afghanistan to devolve into some form of ungoverned space, which then enabled potential adversaries some form of sanctuary.

---

† When I originally wrote this chapter it was in 2009 at Joint and Combined Warfighting School as I was leaving United States Pacific Command (PACOM). As this chapter was being finalized in 2020, we were still in Afghanistan and I don't think anyone could really answer what effect we were trying to achieve there. If we were there to get bin Laden, then we achieved that mission and the question became why were we still there. If we were doing nation-building, then I am not sure that we were doing that very well. What defined success in Afghanistan at that point? I remember saying to myself back in the beginning of the war that maybe we ought to have just empowered the warlords there and maybe we wouldn't still be there. Again, what exactly were we attempting to achieve there? I think that defined what we ought to have been doing but that was a grand strategy discussion that appeared to be absent in all this. Again, as a closing thought on this, maybe that's why were still there because no one and specifically, the NCA, Joint Chiefs, State Department, and CENTCOM could not articulate our end-state goals. Until we did that we were ultimately going to continue to spend our resources and as I have said throughout this book every dollar we spent doing offensive contingency operations was a dollar we weren't spending on developing capabilities to support major combat operations against a peer or near-peer competitor.

Personalities Matter

Over time, any prospective student of this form of warfare understands that personalities matter. In fact, most recently, that fact was evidently not lost on the new USCENTCOM commander, the former MNF-I commander, General Petraeus. With the firing of the senior American commander in Afghanistan, the Obama administration made a statement that personalities do matter and that likely, that decision was supported by General Petraeus. In Iraq, Lieutenant General Sanchez and later General Casey failed to apply the lessons applied by General Petraeus. The United States came very close to packing up and leaving Iraq, inviting further aggression and emboldening future extremist Islamic fanaticism. History has shown us that not everyone is good at this business. Some leaders are exceptional at this endeavor and others are just downright awful. Despite a trend over time, shown repetitively, that most conflicts that the United States becomes involved in are low-intensity conflicts, the Department of Defense continued to plan for the "Russian Horde" attacking through the Fulda Gap.[7] The focus continued conventional emphasis on National Training Center rotations, stressing traditional conventional force-on-force conflicts. It should be no surprise based on these recurring trends that it typically takes the mavericks of any service to bring some order to this messy business. Because of all the above, it should drive one of three logical derivatives. Either we need to acknowledge that we should refocus some of our resources toward these types of fights and invest in developing capabilities or just avoid the problem all together. A better approach would be to find some form of balance rather than what continues to be either one extreme or another. In the opinion of the author, this is a recurring all-or-nothing strategy, which appears to be a recurring problem in our overall approach.

Organize the Armed Forces to Conduct a Counterinsurgency

Unfortunately, for the same reasons that the U.S. military does not typically stress unconventional or asymmetric warfare over the traditional conventional force on force applications, they also do not make changes unless it is absolutely necessary. To date, there have been little if any modifications to traditional force structure to conduct counterinsurgency. While it can be argued that General Petraeus may have altered the approach in Iraq, he still used a conventional troop structure methodology to accomplish his objectives. An interesting observation associated with all of this suggests that either the institution is inflexible, or it is just too rooted in its ways to change. Although the United States may have succeeded in Iraq, it may not in fact be due to anything more than finding a compromise with the Sunni and had nothing to do with any decisions on changing force structure or modifying traditional tactics, techniques, and procedures.‡ To date, there are no known cases of organizing the force structure to conduct a counterinsurgency. Of course, one of the other primary lessons in low-intensity conflict, insurgency, and counterinsurgency warfare is that one cannot separate politics from warfare. The two are inseparable.[8] In 2009, General Stanley McChrystal may have in fact finally started to arrive at changing the makeup of formations, adjusting rotations, personnel, and force structure by attempting to develop a network approach. Had it been successful, it might have maximized the impact on operations in Afghanistan, but he was relieved, and we went back to business as usual which unfortunately was a second-order effect of the fallout of his relief and what we often refer to as the rule of unforeseen circumstances. I have personally known General McChrystal since the early 1990s, when I was a lieutenant in 2nd Ranger Battalion. I often tell a story of having helped plan the evacuation of American citizens from Liberia in 1990 at Fort Bragg for three weeks in an emerging crisis that we might have had to jump into Liberia, seize the airfield, and then conduct noncombatant evacuation operations. The guy I sat across for three weeks while planning that was a promotable major named Stan McChrystal. It's a small world. He was the right guy for the fight in Afghanistan, but it is what it is. A lot of special operators have some pretty wicked senses of humor that border on being cruel and the circumstances that surrounded his relief in my personal opinion were a bit extreme, although one could likely make an argument for or against. That age-old concept of acceding to civilian authority as a soldier comes to mind but at what cost? I think you would be hard pressed to find anyone that said that the circumstances that had people in his immediate inner circle making fun of the vice president was rising to the level of insubordination or something similar to what General MacArthur did in Korea with President Truman.[9] So, in a sense I always asked the question of who in the government didn't know that some of these people didn't have some callous and cruel senses of humor and that they didn't know what they were getting when they hired the guy. Sometimes it just appears we are our own worst enemy.

The Host Nation's Forces Must Fight Most of the Conflict

While there were Herculean efforts at trying to stand up both the Iraqi Security Forces and Afghan National Army, little of the fighting fell on their shoulders. Clearly, that

---

‡ Again, at the time of the writing of this paper, the general consensus was that we had actually succeeded in Iraq and at the time, in 2009/2010 that was true. The decision to leave Iraq in 2011/2012 by Obama was a strategic blunder and only forced us to return later. As I continue to say throughout this book, what exactly were we attempting to do there? Were we trying to empower the Sunni, Shia or be arbiters of the peace? Depending on how you answered that question, the downstream effects of that decision impacted how we should have approached any attempt at some greater solution.

transition was critical to any exit strategy and significant amounts of time, money, man-hours, and resources were expended attempting to achieve that goal. If there is a "takeaway" from this, it is that counterinsurgency is a messy business, and that transferring the bulk of responsibility to indigenous forces is a lofty goal that takes time. Democratic societies typically exhibit minimal patience and Americans in general are an impatient lot. Our collective national conscience and psychological need for immediate gratification increases our political leaders' desires for quick and decisive outcomes. Our leadership should have stressed the need for patience and the long-term benefits associated with a stable and productive Afghanistan and Iraq. Consequently, you would have been hard pressed to find that in either Afghanistan or Iraq that the bulk of fighting was being done by the host nation's forces.

The "Takeaway"

The aim of this portion of the chapter was to compare long-standing lessons learned from previous insurgencies and small wars with respect to Iraq and Afghanistan. There is a long-standing comment about American military officers not reading their manuals and even when they do, they fail to follow the doctrine contained in those manuals.[10] In the spirit of not paying much attention to our doctrine or finding a need to follow it, we also don't pay much attention to previous lessons learned and our collective performance to date would probably rate a C—at best. It took arriving at "near failure" in Iraq before the United States started to change its tactics and leader selection. Additionally, if you gauge the United States's performance by any ability of its major institutions to adjust to the lessons learned provided in this chapter, the grade goes down to one of nearly failing. There is an obvious need to break the traditional paradigm of ignoring previous lessons learned and develop a better understanding of how to conduct small wars and counterinsurgency operations. The force of individual personality might be the only saving grace at this point, but it took untold amounts of blood and national treasure to finally arrive at placing the right people in charge. Clearly, education, mentorship, and changes in our systemic approach to these types of conflicts are better choices than indiscriminate attempts to find the right man for the job.

CHAPTER 5

The Principles of War for IEDs and UAS Platforms

Despite the billions of dollars and thousands of personnel that worked on this problem, I know of no principles of war for C-IED study. This chapter, first initiated in 2007, is an attempt to take a crack at that.

Mass

According to *U.S. Army Field Manual 100-5: Operations*, mass is defined as follows: Mass—the effects of overwhelming combat power at the decisive place and time. Synchronizing all the elements of combat power where they will have decisive effect on an enemy force in a short period of time is to achieve mass. Massing effects, rather than concentrating forces, can enable numerically inferior forces to achieve decisive results, while limiting exposure to enemy fire.[*]

The Principle of Mass for IEDs (Mass)
Friendly
This is straightforward and focuses on massing the effects of combat power at the decisive place and time. Enemy IEDs prevent friendly forces from massing combat power at the decisive place and time because friendly forces don't know where they are. It is typically in the form of an ambush, booby trap, or obstacle. Some are victim-activated IEDs while others are command detonated. From an organizational approach, part of the problem is not concentrating forces. The author in early 2006 suggested that creating a mobile C-IED strike force would facilitate defeating this problem by creating expertise, which enables friendly forces to attack the problem faster and more efficiently. This is analogous to concentrating all the capabilities (or at least a significant amount of them) into a mobile strike force and would have been the actualization of the principle of mass. In addition to this benefit, the force

---

[*] This chapter draws extensively, and almost exclusively, from *U.S. Army Field Manual 100-5: Operations*. www.digitalattic.org/home/war/fm1005/index.php#principles01.

becomes highly proficient in defeating IED networks (familiarity with the problem). Ultimately, this is also what allows what is called the inkblot strategy to succeed. This concentration of power allows friendly forces to attack a network, destroy it, and then move to another faster than the enemy can regenerate it. At the end of the day, if you can destroy them faster than the enemy can rebuild them, you win and they lose.

Enemy

The enemy's ability to mass effects is limited in any IED-enabled asymmetric fight, although, to be sure, they attempt to maximize every strike. They record the event and use that media to maximize propaganda value, which in turn enables the leadership of the organization to advertise and ask for money and manpower (recruits). The strategy itself is a harassing strategy designed to slowly drain the resources and will of the superior actor. It is also a cost-imposing strategy which causes the superior actor to engage in huge investments to overcome what costs minimal amounts of money for the insurgent. Taken at a much larger perspective over time, it is costly and diverts resources from other venues which weakens the United State or any symmetrically superior actor in this type of fight. The enemy typically will not mass their forces in this type of fight because it makes them vulnerable to destruction.

The Principles of War for UAS Platforms (Mass)

Friendly

There is an entire chapter devoted to the emerging capabilities of UAS platforms later in this book. UAS platforms provide a game-changing approach to the IED fight and although investment is significant up front that approach would almost completely invalidate the enemy's ability to conduct their current form of IED-enabled asymmetric warfare that they are waging against us. This approach is called Airborne 24/7 and overwhelmingly reduces the enemy's ability to continue conducting any form of operations because they would be constantly under surveillance. This invalidates their current approach and simultaneously reduces their freedom of maneuver, and their ability to maintain any form of offensive operations.

Enemy

A more concerning issue is that the enemy is attempting to use UAS platforms to attack our forces. This takes what was essentially a counter-punch strategy that took advantage of our predictability and maneuver into a more offensive form of warfare. This further enables remote warfare with minimal risk at the point of attack to enemy forces. A swarm of UAS platforms would allow the enemy to mass firepower without becoming vulnerable to being targeted or destruction. They could cause significant damage to friendly force locations or enable costly attacks on logistical areas and supplies. The more concerning issue is that these same platforms can also be used as delivery vehicles for weapons of mass destruction (WMD, chemical or biological agents). This threat also exists inside the United States and is a significant threat if left unchecked (more about this later).

Maneuver

According to *U.S. Army Field Manual 100-5: Operations*, maneuver is defined as follows: Place the enemy in a position of disadvantage through the flexible application of combat power. Maneuver is the movement of forces in relation to the enemy to gain positional advantage. Effective maneuver keeps the enemy off balance and protects the force. It is used to exploit successes, to preserve freedom of action, and to reduce vulnerability. It continually poses new problems for the enemy by rendering his actions ineffective, eventually leading to defeat.

The Principles of War for IEDs (Maneuver)

Friendly

Immediately, multiple combat tours and countless months dealing with this problem have led me to be extremely pessimistic about this topic. We spend too much time on the FOB, and we don't have enough entry and exit control points, which allows the enemy to establish an effective early warning network. We don't do a good job of operations security (OPSEC), we don't do a good job of rolling back the early warning network, and we don't keep the enemy off guard with differing ways to deceive and then ultimately attack them. The simple truth is that we are way too predictable. As Americans we love routines. We roll out the gate every day at 0530 to clear the roads and are back by 0700 or 0730 at which point our first convoys head out. We must change this type of approach and create stress on the enemy's early warning network. There are multiple ways to accomplish this and later in this book there is an entire chapter designated to tactics, techniques, and procedures, which enable friendly forces to do exactly that. Simply put, if we don't take action to reduce the enemy's IED effort and their early warning network, we will not be able to reduce predictability. At that point, by default we arrive at a point where we lose freedom of maneuver. Yes, there are ways to overcome this and some of those ways will be brought up later but suffice that we are probably violating the intent of this principle of war by failing to take actions that enable our freedom of maneuver.

Enemy

IEDs by their very nature reduce friendly freedom of movement and simultaneously bleed the enemy (our friendly forces as the enemy views the problem). IEDs can be used to create obstacle belts preventing friendly forces from getting into key terrain or areas. IEDs also enable the enemy to engage friendly forces without becoming decisively engaged. Complex ambushes might eventually be a way the enemy achieves mass, but throughout the war, the enemy was limited to an IED-enabled form of irregular warfare. As a form of obstacle, a more advanced enemy may use IEDs as a canalizing strategy or use them to prevent reinforcement of an ambush site thus enabling massing their forces on a smaller Coalition or U.S. element or at least for a limited period. To be sure this is episodic and would have to be mindful of reaction times for close air support (CAS) or available quick reaction forces (QRF).

The Principles of War for UAS Platforms (Maneuver)
Friendly
UAS platforms are a potential game changer because they can simultaneously provide strike and ISR from above in an almost continuous fashion and provide persistent stare capabilities. This also enables friendly forces to use various payloads to find enemy IED factories, reduce enemy freedom of movement, and conduct strike operations. Saturation of the airspace can be achieved by pushing multiple platforms down to the brigade level, which would enable removing the adversary's ability to conduct effective IED-enabled warfare. This in turn enables more freedom of movement and puts the enemy in an even greater defensive role.

Enemy
As stated in the previous mass discussion, UAS platforms can also potentially be used against friendly formations with multiple payloads, swarms, and WMD. This is concerning and another reason why friendly UAS platforms to include an ability to take enemy UAS platforms down must be examined with the utmost haste. In a world where U.S. or Allied air forces dominate the air space, the enemy may resort to a short duration influx of small UAS platforms to attack our FOBs, troops, or critical targets. They may also develop or buy on the open market some type of electronic warfare, cyber, or directed energy weapons which might be capable of attacking any attempt at going "Airborne 24/7" and saturating the battlespace with strike and reconnaissance UAS platforms. If the enemy were able to conduct this type of maneuver operation it would create a recognizable signature that could be potentially exploitable but more than likely extremely short lived. Thought should be given to be wary of the enemy's desire to create a significant propaganda win in some type of spectacular event when examining this threat.

Economy of Force

Economy of force is defined as follows: Employ all combat power available in the most effective way possible; allocate minimum essential combat power to secondary efforts. Economy of force is the judicious employment and distribution of forces. No part of the force should ever be left without purpose. When the time comes for action, all parts must act. The allocation of available combat power to such tasks as limited attacks, defense, delays, deception, or even retrograde operations is measured to achieve mass elsewhere at the decisive point and time on the battlefield.

The Principles of War for IEDs (Economy of Force)
Friendly

IEDs from an enemy perspective are by the very nature of the approach an economy-of-force mission for the enemy. To achieve economy of force when conducting operations against friendly forces, the approach the enemy uses is predominantly utilizing IEDs. We need to go back to a concept of simply finding a way to do more with less. Most people who are reading this with any experience in this fight would say yeah, that's a blinding flash of the obvious but at the same time what is about to be suggested hasn't been done. Three distinct items stick out that defy common sense yet we are either doing the same thing over and over again expecting a different result, or in some cases, failing to take action. So, to those who would say this is a blinding flash of the obvious, take note because none of what I am about to suggest has been done to date. (1) Increase the number of entry and exit control points (ECPs) on our FOBs so that the enemy cannot have any reasonable assurance that our ground-assault convoys rolling out can be continually monitored. This means conducting cordon and knock, and constant measures to ensure that the enemy has limited observation and communication capabilities near our ECPs. This also means actively using deception and conducting radio frequency surveys to conduct pattern analysis around these areas. (2) Push UAS platforms down to the brigade level to saturate their area of operations with both strike and reconnaissance capability. (3) The establishment of a mobile C-IED strike force is in fact an economy-of-force measure because this force's main effort is conducting operations against IED networks.

Earlier, the discussion on seven simple lessons of counterinsurgency provided for organizing the force to conduct operations against the insurgency you are facing. In this case, it is an IED-enabled insurgency. That is the primary means in which the enemy inflicts damage against friendly forces, yet we still haven't changed a damn thing we are doing. If you are like me, you start to question the sanity of that approach and wonder if our leadership at the highest levels is just asleep at the switch. As a primary example, we are still attaching capability to battalions and brigades attempting to fight this fight as if it were a normal fight. It isn't. Someone once said that IEDs are a condition of the modern battlefield and my response to that is that they don't get it. In fact, it is quite the other way around where IEDs are essentially the modern battlefield that we will continue to see and since we are still running the exact same playbook, we make it easy for the enemy to adjust and overcome our sheer numbers and advantages in firepower and maneuver. Establishing a C-IED strike force enables the friendly force to develop expertise in this type of warfare. This enables the strike force to destroy enemy IED networks faster than they can regenerate. That is the true economy-of-force approach, which has been lost in this madness. In essence, what is needed is a change in design that will allow our forces to defeat networks at a faster pace than we have in the past.

Enemy

The entire IED approach is in fact an economy-of-force approach that ties down larger forces as well as creating a losing economy-of-scale battle for friendly forces. We are spending millions and millions of dollars in developing MRAPs and capabilities to find and defeat IEDs and the enemy's approach costs him little in comparison. That makes about zero sense at the strategic level of war. The enemy also uses IEDs in the form of obstacle belts just like we would use engineering assets and mines to prevent an adversary from having access to terrain or to canalize friendly forces into more advantageous engagement areas. Most of the enemy's ability to resist is a strategy based on conducting an IED asymmetric warfare approach.

The Principles of War for UAS Platforms (Economy of Force)

Friendly

UAS platforms provide an unprecedented approach to remove the ability of the enemy to emplace IEDs while also being able to find IED factories. The airspace above the IED-enabled asymmetric warfare battlefield is the critical high ground and key terrain in that fight. Providing persistent overwatch eliminates the enemy's freedom of movement and action. As stated before, although the investment is significant up front, if we spend significantly less time in a place like Iraq or Afghanistan because IEDs are rendered ineffective then the investment more than outweighs the cost up front. This course of action in the context of the problem centers on solving a problem in three to five years vice spending resources to maintain forces in a place like Afghanistan for nearly 20 years. The question one is forced to ask when critically examining this problem is why are we still doing the same thing we have done for the last 20 years? This is one of those examples that requires you to think through what we are trying to achieve and then ask does our organizational force structure architecture make sense.

Enemy

To avoid being repetitive, UAS platforms are both a threat and a potential solution to multiple issues. Within the realm of an asymmetric threat, the Federal Aviation Administration (FAA) is collectively on its ass. There is no enforcement arm associated with the FAA, and I will show that later in this book by proving that the interdiction rate is so low that it is essentially statistically insignificant. If you speed through any town in the United States, you will likely be pulled over by one of three potential law-enforcement organizations (police, sheriff, or the state patrol). If you use UAVs or UAS platforms incorrectly or unlawfully who pulls the user over and stops them from doing what they are doing? The answer right now is, unfortunately, no one.

Think about that for a minute ... that cannot be a good thing. Given the nature of this threat, one would think that this is something the FAA had worked out prior to incorporation of UAS systems into the National Airspace System (NAS), but that is not the case. It is easier for the military to deal with this threat downrange because the rules of engagement are more friendly than the existing laws in the United States. UAS platform payloads could attack infrastructure inside the United States with a lot more ease than the attacks on 9/11 and yet there hasn't been much done about this. Chemicals, biological agents, or explosives could all be attached to UAS platforms. From an economy-of-force perspective, this enemy course of action could be devastating. The return on investment would be astronomical because it would almost certainly spawn a completely new organization much in the same way that the Transportation Security Administration (TSA) now exists to prevent another 9/11. I should not have to expand on the monumental investment that the second- and third-order impact on an economy would require. I will discuss more on this concept later, but I consider the FAA's TSA approach a huge waste of resources because it is extremely unlikely that any plane taking off in the United States with primarily American citizens on board would ever allow itself to be hijacked again. The passengers would simply rise up and take the plane over no matter what the cost because they realize what is in store for them if they don't. Thus, the entire premise is both outdated and costly given the nature of the psychological change in how potential victims deal with this threat. In any strategic-level discussion on resources, this continued approach could potentially be viewed as a significant drain on resources that might be better spent in other ways.

Unity of Command

Unity of command is defined as follows: For every objective, seek unity of command and unity of effort. At all levels of war, employment of military forces in a manner that masses combat power toward a common objective requires unity of command and unity of effort. Unity of command means that all the forces are under one responsible commander. It requires a single commander with the requisite authority to direct all forces in pursuit of a unified purpose.

The Principles of War for IEDs (Unity of Command)
Friendly

Simply put, there is no unity of command in the C-IED fight. Each unit has their own approach and while there have been some efforts at education that I applaud, by organizations like JIEDDO, there is no overall unity where operations are synchronized. I have lived through this firsthand in multiple operations and what one unit does well, others do poorly, and sometimes operations run counter to each other because the synergy of effort focuses more on the traditional aspects of COIN rather than realizing the IED problem is part and parcel to the COIN fight—that recurring theme that IEDs are simply a condition of the battlefield and not how the enemy engages you. I think at times we just missed the boat on this because instead of changing our formations or creating a potential mobile C-IED strike force which enables our COIN goals, we look at it ass-backwards. The enemy uses IEDs to prevent you from getting to places, they attempt to bog you down, they attempt to erode the will of the American public but it's not just a condition on the battlefield. So much has been said about going after the network yet it is a completely fragmented approach and C-IED organizations are not the main effort, so at some point you stand back and question the overall understanding of what the enemy is doing and then attempt to take that away from them. As an example, where we had success, we got off the FOB and stood up combat outposts and denied freedom of maneuver to the enemy. Taking away the enemy's ability to conduct IED-focused operations changes the context of the problem. Going back to the center of gravity and critical vulnerabilities provides ample opportunity to develop critical targets which reduce the network, yet what I have watched over the last 20 years focuses on traditional company- and occasionally battalion-sized operations consistent with episodic presence. So, a lot of the resources that facilitate the enemy's C-IED supply chain come in from Iran and Syria. I always questioned why we didn't go to an old-school approach of conducting battalion- and brigade-sized reconnaissance operations along the Iraq–Iran border and doing the same thing on the Iraq–Syria border thereby making Iraq an island. If you eliminate the enemy's supply, then you increase the host-nation's forces' effectiveness because the adversary has nothing to fight with. You create a defense in depth along the border and then hold in the center with host-nation forces. What I have witnessed over time watching Multi-National Corps-Iraq (MNC-I) dictate throughout Iraq a completely idiotic curfew bifurcating competing objectives to some of the problems. It shows an overall lack of understanding and then consequently a unity of command. Another prime example of this was the decision to focus more on escalation-of-force incidents rather than IEDs. Thus, instead of achieving some greater effect on IEDs, it actually made it easier for the enemy to attack convoys without hitting civilians because they were more concerned about escalation-of-force incidents and in the process created a free fire zone. I have witnessed JIEDDO and CENTCOM put a person on an international state department designation that didn't do anything but alert the same person to the fact they were potentially being collected on. I could go on and on and on, and it's just not worth it. There is no unity of command in this problem set. DOD, FBI, CIA, NSA, DIA, DOS, Treasury, ATF, USDA, DEA, Commerce, DHS, Customs and USAID are all elements that potentially play in this problem set. If there is any unity of command, I challenge anyone to tell me who's running this show because it doesn't exist. It is also important not to discount the fractured nature of conducting operations across the theater of war and the fact that most of the support comes from areas outside the area of combat operations, known as support zones.

Enemy

Given the nature of what was just described above, the enemy has the advantage of a cleaner command-and-control (C2) infrastructure process than we do. Make no mistake there are fissures in this process, namely that their support and C2 is vulnerable to interdiction and there are essentially two competing networks (Sunni and Shia) that do not cooperate on a consistent basis. The enterprise moves manpower, explosive material, IED components, money, expertise, and ideology. Every effort should be made to fracture and reduce their leadership and chain of command. One could make an argument that focusing competing networks on each other reduces resources being focused on U.S. or Coalition forces. Without overstating the obvious, the concept of unity of command for the adversary is focused on a series of infinite small engagements and the structure is likely cellular, but what appears to have some degree of vulnerability is their supply chain to ensure resupply of IED precursors and components. This seems to be where the enemy is most vulnerable because their logistic network is not decentralized.

The Principles of War for UAS Platforms (Unity of Command)

Friendly

This is an emerging problem set that has not been well thought out. As discussed previously, the FAA has no enforcement arm to deal with any UAS threat domestically. It is all basically a good-faith exercise. If 9/11 has shown us anything it is the ability of the enemy to develop cunning ways to attack us and this appears to be a critical vulnerability that we have not protected. This is especially problematic because of the nature of the sector where it appears to be growing exponentially. If someone had said that 19 hijackers with box cutters would have brought down the WTC Twin Towers and attacked the Pentagon prior to that actual event, they would have been dismissed as overly paranoid. UAS platforms offer a similar approach in that it can be done remotely or launched and controlled without committing personnel, providing a form of standoff engagement. Obviously, it is not the same as hijackers, but it is still an asymmetric approach that can potentially cause a disproportionate return to the amount of investment. If you examine the 9/11 attacks in that context, it should be fairly clear that that action and several other similar attacks spawned what is now the TSA. The annual budget for TSA for FY 20 was $7.79 billion.[†] If you examine that in the context of a disproportionate

---

[†] David Pekoske, TSA Administrator, made these remarks to House Homeland Security Appropriations Committee, April 2, 2019. www.tsa.gov/news/testimony/2019/04/02/examining-presidents-fy-2020-budget-request-transportation-security.

response to a threat that is fairly unlikely in the future, we are spending nearly $8 billion a year on that threat. Let that sink in for a moment and realize that the cost to maintain that versus what it cost in terms of 19 suicide bombers (you can make a case that 9/11 was four airborne suicide airplane bombs or guided missiles). So, my immediate comment is that when you examine the threat that UAS systems pose, it's on the same level if not worse and it may in fact be more dangerous because it doesn't even cost a single life, if done correctly. It's truly standoff or remote warfare and it too would likely create a knee-jerk reaction by forcing us to create some form of UAS regulatory or enforcement agency that looks a lot like the TSA but instead focused on UAS systems. In the case of a UAS platform attack in the United States, who is the lead agency in coordinating the response? As a result of all of this, I always ask people who in Homeland Security, the FAA, DOD, or some local law enforcement agencies are regulating this potential threat? As it stands today, the answer is no agency exists and there is certainly no unity of command because of that.

Enemy

There is minimal evidence at this point of any emerging. Not to say there isn't unity of command in various organizations, but this is not a single orchestrated movement and instead a series of smaller, separate movements across multiple operational areas. In some cases, the threats are religious, some are organized crime, some are political, but all resemble various forms of hybrid asymmetric warfare. As I mentioned earlier, it would be advantageous to find ways to make these groups attack each other or at the very least ensure there is minimal or no cooperation between differing movements. To pull off some type of spectacular UAS attack where they mass drones, they would need to achieve some form of localized command and control. In simple terms their task is much easier than ours because when dealing with this type of threat, we must be vigilant and cannot afford to be wrong while they only need to be right once. Considering what is potentially at stake, it sort of surprises me they haven't figured this out yet and maybe that is a testament to several factors that put them on the defensive, e.g., fighting on the other side of the world, increased immigration vetting, and increased border security.

Objective

Objective is defined as follows: Direct every military operation toward a clearly defined, decisive, and attainable objective. The ultimate military purpose of war is the destruction of the enemy's armed forces and will to fight. The ultimate objectives of operations other than war might be more difficult to define; nonetheless, they too must be clear from the beginning. The linkage, therefore, between objectives at all levels of war is crucial; each operation must contribute to the ultimate strategic aim.

The Principles of War for IEDs (Objective)

Friendly

This is a much deeper conversation than simply trying to define a tactical military objective associated with destroy, degrade, defeat, or deter. The problem here is much deeper. The aim is not to defeat the IED but to defeat the insurgency or remove the root cause of the problem, which stirs the population and insurgents to resist. The IED simply enables the insurgent to effectively attack our forces. Removing the ability of the insurgent to effectively attack friendly forces creates a second-order effect of reducing the will of the enemy to fight. It is not to say that this in and of itself will remove the root cause of the problem. If the population is still disenchanted and committed, then they will simply find another way to resist. We must go back to what exactly it is we are trying to achieve in all of this, which begs a bigger strategic discussion, and whether this is a war of ideas, or some greater problem set. If it is something else, we need to be attacking on multiple fronts because we are not removing the conditions that allow our adversaries to flourish. Removing the networks that resist what we are trying to do in whatever location makes resistance more difficult. It's a whole-of-government approach but it begs a better understanding of the environment you are operating in. I go back to the comments I make throughout this book about combining the Strange methodology and the JFK Special Warfare Center methodology into a greater hybrid approach and examining problems from that type of combined perspective.

Enemy

It appears for all intent and purpose the primary objective of the enemy is the establishment of some greater religious or Islamic caliphate, at least in Iraq and possibly Afghanistan although that problem appears more complicated. The root causes in this war are related to those concepts as well as potentially coming to grips with a greater problem which is the entire idea of a zero-sum game in that part of the world. For most of the region's history there weren't enough resources to go around and so their calculus is shaped by an inability to grasp anything other than wins or losses. Water is more important than oil in that part of the world (certainly long-term outlooks) in my opinion. Modern irrigation can build up an agriculturally based economy rather than one based on oil, which changes the construct of a zero-sum game mentality because it creates an agricultural surplus. This enables change, ideally resulting in the belief there is more than enough to go around. That then provides a start to changing the zero-sum game belief so centric to that part of the world. Without further amplification, we need to attempt to get back to the root causes of the problem in that part of the world. Part of it is religious in nature, part of it is that Islam never had a reformation, part of it is education, women's rights, and the existing economic structure. Solving some if not all these types of ongoing issues peels back the resistance's ability to motivate their supporters. It removes potential grievances and underlying motivations for supporting the resistance.

The Principles of War for UAS Platforms (Objective)
Friendly

I contend as I have throughout this chapter that the best way to look at this problem is through what we are trying to achieve. For all the reasons previously established throughout this book, UAS platforms used in a better configuration and approach may allow us to remove the enemy's current ability to conduct effective IED attacks against friendly forces. The problem I see in all this is that we are too stuck in our infrastructure and, as an example, the executive agent for UAS platforms and their integration is the air force. I have devoted an entire chapter to this problem, but with the context of understanding objectives and how it relates to what we are doing, UAS platforms and their inherent organizational structure complicate the way we are fighting this conflict. It appears much more advantageous to make a significant monetary adjustment and push strike and reconnaissance capabilities down to maneuver-brigade level rather than continuing to do things the way we have. This will become apparent later in this book but for the sake of examining objectives, the comment is valid as it creates obstacles to more efficient courses of action. Removal of the adversary's ability to utilize IED-enabled asymmetric warfare forces the enemy to go to more traditional raids and ambushes which decreases their survivability.

Enemy

The enemy's use of UAS platforms is expanding but make no mistake if we don't work to solve this problem, they will use it to attack our critical infrastructure in the United States. We need to fix it now and not wait until it becomes a problem. Unfortunately, like most things we wait until there is a problem. The projected expansion of the UAS platforms in the United States will create huge increases in revenue so there may be a reluctance to restrict any of this growth. This is a significant threat that eventually the enemy will take advantage of. It would be wise to get out in front of this problem rather than be forced into a reactive and cost-prohibitive response.

Offensive

Offensive is defined as the following: Seize, retain, and exploit the initiative. Offensive action is the most effective and decisive way to attain a clearly defined common objective. Offensive operations are how a military force seizes and holds the initiative while maintaining freedom of action and achieving decisive results. This is fundamentally true across all levels of war.

The Principle of War for IEDs (Offensive)
Friendly

IEDs by their very nature are essentially an economy-of-force or defensive tactic at the tactical level of war. In fact, some might even be considered a booby trap (self- or victim-activated). At an operational or strategic level of war, they might actually be seen as an offensive technique but let's be honest, the enemy uses IEDs because they don't have tanks, airplanes, and ships. It's what is available to them, and we haven't quite figured it out, creating a process that is both cost imposing and lengthy. Make no mistake, the enemy's IED campaign is basically a limited offensive to make our efforts at bringing stability to Iraq or any other location costly. If at some point it becomes too costly then a national conversation emerges about what we are doing there and whether or not it is in our national interest to stay there. That conversation already occurred once in 2006 and 2007 during the start of the Iraqi surge when we were experiencing over 100 KIA per month in Iraq from IEDs. So, what's the equivalent issue for friendly forces? How do we go on the offensive? First you go after the network to invalidate the enemy's ability to wage warfare against you through attacking their critical vulnerabilities (COG/Strange) or through understanding political-military factors associated with the area you are operating in. A consistent theme throughout this discussion is the idea of removing the conditions that create the root causes of resistance. That applies to going on the offensive. It sounds easy but it isn't and as a testament to that, we fought and won World War II in less than four years (December 1941 through August of 1945). We have been in Afghanistan 20 years and Iraq seventeen. A good student of warfare would question what we are doing and whether our approaches are working. At the very least that age-old comment about "doing the same thing over and over again expecting to get a different result" comes to mind. We don't appear to be any closer to the finish line than we were when we started this mess. Why is that and what are we doing about it? As a guy who spent over 100 months in combat after 9/11 and over approximately 12 years in combat zones in a 30-year army career, I question our leadership and how we are planning to attack this problem set. Whatever it is we have been doing and how we pick our leaders isn't working. I don't know if I have the immediate answers to fix this but here is what I do know: our previous and current approach hasn't worked. Realization of that fact is the first step to some form of recovery here.

Enemy

IEDs are the enemy's primary offensive capability. The enemy uses them to continue a larger economy-of-scale battle, which imposes significant long-term costs on the United States. Their hope is that we will eventually lose the national will to continue the fight, or eventually the strategy becomes so costly in terms of resources that we determine that the cost is not supportable, especially when there are near-peer or peer threats, which are emerging. As I have said on multiple occasions throughout this book, we need a "come to Jesus" moment in all this. We need to prioritize where we spend our resources and we need to figure out how to offramp some of these missions to local forces rather than continuing to bleed ourselves into ruin. Every dollar we spend in these fights is a dollar we do not spend on emerging threats. At some point, we need to either figure out how to defeat the insurgents and resistance efforts or we need to empower others to do it for us so that we aren't spreading out our forces and continuing to drain our national bank account. Good enough is good enough. We need to stop defining success in terms of our cultural expectations. We often do what is referred to as mirror imaging; what we should do is realize that how they did their business before we got there is probably the most realistic expectation of success, not some form of western democracy. We need to get out of nation-building and reinforce maintaining allies and partners that are supportive of our national objectives not turning the rest of the world into the United States. Quite honestly, most places are ready for it, and it is a waste of time, resources, and national blood and treasure. Good enough is good enough. Define the objective we are trying to achieve and go on the offensive to get there. IEDs create a significant drain on resources and bog our forces down in protracted fights.

The Principles of War for UAS Platforms (Offensive)
Friendly

These platforms enable friendly forces to find, fix, and finish enemy formations and enemy IED network nodes. An airborne 24/7 UAS capability is an attack in a three-dimensional realm by using maneuver in the airspace domain to reduce freedom of maneuver and action by the enemy in the ground domain. The approach I just described truly enables friendly forces to take the fight to the enemy throughout the breadth and depth of the battlefield. This is a game changer if we provide enough platforms, authorities, and infrastructure to have persistent strike and reconnaissance dominance over non-contiguous battlespace.

Enemy

This is the next emerging threat that the enemy will use to achieve their objectives both at the tactical and the strategic level. We need to get out ahead of this problem. As it stands, there is little to no understanding of the threat this capability presents. This is an emerging threat into which we are flying blind.

Security

Security is defined as the following: Never permit the enemy to acquire unexpected advantage. Security enhances freedom of action by reducing vulnerability to hostile acts, influence, or surprise. Security results from the measures taken by a commander to protect his forces. Knowledge and understanding of enemy strategy, tactics, doctrine, and staff planning improve the detailed planning of adequate security measures. Risk is inherent in war; however, commanders must not be overly cautious. To be successful, commanders must take necessary, calculated risks to preserve the force and defeat the enemy. Protecting the force increases friendly combat power.

The Principles of War for IEDs (Security)
Friendly

This has been said before throughout this book and it should be noted that the definition above provides that we should never allow the enemy to acquire unexpected advantage but that is exactly what we have been doing on an industrial scale for most of the conflict. We don't use OPSEC or deception very well, we go in and out of one entry and exit control point on an FOB, we don't roll back the early warning networks, we haven't addressed the root causes of the conflict, and we don't think outside the box. We haven't adjusted our formations to the fight that we're in, instead choosing to augment the traditional platoon, company, battalion, and brigade formations with additional capabilities rather than potentially build formations that are designed specifically to deal with the threat. As a result of all these mistakes, we have allowed the enemy to operate with some degree of impunity, but, make no mistake, it is because of our lack of critical thought and application of these type of issues. We must assume some greater degree of risk in all this and to a degree the effort to get off the FOB and take back battlespace form the enemy was an effort to do some of that but in my personal opinion a lot of this stems from our senior leaders and the amount of risk that they are willing or in this case unwilling to take. In life, you typically are rewarded or punished for the choices you make; security is a similar concept. If you violate security, you typically get punished, and in this business, people die.

Enemy

The use of IEDs allows the enemy to maintain some degree of security by placing them as obstacles to friendly force access. The enemy uses these for multiple purposes to include obstacle belts to prevent friendly forces from entering specific areas. The enemy uses IEDs to harass, kill, and strike their adversary without becoming decisively engaged. They also use IEDs to protect their force. To overcome some of this you need to engage in TTP like out of sector rotary-wing assaults, use of cameras covered by snipers or some form of indirect fire/interdiction.

The Principles of War for UAS Platforms (Security)
Friendly

Emerging UAS capabilities allow for airborne surveillance as well as strike capabilities. Electronic warfare payloads could also be configured to do constant RF surveys in conjunction with pattern analysis to shake out and identify elements of the enemy's early warning network. Tactical patience and these capabilities would allow for significant reduction of the enemy's ability to conduct IED emplacement with confidence that they will not be interdicted or rolled up. The critical high ground is the airspace that allows for persistent stare and strike. It should also be noted that if we do not dominate this space then some other entity will eventually fill it and in doing so there will be a high price to pay in catching up. Additionally, while not focused on this problem set, a smarter approach would be to task-organize our efforts into two distinct problem sets, namely overseas contingency operations (OCO) and major combat operations (MCO). Most of this book focuses on OCO problems but MCO is just as much of a concern. It probably makes more sense to keep the MCO requirements with the air force and the navy while pushing the OCO requirements down to maneuver units in the army and the Marines but that is based on mission sets and a concept that has not been approved yet.

Enemy

This will be an emerging threat to our security through surveillance, electronic warfare packages, cyber threats, or WMD placed on these platforms. If we cede this space to the enemy, the enemy will make us pay. This means we must take an active role in reducing the enemy's ability to use this space and these types of capabilities. It also means that we need to solve who takes lead for this inside the United States. As this book is being finalized, no agency has any law-enforcement responsibility for this problem set and this is an accident waiting to happen. As discussed, this is a significant vulnerability and requires fixing. At some point, the enemy may also use these types of platforms to enhance their own security, and it will create a counter-ISR/ISR (intelligence, surveillance and reconnaissance) context that will require us to devote efforts to removing this type of ISR capability from the enemy's arsenal.

Surprise

Surprise is defined as the following: Strike the enemy at a time or place or in a manner for which he is unprepared. Surprise can decisively shift the balance of combat power. By seeking surprise, forces can achieve success well out of proportion to the effort expended. Rapid advances in surveillance technology and mass communication make it increasingly difficult to mask or cloak large-scale marshaling or movement of personnel and equipment. The enemy need not be taken completely by surprise but only become aware too late to react effectively. Factors contributing to surprise include speed, effective intelligence, deception, application of unexpected combat power, OPSEC, and variations in tactics and methods of operation. Surprise can be in tempo, size of force, direction or location of main effort, and timing. Deception can aid the probability of achieving surprise.

The Principles of War for IEDs (Surprise)
Friendly

IEDs provide the enemy with the ability to strike at the time and place of their choosing through various techniques. VBIEDs and SVBIEDs have been exceptionally lethal and serve as something like the ability to mass on critical targets and infrastructure in a COIN type of fight. VBIEDs, SVBIEDs, and suicide vests can create mass casualties while creating terror and sow doubt in the ability of the existing government as legitimate when they cannot protect the population from attacks like this. It decreases confidence in the established government. Personally, I have always viewed this as the enemy's higher-caliber weapon systems or when used as a suicide technique it is a guidance system that enables the weapon to be employed to its maximum effect. As I have said, one can make an argument that the events of 9/11 and the airplanes were essentially improvised suicide airborne IEDs. The bigger issue in all of this is the amalgamation of all the things we aren't doing that enable the adversary to use IEDs to engage us without an ability to interdict them and that is what we need to eliminate. As a force, when you start to roll back the early warning network, when you interdict their resupply, remove IED precursors and critical components and take away their money, and then place persistent ISR above the area of operations, you take away their ability to engage you. That's the

United Nations Office of Humanitarian Coordinator Building in Baghdad after being hit by VBIED truck bomb, August 22, 2003. (Wikimedia Commons/United States Air Force ID DF-SD-04-02188)

Weapons cache and VBIED found in Al Anbar, April 26, 2005. (Wikimedia Commons/Official USMC photo by LCpl Brian M. Henne)

problem—folks don't see it in that prism, they see it in stovepipes and that is what we have been doing for most of the last 20 years driving folks like me crazy who keep preaching that we aren't attacking this problem the right way.

Enemy

Not much more can be said about surprise that hasn't already been said. IEDs provide the ability to use the concept of surprise, and it is the crux of how the enemy conducts attacks against friendly forces. Taking away this ability is critical to reducing the insurgency and their collective will to fight. When the enemy can no longer attack friendly forces with minimal loss of life or impunity for all the reasons stated above, they will have to adapt. They will likely adapt by moving to UAS platforms or going back to traditional raids and ambushes which makes them more vulnerable to destruction.

The Principles of War for UAS Platforms (Surprise)
Friendly

Taking the high ground using the airspace and an airborne 24/7 UAS capability with persistent stare and strike solves a lot of the surprise issues because it severely degrades the enemy's ability to plan, emplace, and execute IED attacks. This essentially changes the opaque attributes in this fight because it removes the enemy to theoretically attack us based on our operational patterns and security weaknesses without being engaged. There is no silver bullet in any of this but as I said throughout this book when you take multiple actions designed to strip away the enemy's ability to engage you, then you start to reduce freedom of movement and maneuver and you put the enemy on the defensive. For reasons that I simply cannot explain, what seems so obvious to me hasn't been done and we aren't much closer to changing the status quo so I have failed in trying to get people to change what they are doing. Again, this is a recurring reason why I wrote this book and the idea that maybe someone reading this, who can make a difference, will start to change things. The definition of insanity comes to mind, which is that we are doing the same thing over and over and expecting a different result. Ultimately, if we are smart enough to use these types of platforms to change the nature of this fight it will force the enemy to adapt. In doing so, the enemy will adapt to new forms of warfare or be outpaced, and consequently their ability to resist becomes exceptionally problematic.

Enemy

Surprise will come in the form of a swarm of the enemy utilizing UAS platforms or a fleet of these when we are least prepared for this or in combination with complex attacks utilizing IEDs, ground forces, and UAS platforms. UAS platforms are problematic because they can enable other attacks and in and of themselves with the right payloads could cause devastating attacks. UAS platforms can appear out of nowhere which is consistent with enabling enemy forces to achieve surprise. Without being overly simplistic, taking away this capability through the dominance of this space allows friendly forces to avoid these types of problems because we optimally have persistent stare throughout our area of operations and could potentially react to any type of scenario like this. Additionally, it might serve our interests if we developed TTP and platforms that can incapacitate or disable these types of platforms while simultaneously protecting our own. As an observation over the last couple of years, the military has seen the potential for these types of attacks and taken some precautionary actions but probably not to the level that this book believes should be taken. In simple terms, not to the level necessary to combat these types of problems.

Simplicity

Simplicity is defined as follows: Prepare clear, uncomplicated plans and concise orders to ensure thorough understanding. Everything in war is very simple, but the simple thing is difficult. To the uninitiated, military operations are not difficult. Simplicity contributes to successful operations. Simple plans and clear, concise orders minimize misunderstanding and confusion. Other factors being equal, the simplest plan is preferable. Simplicity is especially valuable when soldiers and leaders are tired. Simplicity in plans allows better understanding and troop management at all echelons and permits branches and sequels to be more easily understood and executed.

The Principles of War for IEDs (Simplicity)

Friendly

The overall response to the IED has been less than simple. If anything, we have created gigantic monstrosities to deal with this problem that have been highly unproductive. A couple of small victories here and there but the overall principle of simplicity is not something that most people would characterize various C-IED efforts as. The organizational structure associated with all this has no unity of command, no common objective, no coordination authority, and is ultimately ineffective while consuming incredible amounts of resources with minimal impact on the overall outcome. Without stating the obvious, for most of the war, the greatest killer on the battlefield for the enemy was some form of IED. Despite that, we were still in traditional formations and attempting to tell people that IEDs are just a condition of the modern battlefield. I am sorry but that tells me we don't get it; it tells me we need to critically examine our efforts and the impact (or lack of impact in many cases) that we have had on this fight. We need to change the way we are approaching this problem and maybe it wouldn't hurt to figure out how to put the IED and the network at the top of our target list. We need to change what we are doing.

Enemy

The enemy's approach is if nothing else simplistic in nature. There aren't using complex devices that require a master's degree or significant amounts of training. They teach their soldiers and IED builders how to build fairly simple but deadly bombs and run a clandestine network that transports manpower, money, resources, bomb making material, and a supporting ideology. Their approach is making us pay a lot of money and putting a lot of resources into this problem and to tell the truth we aren't doing a great job at destroying their network.

The Principles of War for UAS Platforms (Simplicity)

Friendly

Using UAS platforms in mass quantities provides both specific and wide-angle stare which reduces an enemy's ability to conduct IED-enabled asymmetric warfare. This is simply achieved by dominating the airspace 24/7 with an unmanned, cheap capability (in comparison to manned approaches) and should be run by the ground forces themselves, rotating operators and front-line soldiers through the operation and support requirements associated with various UAS platforms. This provides a simple and straightforward chain of command as well as a method to deny freedom of action.

Enemy

Not a lot has been done at this point with UAS platforms but the ideal approach for the enemy would be to appear suddenly, launch a swarm of these platforms for whatever mission they were executing and then disappear—in a sense guerilla warfare tactics with UAS platforms. They will not own the airspace, but these platforms could create significant challenges for friendly forces especially if some of these platforms came with WMD and the enemy was able to use that WMD against larger base complexes to create mass casualty events.

Resource Allocation

What are the implications of how IEDs could potentially enable asymmetric actions? Why is this important? It doesn't take a rocket scientist to figure out that this latest trend in warfare enables the traditional model of guerrilla warfare. It is a cheap and easy method to attack the traditional institution of the nation-state, is plentiful, and easy to construct. Traditional models of guerrilla warfare will benefit from the concept and tactics of IEDs. Above and beyond that concept, the IED now has reached mythical "rock star" status. This is the weapon and strategy that brought the world's only superpower to the brink of failure in Iraq. Warfare in general is basically about adjustments and innovation. History is full of examples of failure to adapt to new forms of warfare. The French belief in the static defense resulted in the German Army completely defeating the French army in six weeks in 1940. The Maginot Line was the cornerstone of the French defensive plan. Fixed fortifications are not flexible. The German adaptation of blitzkrieg warfare in World War II overwhelmed the French military. A recurring message throughout history is that it treats ruthlessly those who fail to adapt. Terrorists, jihadists, and rogue actors will undoubtedly benefit from the current proliferation of IED technology and tactics. Terrorists and religious terrorists exhibit traits and tendencies that will undoubtedly benefit from the expanded use of IEDs. Their mental predisposition to violence through an attitude of "the ends justify the means" and willingness to die for their cause makes them one of the most dangerous organizational models who could adapt to the new tactics learned from current successes in Iraq. The independent nature and remote characteristics of the IED is readymade for terrorist campaigns and objectives. Of all the potential proliferation problems associated with IEDs, this potential branch poses one of the most significant threats. The rise in numbers of IEDs throughout Iraq and Afghanistan foretell future difficulties and proliferation. It was and continues to be my prediction that sooner or later this trend will find its way into the world of international terrorism, beyond simply the confines of the United States' current Global War on Terror.

In the current world we live in, the IED is a significant threat to undermining the stability we have. Tribalism, religious zealotry, ideological strife, and routine conflict are the norm. What stability we have gained is in large part due to the current construct of nation-states that for the most part are freely elected democratic regimes. The IED can significantly destabilize this system and create stateless areas ruled by tribal warlords. This is not in the best interest of nation-states or mankind. To prevent future instability, it is essential that we find a way to combat IEDs and identify where traditional nation-states are most vulnerable to prevent future instability. Supply-chain management procedures and understanding various cultural predispositions to violence are other areas that we need to make greater inroads into as they influence the problem sets we deal with. Dual-use products like fertilizer can be made into explosives, which are used for IEDs, but if a particular culture is not prone to effective supply-chain management procedures, then you have a huge gap in law enforcement, customs, or regulatory agencies being able to account for supplies, which invariably make their way into enemy hands. This concept also applies to money and how money is moved around.

When you arrive at that observation, you juxtapose the choice between dealing constantly with what the Department of Defense refers to as overseas contingency operations (OCO) and realize that every dollar we spend on OCO is a dollar we don't spend on major combat operations (MCO) preparation or capability development. Taking this into account forced me to arrive at a conclusion that the IED and specifically IED-enabled asymmetric warfare enable the asymmetric actor to tie down or defeat superior actors. This is further compounded by the fact that IED defeat strategies and approaches have typically put the symmetrically superior actor in cost-prohibitive approach. It requires a losing economy-of-scale equation that even when the symmetrically superior actors win, it is so cost inefficient that it causes irreparable damage.

The resource methodology used here aimed at analyzing how IED-enabled asymmetric warfare might impact our goals and objectives from national interest perspective. In a sense, examining this entire construct suggested to me that we should be cognizant of where we spent our resources and understand where there were danger zones. In simple terms, we should invest in places that make sense and provide some form of benefit. That benefit could come in retaining the status quo, stopping an insurgency, or even assisting in regime change if we felt that was in our national interest. At a very macro level, it's nothing more than resource allocation and alignment of resources against objectives. Another perspective says that we ought to be investing in capability that aligns against increasing structure in locations that support infrastructure support for major combat operations and ensuring that where there is convergence that we focus our resources. While this makes perfect sense, or put another way appears to be common sense, it appears that that construct is all too uncommon.

Conclusions

UAS platforms are the next issue that we are going to face and just like IEDs, we are not prepared. In the spirit of that thought process, here are some general comments that fall under miscellaneous subjects that require addressing or expanding. These are general comments and are meant to help how the people fighting this fight ought to view this problem.

(1) An IED manual must be written at three levels: the first, a user level, the second, an intermediate level for company and battalion leadership, and finally at an operational to strategic level to understand the operational goals of the IED network. Understanding the network and how to reduce it is something that ideally should be understood at all levels but in reality, it is really something that should be understood by leaders and less by the people on the front line of this fight, although the more people that understand this fight the better off we will all be. At opposing extremes, one is simply a matter of dealing with the problems associated with IEDs and how you conduct operations while the other end understands the vulnerabilities associated with an individual network.

(2) Any manual must start with a chronological approach to the problem. Welcome to Iraq, Afghanistan or wherever it is you are going. The threat: Types of IEDs that the enemy uses. Pattern analysis: Friendly operational pattern analysis. Freedom of Movement: Example … roll back the early warning network. How the enemy uses IEDs and what their goals are (the why). What we think the enemy is trying to do. How the terrain impacts where you are fighting. This could include but is not limited to Lidar data and historical IED reports. This saves lives. Ideally all this is done prior to deployment and there is no reason that it can't be. As far back as 2007, I pointed this out to the JIEDDO COIC in Reston.‡ With the state of gaming in the United States, there is no reason that we cannot contract with any number of corporations to come up with a way to reproduce the environments

---

‡ On one of the deployments back into Iraq for General Petreaus, when returning from Iraq to Hawaii, I stopped into JIEDDO and spent a day with them assisting them with how to solve some of the problems they were facing. My first observation was that, as a group, they really had no understanding of how this fight was really going down. I could provide example after example of this but a lot of this data is still classified. What I can offer is that in my opinion, reach-back support should truly be led by people who have been in this fight and from what I can see that is not the approach that they took. Most of the people I interacted with hadn't been forward and as I went through what I thought were fairly simple conclusions about what the enemy was doing, I was shocked to see that they didn't see it the same way I did. I also stopped into an Elite Special Operations Headquarters that I used to be part of and provided them what I had done to date to assist them in destroying the networks they were facing. I found out later that they used some of the TTP I had provided to interdict targets. Again, a recurring theme in this work is that I don't care about credit, I care about impact and this entire manual, book, or work should be a living breathing document constantly updated to provide the most.

and the threats our soldiers are going to face. Quite honestly, I am still amazed we haven't. It saves lives.

(3) Understand the operating environment. What are the tribal, religious, and economic affiliations in the region? What is it that the enemy is trying to do there and how do they fit into those groups? Ultimately, this is entry-level and survival type of stuff. Playing defense doesn't solve this problem. Go back to the principles of war, go on the offensive. Staying on the FOB doesn't solve the problem. Transition from the defense to the offensive. Again, this is basic principles of war stuff. At an advanced level leaders should tie in the centers of gravity and political-military factors. State objectives in effects and use PMESII-PT (political, military, economic, social, information, infrastructure, physical environment, and time) as a framework to understand the art of the possible. Target the enemy's support zones. Attack the root cause of the problem, don't fight the symptoms. Go airborne 24/7 by taking away the airspace with persistent stare and strike. Finally get after the network. Take away the enemy's freedom of action, reduce available resources, and degrade enemy critical requirements through vulnerabilities.

While in MND-N, I tasked our chaplain to engage specific targets. We tasked our chaplain as an asset to get after problems that involved religion. Religion is something we steer away from because of our own history where we always approach this problem from an American civics' perspective and steer clear of this subject because of our history of separation of church and state. I am not a religious expert, I make no claim to be one, but I do know enough about history and I do know that you ought to look at this from their lens not ours, and that means that I should make sure that we understand and use religion in this fight with people a lot smarter than me on this subject. Religion is a critical part of this fight. We haven't done a damn thing with all of this and therefore, anything we do to start moving toward trying to solve these issues can do nothing but potentially create a dialogue that informs this problem set.

CHAPTER 6

Playing Hardball: Getting After the Network

This chapter, first written in the summer of 2007, provides a start point for reducing the support system that sustains the production, assembly, and emplacement of the IED. To intelligently discuss this problem, we must state exactly what the definition of a generic IED network is. Despite volumes of information out there on IEDs (mitigate blasts, how to jam IEDs, varying types of IEDs, etc.), there is no common definition, which succinctly states exactly what an IED network consists of and its purpose. The following definition is submitted for ease in defining the IED network:

> IED NETWORK: The IED Network is the supporting activities and infrastructure, which assists in the delivery of the IED to its intended target.

Given this definition, we can now start to break down the various activities and structures supporting the delivery of IEDs to their intended target and what that process encompasses. Through understanding this network, warfare practitioners can define objectives, tasks, and goals, supporting the destruction of enemy warfighting capability. Make no mistake, IEDs are currently the enemy's primary offensive capability. The most effective model categorizing this problem is the center-of-gravity approach, which utilizes subcomponents, which consist of the following: Center of gravity, critical capabilities, critical requirements, and critical vulnerabilities. From *Perspectives on Warfighting, Number Four, Second Edition, Centers of Gravity and Critical Vulnerabilities: Building on the Clausewitzan Foundation So That We Can All Speak the Same Language* by Dr. Joe Strange:[1]

> **Centers of Gravity:** Primary sources or moral or physical strength, power, and resistance.[2]
> **Critical Capabilities:** Primary abilities which merits a Center of Gravity to be identified as such in the given context of a given scenario, situation, or mission.[3]
> **Critical Requirements:** Essential Conditions, resources and means for a Critical Capability to be fully operative.[4]
> **Critical Vulnerability:** Critical Requirements or components thereof which are deficient, or vulnerable to neutralization, interdiction or attack (moral/physical harm) in a manner achieving decisive results—the smaller the resources and effort

applied and the smaller the risk and cost, the better.[5] As a result, the following analysis will attempt to break down the general description of the IED network into subcomponents ultimately allowing units to develop a targeting methodology and go after the Critical Vulnerabilities associated with IED Network Center of Gravity.

IED Network Center of Gravity

CRITICAL CAPABILITY # 1: Resources

Critical Requirement 1: Ammunition (Ordnance), Fragmentation Devices
- Critical Vulnerability 1: Movement of ammunition, resupply operations, cache sites.
- Critical Vulnerability 2: Signatures.
- <u>Potential friendly actions to attack critical vulnerability</u>: (1) Mobile X-ray vans along critical chokepoints hinder enemy movement of resources and reduce freedom of maneuver and action. (2) Develop and track movements with national ID card. (3) Full motion video (FMV) and ground moving target indicator (GMTI) backtracking capability provides units with the opportunity to backtrack IEDs to bombs in areas where they are consistent problems. (4) Target prioritization and cache relationships to IED patterns provide the opportunity for units to focus assets in areas where they are likely to produce high returns.

Critical Requirement 2: Technology Supplies (stuff to make bombs with)
- Critical Vulnerability 1: Reduce availability of components
- <u>Potential friendly actions to attack critical vulnerability</u>: (1) Import control mechanism tracking methodology on dual-use/IED components. (2) Tracking, tagging, locating (TTL) technology placed in critical IED components. (3) Higher tariffs/taxes on dual-use critical IED components. (4) OGA collection/surrogate interdiction against component suppliers outside of Iraq.

Critical Requirement 3: Funding (Money) and Monetary Transfer System (Hawala)
- Critical Vulnerability 1: Financial resources
- <u>Potential friendly actions to attack critical vulnerability</u>: (1) Reduction of black-market oil revenue: tracking, tagging, and locating (TTL) against illegal oil transactions and deliveries. (2) Cross-reference intelligence, cyber network operations (CNO), and high-volume, high-dollar transactions (5 million or higher) against known/suspected IED network supporters and financiers as well as all high-dollar value transactions in Kuwait, Saudi, Jordan, and Syria (if possible). (3) Cross-reference money transfers against import-export dealers, car dealers, bankers, major Coalition contract supporters.

Critical Requirement 4: Labs/Factories to Build Bombs
- Critical Vulnerability 1: Signatures, sustenance (food, water, place to house personnel)
- <u>Potential friendly actions to attack critical vulnerability</u>: (1) Measures and signatures intelligence (MASINT) signatures associated with electronic emanations of equipment used to assemble IEDs, unintended radiations, and higher pedestrian and automobile traffic provide valuable indicators to find and fix IED labs and factories. (2) Increased food purchases, stores, feeding requirements create unusual signatures, which could potentially identify these areas. (3) Residual chemical signatures associated with bomb-making operations also seem like a likely byproduct.

CRITICAL CAPABILITY # 2 Personnel:
Critical Requirement 1: Recruiting
- Critical Vulnerability 1: Education, tolerance, women's rights.
- Critical Vulnerability 2: Information campaign.
- Critical Vulnerability 3: Key tribal and religious leader support
- <u>Potential friendly actions to attack critical vulnerability</u>: (1) Adult literacy program, children's tolerance products in Arabic (i.e. Dr. Seuss), democratic awareness and historical perspective of Christian reformation classes (texts for adult literacy). (2) Exchange program for key tribal and religious leaders. Unit cultural advisors recruited from Arab-speaking Americans (preferably religiously aligned against sectarian makeup of assigned areas). (3) Increased recruiting of Arab American IO capability to assist with counter-propaganda campaign. (4) Active computer network attack against "hostile IO sites" to reduce internet availability to the enemy. When required, shut down all neutral or hostile propaganda conduits out of Iraq using (EW, STO, and CNA), while we buy time to get our messages out first. (5) Actively seek key tribal and religious leader support using cultural and religious experts.

Critical Requirement 2: Religious Support (Tacit or Direct Approval of Activities)
- Critical Vulnerability 1: Actions inconsistent with Islam and which run counter to requirements for jihad.
- Critical Vulnerability 2: Leaders never conduct suicide bombings. This is inconsistent with jihad?
- <u>Potential friendly actions to attack critical vulnerability</u>: (1) Rapid exploitation of enemy acts of brutality and attacks against women, children, and civilians. Exploit themes that are inconsistent with Islam using cultural experts recruited from Arabic-speaking American Iraqis and Sunni/Shia. (2) Aggressive campaign to separate the generic Islamic fanatical leader from their troops by highlighting that they never conduct the missions which they send out people to die on.

PLAYING HARDBALL: GETTING AFTER THE NETWORK • 97

CRITICAL CAPABILITY # 3 Operations, Planning and Training
Critical Requirement 1: Early Warning and Surveillance Network
- Critical Vulnerability 1: Early warning networks are reliant upon schedules and complacency.
- Critical Vulnerability 2: Communications modes.
- Critical Vulnerability 3: Early warning requires observation of entry and exit points.
- <u>Potential friendly actions to attack critical vulnerability</u>: (1) Modify schedules to the point of it being painful. If units and personnel are getting comfortable, they are probably developing a predictable schedule. Using a "lines of visibility" analysis, determine the likely observation points on entry and exit control points and airfields. (2) Constantly and in an unpredictable manner, do cordon and knocks in these areas to roll back the early warning network and force the enemy to rely on alternative modes of communication. (3) Communications modes are vulnerable to geolocation. Exercising tactical patience in conjunction with SIGINT, MASINT, and HUMINT helps to map a significant portion of the network and can lead to substantial secondary and tertiary target sets. (4) Create alternative entry and exit points from FOBs and static locations to confuse the enemy and reduce friendly forces predictability.

Critical Requirement 2: Ordnance Storage/Caches
- Critical Vulnerability 1: Movement of ammunition, resupply operations, cache sites.
- Critical Vulnerability 2: Signatures.
- <u>Potential friendly actions to attack critical vulnerability</u>: (1) Mobile X-ray vans along critical chokepoints hinder enemy movement of resources and reduce freedom of maneuver and action. (2) Develop and track movements with national ID card. (3) FMV and GMTI backtracking capability provides units with the opportunity to backtrack IEDs to bombs in areas where they are consistent problems. (4) Target prioritization and cache relationships to IED patterns provide the opportunity for units to focus assets in areas where they are likely to produce high returns.

Critical Requirement 3: IED Delivery
- Critical Vulnerability 1: Early warning network (previously discussed).
- Critical Vulnerability 2: Perception of unobserved, unmanned areas to place IEDs along likely Coalition avenues of approach.
- <u>Potential friendly actions to attack critical vulnerability</u>: Discussed in detail in the "The Counter-IED Playbook" (Chapter 7). (1) Push/herd IED delivery/emplacement teams to engagement areas or kill zones. (2) Show strength in one area to drive enemy to another. The area the enemy is driven to should appear to be unmanned and along a known Coalition route or avenue of approach.

Critical Requirement 4: IED ASSEMBLY
- Critical Vulnerability 1: Labs/factories to build bombs (previously discussed).
- Critical Vulnerability 2: Knowledgeable bombmakers to either train local personnel or conduct mobile training.
- Critical Vulnerability 3: Internet transfer of knowledge
- Potential friendly actions to attack critical vulnerability: (1) Expert bombmakers are not likely to be local although they could be in time. It is also likely that when expert bomb-builders are in a particular location that IEDs will be utilized in a belt technique to provide protection from U.S. or Coalition forces. Deviations in traditional patterns could indicate that bombmakers are in a particular area. When IEDs move from a constant casualty-causing pattern to one of protecting or denying a particular area, it is likely that a high-value target exists (bombmakers, leadership). It is also likely that with an increased number of checkpoints and population control measures there will be an increased need to utilize some form of internet connectivity to reduce source material. (2) Cross-referencing SIGINT, access to internet connectivity, HUMINT, and IED activity deviation provide the baseline for potential bombmaker presence. There is no magical solution to all this—it just requires hard police work that will lead to the discovery of potential bombmakers. (3) When the opportunity presents itself, and we roll up bombmakers, every effort should be made to affix blame to internal elements of the same organization to create havoc and sow distrust among that network. (4) Internet transfer of data is subject to corruption, alteration, and degradation through denial or usurpation.

Critical Requirement 5: Command and Control.
- Critical Vulnerability 1: C2 requires communications modes. Movement of ammunition, resupply operations, cache sites.
- Critical Vulnerability 2: Signatures.
- Potential friendly actions to attack critical vulnerability: (1) Deliberate jamming of nets when mapping and geolocation are either unavailable or impractical will result in a corresponding degradation in the enemy's ability to direct operations, conduct early warning, direct surveillance, or focus combat power. (2) Signatures of all electronic equipment can be tracked if it is "base lined" and the appropriate equipment is present to detect it.

CRITICAL CAPABILITY # 4 *Propaganda*
Critical Requirement 1: Connectivity, Access, and Command and Control
- Critical Vulnerability 1: Access to internet.
- Critical Vulnerability 2: Command and control (communications).
- Critical Vulnerability 3: Recording devices (camcorders etc.).
- Critical Vulnerability 4: System is subject to suspension.

- Potential friendly actions to attack critical vulnerability: (1) Access to the internet can be denied, shut down, or utilized to target organizations or individuals. (2) Command and control can be shut down with EW and is another way to geolocate targets if they are on exploitable mediums. (3) Devices used to record events create recognizable signatures and are subject to geolocation with the proper equipment. (4) All the above systems can be shut down, geolocated or exploited one at a time or simultaneously. (5) The ability to take control of events rather than allowing events to control you is critical to defeating the enemy's propaganda campaign. (6) No discernable effort has ever been made to get ahead of this problem and create a current ops capability to place the "cone of silence" over Iraq. The capability to shut down the enemy propaganda cycle can pay huge dividends in mitigating or exploiting events that are either favorable or unfavorable.

Critical Requirement 2: Content That Resonates with the Local Population (the Message)
- Critical Vulnerability 1: Not consistent with majority of Muslim teachings (previously discussed).
- Critical Vulnerability 2: Subject to scholarly rejection.
- Potential friendly actions to attack critical vulnerability: Coalition forces can defeat much of the effect of the enemy propaganda campaign by seeking recognized religious scholar condemnation of insurgent and jihadist actions.

(1) The above center-of-gravity approach was an initial start point to provide planners and operators with a conceptual jump start on how to go after the IED network. In doing so, this effort is not all encompassing and represents a philosophical ground zero designed to attack the IED network centers of gravity to degrade and destroy the enemy's primary weapon system. Over time it has been apparent that we do not have a well-coordinated effort. Mao once said that everything is propaganda. The enemy cannot defeat our forces on the battlefield in the current environment we operate in. The enemy's hope is to outlast us and make it so painful that we eventually leave on our own accord. The less publicity they get in this fight and the more we reduce casualties the more likely it will be that the enemy's will to fight will evaporate. Reducing the avenues with which they can get the message out also has a corresponding effect on the amount of money that they receive from donors. Less money equals less IEDs.

(2) Ask yourself what nodes the enemy's IED network requires in the environment where you are operating. They may not always be the same. Every problem is different, but this might serve as a template to start to analyze the problem that you might be facing when dealing with an emerging set of issues.

(3) As I look back on this and then consider my own personal experience that was expanded on by serving as the USF-I J39 and then as the A/DCG OPS in Pakistan, I expanded my own view of the problem. I tend to see the entire problem as an

attempt by the enemy to move commodities now. Those commodities are typically money, manpower, bombmaking materials, resources, ideology, equipment, and bombmaking expertise. All those things eventually shake out in a COG analysis and should lead any decent planner to start to look at other issues in whatever existing situation they find themselves in.

Flowchart Annex

1. While no situation is ever going to provide a cookie-cutter approach, there is a natural logic, which suggests you move from left to right along the continuum from engagement through non-kinetic solutions, finally to force and kill/capture operations.
2. What that might look like is the following approach.
    a. Conduct a meeting, meet and greet, develop a relationship or have your three cups of tea, if that is what you want to call it.* Attempt to assess whether the element, tribe, individual, or faction is supportive of your cause or not. If they are supportive of your cause, try to evaluate why. Is there some ulterior motive behind their potential non-cooperation for the people you are dealing with? What might be motivating their resistance to cooperating with you? This is a thinking man's game; you must evaluate each situation differently. It's problem-solving on an individual basis where you must take a general pattern that has emerged and evaluate it for inconsistencies and then apply common sense to what you are attempting to do. As said before, there is no cookie-cutter approach, its complex problem solving on a nonlinear basis. Often in Iraq, we empowered the wrong people at the expense of alienating the existing power base because we took everyone at face value, and assumed they were telling us the truth when in fact they were not the folks with all the *wasta* and in doing so we took a neutral situation and made it worse.† Always evaluate the other party's motives.

---

* This is a reference to the book written by Greg Mortenson, and David Oliver Relin in 2007. There is a debate over some of the claims in that book were severely exaggerated but it's not the book in this discussion that I care about but instead the euphemism of making the effort to work through cultural differences and resolve issues.

† *Wasta* is the Iraqi term for power. In my sector, I had what was called the Iraqi Advisor Task Force working directly for me. I had a retired CW3 Special Forces Warrant running that program as a contractor for me. It was for all intent and purposes a survey or sampling approach that allowed you to get feel for how the folks on the ground in a particular area felt about things, it also served as an informal intelligence network. You always had to take things with a grain of salt and realize that it was a prism that you were seeing with a particular slant. I often used to confirm or deny the people who made claims to be things that sometimes they were not. It was a valuable tool.

b. Provided there are no ulterior motives by the party you are seeking cooperation from, attempt to develop a common consensus position. What is good for them is good for you and what is good for you is good for them. How do they benefit from shared goals and objectives? Can you offer them assistance, carrots, enticements which reward them for cooperating? Make it in their best interest to do so. These are some of the ways you can help them.
   i. CERP projects.
      1. Schools, wells, small business incentives.
      2. SWET improvements: sewage, water, electricity, trash.
      3. Religious outreach. Can you help the local mullah/imam?
      4. Economics. How do the locals do what they do and how do they eat? These should drive how we think about the local economy. You should be able to answer these questions and figure out if there is anything that you can do to improve things if you are looking for their cooperation. This of course must be weighed up against understanding the existing objectives in the greater area you are operating in. If empowering one tribe or group derails the balance, then any actions must be both coordinated and judged on their potential impact. The obvious takeaway is that while your unit may personally see things get better by taking that approach, your hands may be tied by the overall goals of higher headquarters and taking these types of approaches may run counter to other goals. You can't do things in a vacuum.
c. You must monitor the local religious leaders and their sermons. Failure to do this can result in mission failure or additional expenditures of resources to the point of being counterproductive. An obvious statement is required here but this cannot be done overtly. You must find a way to monitor these through low-visibility means or methods. On occasion, it may also require overt monitoring to provide the guise that you occasionally monitor what they do, even if they are unaware that you constantly monitor what they do. You want them to believe you monitor what they do but not to the point where they think you are constantly watching them.
d. If these actions fail to succeed and the resistance level in your sector remains constant or increases through ambushes or IED-centric warfare then you will have to progress to the next level of engagement, namely threats and consequences.

Threats and Consequences

1. When at any time, you arrive at a point in the engagement process where the person, organization, tribe, or faction you are trying to influence makes

it clear through either their words or their actions that they are not willing to work with you of their own accord, then it becomes time to take the next step toward compelling them to comply. In essence, making them comply with your will or objectives. This may require threats, and even kinetic actions where you step up the operational tempo, devote resources to reducing their resistance level. This is both an opportunity and a period of caution. Often there is still time to achieve what you set out to do without potentially creating a permanent adversary but instead one who comes around to support our objectives albeit with some degree of coercion. A note about this: Do not be afraid to reward these same people if they retain their support for a period.

2. When it becomes necessary to increase offensive operations in a particular area because of the conditions, then refer to the counter-IED portion of this manual. Start or increase offensive C-IED operations. These types of operations can range from singular events or techniques like mobile "hajji" strike vehicles (see Chapter 7) to complete brigade-sized security operations (screen, reconnaissance in zone). The point of this comment is that you now must take things to a different level because force may be the only approach that is going to work with some of these people. When you arrive at that point, in this part of the world, there are a lot of people who only understand force. Don't go straight to it but don't hesitate to use it you have to.

3. Get off the FOB and apply critical reasoning. To defeat the insurgent, one of the primary objectives you must achieve is to protect the population. In any insurgency where the enemy attempts to hide among the population, you must protect the population from reprisals, threats, and coercion. To do this, you cannot be on the FOB 18 hours a day or even four hours a day, you must provide a limited degree of permanent presence in the population centers. Every insurgency is different but there are basic principles that you cannot ignore and that is one of them. A reading of a Roger Trinquier's *French View of Counterinsurgency*, John Nagl's *Learning to Eat Soup with a Knife*, or T. E. Lawrence's *Seven Pillars of Wisdom* and half a dozen other books on various insurgencies serve as a start point for understanding where any given situation might present similarities. Remember it is not a cookie-cutter recipe, it's a start point. You must adapt to what each situation presents indicators for. I have taught jiu-jitsu for years starting in Aikido at 6 years old and then moving over to jiu-jitsu. The analogy I use with students all the time goes like this; everyone's jiu-jitsu is different, what works for you may not work for me. I teach you techniques and it is like having all the ingredients for a salad, but ultimately you make your own salad. Dealing with insurgency or irregular warfare is the same. You must learn what makes individual techniques and situations work for the problem that you are in and then adapt. When the enemy starts to deviate, you must recognize it, and then you must counter it.

4. As a military force, the U.S. has become too restricted to our safety zones. We are still casualty-prohibitive. We are afraid of taking risk. This trend has been exacerbated by recent political correctness and grand attempts at emasculating the combat arms branches of the military. In Iraq and Afghanistan, the obvious fix to an ingress of manpower, material, and armaments infiltrating from either Iran (Iraq) or Pakistan, and specifically the FATA, Baluchistan, and Northwest Frontier provinces was to go old school and go to the field. In essence, create a defense in depth along the border along the primary ingress routes. I always referred to this as the "Make Iraq or Afghanistan an island course of action." In essence, cut off the insurgent's ability to access their resupply. Once they shoot their basic load, they become combat ineffective and are unable to sustain the fight. As a result, the local military forces become more effective against this target set by reducing the enemy's ability to retain their logistical supply requirements. Yet, to date, we have not ever attempted this course of action in either Iraq or Afghanistan. To put it mildly, it has been a source of frustration for years and throughout my 100-plus months of combat deployments, I have constantly questioned the existing approach. We are too risk averse to ever attempt something like that. We need to think outside the box and look at where the source of the insurgency or resistance receives most of its aid. If you look back at Vietnam or Korea, it is understandable why we chose not to deal with either Soviet or Chinese Communist aid for obvious escalation reasons and geographic considerations. In Iraq and Afghanistan, that excuse or consideration no longer exists. Yet, it is as if we have not learned a thing from our past experiences or taken the time to read about other's past experiences to avoid repeating the same mistakes.

5. Religion and specifically Islam. Do not be afraid to address this issue. As of today, we are afraid to touch this subject because of the risk of offending Muslims. I have news for folks who think this way—the people you are going to piss off are already there. Nothing you do is going to change their mind; they are the ones we most likely must kill. The ones who are moderates are going to embrace a reformation in Islam because they are already there but are afraid of reprisals. This is ultimately the 800-pound gorilla in this fight and is something no one in our leadership has wanted to touch for the last 25 years. You must address this because it is a potential root cause in the greater strategic framework. Almost 95 percent of the people we are fighting today have this as a critical issue and we have not touched it. It is a war of ideas and a clash of cultures. Use your chaplain, he is an infidel, but he is a holy man and that is at least respected.

6. You must attack their supply chain. You can cut it off by going to the border and creating a defense in depth. You can also corrupt their supply chain or illuminate it so that you can interdict it. You can reduce it through direct and

indirect action, but it is ultimately police work and intelligence-driven operations that will enable you to make those decisions. Money is a weapon.

7. Constantly question the organizational approach. Do not try to fit a round peg into a square hole and force a C-IED capability into a traditional army structure if it doesn't belong there. Adjust the organizational approach to the problem, not make it work into a conventional paradigm built for entirely different conflicts. In the end if you are not achieving the effects that you set out to accomplish, then you need to ask the following question: So, who gets punched in the face? If you are failing and no one is getting punched in the face, whatever you are doing isn't working.

CHAPTER 7

The Counter-IED Playbook: Break out the Sledgehammer

When I originally wrote this chapter in 2007, it was called the "Counter-IED Playbook," and it was written while I was deployed to Iraq acting as General David Petraeus's personal C-IED advisor. I was out and about in Iraq attempting to assist anyone I could in destroying C-IED networks. We were in the middle of the Iraqi surge and we needed to bring down the number of casualties, so anything we could do to kill the folks putting in IEDs and destroy their networks was a win. This chapter was the start of the written effort to get people to understand the challenges we were facing and make them smarter on how to defeat the whole concept of the IED. Minus a few adds to this chapter and some changes I had to make to get DOD to approve this (security concerns), I have left this as I wrote it.

If the cultural winning of hearts and minds didn't work, and all else fails then you must kill your adversary. This chapter was designed to help you figure out how to do that. Ideally, you don't have to do what is listed here but my experience has been that often it never works out the way you want it to and despite our best efforts this approach is often necessary to establish that we are willing to take to this level. If you don't cooperate, this is what you are going to face. That's what this chapter is all about. It's not designed to be nice to your adversary and the network, it's designed to kill and destroy them.

This is by no means exhaustive, it's a start point that was further watered down by the Defense Office of Pre-Publication Security Review Process and a lot of other organizations that redacted some of the concepts and explanations in this book. It's a start point and if one understands operations, then it's straightforward but it's not a cookbook—it's a conceptual framework that is designed to help people in this business learn to fish for themselves.

Structural Framework

Philosophically, an IED is designed to be a standoff engagement system, initiated through some type of remote control, command wire, or self-initiated that allows the opposing force to disengage rapidly and escape detection by friendly forces. This type of attack allows the enemy to asymmetrically overcome firepower and disadvantages that are inherent in an insurgent force. The insurgent does not want to become decisively engaged. Direct engagement usually results in the enemy getting killed or captured. IEDs serve an additional purpose by decreasing Coalition forces' freedom of action and increasing the insurgents' ability to move around the battlefield at significantly lower risk of detection or interdiction. The key to defeating or disrupting the concept of IEDs is understanding the development cycle, employment cycle, and vulnerabilities that are intrinsic in the IED system. The crux of this chapter will address how to offensively attack the IED network and focuses primarily on destroying IED emplacement times through (1) air-to-ground operations and (2) ground operations.

IED Early Warning Network and Placement

The diagram below depicts a generic IED targeted area of interest (TAI). It is important to try to visualize how the enemy employs the placement of the IED and the tactical early warning network that supports it.

This diagram is an effort to try to characterize the nature of what routinely goes on with regard to IED hotspots or IED targeted areas of interest (TAIs). The enemy utilizes an early warning network to alert the IED controllers and emplacers of route-clearance teams and any other major movements that may affect the emplacement of IEDs. We have not yet defined whether the early warning

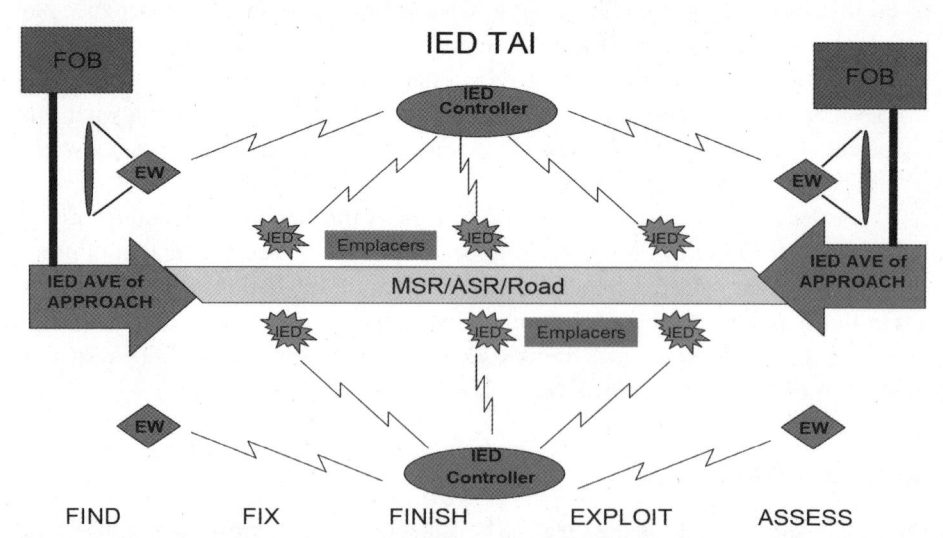

One of the first attempts at trying to define how the IED attack networked with a diagram during the Iraqi Surge, 2007. (M. D. Matter)

network communicates directly with an IED controller, or they go straight to the IED placement teams. Likely, the probability exists that there is in fact an IED controller. This is based on the following assumptions and logic: as the number of IED placement teams increase the number of phone calls would also increase to a point where it was counterproductive to the overall early warning network. Thus, the viability of the early warning node requires fewer phone calls when the primary purpose of an early warning network is to prevent compromise of its leaders and avoid risking the discovery of the IED placement teams. Probably, the early warning node makes one phone call to the IED controller who then makes multiple phone calls to IED placement teams. It is also probable that the early warning network has at least a primary and an alternate means of communications and a no-communications signal setup in case of a loss of communications.

The following diagram represents a basic departure point where we assume that all IED hotspots and TAIs have some form of early warning network and a relatively well-rehearsed and informed set of teams which have various responsibilities leading up to the final placement and detonation of an IED. Given this data, most of the remainder of this chapter will focus on providing basic TTP, which allow Coalition forces to take offensive operations and destroy IED networks. Embedded in the diagram and each TTP is a find, fix, finish, exploit, assess (F3EA) methodology to assist as a guide to attacking each IED hotspot/TAI.

FOB Concentric Circles

Every FOB should be looked at as if it is at the center of multiple concentric rings. Those concentric rings correspond to sensor/shooter zones. The further out you go out from the FOB the more likely the unit will have to rely on airborne ISR assets or some kind of organic airborne surveillance. Within the inner ring, units can often rely on some kind of direct observation or persistent surveillance. The point of this is that it should be looked at as though it was a range card on a crew-served weapon system. Units must also note dead space and when a patrol is entering an area where there is dead space, then they would probably go into bounding overwatch or even request an aerial weapons team, or some form of airborne overwatch provided the assets exist to that.

The enemy will continue to show up on these roads or routes around the FOB to place IEDs until we make them pay for it. A reconnaissance and surveillance plan plus a fires plan to interdict any IED placement teams along every route should be one of our intermediate aims. If units are short assets and are incapable of monitoring all the areas, then those areas are viewed as dead space and can be mitigated through devices like unattended ground sensors or sweeps with coherent change detection. This TTP and methodology provides the unit with both an offensive and defensive approach to approach the IED problem. As stated, if units are entering an area

FOB CONCENTRIC CIRCLES

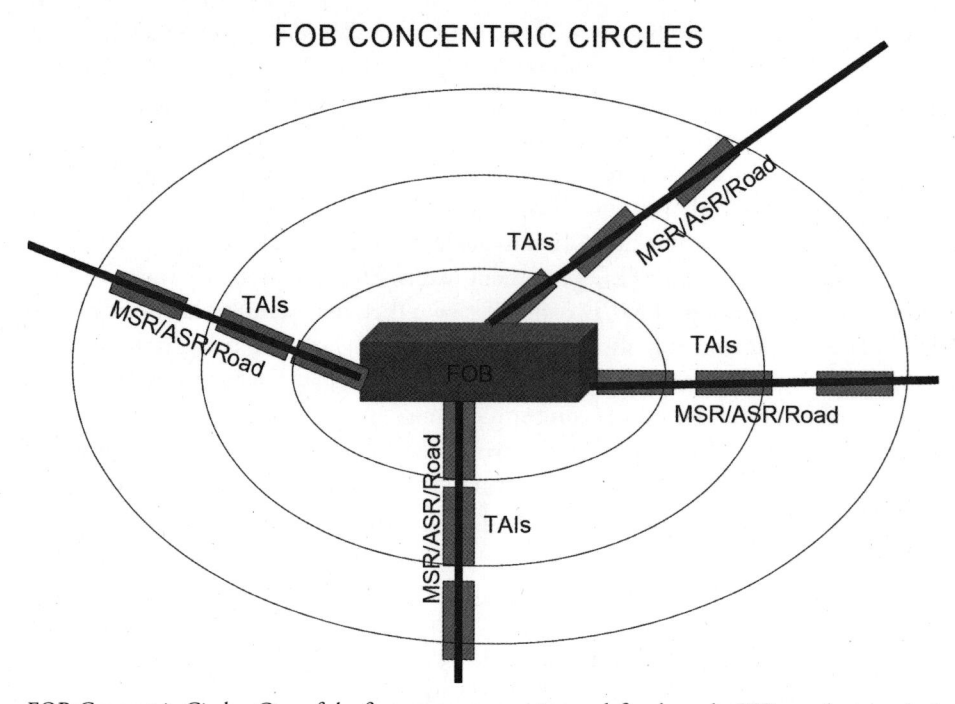

FOB Concentric Circles. One of the first attempts at trying to define how the IED attack networked with a diagram during the Iraqi Surge, 2007. (M. D. Matter)

where there is no sensor or shooter, they are entering dead space and should take appropriate action. Additionally, doing some form of correlational analysis allows the units to focus their resources on high-volume sensor-shooter zones/TAIs, ideally based on corresponding enemy activity.

The figure below is a depiction of an FOB with roads or routes leading out of the FOB or near the FOB. On these routes, the enemy will eventually show up to place IEDs. TAIs are specific hotspots that may have greater activity than others have and warrant 24-hour coverage. Every unit should have a diagram like this with an associated reconnaissance and surveillance matrix as well as a direct fire/indirect fire coverage matrix. Providing this kind of detail will allow units a methodology to defeat or mitigate the IED problem. If nothing else this allows for more intelligent decision-making about what areas are covered and what areas are not which in turn ought to reduce casualties, while focusing offensive efforts where they make the most sense.

Break out the Sledgehammer

1. Offensive counter-IED operations and TTP.
2. IED early warning network and placement.

3. FOB concentric circles.
4. Tactics, techniques, and procedures.
5. Air-to-ground operations.
   a. Gunship with follow on intra-theater airlift.
   b. NT-ISR/sniper/listening pod.
   c. Dedicated CAS w/ground JFACs.
   d. Rotary-wing attack weapons teams.
   e. EA aircraft (airborne electronic attack platform).
   f. EA aircraft/ISIS/Stingray.
   g. Airborne jamming platforms.
   h. Unintended radiated emissions.
   i. Highlighter/task force ODIN/MULTIINT coupling.
   j. RAID/nontraditional SR (air to ground).
6. Ground Operations.
   a. Guided multiple-launch rocket systems.
   b. Sniper.
   c. Mobile hajji vehicles/strike teams.
   d. Military free fall.
   e. Cameras/fake cameras/camera kits.
   f. Mobile X-ray vans.
   g. Roll back the early warning network.
   h. National identification card.
   i. ISIS/Stingray on clearing teams.
   j. Unintended radiated emissions.
   k. SIGINT-focused operations.
   l. Multiple band clearing.
   m. Clearance w/simultaneous AASL T to the flanks of RC.
   n. Demographics/mosque monitoring/cultural.
   o. Diming out the snitch.
   p. Prison ops/releases/taxis and audio recordings.
   q. Tracking tagging locating (TTL).
   r. Deception/drop-off patrols.
   s. OPSEC pattern analysis/visibility diagrams.
   t. HUMINT (OSS-type ops).
   u. PSYOP loudspeakers (deception).
   v. Baited ambushes (concrete, posters, etc.).
   w. VIN registration/VBIED pattern analysis.
   x. FLASH TCPs.
   y. Dummies/mannequins.
   z. Special category IEDS.
   aa. Large buried IEDs.

ab. Explosively formed penetrators.
ac. SVBIEDs/VBIEDs.
ad. Inculcating the C-IED mindset.

Tactics, Techniques, and Procedures: Air-to-Ground Operations

1. Gunship Aircraft with Follow-On Intra-theater Airlift

This method was used in MND-N to bring the worst TAI in MND-N from 55 IEDs a week down to zero in a single reporting period (we tracked by the week and the month). Initially, we hoped to catch the IED placement teams in the act of placing the IED but there was only one incident during a two-week period when we came close to placing ordnance on a potential target.[*] In the end, it became apparent that the sound of the airplane at 8,000–10,000 feet was audible and as a result no IED placement teams would enter the TAI or for that matter were any IEDs placed in the general vicinity. It is interesting to note that although we failed to interdict any of the IED placement teams, we achieved the effect we were after. We had taken the worst TAI in MND-N (actually, the worst in Iraq) and brought it down to zero IEDs during that time frame (reporting period). I asked our USAF ALO to go back to the CAOC and request that any intra-theater airlift going through our sector do three turns around whatever TAI we designated, as they were flying from one location to another. This would recreate an illusion that an aircraft was above whatever TAI we designated and that a gunship aircraft at night sounds like every other aircraft at 8,000–10,000 feet.

Find: Gunship aircraft onboard sensors seeking IED placement teams.

Fix: Gunship aircraft targeting systems.

Finish: Gunship aircraft onboard weapons systems and capabilities.

Exploit: Recommendation to use intra-theater airlift to do three turns around multiple TAIs as they fly from one location to another. This creates an opportunity for tactical deception ISO reduction of IEDs.

Effect: Task (1): Destroy IED placement teams. Purpose (1): Reduce effectiveness of enemy IED campaign. Task (2): Deceive IED placement teams into believing that gunships are actually above TAI/IED hotspot. Purpose (2): Reduce effectiveness of IED campaign. Increase IED placement team propensity to venture into gunship kill zone. Task (3): Increase the "going rate" price of planting IEDs. Purpose (3): Reduce available cash (logistics) to the enemy.

---

[*] In this particular case, we could not get positive identification that the vehicle stopped on the MSR was digging in an IED because they probably had a vehicle with a latch in where they just stopped over the road and then placed the IED on the road. I was flying on a different ISR platform that night but we could not clearly identify any hostile action.

2. Nontraditional ISR/Airborne Targeting PODs

As an alternative to a gunship aircraft which is a high-demand, low-density asset and usually unavailable to conventional forces, units can use nontraditional ISR (NT-ISR) by using close air support aircraft with airborne targeting pods or other applicable pods to detect IED-emplacement teams. The advantage of using this type of platform is that they can fly at 18,000–20,000 feet and get the same resolution that the gunship aircraft would get at 8,000–10,000 feet. Used by itself, or in a sequential fashion, after establishing a pattern of aircraft presence would likely entice the enemy to venture into IED hotspots/TAIs where we can engage them. This platform can also spot for itself and carry the ordnance necessary to serve as both the sensor and the shooter. It is likely that under the current ROE, that we would have to establish a digital downlink into the unit that owned the battlespace that the IED hotspot/TAI was in, to clear fires.

Find: NT-ISR platform (F-18 w/targeting POD) or F-16 w/ targeting POD with downlink to tactical TOC.

Fix: Onboard targeting systems of NT-ISR platform.

Finish: Onboard weapons platforms.

Exploit: Camera systems on board will provide potential information operations products for post-interdiction use. Onboard tapes can also be cross-referenced against other intelligence systems to determine if some form of analytical correlation can determine greater targeting value for intelligence value.

Effect: Task (1): Destroy IED placement teams. Purpose (1): Reduce effectiveness of enemy IED campaign. Task (2) Gain further intelligence and targeting information through correlational analysis from other overhead platforms. (2) Purpose: Reduce IED networks and support to the IED network. Task (3): Increase the "going rate" price of planting IEDs. Purpose (3): Reduce available cash (logistics) to the enemy.

3. Dedicated CAS w/Ground JFAC/JTACs

Dedicated CAS can be offset while JFAC/JTACs or designated recce teams overwatch designated IED hotspots/TAIs to provide additional alternatives and avoid establishing patterns in any location, which will increase the effectiveness of our counter-IED operations. This technique focuses on the use of standoff weapon systems which allow JFACs, JTACs, and units to use joint fires platforms that are significant distances away from the IED hotspot/TAI, thereby lessening the signature of overhead platforms.

Find: JFAC/ground unit.

Fix: JFAC/ground unit.

Finish: CAS/J-FIRES platform with associated ordnance.

Exploit: Precision-guided munitions (PGM) seeker head tapes provide a huge IO opportunity to incite fear and doubt among IED placement teams and raise the "going rate" for placement of IED teams, ultimately requiring more cash from IED financiers provided we declassify and publicize these events.

Effect: Task (1): Destroy IED placement teams. Purpose (1): Reduce effectiveness of enemy IED campaign. Task (2): Increase the "going rate" price of planting IEDs. Purpose (2): Reduce available cash (logistics) to the enemy.

4. Rotary-Wing Attack Weapons Teams (AWTs)

Use of AWTs provides another air-to-ground system that can be utilized independently or in conjunction with some of the other assets discussed previously. AWTs can provide weapons platforms to detect as well as strike IED placement teams. The sensor suites on gunship helicopters enable these platforms to find, fix, and finish any IED emplacement teams. These systems also provide a capability to influence insurgents by their mere presence. Like the gunship aircraft, helicopters can be heard. Using this system to portray that one area is being monitored and turning the IED emplacement teams toward another area, which is a designated kill zone, provides opportunities to increase doubt and degrade the enemy's confidence in their TTP.

Find: Gunship helicopters onboard sensors monitoring designated IED hotspots/TAIs.

Finish: Onboard weapons platforms.

Exploit: AWTs provide another asset that by its presence can deter or push IED placement teams to a designated kill zone.

Effect: Task (1): Destroy IED placement teams. Purpose (1): Reduce effectiveness of enemy IED campaign. Task (2): Increase the "going rate" price of planting IEDs. Purpose (2): Reduce available cash (logistics) to the enemy.

5. Airborne Jamming Platforms (AJPs)

Although most platforms are used primarily to disrupt enemy communications and provide defensive electronic attack against radio-frequency-controlled IEDs (RCIEDs), there is an opportunity to use the system to disrupt the early warning networks associated with the IED placement teams. Using them at the correct time and place based on our estimates of when IED placement teams are given their orders provides potential opportunities to take advantage of the IED controller and his network after they have given their teams instructions to insert IEDs. Essentially, by waiting till after the IED teams have been given their marching orders, we effectively isolate the IED teams and ensure that they are incapable of receiving additional instructions after we introduce new forces or elements to kill/capture these placement teams, making them more susceptible to interdiction. This technique requires greater fidelity than we currently possess.

Find: Assist ground units in isolating IED placement teams after they have departed for the IED hotspot/TAI and prevent additional communications from giving them recall instructions.

Fix: Ground forces or aerial platforms arrive on station to fix IED placement teams after they have received their instructions.
Finish: Maneuver forces kill/capture IED placement teams.
Exploit: Captured elements or isolated communication nodes.
Effect: Task (1): Destroy IED placement teams. Purpose (1): Reduce effectiveness of enemy IED campaign. Task (2): Increase the "going rate" price of planting IEDs. Purpose (2): Reduce available cash (logistics) to the enemy.

6. *Airborne Electronic Attack Aircraft and Tracking, Tagging, and Locating*

The goal of using this capability is to use the high ground to make insurgent freedom of movement untenable. It takes away their ability to retain the offensive. It also allows friendly forces to track and geolocate enemy high-value targets HVTs. Movement of these capabilities to an air-centric approach increases their speed and lethality.

Find: Use airborne special capabilities to find targets. Speed and line of sight.
Fix: Ground forces or aerial platforms arrive on station to fix HVTs, IED placement teams, or other designated targets.
Finish: Multiple approaches to include airborne handover and coordinated air ground teaming to execute kill/capture operations.
Exploit: Captured elements or isolated communication nodes.
Effect: Task (1): Destroy IED placement teams, or HVTs. Purpose (1): Reduce effectiveness of enemy IED campaign. Task (2): Increase the "going rate" price of planting IEDs. Purpose (2): Kill/Capture HVTs, attack network capabilities.

7. *Unintended Radiated Emissions (UREs)*

Air platforms with URE-calibrated equipment can detect electronic equipment from significant distances if the equipment is baselined to find the specific system they are looking for. As a result, the types of specific equipment we might be looking for have a recognizable MASINT baseline that can be seen and verified from long distances away. If this equipment is coupled to a coherent change-detection platform that provides a real-time response that can be sent via downlink to the ground unit, there is the possibility of finding IEDs and the triggermen prior to the device being activated. This same technology can also be used to find devices like video cameras which the enemy uses to record events for propaganda purposes. It is also likely that the signatures put out by IED factories create a discernable and recognizable pattern that differs distinctly from areas that do not contain IED factories. In very simple terms, the URE signature, the increased use of electricity, heat, increased traffic all create discernable patterns that are indicators of enemy activity. It is fishing with a better fish finder.

Find: Utilize URE technology with coherent change to detect RCIED devices and other devices that are typically associated with enemy attacks.

Fix: Devices will provide a line of bearing (LOB) to the target providing opportunity for intersection and triangulation which can be then turned into a geo-coordinate.

Finish: Utilize ground maneuver forces or precision fires to kill/capture associated enemy forces.

Exploit: Captured equipment and devices can be baselined as well as exploited.

Effect: Task (1): Detect the IED and the IED placement team to include the triggerman. Purpose (1): Reduce effectiveness of enemy IED campaign. Task (2): Increase the "going rate" price of planting IEDs. Purpose (2): Reduce available cash (logistics) to the enemy. Task (3): Create doubt and confusion among IED builders and placement teams. Purpose (3): Reduce confidence in TTP.

8. *Highlighter/Task Force ODIN Multi-Intelligence Coupling (Air to Ground)*

The discussion focused earlier on the coupling of unintended radiated emissions (UREs) with coherent change detection. That is just one example that assists the ground commander in getting to the left-of-boom concept. There are other technologies in existence which when stacked in locations can assist in identifying where the IED cells are located. As an example, pattern analysis can reveal where large and buried IEDs are located. This then allows assets to be redirected to cover those areas so that we can use GMTI backtracks or full motion video (FMV) to assist in determining where the personnel who are originating these attacks reside and then eliminate them. The prioritization of assets and stacking of assets where American soldiers are being killed is an extension of the same theory that was published in the January of 2006 by this author, during the initial suggestion of creating a multi-functional, multi-intelligence, counter-mobile IED strike force. We are at the cutting edge of combining nontraditional methods and ISR into a synergistic effort. The bottom line is that we need to stack multi-intelligence assets in the places where they make the most sense and destroy the IED cells that are causing the most casualties.

Find: Utilize state-of-the-art nontraditional ISR and multi-intelligence coupling to detect previously undetectable high-value IED cells.

Fix: The same system coupling can both find and fix the enemy IED cells.

Finish: Organic or designated maneuver forces engage identified exposed or isolated nodes.

Exploit: (1) Potential deception/disinformation to provide plausible explanation as to why potential targets are killed or captured on a disinformation basis. (2) IO and face-to-face engagement with specific tribal and religious leaders.

Effect: Task (1): Detect then destroy high-value IED cells killing American soldiers. Purpose (1): Decrease effectiveness of enemy IED attacks.

9. *RAID/Nontraditional ISR (Air to Ground)*

Any type of persistent surveillance creates enormous problems for the insurgent, which amounts to a blocking obstacle that should be part of a greater obstacle belt, which turns the enemy toward desired engagement areas or kill zones. It also provides a targeting package, which units can use to provide fires in the form of a sensor shooter platform. For every obstacle or sensor there should be a corresponding shooter. If units cannot answer who the shooter is, they need to go back and have a corresponding fire-support execution matrix, which delineates which units are in support as primary and alternate fire-support means to interdict anyone doing "bad things" in the zone of reconnaissance. This amounts to a pre-combat check, which should always be in place. If we are scrambling to find out how to engage then we have failed in our preparation for combat. Bottom line, units need to do a better job ensuring that all forms of observation are covered with some form of fires, which amounts to primary, alternate, and emergency measures.

Find: Persistent surveillance locates enemy IED formations and pushes IED-placement cells to likely engagement areas.

Fix: Surveillance packages on platforms can geolocate through optical and FMV means while some thought should be given to adding electronic attack, close-0target reconnaissance capabilities and persistent surveillance platforms above FOBs, provided the potential loss of the platform is mitigated by the likelihood of recovery or destruction.

Finish: Organic or designated maneuver forces engage identified exposed or isolated nodes.

Exploit: (1) IO products advertising the success of the platform made available to the local population will increase the number of tips as well as drive potential insurgents to move to areas not covered by the platforms. The areas that they could potentially move to should be "fires ambush sites" in which there are both sensors and shooters dedicated to the potential destruction of IED placement teams. (2) IO and face-to-face engagement with specific tribal and religious leaders following successful engagements will reinforce the shift in the tide of war and will separate the insurgents from their support base (should be a battle drill).

<u>Effect</u>: Task (1): Deny actionable information to insurgents and IED networks. Purpose (1): Decrease effectiveness of enemy IED attacks.

Ground Operations

1. GMLRS: Guided Multiple-Launch Rocket System

This is simply another precision fires platform that provides units the capability to strike IED placement teams without being heard or presenting any signature. It also has a 70-kilometer range and can be utilized with multiple forms of observation. This is an economy-of-force platform. If you utilize a concept of extending concentric rings away from the FOB and show strength or capability using AWTs, aerial platforms, etc. at the outer concentric rings, it appears easier for the insurgent to place the IEDs at the location that appears to be uncovered/unobserved. Utilizing some of the less-observable assets, or in conjunction with cameras and camera kits, you drive the insurgent and IED placement teams toward the kill zone. This could be used in conjunction with herding as a concept.

Find: Utilize the organic assets of the task force to find the IED placement teams.

Fix: Sensor capabilities provide targeting data and transmit data to maneuver unit, which owns the battlespace. Unit clears battlespace.

Finish: GMLRS fires precision warhead in support of observer and maneuver unit.

Exploit: Post-event, IO engagement with local tribal and religious leaders reference turning in insurgents, AQIZ, and inevitability of defeat provides opportunities to additionally degrade IED network.

Effect: Task (1): Destroy IED placement teams. Purpose (1): Reduce effectiveness of enemy IED campaign. Task (2): Increase the "going rate" price of planting IEDs. Purpose (2): Reduce available cash (logistics) to the enemy. Task (3): Create doubt and confusion among IED builders and placement teams. Purpose (3): Reduce confidence in equipment and create an atmosphere of confusion and fear among potential IED placement teams.

2. Snipers

Units are doing fairly well at utilizing snipers to cover IED placement zones but we can improve by herding IED placement teams to kill zones through the creative use of control measures designed to push IED placement teams to areas where we can interdict them. We need to push hard for an expansion of persistent electronic intrusion camera kits and mobile X-ray vans. We had huge success in MND-N during OIF 5-7 rotation doing exactly this.

Find: Utilize unit snipers to overwatch obstacles to IED emplacement that may induce reaction from the insurgent to remove the obstacle. Snipers to overwatch obstacles to IED emplacement that may induce reaction from the insurgent to remove the obstacle.

Fix: Self-contained system with use of persistent surveillance and direct line of sight.

Finish: Sniper/sniper teams and potentially other indirect fire systems.

Exploit: IO value goes up significantly as we interdict IED placement teams. This increases the prices to pay IED emplacement teams and reduces IEDs. It also reduces the will to fight or resist because of the psychological impact of the sniper.

Effect: Task (1): Destroy IED placement teams. Purpose (1): Reduce effectiveness of enemy IED campaign. Task (2): Increase the "going rate" price of planting IEDs. Purpose (2): Reduce available cash (logistics) to the enemy. Task (3): Create atmosphere of fear among placement teams. Purpose (3): Reduce confidence in successful placement of IEDs and reduce perception of catch and release program.

3. Mobile Hajji Vehicles/Strike Teams

Place indigenous-looking soldiers in local vehicles w/ relaxed grooming standards on roving patrols throughout the AOR to engage IED placement teams and defeat enemy early warning network. This technique will wreak havoc throughout the IED placement teams and the enemy's internal OODA loop. Currently, the enemy has an early warning network that knows when a Coalition patrol leaves the entry/exit control point. This technique eliminates the ability to comfortably predict when and where friendly forces will show up. In very simple terms, this technique will foster fear and doubt and create significant confusion in the IED placement network. Currently, friendly forces are consistently predictable. This technique eliminates one portion of that problem and sows fear and doubt in the enemy.

Find: Hajji vehicle strike teams roam the MSRs looking for IED placement teams.

Fix: Teams organically engage IED placement teams.

Finish: Teams organically kill or capture IED placement teams and call for follow-on support as required.

Exploit: IO values go up significantly as we interdict IED placement teams with this technique because of the nature of its unpredictability.

Effect: Task (1): Destroy IED placement teams. Purpose (1): Reduce effectiveness of enemy IED campaign. Task (2): Increase the "going rate" price of planting IEDs. Purpose (2): Reduce available cash (logistics) to the enemy. Task (3): Create atmosphere of fear in placement teams. Purpose (3): Reduce confidence in successful placement of IEDs and reduce perception of catch and release program, Increase unpredictability of Coalition forces.

4. Military Free Fall (MFF)

Use MFF to insert sniper teams or electronic attack close target reconnaissance teams to detect IED placement teams and or geolocate potential IED-related network associates. This TTP provides an option that is a low-visibility insertion, which increases the likelihood that the team will be successful in locating adversary capabilities and enabling the action element to successfully prosecute the target, be it interdiction or reconnaissance. This is very simply another method of insertion that we have not used to date and would provide additional options, which make detection by the enemy less likely.

Find: Utilize this low-visibility insertion method to decrease the probability of detection.

Fix: Self-contained with organic weapons (sniper or EA CTR).

Finish: Snipers can engage, EA CTR team can direct forces on to the target when the trigger event occurs, or we can use indirect fires or airborne platforms to finish.

Exploit: Increases the unpredictable nature of Coalition forces showing up at any time on the battlefield to interdict IED placement teams, triggermen, or network support associates.

Effect: Task (1): Destroy IED placement teams. Purpose (1): Reduce effectiveness of enemy IED campaign. Task (2): Increase the "going rate" price of planting IEDs. Purpose (2): Reduce available cash (logistics) to the enemy. Task (3): Decrease the detection rates of sniper/EA CTR insertions. Purpose (3): Increase the lethality/effectiveness of IED interdiction teams ultimately reducing confidence in successful placement of IEDs and reducing perception of catch and release program.

5. *Cameras/Camera Kits*

Cameras and camera kits provide limitless opportunities to shape the battlefield through direct engagement (direct or precision fires) or herding IED placement teams toward a designated kill zone. Cameras placed in high-density IED hotspots and TAIs near FOBs where they can be covered by direct fire typically reduce IEDs drastically in that area. This is the equivalent of a turning/blocking obstacle. It forces or herds the enemy to another location. Often it is turned into a baited ambush where the insurgent will choose to try to destroy the camera rather than move to another location. This technique has worked in the past and will continue to work in the future. This TTP will either force insurgents away from a particular IED placement area or it will likely increase the lethality of our engagements with the enemy as he tries to contest our ability to place persistent surveillance in an area that they want to utilize to attack our forces.

Find: Utilize cameras as baited ambushes to draw insurgents into kill zones. Additionally, utilize cameras kits to herd IED placement teams into kill zones. Snipers/JFACs can also provide additional capability to either strike the target directly or indirectly.

Fix: Persistent electronic intrusion provides the capability to target IED placement teams with multiple weapons systems.

Finish: Ground unit direct fire or precision guided fires provide the capability to finish the target.

Exploit: Post strike IO, SIGINT analysis, reinforce capability and influencing IED placement teams to move toward designated kill zone.

Effect: Task (1): Turn/Conduct reconnaissance/deceive insurgents/IED placement teams. Purpose (1): Kill/Capture/Herd IED placement teams toward kill zone. Task (2): Destroy IED placement teams. Purpose (2): Reduce effectiveness of enemy IED campaign. Task (3): Increase the "going rate" price of planting IEDs. Purpose (3): Reduce available cash (logistics) to the enemy.

6. *Mobile X-Ray Vans*

This capability presents incredible opportunities to reduce IED freedom of movement. Large numbers of mobile X-ray vans placed in concentric circles and along enemy logistical resupply routes could restrict movement of IEDs and VBIEDs to a bare minimum in cities. In addition, positioning this capability along major avenues of approach and key ingress routes into a city while simultaneously protecting them would restrict the enemy's ability to move munitions, EFP components, and VBIEDs. This same capability has the potential to limit/reduce the flow of EFP and EFP-related materials into the country by positioning these assets along the border as a defense in depth.

Find: Mobile X-ray vans find IED components or deter freedom of movement.

Fix: Turn IED component suppliers to alternate routes that eliminate "hiding in plain sight." Denying access to traditional routes will make discovery and interdiction of IED component suppliers easier as they move toward less-traveled routes.

Finish: Ground units will detect and then seize IED components as they become apparent.

Exploit: IO Follow-on operations will announce success and influence IED/EFP component suppliers as well as potential third-party actors to seek alternative means to supplying insurgents. This will cause delays in their logistical resupply.

Effect: Task (1): Locate/deter IED and EFP component suppliers. Purpose (1): Reduce total number of EFP/IEDs coming into theater from neighboring countries. Task (2): Enhance ISR capability by driving IED/EFP suppliers to nontraditional, less-traveled routes. Purpose (2): Degrade/reduce enemy IED logistical resupply. Task (3): Increase the "going rate" price of planting IEDs. Purpose (3): Reduce available cash (logistics) to the enemy.

7. Roll Back the Early Warning Network

Across the board, we have done a terrible job at trying to roll back or neutralize the early warning network. There is an early warning network near every major FOB. We may not be able to define it, but it is there, and it observes our actions constantly to provide greater freedom of movement to our enemy. There are electronic warfare assets (EA CTR and SIGINT assets) that can be utilized to start to define the early warning network. Degrading the early warning network reduces the freedom of movement of the enemy and has a corresponding effect on the enemy's ability to confidently place IEDs without compromise, detection, or interdiction. One example of how to accomplish this task is the following: As we roll out for other than routine missions, we need to have SIGINT collecting on the areas immediately around the FOB and the entry and exit control points. Over time, we will likely see the same phone numbers unless they routinely switch phones. If the enemy routinely switches phones, we can attempt to gain a line of bearing of the immediate hits and see if there is a recurring pattern in that area that can be effectively defined and then targeted through EA CTR or cordon-and-knock operations. Finally, if we are unable to define the early warning network, we can always jam their ability to communicate by using airborne jamming platforms to shut down their ability to communicate. Another technique is to conduct routine cordon-and-knock operations in areas that have immediate visibility of the entry and exit control points. Recurring operations of this nature can potentially capture the EW nodes provided it is done with some degree of surprise. As we continue to conduct these types of operations, more than likely, the result will be that the enemy will pull back to a "less visible" position and attempt to achieve the same results but will operate in a safer but less effective network.

Find: Utilize SIGINT and EA CTR assets to find EW nodes in vicinity of entry and exit control points.

Fix: ICW ISR and EA CTR assets and coordinated ground operations, CF conduct sequential operations to define and then reduce EW nodes of enemy EW network ISO counter-IED ops.

Finish: Ground units will detect and then neutralize EW nodes.

Exploit: IO Follow-on operations will advertise the success of the reduction of the EW network, reinforcing the inevitability of insurgent defeat with local tribal and governmental leaders through key leader face-to-face engagements.

Effect: Task (1): Map/locate/ EW nodes located near FOBs. Purpose (1): Reduce predictability of CF as well as increase effectiveness of combat forces by reducing available notification/reaction time to insurgent networks. Task (2): Deny actionable information on Coalition forces by reducing effectiveness of EW network. Purpose (2): Reduce/degrade enemy freedom of movement. Task (3): Decrease the insurgent confidence in their ability to conduct unfettered placement of IEDs. Purpose (3): Reduce effectiveness of IED network.

8. *National ID Card*

The establishment of a national ID card enables the government and Coalition forces to remove the "opaqueness" of this fight and reduces the ability of foreign fighters to hide in plain sight. An individual barcoded ID, cross-referenced against the "Muqtar Books" (equivalent to Iraqi birth certificate) will allow Coalition forces to discern who is supposed to be here and who is not. A second-order derivative of this capability is that it will create a virtual berm and restrict insurgent freedom of movement while providing an ancillary benefit of analyzing where people go to (patterns), which may provide valuable information regarding movement of resistance fighters and insurgents. When combined with SIGINT and electronic attack close target reconnaissance a national ID can alter the current condition of the battlefield providing substance where none exists currently.

Find: Categorize/detect non-locals and personnel who do not possess a legitimate ID.

Fix: Security force and Coalition force checkpoints reduce freedom of movement and funnel foreign fighters and insurgents to utilize alternative means to move manpower, material, IED materials in our battlespace, increasing the likelihood of detection.

Finish: Forcing the adversary out of his traditional movement pattern increases the Coalition forces' capability to find and fix networks. As targets become apparent, units will increase their ability to interdict IED support/networks.

Exploit: Emphasize inevitability of the process by promoting the local security forces defining their operating environment.

Effect: Task (1): Categorize/define population in the country. Purpose (1): Delineate between civilians who are supposed to be in the country and those who are not. Task (2): Reduce freedom of movement of enemy forces by defining operating environment. Purpose (2): Reduce the ability of insurgents to move IEDs around the battlefield. (3): Decrease confidence in insurgent ability to conduct unfettered placement of IEDs. Purpose (3): Reduce effectiveness of IED network.

9. Unintended Radiated Emissions (UREs)

All electronic devices emanate emissions. The routine use of cell phones and other electronic equipment to detonate IEDs can and should be exploited. Technology exists today, which can provide our forces with the capability to detect electronic equipment through these emissions, ultimately allowing discovery of IEDs utilizing electronic devices before they go off. Combining this technology with coherent change detection will assure detection of change and provides an ability to cross-cue to other electronic baseline signatures. This provides friendly forces the capability to detect the IED before it goes off while potentially being able to find the IED triggerman as well.

Find: Utilize URE equipment and couple it to coherent change-detection technology (highlighter) to detect "coherent change" associated with electronic emitting equipment.

Fix: Detection provides friendly forces an opportunity to fix the IED triggerman and engage him with direct or indirect fires before the IED goes off.

Finish: Organic maneuver forces utilize detailed targeting information to kill/capture identified triggerman and associated IED placement teams.

Exploit: Utilize change and increased frequency of detection to initiate deception and instill the belief that the IED networks are compromised. Increase red-on-red violence by making it look like snitches or other factions are turning them in.

Effect: Task (1): Find/detect IEDs, IED emplacement teams/members and triggermen through use of UREs and coherent change-detection technology. Purpose (1): Reduce effectiveness of enemy IED campaign and get left of boom. Purpose (2): Reduce confidence in IED as a weapon system.

10. SIGINT-Focused Ops

Units must do a better job at focusing SIGINT-collection assets on the IED network. A routine comment one hears is that IEDs are a condition of the battlefield. Each time an IED is placed or explodes, Coalition forces cease doing whatever it was that they were originally doing. Although it may seem counter-intuitive, if units place more emphasis on degrading the IED network, they would find that many of their problems would go away. Likely, as the number of IEDs are reduced, the effectiveness of a unit's operations increases and the effectiveness of insurgent forces decreases. IEDs are the moral equivalent of death by a "thousand cuts." Although not totally correct, if units focus more effort on defining the early warning network, and the IED network, they would see a corresponding rise in their freedom of movement and simultaneous reduction in the enemy's freedom of movement. A very simple fact of life is that every IED (even if it doesn't go off) must be cleared. Those that go off typically require a quick reaction force response, medical evacuation, and sometimes result in more casualties than were originally encountered by the initial set of forces when they were hit by the IED. By focusing our SIGINT assets on the early warning network and the IED network, our ability to target and interdict this network will start to change the current dynamic of the battlefield. In essence, as we start to turn this trend around, we will see a corresponding drop in IEDs, less freedom of movement of the enemy, less friendly casualties, more tips because of the population seeing a shift in success, and a reduction of enemy confidence in their ability to conduct effective operations. Over time, this will allow units to conduct more effective operations against local insurgents. A reduction in the enemy's freedom of movement has profound effects on the battlefield. Ultimately, we need to focus our collection assets toward defining the early warning and IED networks. This is a sequential fight. By defeating the early warning network and the IED placement networks, we enable future operations and increase our freedom of movement and reduce the enemy's freedom of action.

Find: Utilize SIGINT-collection assets to define early warning network and the IED placement teams.

Fix: Utilizing data derived from SIGINT collection fused with other intelligence and operations objectives, roll back the early warning networks and the IED placement network.

Finish: Organic maneuver forces utilize detailed targeting information to kill/capture identified networks.

Exploit: Reduce enemy freedom of action, which increases likelihood of detection.

Effect: Task (1): Collect on early warning networks, IED placement teams IOT define these networks. Purpose (1): Reduce effectiveness of enemy IED campaign and get left of boom. Purpose (2): Reduce enemy freedom of action.

11. *"Multiple Band" Clearing*

Units typically conduct predictable sequential operations to clear roads. As Americans, we have a predisposition to schedules, timetables, and systems. In this environment, all the above can have deadly consequences. Typical observations of current clearing operations depict the same sized force with the same equipment going out and doing exactly the same thing time and time again. It is the moral equivalent of running the same play in football every down. In very simple terms, we are predictable. When we stop being predictable, the enemy cannot plan around that predictability. Although only one technique, multiple band clearing or multiple technique clearing, can cause severe consternation and create an unpredictable nature of friendly operations, sending out sequential clearing teams and staggered operations coupled with simultaneous electronic attack of enemy communications can create an atmosphere of uncertainty and anxiety for our adversaries. Sending out two or three clearing bands where we used to send one and doing so in a totally random fashion increases the likelihood that the enemy will be forced to observe what we are doing rather than use our predictability as a weapon against us. Clearing from different directions or doing "crazy Ivans" or similar techniques with simultaneous air movement of clearing assets can make our operations more likely to gain some degree of surprise, and if nothing else become less predictable.

Find: Remaining completely unpredictable through operations like multiple band clearing reduces enemy freedom of action and increases the chances of mistakes by the enemy.

Fix: The unpredictability of operations increases the effectiveness of our operations while simultaneously reducing the effectiveness of enemy IED operations.

Finish: Organic maneuver forces gain more chance contacts through being less predictable.

Exploit: IO campaign, civil military operations, and tribal face-to-face engagement follow-on operations reduce sanctuary and local support to IED/insurgent network.

Effect: Task (1): Conduct nonstandard unpredictable clearing operations (multiple band clearing) Purpose (1): Reduce enemy confidence in Coalition predictability and limit freedom of action. Purpose (2): Reduce effectiveness of enemy IED campaign.

12. Clearance with Simultaneous Air Assault to the Flanks of Route Clearance Areas

In attempting to remain completely unpredictable, another technique that can be used is simultaneous or sequential rotary-wing air assaults to the flanks of route-clearing operations. Utilization of this technique can bag triggermen and portions of the early warning network. Simultaneous use of "man in the middle" electronic attack close target reconnaissance operations will yield capture of IED placement teams, early warning network nodes, and triggermen. This technique will also reinforce the unpredictability of Coalition force operations while securing egress routes of the enemy. This in turn will impact what the enemy is willing to risk and likely reduces the enemy's confidence and subsequent willingness to conduct placement of IEDs and attacks utilizing IED triggermen.

Find: Remaining completely unpredictable through operations like simultaneous air assaults to the flanks of route-clearance operations reduces enemy freedom of action, increases the chances of mistakes by the enemy, and reduces enemy confidence in Coalition force predictability.

Fix: IED placement teams, triggermen, and early warning nodes through simultaneous, near simultaneous flanking movements.

Finish: Organic maneuver forces engage exposed/isolated nodes.

Exploit: IO campaign, CMO and tribal face-to-face engagement follow-on operations reduce sanctuary and local support to IED/insurgent network.

Effects: Task (1): Conduct nonstandard, unpredictable clearing operations (simultaneous air assault to flanks of clearing operations). Purpose (1): Reduce enemy confidence in Coalition predictability and limit freedom of action. Purpose (2): Reduce effectiveness of enemy IED campaign.

13. *Demographics/Mosque Monitoring/Cultural-Tribal-Religious Affiliations*

Units must make every effort to understand their operational environment and the consequences that the atmospherics have on the counter-IED fight. If one visualizes a series of overlays which provide the following: (1) Problem mosques preaching sedition and resistance, (2) Tribal/religious fault lines depicting violence and violent acts, (3) Potential communication nodes (e.g., internet access points), (4) Known and suspected cache sites, (5) Militia activity, and (6) Geographical demographics, there is a likely correlation between these areas and IED activity. When evaluating the overall situation given an understanding of the above factors, our ability to address potential grievances transcends the basic kinetic aspects of this fight into the political and informational realm. Addressing the potential grievances by parties that express some discontent with whatever situation it is where they see some perceived flaw, can accomplish significant strides toward peeling back substantial portions of the resistance. The perception of inclusion and a method to address grievances makes all the difference in the world in this fight and potentially removes much of the motivation for violence but is just part of a greater effort to strip off motives to resist the government or our objectives.

Find: Use soft IO and engagement to separate IED networks from their support base. Use multi-intelligence and nontraditional analysis to define problem areas. Use of capabilities like the Iraqi Advisor Task Force to monitor general attitudes. Fuse this with open-source intelligence.

Fix: Pattern analysis and tips garnered from middle-of-the-road local personnel who view Coalition forces as the greater of two evils (change perception of this to the insurgent being the greater of the two evils).

Finish: Organic maneuver forces engage exposed/isolated nodes. Provide services and methods to remove obstacles that encourage violence. Provide method of airing grievances and effecting change politically.

Exploit: IO campaign, CMO, and tribal face-to-face engagement follow-on operations reduces sanctuary and local support to IED/insurgent network.

Effect: Task (1): Conduct nonstandard analysis to define IED operating environment. Purpose (1): Provide nontraditional glimpse at likely IED emplacement areas. Task (2): Enfranchise disaffected groups and insurgents. Purpose (2): Reduce motivation for violence and resistance.

14. Diming Out the Snitch

Right up front, there is nothing that prevents you from lying to the enemy. What is suggested here will likely garner a lot of resistance in conventional circles, but it has been done before and it works. Selective release with hard liners diametrically opposed to any cooperation can, when done correctly, create significant amounts of distrust among insurgent organizations. As a result, I would suggest that opportunities exist to create insurgent on insurgent violence through the timely use of deception or disinformation. As an example, if you have personnel who are unwilling to talk for whatever reason, an option is to release them, providing an impression that they cooperated with Coalition forces. This is especially effective after a successful operation where insurgents have been killed or captured. Releasing an individual in the general vicinity and providing an appearance of some kind of reward can cause extreme turmoil among insurgent and terrorist organizations to the point that they will likely turn on each other. In essence, you are introducing doubt and fear into a society that is already distrustful. You can combine this technique with a tracking, tagging, or locating operation where the released individual is unwittingly tagged. The tag acts as an insurance policy against potentially releasing an individual who escapes the wrath of the terrorist organization. If in fact, the insurgent can convince the others that he was actually not involved in providing information to Coalition forces, then the tag will provide locations to where other insurgents are hiding or other locations of significant interest.

Find: Use tactical deception and disinformation to cause red-on-red violence. Use TTL capability to tag and track released individuals.

Fix: Utilize released individuals to lead Coalition forces to insurgent forces.

Finish: Insurgent forces could break out in red-on-red violence if they believe released individual was responsible for providing information to Coalition forces. Organic maneuver forces engage exposed/isolated nodes. This approach offers huge opportunities to fracture insurgent and resistance networks and provides an incentive for fence-sitters to be brought back into the fold of our objectives.

Exploit: Follow-on operations to reinforce success and encourage additional red-on-red violence.

Effect: Task (1): Deceive/misinform insurgents. Purpose (1): Incite red-on-red violence and fragmentation.

15. Prison OPS/Release/Taxis and Audio Recordings

Units must take every opportunity to gain actionable information through nontraditional means. This equates to potentially tagging individuals being released from prison to gain further information on their networks. We can place recording devices and tracking devices in the taxis that take them to their first location after being released. We can place recording devices and tracking devices in the taxis that take them to their first location after being released. There is nothing to prevent us from incorporating the taxi and the taxi driver as a clandestine arm of the government military to further uncover IED/insurgent networks. This is the tip of the iceberg. At every turn, whether it is through incarceration or release, we should aim to gain further actionable information on the insurgent networks through use of technical surveillance, tracking devices, or operations that are routinely perceived to be neutral or even passive.

Find: Track/tag/use nontraditional means like prisoner releases, taxi drivers, to gain actionable targeting information.

Fix: Assets unwittingly self-locate insurgent/IED networks.

Finish: Organic maneuver forces engage exposed/isolated nodes.

Exploit: Tactical deception and disinformation can enhance overall objective by inciting red-on-red violence.

Effect: Task (1): Locate/reconnaissance through nontraditional means to deceive/misinform insurgents. Purpose (1): Incite red-on-red violence and fragmentation. Task (2): Track/tag/locate insurgent networks. Purpose (2): Destroy/degrade IED and resistance networks.

16. *Tracking, Tagging, and Locating (TTL)*

Some of the techniques above have suggested the use of tracking, tagging, and locating devices. It is limited to one's imagination and can provide new ways to validate sources, gain actionable information, and attack problems typically unapproachable with common military equipment. As an example, the corruption associated with oil smuggling at the Bayji refinery is a perfect target for multiple TTL operations. Even if the techniques are eventually compromised, the value gained from the insurgent networks knowing that this type of operation is ongoing could potentially slow their operations and decision-making substantially. TTL operations are limited to the imagination and can assist a variety of operations. Knowledge of how to employ the systems is critical to success while a vibrant imagination and perceptive ingenuity can provide multiple opportunities, leading to extensive increases in actionable targeting information. Additional cross-cueing of assets, correlation of data, and association of common patterns derived from TTL operations will provide substantial advantages to Coalition forces.

Find: Locate using TTL devices to gain greater targeting information.

Fix: TTL devices can be either self-radiating or can be retrieved through radio frequency or manual downloads. It is a system-dependent capability, which provides targeting data to include real-time interrogation and GPS data.

Finish: Organic or designated maneuver forces engage identified exposed or isolated nodes.

Exploit: Potential deception/disinformation to provide plausible explanation as to why potential targets are killed or captured. Second-order **effect:** If compromised, be prepared to expand on potential value of enemy knowing all kinds of things are being tagged. Potential disinformation as well about cooperation of certain elements within enemy cells that could expand red-on-red violence.

Effect: Task (1): Locate/reconnaissance through nontraditional means to find IED nodes, insurgents, deceive/misinform insurgents. Purpose (1): Incite red-on-red violence and fragmentation. Task (2): Track/tag/locate insurgent networks. Purpose (2): Destroy/degrade IED and resistance networks. Task (3): Decrease the insurgent confidence in their ability to conduct unfettered placement of IEDs. Purpose (3): Reduce effectiveness of IED network.

17. Deception/Dropoff

We have not historically done tactical deception well. This is also because our operational security and propensity for schedules and patterns makes units vulnerable as well as predictable. Neither of these problems assist in the deception process. Even the smallest amount of tactical deception assists in the overall OPSEC process since the enemy is forced to deal with the fact that maybe the information is incorrect. Dropoff patrols and misrepresenting what your intended target is or where it is, are examples of potential ways to mitigate an early warning network. Currently, there are many FOBs, which have only one way in and one way out. In instances where there is only one entry and exit point, we are our own worst enemy. There are multitudes of examples where we have shut extra entry/exit control points because they are manpower extensive. The unintended consequence is that we become creatures of habit and become predictable, making the enemy's job much easier. Rotating our primary entry and exit control points randomly could make our enemy's task exponentially more difficult. Another example of a tactic that creates huge difficulties for the enemy is assigning target packages to outside agencies. Doing an out-of-sector air assault to service a target in another brigade's sector causes huge problems for the enemy's early warning network. It is nearly impossible for the enemy's current early warning network to pick up an out-of-sector air assault when their early warning network is set up on a local scale. As a general observation, units can do a much better job at utilizing OPSEC and deception and finding ways to counter the early warning network.

Find: Deny information to the enemy, misrepresent intentions, and deceive them resulting in increased effectiveness of our own maneuver forces.

Fix: Deception results in increased effectiveness of targeting efforts and decreases effectiveness of enemy early warning network. The result is a greater find and fix percentage of enemy IED network personnel, reducing the total number of IED attacks.

Finish: Organic or designated maneuver forces engage identified exposed or isolated nodes.

Exploit: Potential disinformation about cooperation of certain elements within enemy cells, which could expand red-on-red violence.

Effect: Task (1): Deny Information, deceive/misinform insurgents. Purpose (1): Deny information; increase effectiveness of Coalition IED-defeat forces, incite red-on-red violence and fragmentation. Purpose (2): Decrease enemy confidence in their early warning network information, reducing the number of IEDs.

18. OPSEC/Pattern Analysis/Visibility Diagrams

Units must make every effort to avoid creating repetitive patterns. It starts from clearing the MSR and roads at the same time, to going the same way to an objective over and over. The U.S. military runs on schedules and timetables, and we love repetition. Unfortunately, the enemy thrives off our schedules and patterns as well. Units should change times when they clear roads, entry and exit control patterns, internal graphics and control measures to eliminate perceived seams. Units should also make efforts to change how they get to objectives. Go by air, return via ground, when possible, to achieve some degree of surprise. When conducting raids, stage out of different FOBs, send a different unit, don't clear routes from the same direction each time, change times routinely. Bottom line, be unpredictable.

Units must visualize roads as areas that require visibility lines and that each road that leads out of the FOB, that we frequent, should have a corresponding range card associated with the length of that road, and that units should have, as a minimum, a set of concentric circles moving outward from the FOB with associated sensors and shooters assigned to each portion of the road. Where there is dead space, there should be an associated collection plan, or an asset designated to collect against that area. Units should also consider two additional considerations when addressing this problem set. (1) When addressing dead space and planning in general, the aim should be to drive the enemy to emplace IEDs in areas where we have a kill zone set up. In essence, what we are striving for is to herd the enemy to an area where we can kill them. Finally, if we must accept that we are going to have to drive or move into areas that we know we have uncovered dead space, then we do so consciously with a plan of mitigation. Assume that there are IEDs buried in this location and assume that that there are triggermen present and plan accordingly to defeat them through innovative maneuver or through use of fires or ISR for that period. Without a doubt, the enemy will have figured out where we are not and will have a plan to utilize that space to kill friendly forces.

Find: By increasing our OPSEC vigilance and understanding our operating environment, we increase our efficiency.

Fix: Understanding the operating environment through the method described balancing dead space and pattern analysis will assist in fixing and herding the enemy to kill zones.

Finish: Organic or designated maneuver forces engage identified exposed or isolated nodes while protecting our own operations.

Exploit: Several avenues to proceed on as units see success. (1) Potential deception/disinformation to provide plausible explanation as to why potential targets are killed or captured on a disinformation basis. (2) IO and face-to-face engagement with specific tribal and religious leaders.

Effect: Task (1): Deny actionable information to insurgents and IED networks. Purpose (1): Decrease effectiveness of enemy IED attacks.

19. HUMINT (OSS-Type Ops)

Where is the modern-day Office of Strategic Services (OSS) or equivalent where we can employ Americans who speak the language and look like the indigenous personnel? It does not exist, but the requirement to do these types of operations has not gone away. In fact, there is nothing we need more desperately than an indigenous-type organization, capable of infiltrating areas to gain access to information that we would otherwise be incapable of obtaining. To some extent, there exists a capability on the battlefield that provides a similar capability but not what is really needed. The Iraqi Advisor Task Force (IQATF) probably provided a battlefield atmospherics capability that can be leveraged for IO purposes and general atmospherics but doesn't provide HUMINT or the capability to do clandestine/covert operations with no association to the U.S. government. To interdict the enemy's resupply system, we need assets capable of doing exactly these types of operations. The Hawala system of moving money creates huge problems for Coalition forces and joint agencies trying to reduce the flow of money to the insurgents.[†] Gaining information and determining how to reduce the effectiveness of that system would reduce the effectiveness of the overall IED network. This is but one example but could have an enormous impact on the insurgents' ability to wage war through the placement of IEDs.

Find: Utilize OSS-type indigenous capability to infiltrate areas previously denied, gaining actionable targeting information.

Fix: Unique access will allow detailed targeting of desired networks over time.

Finish: Organic or designated maneuver forces engage identified exposed or isolated nodes.

Exploit: Several avenues to proceed on as units see success. (1) Potential deception/disinformation to provide plausible explanation as to why potential targets are killed or captured on a disinformation basis. (2) IO and face-to-face engagement with specific tribal and religious leaders. (3) Economic incentive to strip away/replace alternative economy provided by IED network.

---

† Julia Kagan, "Banking and Finance: Hawala," 2019. www.investopedia.com/terms/h/hawala.asp. Hawala is a method of transferring money without any money actually moving. Interpol's definition of Hawala is "money transfer without money movement." Another definition is simply "trust." Hawala is an alternative remittance channel that exists outside of traditional banking systems. Transactions between Hawala brokers are made without promissory notes because the system is heavily based on trust and the balancing of Hawala brokers' books.

Effect: Task (1): Gain actionable information for targeting to destroy IED networks. Purpose (1): Decrease effectiveness of enemy IED attacks.

20. PSYOP (Now MISO) Loudspeaker (Deception)

We discussed earlier the use of the gunships against potential IED-placement teams in specific high-density NAIs. A complementary technique is to use loudspeakers to replicate the sounds associated with a gunship. This principle also applies to other assets that create the same fear or doubt in the enemy's IED-emplacement approaches. This technique can add further confusion to the battlefield and increase the effectiveness of an existing system or potentially replicate the belief that the system is where it is not and achieve the same effect as if it were present. The overall point is that loudspeaker operations should be incorporated wherever possible to assist in tactical deception in either an ambiguity-increasing mode or an ambiguity-decreasing mode. Essentially, this asset may have potentially dozens more uses in similar concepts, but we are hard pressed to provide examples of usage of this asset. Units should make a greater effort to incorporate this type of asset and assets like loudspeakers into their counter-IED operations.

Find: Herd/push IED placement cells to areas where they can be engaged and killed. Loudspeakers create confusion and increase likelihood that IED-placement teams will be unsure of their environment or can be used to herd them to areas where they believe they are safe but instead are in some form of interdiction ambush.

Fix: Use organic targeting capabilities to set conditions for kill/capture of insurgent IED cells.

Finish: Organic or designated maneuver forces engage identified exposed or isolated nodes.

Exploit: Increase confusion and push IED cells to areas where they can be engaged and destroyed.

Effect: Task (1): Deceive IED-placement cells as to the presence of gunships and other IED-destruction assets. Purpose (1): Decrease effectiveness of enemy IED attacks.

21. Baited Ambushes (Concrete, Posters, POO Stickers, and Abandoned Vehicles)

There are considerable opportunities to use baited ambushes to lure the enemy into kill zones. Examples include but are not limited to deliberately leaving certain areas of roadways with holes that we know the enemy will reuse and covered with some form of observation and fires. Thus, it should be a given that we fix the areas that we cannot maintain constant observation on first, while leaving the more enticing areas for the enemy to use. Other examples include using posters or point-of-origin stickers that will draw the enemy's attention and cause some reaction, which can ideally, then, be targeted. This is like the technique that was discussed in placing cameras on the battlefield, which are then covered by snipers. The key is finding some device or perceived advantage that the enemy is looking for to take advantage of in placing an IED or potentially using the bait as a future potential weapon. Other techniques include providing a sensor shooter link near abandoned vehicles or broken-down Coalition vehicles. The bottom line is that we need to get into the enemy's decision cycle and determine what the enemy is looking for in terms of opportunity and then take advantage of that requirement by creating conditions that allow units to kill or capture the enemy using these enticements.

Find: Utilize baited ambushes and enticements to draw insurgents and IED-placement cells into areas where we can engage them with precision fires and snipers. Utilize a variety of methods to attract them to the kill zone.

Fix: Targeted areas will have both sensors and shooters to kill or capture insurgents or IED placement cells.

Finish: Organic or designated maneuver forces with precision and long-range fires or CAS engage IED cells or identified insurgents.

Exploit: Several avenues to proceed on as units see success. (1) Potential deception/disinformation to provide plausible explanation as to why potential targets are killed or captured on a disinformation basis. (2) IO and face-to-face engagement with specific tribal and religious leaders. (3) Economic incentive to strip away/replace alternative economy provided by IED network.

Effect: Task (1): Draw enemy into baited ambush IOT kill or capture IED placement cells and insurgent network. Purpose (1): Decrease effectiveness of enemy IED attacks.

22. Vehicle Identification Registration (VIN)/Vehicle-Borne IED (VBIED) Pattern Analysis

Gaining or obtaining information (analysis) on vehicles and where they originate from can potentially lead to relevant information which points to VBIED factories. Additionally, GMTI and full motion video backtracking over areas where VBIEDs are used extensively will provide the capability to follow the vehicle back to its source. Although the information is determined post-blast, the enemy does not likely have the ability to reconstitute VBIED assembly factories quickly. Therefore, in areas where there is a high concentration of VBIEDs, it is advantageous to provide continuous overhead full motion video until the factory/network is found and destroyed. This type of operation is resource-intensive but should be prioritized to reflect the sensitivity of VBIED operations. In an insurgency, it is critical to protect the population and the current enemy Al-Qaeda/Jihadist TTP is to use these weapons as one of their primary sources of instilling fear and reducing confidence in the government. This is as much a propaganda weapon as it is a weapon designed to maximize casualties and incite religious/ethnic hatred. Reducing this enemy capability will directly increase the people's confidence in their government, enhance legitimacy, and degrade the enemy's influence operations.

Find: Utilizing FMV, MASINT, HUMINT, and police work-type techniques focus in on areas that have high VBIED detonation rates. Electronic signatures, higher traffic rates, and supplies associated with VBIEDs provide starting points.

Fix: Multi-INT capabilities and FMV provide the opportunity to do forensic backtracking to find and fix VBIED factories.

Finish: Organic or designated maneuver forces with precision and long-range fires engage IED cells or identified insurgents.

Exploit: Several avenues to proceed on as units see success. (1) Potential deception/disinformation to provide plausible explanation as to why potential targets are killed or captured on a disinformation basis. (2) IO and face-to-face engagement with specific tribal and religious leaders to expand on why they should not provide support to criminals and terrorists. Reinforce inevitability of discovery and the negative impact it brings to their communities. (3) Economic incentive to strip away/replace alternative economy provided by IED network. (4) Placing TTL devices into the network where opportunities exist provides an ability to illuminate an entire network simultaneously. (5) Opportunities to create confusion, distrust, and red-on-red violence also exist with these types of operations.

Effect: Task (1): Reduce total number of VBIEDs. Destroy VBIED factories. Purpose: (1): Decrease effectiveness of enemy IED attacks.

23. Flash TCPs

Increased use of flash TCPs with electronic attack close target reconnaissance capabilities with overhead SIGINT collection. This can provide a significant amount of targeting information provided we have the tactical patience to do the analysis and collection necessary to identify higher-value targets. We can use this technique to expose early warning networks and force HVTs to carry exploitable devices, which provide friendly forces with the capability to geolocate these devices. In a worst-case scenario, this technique can significantly reduce the freedom of movement of HVTs and key enablers. As part of a greater mobile counter-IED strike force, we can use maneuver flash TCPs to block in emplacement teams once they have started to reseed areas just cleared.

Find: Utilizing electronic attack close target reconnaissance techniques cause enemy cell-phone early warning network to light up.

Fix: EA CTR will be able to pick up cell phones that call in as a result of flash TCPS. This is the start of the police work phase to collect more information, discern legitimate targets, and then geolocate them.

Finish: Organic or designated maneuver forces with precision and long-range fires engage IED cells or identified insurgents.

Exploit: Several avenues to proceed on as units see success. (1) Potential deception/disinformation to provide plausible explanation as to why potential targets are killed or captured on a disinformation basis. (2) IO and face-to-face engagement with specific tribal and religious leaders. (3) Economic incentive to strip away/replace alternative economy provided by IED network.

Effect: Task (1): Detect and map enemy cell-phone early warning system. Purpose (1): Decrease effectiveness of enemy IED attacks. Task (2): Reduce enemy freedom of movement. Purpose (2) Degrade C2 and enemy ability to engage friendly force convoys/patrols.

24. Dummies/Mannequins

Utilization of dummies or mannequins in conjunction with cameras and observation posts (OPs) can create confusion and reduce enemy freedom of maneuver. This technique helps to confuse the enemy, increase apprehension, and prompt the enemy to question even the most obvious information. The result of this kind of obfuscation causes issues in the responsiveness in the enemy's decision cycle. It also serves as an economy-of-force measure by providing the enemy with a signature where potentially friendly forces could have no representation. Overall, this technique causes the enemy to question even the most basic information. The cost associated with this kind of measure is minimal and can enhance potential deception efforts with other measures discussed throughout this chapter. Examples of this could be routine false rotary-wing insertions utilizing dummies as part of the plan. This kind of technique is limited to the imagination and the particular METT-TC factors influencing any individual mission.

Find: Push enemy to areas where he thinks we are not (designated kill zones/engagement areas).

Fix: Targeted areas will have both sensors and shooters to kill or capture insurgents or IED placement cells.

Finish: Organic or designated maneuver forces with precision and long-range fires engage IED cells or identified insurgents.

Exploit: Several avenues to proceed on as units see success. (1) Potential deception/disinformation to provide plausible explanation as to why potential targets are killed or captured on a disinformation basis. (2) IO and face-to-face engagement with specific tribal and religious leaders. (3) Economic incentive to strip away/replace alternative economy provided by IED network.

Effect: Task (1): Draw enemy into baited ambush IOT kill or capture IED placement cells and insurgent network. Purpose (1): Decrease effectiveness of enemy IED attacks.

25: Out-of-Sector Rotary-Wing Assault

The obvious idea here is to overcome the enemy's early warning network, and their early warning network is built locally not regionally. The more unpredictable our operations are, the more difficult it is for the enemy to have freedom of maneuver. This stifles enemy offensive operations and capability when they are hit from locations that they did not anticipate or for that matter even considered. This can be done in diverse ways by using units from out of traditional sectors or using intermediate staging bases (ISBs). To some degree it is really limited to operational planners' imaginations.

Find: Targeting folders or objectives pushed to other units to strike and coordinated with the units owning the ground so as not to create blue-on-blue surprises or fratricide. This creates surprise on the battlefield.

Fix: Objectives are fixed via both internal forces and external forces.

Finish: Accomplished through strike forces from out of sector.

Exploit: Several avenues to proceed on as units see success. (1) There are multiple options with this TTP, which include l deception/disinformation to provide plausible explanation as to why potential targets are killed or captured on a disinformation basis. (2) IO and face-to-face engagement with specific tribal and religious leaders to make sure they understand that they are vulnerable and that Coalition forces remain unpredictable, reducing their will to resist. (3) Economic incentive to strip away/replace alternative economy provided by IED network. (4) Confirms inevitability of inadequate defense and reduces freedom of action and maneuver for the enemy.

Effect: Task (1): destroy/defeat targets through air assault or long-distance rotary-wing strike. Purpose (1): Reduce enemy freedom of action and freedom of maneuver.

Special Category IEDs

1. Large Buried IEDS

Large buried IEDs represent a category of IEDs that are killing a high percentage of our soldiers in the overall IED problem set. A more simplistic approach to large buried IEDs suggests that insurgents require time to dig them in (placement) and the insurgent must have a quantity of explosive ordnance in reasonable proximity to the planned IED attack location. Two primary approaches to the problem will potentially provide a way to attack large buried IED cells. The first is to establish where they are operating. Once we can establish this then we can utilize some form of forensic backtracking or establish a 24 hour/7 day-a-week ISR coverage to find the cell members then kill or capture them. Obviously, we have not achieved getting left of boom in this approach, but it does provide a way of destroying the cells. The second method of interdicting this type of capability is with mobile X-ray vans. Mobile X-ray vans will pick up transported IED materials like artillery shells, mortar rounds, and fire extinguishers. These vans create an obstacle that the enemy has difficulty bypassing. By placing these vans at critical road junctions and around areas where large buried IEDs occur, we will be able to reduce the enemy's resupply capability by making it harder for him to move ammunition around the battlefield. In doing so, the number of large buried IEDs will decline.

Find: Utilizing Mobile X-ray vans and full motion video we can either deny ingress of the materials at critical checkpoints or deny the ability of the enemy to place the large IEDs in areas of their choosing. Overhead FMV can also forensically backtrack IEDs and where they came from. This provides us with an ability to dedicate the coverage to areas where we are losing the most soldiers to large buried IEDS.

Fix: This type of capability either designates the target on the spot as in the case of mobile X-ray vans or provides data to directly locate where the IED emplacement team originated.

Finish: Organic or designated maneuver forces with precision and long-range fires engage IED cells or identified insurgents.

Exploit: Several avenues to proceed on as units see success. (1) Potential deception/disinformation to provide plausible explanation as to why potential targets are killed or captured on a disinformation basis. (2) IO and face-to-face engagement with specific tribal and religious leaders. (3) Economic incentive to strip away/replace alternative economy provided by IED network.

Effect: Task (1): Detect large buried IEDs and their origination points. Purpose (1): Decrease effectiveness of enemy IED attacks. Task (2): Deny access of materials through use of mobile X-ray technology. Purpose (2): Decrease effectiveness of enemy IED attacks.

2. Explosively Formed Penetrators (EFPs)

These types of IEDs are one of the major causes of death among American soldiers. Finding a way to significantly impact the logistical resupply of the insurgents using these IEDs will have a critical impact on the enemy's ability to sustain his IED campaign. Mobile X-ray vans create a distinct problem for insurgent groups transporting EFPs because they show up readily on X-ray technology. As a result, the placement of these vans will create a significant problem for the insurgent trying to transport these devices or the materials that help create these devices into the general urban areas. Placement of mobile X-ray vans at key crossing points along the border and ingress routes creates an additional burden for the enemy. The enemy will be forced to use alternative methods or attempt to attack the capability. The potential use of the same capability in a mobile flash TCP context will also serve as an additional deterrent to the enemy overcoming static acknowledged locations. The use of the mobile X-ray van can have far-reaching impacts on the movement of arms and material and specifically the EFPs. ISR can also be utilized in areas where recurring EFPs are being utilized. Adding an enduring ISR coverage capability over an area, which routinely has EFPs will likely result in identifying the placement nodes as well as providing information to interdict potential storage facilities.

Find: Utilize Unintended Radiated Emissions technology to locate EFPs and EFP assembly areas as well as Full Motion Video platforms to forensically backtrack EFP delivery vehicles. Utilize Mobile X Ray vans to deny access or detect inbound shipments of EFPs.

Fix: Targeted areas will have both sensors and shooters to kill or capture insurgents or IED placement cells or designated assembly points.

Finish: Organic or designated maneuver forces with precision and long-range fires engage IED cells or identified insurgents.

Exploit: Several avenues to proceed on as units see success. (1) Potential deception/disinformation to provide plausible explanation as to why potential targets are killed or captured on a disinformation basis. (2) IO and face-to-face engagement with specific tribal and religious leaders. (3) Economic incentive to strip away/replace alternative economy provided by IED network.

Effects: Task (1): Detect EFP type IEDs and their origination points. Purpose (1): Decrease effectiveness of enemy IED attacks. Task (2): Deny access of materials through use of mobile x-ray technology. Purpose (2): Decrease effectiveness of enemy IED attacks.

3. SVBIEDs/VBIEDs

In a similar sense to the above two types of special category IEDs, VBIEDS and SVBIEDS cannot get through X-ray-capable technology without being detected. Strong pointing in any form of X-ray technology, in this case a potential "backscatter" van, will degrade the enemy's capability to move these devices around the battlefield. Placed at critical junctions and potentially combined with an offensive pre-detonation capability or high-power microwave could significantly degrade the enemy's capability to employ these devices effectively. An additional benefit of using this technology is that it forces checkpoints to enforce vehicle inspections. This of course assumes that a unit would use an intermediate checkpoint/inspection area prior to the strong-pointed X-ray capability (to avoid the attack of a suicide VBIED). As discussed, ISR platforms can be utilized to focus on areas where there are patterns using either persistent surveillance or dedicated airborne ISR assets to isolate and backtrack where the sources of these problems are. Thus, if we can establish a trend or pattern of where these events are taking place, we can dedicate assets to try to kill the problem.

Find: Utilize unintended radiated emissions technology to locate EFPs and EFP assembly areas as well as full motion video platforms to forensically backtrack EFP delivery vehicles. Utilize mobile X-ray vans to deny access or detect inbound shipments of EFPs.

Fix: Targeted areas will have both sensors and shooters to kill or capture insurgents or IED-placement cells or designated assembly points.

Finish: Organic or designated maneuver forces with precision and long-range fires engage IED cells or identified insurgents.

Exploit: Several avenues to proceed on as units see success. (1) Potential deception/disinformation to provide plausible explanation as to why potential targets are killed or captured on a disinformation basis. (2) IO and face-to-face engagement with specific tribal and religious leaders. (3) Economic incentive to strip away/replace alternative economy provided by IED network.

Effects: Task (1): Detect VBIED/SVBIED-type IEDs and their origination points. Purpose (1): Decrease effectiveness of enemy IED attacks. Task (2): Deny access of materials through use of mobile X-ray technology. Purpose (2): Decrease effectiveness of enemy IED attacks.

Inculcating the Counter-IED Mindset and Recommended Changes to Existing Task Organization

Always ask yourself what you are attempting to achieve. The fight here has always been about destroying IED networks and reducing the number of casualties caused by IEDs. To do that, we must change the way people think about this problem and to some extent, we need to change the way the leadership thinks about this problem. I cannot tell you how many times I have heard that "IEDs are simply a condition on the modern battlefield." Maybe, but if that were true, we would see traditional raids and ambushes and we don't, so it becomes harder to buy into that logic when it appears that the vast majority of engagement suggests that IEDs are the modern battlefield in a COIN or low-intensity conflict type of environment. It is interesting to note that while this debate originally centered on whether divisions should be enabling brigades to conduct counter-IED operations or whether the focus should be a division-run operation, the nature of the IED fight has changed. The Army Corps must also have a role in this fight, even if it is primarily as a resource provider. The following recommendations are proposed to assist in establishing the most optimal force structure to destroy IED networks faster than the enemy can reconstitute them. This also assists in developing understanding and inculcating the desired mindset and organizational changes necessary to defeat the IED network.

(1) Each major MND should stand up a dedicated mobile counter-IED strike force (yes, this is a thing, a unit). The division mobile counter-IED strike force should consist of, but not be limited to the following organizational elements:

    a. Two light infantry companies.
    b. Dedicated aviation assets to support the unit.
    c. Sniper platoon.
    d. Dedicated JTACs (twice the normal complement).
    e. Electronic attack close target reconnaissance detachment.
    f. Tracking, tagging, and locating detachment.
    g. Electronic warfare detachment.
    h. Dedicated Intelligence Support with SIGINT equipment and UAVs.

Each MND should have a mobile counter-IED strike force working for it although at times based on battlefield requirements; the Army Corps could reallocate the forces. The force should be sent to the locations where we are losing the most American soldiers. In quite simple terms, we need to utilize the inkblot method of stamping out hot spots in our AOR. Therefore, the highest density of loss of American lives would be the very first target area that we dedicated these forces to attack. As discussed, there will be many opportunities to achieve economy of force and deception once successful employment of these types of operations occurs.

The threat of kinetic operations following effective employment of these assets increases the success of our perception and information operations.

An alternative to the above course of action is to attach the assets to the brigade combat team (BCT) to attack this problem. This is a less favorable course of action for several reasons. Primarily, the BCT would be sourcing the mission and is already tasked with existing maneuver forces organically, which would take them away from their current existing missions. Additionally, it is likely that this force would be of an ad-hoc nature. Most of the assets would have little familiarity with regards to collaborating with each other and would be less likely to develop effective CONOPS. The first course of action (division approach) would be a force dedicated solely to the elimination of IEDs develop SOPs and CONOPS rapidly and efficiently vice the second force, which would have greater difficulty achieving similar effects. It is also probable that the division approach would have significantly more success than the second given the nature of unfamiliarity of the brigade-level force in conducting mobile counter-IED strike force operations. This is exacerbated by the fact that they are tied between existing missions and the C-IED mission focus. Finally, by conducting operations in a division-centric mobile counter-IED strike force mode, we relieve the brigade commander of the responsibility to dedicate command-and-control assets for these operations. Simply put, the task force shows up and comes as a complete package and works for the brigade commander in his battlespace and leaves when they have completed the mission.

(2) There is an obvious requirement to change the way we are currently conducting our preparation for deployment and training against IEDs. We must make every effort to change the way we conduct rotations. The most effective way of maintaining situational awareness and retaining familiarity with the terrain is to ensure that units return to the same areas. It is imperative to assign divisions a sector responsibility and require of the division to rotate units in and out of that sector. One brigade in the 101st, 3 BCT is on its third rotation to Iraq and it is also on its third different operational area. This makes absolutely no sense at all. Imagine how much more effective this unit would have been had it returned to the same sector. This would allow units to be solidly familiar with the terrain, have established contacts and understand all the political and religious nuances associated with that particular area. The way we are currently conducting rotations is not optimal and borders on insanity. Personally, I cannot think of a more ineffective approach.

(3) Technology solutions exist today to provide computer-based scenarios that can detail and provide virtual training on the exact areas and sectors that units will enter in Iraq. A year out or whenever these units are identified if they don't know where they are going—the optimal solution is for units to return to their previous location—so they can utilize this technology to train up and provide 3D modeling and simulation to train every day on these areas. This will increase their awareness and significantly increase their on-the-ground situational awareness before they

show up, which contributes to when units take the most casualties (the first three months). Additionally, we should make every effort to integrate all IED events in updates to the programs to gain any additional insights to potential patterns as well as preparing units for identified hotspots. Technology exists to accomplish exactly this type of modeling and simulation.

(4) We need to develop a divisional-level OPFOR IED targeting cell which incorporates all this information and actively plays the adversary role to gain insight into what the likely enemy courses of action are, and then utilizing that data, units can start to develop counter-strategies to address potential shortfalls. Personally, I have never seen this and would welcome it as an addition to our existing approach. Ideally, these targeting cells would be directly associated with the previously discussed mobile counter-IED strike force. As an aside, one outlook on this process is that the enemy has its own targeting methodology as well as a potential fire-support system, which they utilize in their internal approach to attack us. While that fire-support system is not conventional, it nonetheless has a hierarchy. For example, a regular IED might be the equivalent of a mortar round or a direct-fire engagement. A suicide bomber is the moral equivalent of a precision-guided munition of greater magnitude depending on whether it is an individual suicide bomber with a vest or a suicide vehicle bomber. The EFP is the moral equivalent of a precision-guided artillery round. Developing an analytical methodology to determine where and why the enemy uses varying types of weapons system could be extremely valuable and assist in revealing their motivations, capabilities, and intent.

(5) The current task organization and independent nature of JIEDDO–IRAQ, JCCS 1, TF TROY, and the MNC-I COIC is unsound. All these elements should be under one command structure at the brigadier or major general command level to task-organize, share resources, and prioritize efforts in support of the commander's intent. This is currently not the case and makes absolutely no sense.

(6) We need to actively recruit cultural and religious experts and push them down to the battalion level to advise the commander on how to address cultural issues. Every effort should be made to educate locals on the economic benefits of cooperation. We need to find ways to bring jobs in and provide sources of revenue for the average citizen. These types of programs eliminate the roots of resistance. Additionally, we need to expand adult literacy programs and provide Iraqis an opportunity to discuss what they perceive democracy to be. This debate needs to occur at the grass roots level and only then will Iraqis be truly invested in this cause. When Iraqis understand what freedom means to them and they want it, our success is secured.

(7) This book, in manual format, needs to be implemented and then modified with every success story, updated with ongoing lessons learned, and instituted at the training centers during every rotation.

***

This chapter was initially one of the major efforts in this work. During the surge, I wrote most of this to help anyone who would listen on how to solve many of these problems with some degree of success. If you ask me how I would rate some of this effort, my answer is that we failed in truly defeating the enemy's approach, but we succeeded in achieving our goals. This entire process is so complex that it remains open to debate about what we were truly attempting to achieve. I discussed this earlier when I explained the concept of "what is the effect you are trying to achieve?" In that context, were we trying to simply get rid of a bad man (Saddam Hussein) and replace the government with some form of democracy (yet to be truly determined)? On the other hand, were we really after that or also adding some form of counter to Iranian influence in the region? If we were after countering Iranian Influence, then why would we get rid of Saddam? Then replace him with a democratically elected government knowing that it will be predicated by the fact that there are more Iraqi Shia than Sunni in Iraq? Then, would it be a surprise to anyone when you go down a path toward democracy but have not figured out that there are more Iraqi Shia than there are Iraqi Sunni, then the result you are potentially looking for is not going to occur. If that is what we were after, then we failed.

Additionally, by the time of the Iraqi surge, there were several factors that also contributed to the jam we had gotten ourselves into, specifically with IEDs. Again, to add insult to injury in this process, one of the primary reasons we ran into the IED problem was because we didn't have enough forces on the ground during stabilization operations. This of course was compounded by the fact that Secretary Rumsfeld discarded the recommendation made by Genera Shinseki prior to the invasion, which would have solved those issues. On the other hand, the requirement was not specific about what forces could have served as some form of constabulary force. Put another way, we could have used the Iraqi security forces for that mission but the minute we made the decision to DeBa'athify, that option was out and then required us to use our own forces. In either case, it really didn't matter how we got to that point; by the time of the surge we had probably exited too much force from Iraq, and we were getting hit with IEDs constantly to the point where at the height of the surge we had 127 KIA in one month. That was the backdrop to why I was called back and went out to help as many units as possible and while doing so wrote most of what is in this chapter.

So, with the above as a caveat, I wrote this chapter to simply help units kill the IED-emplacement process and destroy networks. It is that simple. I also intended this chapter to be a start point not an all-inclusive process. It is good enough to help units figure out how to start attacking the problem and in doing so they will produce their own TTPs and move beyond what I have suggested in this chapter.

PART II

Institutional Paralysis

I wrote Part I primarily in combat to deal with the IED threat. Part II about "institutional paralysis" was written after significant reflection in dealing with the first set of problems that Part I tackled. I kept asking myself if there were better ways to attack these problems. From my foxhole, the two biggest threats that have emerged over the last 10–20 years are unmanned systems and 21st-century all-domain fires integration challenges. The next five chapters attempt to frame these problems and provide recommendations to fix them. This is no easy task because our institutions are so inflexible and parochial that they put their own welfare before the defense of the country. They become more concerned about their own rice bowl and funding than they do about defeating our adversaries, somehow rationalizing that if they lead these fights then they can win it all rather than looking for the best solution even if means that your service or organization isn't in the lead. The extension of that is institutional paralysis and the inability to adapt. The extension of that is the inability of the institution to pivot regarding these emerging threats. To expand on that concept, what I just said was that even if someone comes up with a better way to approach some of these problems, the institution is so inflexible that it cannot change without some outside force or significant failure as the triggering mechanism. As a primary example, I often make the point that we are still devoting significant resources to guarding airports with TSA for a threat that will likely never happen again while simultaneously ignoring a much greater threat—the potential asymmetric use of UAS systems by rogue actors.

As it became evident that there were serious shortcomings in the way that the army and Department of Defense were approaching the asymmetric and irregular warfare issues associated with the first part of this work, it became necessary to also address long-standing shortfalls in the approaches covered in the last three chapters of this book. I believe we are witnessing a revolution of military affairs in this process. Much of what I have offered here has been said for the better part of 20 years, maybe 30 if you want to truly get technical about it, because some of these discussions go back to 1994. The American way of war is empowered by this concept, we have always attempted to mass fires and capabilities at the time and place where necessary. It is what makes us different and when done correctly makes us hard to beat.

The IED problems and the C-IED approaches that emerged started exacerbating many of the issues that we faced and some of the most successful practitioners in this fight were hybrid infantry/fires/SOF/IO network attack designs by people who had those skillsets, often multiple disciplines. Despite those successes the institution wasn't willing to change, and this became apparent in doctrinal discussion between 2006 through 2009 and then again in 2011 through 2013. I know of no other way to put this, but we weren't willing to change our traditional approach and adjust to the problem that we were facing. As this work matured and there were many discussions about this, with multiple people that assisted in this work, we came to a collective conclusion that this was best described by the concept of "institutional paralysis." No change will occur without some type of "black swan" event akin to Pearl Harbor. For argument's sake, evidently 9/11 wasn't enough to change what we were doing and were still doing, over and over but somehow expecting a different result.

For the record, this is really the concept of institutional paralysis. What is that concept? From my foxhole, it's where there are a multitude of personnel that speak up about how we aren't effectively approaching problems as an institution and despite these critiques, the institution is unable to pivot or adjust to new paradigms.

Conflict	Type of War	Result
Korea	Conventional/MCO	Armistice
Dominican Republic	Small War	Restore stability
Vietnam	COIN	Left in 1975
Grenada	Small War	Removed communist govt.
Beirut	Peacekeeping	Left in 1983 after VBIED
Panama	Small War	Removed dictator
Gulf War I; Restore Kuwait	Conventional/MCO	Removed Iraqi forces
Bosnia	Peacekeeping	Restored stability
Kosovo	Air War/bombing	Removed FRY forces
Afghanistan	UW/Small War/COIN	20 years/withdrew
Iraq: OIF	MCO/COIN/nation-building	Removed dictator/still there
Syria: Inherent Resolve	*Inherent Resolve* (defeat IS)	Initial success/ongoing

US conflicts and interventions: results of the last 75 years.

CHAPTER 8

Organizational Change: IEDs and Unmanned Systems

Throughout the wars in Iraq, Afghanistan, and the constantly expanding areas associated with the Global War on Terror, the single greatest challenge our military forces have faced is how to deal with the ongoing threat of IEDs. Short of success in the surge in 2007/8, our adversaries created significantly more challenges for us than we ever created for them. The U.S. and its Allies continue seeking technological solutions to a losing economy-of-scale battle. This chapter, written in 2017, examines the current state of counter-improvised explosive device (C-IED) and improvised threat organizations in the U.S. government and compares that against what it ideally ought to be based off alignment of mission sets. The most basic questions we should ask ourselves are: (1) what is the threat? (2) what is the mission? and (3) assuming that the mission is aligned properly with the requisite resources, where does it belong organizationally? To accomplish this task, this chapter will examine the evolution and development of counter-IED efforts in the American government and ask some extremely critical questions about where it belongs as well as what requirements are associated with the overall mission. As this book is finalized, the organization in government that is now responsible for this effort is the Joint Improvised Explosive Device Defeat Organization (JIEDDO), now renamed Joint Improvised Threat Defeat Organization (JIDA). When I started on this book, I thought that DTRA was the right place but I am convinced this is no longer the case. I am now in favor of creating a civilian-led agency with the following features that enable attacking along multiple lines of effort, which will become clear as the reader makes their way through this chapter. JIEDDO/JIDA was created with the following mission statement:

> The Joint Improvised Explosive Device Defeat Organization shall focus (lead, advocate, coordinate) all Department of Defense actions in support of Combatant Commanders' and their respective Joint Task Forces' efforts to defeat improvised explosive devices of strategic influence.
> —Mission Statement, DoD Directive 2000.19E, February 14, 2006.[1]

An initial examination of this problem highlights several immediate issues. First, why is this simply limited to Department of Defense (DOD) actions? By default, there is an entire network of support zones routinely outside the existing combat zone or area of operations, which influences this conflict. Immediately, that means that other organizations other than DOD are the lead in those areas. DOD has no tasking authority over other government organizations that oversee these support zones and threats. Beyond that critical observation, the effect of the action of IEDs occurs primarily in the area of operations while the majority of the IED support network resides outside the area of operations. This is problematic because the combatant commander and/or the joint task force commander do not even own that battlespace where most of the support comes from. Thus, while DOD may be the lead organization in the theater of war, they are not the lead in the support zones, and instead Department of State (DOS) is typically the lead. This creates significant problems when one organization is not in the lead and cannot task the others with requirements. Finally, without appearing overly skeptical, it is a well-known principle that asking DOD to lead outside of a theater of war is both impractical and nearly impossible because of the interagency politics involved.

On October 1, 2016, JIEDDO transitioned to the Joint Improvised-Threat Defeat Organization (JIDO) under the Defense Threat Reduction Agency (DTRA), moving from a jointly manned activity to a combat support agency (JIDO, 2018).[2] Their new mission statement follows:

> MISSION: JIDO enables Department of Defense actions to counter improvised threats with tactical responsiveness and through anticipatory, rapid acquisition in support of Combatant Commands' efforts to prepare for, and adapt to, battlefield surprise. This supports counter-terrorism, counter-insurgency, and other related mission areas, including counter-improvised explosive device.[3]

Honestly, when examining the above definition, it is fairly clear that not much has changed, except that instead of simply focusing on IEDs, the aperture of the organization expanded to "improvised threats," yet the organization is still led by a Department of Defense entity. Even JIDO's parent headquarters is in DOD, which although aimed at various degrees of proliferation or threat reduction, brings into question the entire alignment of the organization. JIDO's parent headquarters is the Defense Threat Reduction Agency (DTRA) and their mission follows:

> DTRA enables DoD and the U.S. Government to prepare for and combat weapons of mass destruction and improvised threats and to ensure nuclear deterrence.[4]

This is certainly an interesting pairing and runs the gamut from booby traps, UAS platforms, and IEDs to nuclear threats. Questions immediately arise about the scope, breadth, and depth of that requirement. Should the mission be that broad? Does the expertise really reside in that organization? We will examine these questions later after establishing the foundation for this problem set and looking at what the requirements for an organization like this ought to be.

Foundational Understanding

Any attempt at understanding this issue requires a basic understanding of multiple issues, which affect the ability of an adversary to bring IEDs and asymmetric or improvised threats to bear on the battlefield. For the purpose of both ease of the reader as well as structure, this effort will now present information for this case in the following format in a way that the U.S. government examines their organizations with five major core competencies: These are (1) leading people, (2) leading change, (3) moving to results-driven or effects-based strategies, (4), business acumen, and (5) building coalitions. As a leader, the first question one must ask is what is it that my organization does?

Analyzing the Organizational Approach

As an effective leader, it is always best to start out by analyzing what the mission is and how to accomplish it. As such, one way to achieve that is to start with the following five questions:

1. What is the mission?
2. What are the requirements the organization must achieve?
3. What is the end state we want to achieve?
4. Who are the other stakeholders?
5. How does the organization aim to achieve the effects it is aiming to achieve?

Critical examination of our C-IED organizational approach requires understanding these questions and several critical elements providing foundational understanding of the greater issues. Familiarity with irregular warfare, asymmetric warfare, and historical uses of IEDs enable an understanding into the current governmental organizational construct. This enables an effective analysis on whether the approach is aligned appropriately, or we are spinning our wheels (more commonly referred to as a suboptimal approach). Effective leaders must occasionally take a hard look at what return we are getting on our investment. The analysis in this chapter examines JIEDDO/JIDA's organizational approach and alignment. This provides our leadership, anyone reading this chapter, and our government with the ability to examine the effectiveness of our current approach. Ostensibly, although the mission focus might have changed, it is still basically the same and we are trying to defeat the networks, organizations, and movements that are using IEDs and improvised threats. What exacerbates the problem set is that we are also all under the same organization, adding nuclear deterrence to all of this. As a result, and to be brutally honest, I struggle with the nuclear deterrence issue being in the same skill set of the joint improvised threat wheelhouse. This is not to say that each of these opposing ends of the spectrum could not learn a thing or two from their efforts; I am just not sure that entire effort all passes the common-sense test. Here is what I do believe though: it is the concept that we should be a hell of a lot more worried about chemical or biological agents being strapped to UAS systems than we should be about nuclear threats. All of this and the government's current approach is something one might take under evaluation as they examine the efficiency and approach to this mission set.

How Did We Get to Where We Are?

First off, IEDs did not just magically appear, nor did irregular or asymmetric warfare concepts. Multiple resistance efforts throughout history used bombs, booby traps, other types of ambushes, victim-initiated mines, or other types of explosives to attack friendly forces to attain military or political goals. The Irish Republican Army (IRA) used bombs for years to attempt to gain Irish independence from Great Britain.[5] To be sure, these efforts were not aimed at winning over any insurgents or even expelling occupiers—it was a campaign of terror. On the other hand, varying organizations from Basque separatists, differing communist movements, and Middle Eastern terrorists have used bombing for political and terror purposes for years. So, how did this suddenly emerge as an issue driving spending in the range of billions of dollars and creating an entirely new organization in the DOD? I and a lot of others always questioned this because IEDs were really a fringe activity and viewed as a criminal act rather than an act of legitimate resistance for most of the last 100 years. The U.S. invasion of Iraq changed the entire way this problem was viewed. The IED-enabled resistance became the "rock star" of asymmetric warfare techniques because it nearly ejected the United States from Iraq. That is not lost on a lot of military observers in this business. The U.S. nearly failed in Iraq because of the enemy's approach utilizing IEDs. Were it not for the surge and a handful of out-of-the-box thinkers, Iraq would have likely resulted in a humiliating defeat and retrograde, failing while simultaneously leaving the entire region a mess.

Honestly, one of the most glaring mistakes the U.S. made at the outset of the war was not putting enough forces on the ground to deal with the nature of the threat that was present. Iraq had tons of explosives. For all intent, Iraq was nothing more than a big ammunition depot dump. It is interesting to note that General Shinseki advocated for a 300,000-man force in Iraq to serve as the constabulary force once combat operations were over.[6] This ran counter to the Secretary of Defense's opinion that advocated and ultimately directed conducting the attack with significantly less force. Instead, he suggested that the Iraqi Army could be used as a constabulary force in Phase IV, Stability Operations.[7] While this was true, it did not consider three converging factors that impacted this problem set. Because of these three distinct factors converging simultaneously, a situation developed in Iraq in which there were not enough forces to secure all the sites where ammunition was stored. When the

Iraqi Army and Iraq ceased to exist, there was no capitulation or formal surrender resulting in utter chaos and confusion. This was exacerbated by one of our primary operating assumptions and directives provided by Secretary Rumsfeld, stating that the Iraq Army could serve as the constabulary force once Saddam Hussein was killed or captured, and they would welcome the opportunity to do so. Immediately, one is struck with the presumptive nature of this prediction. Not only was there no formal surrender or capitulation, which would have officially signaled that the conflict was over, the Coalition Provisional Authority (CPA) went further to antagonize this exact same population by conducting DeBa'athification.[8] Essentially, every Iraqi Army officer over the rank of major was purged, resulting in thousands of professional military officers being put out of the army, without a job. The tactical ignorance associated with that approach is significant. If that is not a recipe for insurgency, one would be hard pressed to find more permissive conditions or motivation: no capitulation, easily available ammunition stores, professional military officers purged from service now out of work, and not enough Coalition forces on the ground to secure ammunition stores. Should it be any surprise that the United States suddenly found itself in a low-intensity conflict/insurgency? It was incompetence of the highest order. To further add insult to injury, Secretary Rumsfeld knew better because he knew the operating assumptions going into the conflict. I served as an operational planner and saw the initial plans for the invasion of Iraq while deployed forward in Afghanistan and Qatar during early 2002, over a year before the actual invasion, and then participated in multiple planning sessions leading up to the invasion. The entire planning premise, what planners call an assumption, was predicated on using the Iraqi forces for that constabulary force. When that assumption was no longer valid, then you must assume that you now must make up for the lack of forces you had planned on using.

What has always fascinated me about this is how politicized it became. My own observation was always that General Shinseki was correct but to a significant degree so was Secretary Rumsfeld in the context that there was no requirement for the constabulary force to be from the United States. Put another way, the Iraqi Army could have easily served as the constabulary force in post-Phase III Decisive Operations while attempting to establish stability in Iraq.[9] All that was in fact true until the decision was made to DeBa'athify. Once that decision was made, Secretary Rumsfeld knew that the entire premise was invalidated because the Iraqi Army could no longer serve as that constabulary force.[10] Thus, the moment that decision was made we should have sent more troops to make up for the constabulary force requirements no longer met by Iraqi Army. That was not a simple mistake; it was a conscious act to ignore previously validated requirements and borders on professional incompetence. Thus, an insurgency was born with a plethora of war-making materials and no other means to attack the occupier of their country (the U.S. led-Coalition). IEDs now had a purpose, and the U.S. and the Coalition were caught completely off guard and unprepared. Iraqis were limited to an IED approach because they had nothing else to resist or fight with and so they resorted to IEDs more out of desperation than by design. Iraqi Shia with the help of the Iranians utilized one of the deadliest IEDs, known as explosively formed penetrators (EFPs), which had been perfected in combat against the Israelis in Lebanon.[11] Over time, the IED approach nearly brought the most powerful nation on earth, the United States, to near mission failure in Iraq.[12]

Why Are IEDs Such a Big Problem?

Without being overly dramatic, the most obvious reason that IEDs are a problem is that they kill, wound, and maim our troops. More importantly, this is an operational/strategic approach designed to hinder our ability to accomplish our mission wherever we are operating and enables our adversaries to drain our resources. Additionally, IEDs create a losing economy-of-scale battle where for mere cents on the dollar the enemy is making the United States spend inordinate amounts of resources on overcoming this issue, and to date, we haven't achieved victory. Importantly, creating bomb-resistant equipment, or things like mine-resistant ambush-protected (MRAP) vehicles is awesome—they reduce casualties—but it is still a losing economy-of-scale problem. You might protect folks from IEDs, but you are losing the war because the cost, over time, bankrupts you while your enemy spends mere cents on the dollar. If we are being honest with ourselves, we almost left Iraq because of IEDs, and then that exact same technique proliferated to another theater of war where it was not even present prior to events in Iraq. Finally, because of all of this, these techniques proliferated to other areas of the world where our allies and friends do not have the same resources we do. It is exactly this phenomenon which should scare the hell out of our leadership and other students of warfare. This trend is extremely concerning because IED-enabled asymmetric warfare enables asymmetric actors to take a tie and make it a win and take a loss and make it tie. That is extremely dangerous. It creates significant issues in terms of both resources and stability concerns in the existing nation-state order. If left unchecked, it will create increased instability and ungoverned space throughout the world. This pattern will continue to expand until we learn to overcome and defeat this approach. Take notice of the key word that was used in that discussion. We must learn to defeat this approach, not simply degrade it. Unfortunately, while we continue to struggle with this threat, a new one emerged, and that threat was unmanned technologies being utilized in asymmetric approaches.

IED and UAV Threat Convergence

Unmanned technologies present both opportunities and threats. What has emerged with the convergence of unmanned technology on the threat side is extremely dangerous. It is true that UAS platforms represent both a threat and a solution for these problems, but the threat provides serious challenges if left unchecked. Recently, the Pentagon discussed a shift toward utilization of spy planes and airborne sensors in the IED fight, increasing the efficiency of C-IED efforts in Afghanistan.[13] In an article about UAV use to mitigate IEDs, Caroline Rees points out the impact that airborne sensors have had in their short time on the battlefield, creating significant challenges in maintaining force protection. This capability in enemy hands unchecked provides the enemy another opportunity to engage friendly forces without becoming decisively engaged. Others see an opportunity to go airborne 24 hours a day, seven days a week with a massive UAS fleet potentially invalidating the enemy's entire IED approach.[14] In either an IED approach or a UAS attack, the critical terrain is the airspace above the battlefield because if you remove the enemy's ability to engage friendly forces through persistent stare and strike capability, the task for the enemy to engage becomes exponentially more difficult. Additionally, the army is adapting the C-RAM antimissile system for use against small UAVs to shoot down enemy UAV IEDs.[15] As a result of these emerging threats, key leaders in the army appear concerned over the potential uses of UAVs as IEDs and are investing in countering them.[16] Critical to understanding this issue is the fact in 1999, there were 20 UAV system types and 800 aircraft and by 2010 there were 200 system types and 10,000 unmanned aircraft. That amount of growth leaves gaps and seams in any type of law-enforcement requirement for these types of capabilities. Current estimates indicate that by 2025 UAS platforms inside the United States will have increased tenfold.[17]

UAVs as IEDs or Attack Platforms

The greater concern in this overall context is that some of this is so new (or foreign to planners' thinking) that there has not been a lot of thought put into all of this. Where threats have existed on the battlefield, they have manifested themselves against the military and not law enforcement. This is one of the most concerning factors in this equation. The law-enforcement community and National Airspace regulation apparatus is simply not prepared to deal with this threat. One only needs to look back at the events of September 11, 2001, to see how an asymmetric threat can be utilized to attack the infrastructure of the United States. The enemy with nothing more than box cutters and the willingness to sacrifice their lives hijacked four airline platforms and turned them into suicide cruise missiles. Forward in combat zones, the army is now seeing a significant increase in enemy small drone attacks.[18] (One only needs look at what's going on in the Red Sea with the Houthis in 2024 and what that is creating in terms of another cost-imposing strategy. Conceptually it's the same type of problem—we are shooting million-dollar missiles at drones.) While clearly not focused on domestic targets, it does not take much imagination to potentially see how an adaptive enemy could utilize small UAS platforms to conduct a multitude of attacks inside the United States. This reveals clearly that there are extensive vulnerabilities inside the current National Airspace System (NAS) with no fix on the horizon. Kris Osborn also wrote an article on emerging technology in 2016, which focused on how industry was assisting government agencies in usurping the command signal of attacking enemy drones. This reinforces the nature of a simultaneous opportunity and threat. Fox News detailed an attempt by IS to conduct an attack on Incirlik Air Base in Turkey using drones. The attack was foiled because Turkish authorities arrested the suspect before the event occurred, but post-arrest interrogation revealed that the IS jihadist had conducted reconnaissance to attempt to conduct a drone attack. More problematic is the apparent lack of concern for this threat by the Federal Aviation Administration (FAA). The massive influx of UAS platforms is a serious threat. A litmus test on this issue is to examine if there is an enforcement arm for the FAA like a state highway patrol or law-enforcement arm. While exploring that concept, the next question that might be asked in all of this is, if a massive attack using drones occurred, what agency responds? Is it the military or is it some form of yet-undetermined law enforcement? Little attention has been paid to this threat domestically. In the opinion of the author, it is just a matter of time before our adversaries figure this out. Recent testimony by the Federal Bureau of Investigation (FBI) Director Christopher Wray informed a Senate panel recently that an attack is imminent.[19]

Convergence

The convergence of various threats across multiple organizations and various communities creates seams and gaps in the government's approach. UAS threats appear from all logic to be squarely under the FAA's umbrella while IEDs are under JIDO. What happens when UAS platforms start being used as IEDs or attack platforms?[20] Is that potential problem an IED issue or, is it a law-enforcement issue, or is it a DOD/military issue? These sets of issues crosscut existing responsibilities and challenge previously established paradigms. A deeper examination of UAS integration into the NAS illustrates these problems. The NAS contains extensive vulnerabilities associated with integrating UAS, which provide our adversaries another significant avenue to inflict damage to the United States. While it may seem obvious that the above makes sense, if the current level of enforcement is all that exists, then the system that the government has set up might have more problems than one would really care to admit. The future of UAS use in the United States appears to be on track for a massive amount of growth in a very short amount of time.[21] If that prediction holds true, then the FAA is in for a rude awakening when there is zero corresponding growth in the air traffic control, management, or enforcement capabilities. More troublesome, the integration of those systems into an already busy NAS creates significant risks that have not been mitigated. Daily, more than

42,000 manned aircraft transit the NAS.[22] Couple with that, the massive influx of the UAS into that same infrastructure and there is an undeniably increased risk of accidents and vulnerabilities that a cunning adversary can exploit.

What a Smart Terrorist Would Do

Any serious asymmetric warfare approach applied with the assistance of UAS platforms creates significant concerns for the protection of U.S. infrastructure. The following short list of obvious terrorist, criminal, or rogue-actor techniques are not all inclusive of potential threats that exist. Nuclear, biological, or chemical agents attached to a UAS delivery platform flown into a public gathering. This same approach applies to contaminating water supplies. UAS platforms with explosives attacking fuel yards, petroleum plants, electrical power plants, or similar facilities like nuclear power plants, and airports. Electronic attack and cyber-attack payloads attached to these same platforms to attack infrastructure. Creative adversaries acting asymmetrically could cause considerable damage to the domestic infrastructure.

Results-Driven Requirements

This discussion started with a series of questions about analyzing the mission of an organization that is dedicated to defeating asymmetric and improvised threats. A quick analysis of the potential requirements follows. The IED problem is fairly simple. Any organization that is engaged in an IED-enabled asymmetric warfare campaign requires four basic requirements: (1) people, (2) money, (3) IED resources, and (4) a supporting ideology. These capabilities are managed through a network that employs these capabilities to build and employ IEDs against our forces in areas like Afghanistan, Iraq, and other locations where our forces are conducting operations. While it sounds simple, it is not, it is a lot more complicated and the next portion of this dives deeper into this issue, making general assessments on which government agencies typically deal with these problems. When examining this it is important to be able to project similar support requirements for UAS platforms as our adversaries move from IEDs to other technologies that involve unmanned systems like UAS platforms or submersibles.

1. IED resources: This typically includes items like ordnance, explosives, fertilizer, chemicals to make explosives, electronic parts, vehicles for suicide bombs, telephones, and communication devices.
    a. The various government agencies that are involved in these types of issues are the FBI, CIA, ATF, Commerce, Agriculture, DOS, DIA, DHS, Customs, and DOD.
2. Money: This is used to pay their fighters, establish bases, and for logistics. It buys supplies and the commodities used to make bombs.

a. The government agencies typically involved in this are the Treasury, DOS, FBI, CIA, ATF, DEA, DIA, and DOD.
3. People: The cause requires fighters, IED-emplacement teams, IED assembly, religious leaders, facilitators, financiers, logistics personnel, and propaganda personnel. In many cases these people do more than one job as in any type of resistance movement or irregular warfare campaign. The most important thing to realize is that this campaign cannot exist without the tacit support of the population and personnel to conduct operations.
   a. The government agencies typically involved in this requirement are DOD, DIA, CIA, and DOS.
4. Supporting ideology. This is intricately linked to recruits and personnel because any movement requires a supporting ideology. In simple terms if there is no belief in the cause (whatever it is) then recruits, money, and commitment do not follow.
   a. The government agencies typically involved in this requirement are CIA, DOD, DIA, and DOS.

At this point, it should be blatantly obvious that there are many organizations dealing with this problem. Currently a multi-organizational approach, it should be a singular agency. Unified action, when led by DOD in a non-combat zone should be renamed "unified purgatory" because like purgatory, the poor pilgrim (DOD) is stuck and lacks the authority to synchronize, coordinate, or execute as a lead agency in anything but a war zone.[23] Looking back above at the various organizations in this problem set, it is obvious that this is analogous to the same satire that Dante wrote hundreds of years ago. The pilgrim's ascent beyond purgatory through cleansing of his sins becomes impossible. No program or plan of action to gain entry to heaven exists, thus condemning the participants to eternal purgatory. Asking the DOD to lead this effort is analogous to pilgrims attempting to get out of purgatory when every other organization doesn't help you because they dislike being told what to do by the military and hence why it only works in war theaters. Unfortunately, most support zones enabling IED networks in combat zones/theaters of war, do so from outside. It creates a frustrating situation that is often too hard to fix.

The approach that makes the most sense is something that looks like the Office of Strategic Services (OSS) in World War II, but not the present-day CIA although there are clearly proliferation issues, in all this.[24] Intelligence is interwoven throughout this problem set yet requires a massive whole-of-government approach to defeat. DOD led is clearly not the right approach, and frankly, no single agency approach will ever likely work. Instead, an "improvised threat asymmetric warfare czar" with three distinct capabilities is the best course of action. That organization requires people, resources, and authority. It requires the right people in an interagency task force headed by a political appointee with military and intelligence personnel organically assigned with a policy coordination committee or presidential decision directive like authority to direct, coordinate, and synchronize across the entire government. The answer has never been a DOD-led approach, will never be a DOD-lead approach but that is the path that we continue to pursue.

Persistent Asymmetric Conflict and Organizational Alignment

Our adversaries will not attack the United States using traditional tactics or weapons systems.* There is little debate that United States has no true peer but every day that goes by where we do not solve these problems, we allow our closest competitors the ability to gain ground on us. Put another way, every dollar we spend on conflicts in the Middle East, Africa, or the Philippines is a dollar we don't spend on increasing our lethality and capabilities against rising near-peer adversaries like Russia and China. We must enable stability in these areas and then extricate ourselves from these problems so we can concentrate on the greater challenges of major combat operations. Consequently, adversaries will continue to attack our vulnerabilities, and our competitors will assist in bogging us down in these conflicts. Despite the obvious nature of that reasoning, policy, resources, and strategy efforts fail to account for asymmetric and irregular warfare efforts. Resources are not aligned efficiently, and organizations are not aligned logically. Asymmetric and irregular warfare creates significant challenges when coupled with technology. We do not pay attention to the lessons of the past. It should be obvious, that these concepts are no different than we used in our own Revolutionary War against the British. A large part of the Revolutionary War was conducted using asymmetric techniques.[25] Colonial militia and irregulars simply refused to engage the British Army in a formation-on-formation battle, which was seen as both the proper and courteous conduct of warfare. Noted guerilla warfare commanders like Francis Marion and Nathaniel Greene fought campaigns designed to tie down better-equipped British units. As you read this, the description of this problem should make the hair on one's neck stand up as it is eerily familiar. Insurgents directly engaging U.S. forces get killed or captured. That is why insurgents utilize IEDs to engage U.S. military forces and are now moving toward unmanned capabilities. If nothing else, our efforts have certainly not achieved a level where we are creating significant dilemmas for the enemy. Extensive reflection on these problems should drive one to conclude that the current approach is failing, is improperly aligned, and creates significant seams and gaps. IED and unmanned

---

* At the time of the initial writing of this book this held true but later chapters that deal with joint all-domain fires attempt to negate where we have allowed the Chinese to catch up or surpass us, which the approach on joint all-domain fires ideally negates—one of the reasons why this concept is so important.

platform-enabled asymmetric warfare as well as emerging techniques involve both national and local law enforcement but there isn't even the slightest indication that any of this is registering as a threat domestically.

Losing the Battle of Cost-Imposing Strategies

All this leads directly to a more dangerous indication associated with IED, UAV and other irregular approaches. We appear to have missed the boat in all this. Our resources appear focused exclusively on solving tactical problems and not on any greater strategic vision to remove the conditions which enable these types of asymmetric approaches, which again begs the question: Why in the world would DOD lead this? If nothing else, it certainly appears that it should be a whole-of-government approach involving diplomatic, economic, and informational capabilities. Some have even said that this is a clash of cultures—that may in fact be true. What does that imply in this greater problem? Should not our entire approach potentially be guided by trying to solve the greater problem of a clash of culture rather than running away from it? Some might even call that the root cause of this problem,

Russia presents an interesting dilemma because we should be cooperating with them in some areas while ensuring that our national interests are not challenged in others. There is an opportunity for cooperation, which enables discussion on those areas where we see potential conflict. An additional observation on some of this problem is that we ought to encourage some of our allies and partners to develop a strong IED and EFP capability to potentially resist any potential Russian aggression. A prime example of this is in the Baltics, the terrain and geography are extremely canalizing and if the Russians ever decided to attempt to go back into those NATO allies' areas, it would take a while for the U.S. and NATO to get back in because of Kaliningrad and the fact that ground force presence in Europe is a shell of what it once was. I think what would absolutely scare the shit out of the Russians, and Russian armored and motorized formations is organic Baltic EFP and IED capability. Around every corner and narrow road is an EFP.

IEDs and unmanned platforms provide an attractive asymmetric tactic available to the weaker adversary. The strategy behind IED use can vary and range from a "death by a thousand cuts" approach designed to break the popular will or incite terror in the population of the stronger contestant; it can also include efforts to destroy confidence in or impose costs to the transportation, economic, or communications systems of an opponent. The expected outcome is that IEDs and unmanned approaches will remain a weapon of choice for U.S. adversaries in both current and future conflicts. History treats ruthlessly those who fail to adapt. Failure to change the status quo provides a significant advantage to our opponents. For most of this fight, our strategy emphasized defensive measures, such as the use of heavily armored vehicles and defensive electronic warfare. There is a role for this type of defensive approach but sole reliance on defensive tactics, techniques, and procedures is analogous to the faith placed by the French in the Maginot Line. It failed then and it will fail again. This approach puts us on the wrong side of a cost-imposing strategy where expenses significantly exceed a relatively inexpensive strategy used by the enemy. Finally, after almost two decades at war in two major operations, the approach has not worked. When comparing this issue to something like the atomic bomb and the Manhattan Project, we have been in persistent conflict for that period, and we have not really made a dent in some of these problems. How is that possible? As long as the DOD has been working on these problems, what impact at the strategic level have they had? From what I have witnessed, some tactical successes but no major operational or strategic impact.

CHAPTER 9

Unmanned Systems

This chapter, written in 2017, focuses on emerging unmanned systems that make UAS platforms both a threat and a simultaneous opportunity in the asymmetric warfare realm. Further, the security issues these platforms and concepts present with an expanding evolution of asymmetric warfare threats, demand examination. These technologies also impact potential peer/near-peer fights with adversaries like China or Russia. There are opportunities to focus on some of the emerging technologies that exist out there. This chapter focuses specifically on UAS operations and payload opportunities and threats.

Problem Frame

Within the counter-improvised explosive device (C-IED) fight, UAVs provide an approach, potentially providing a game-breaking methodology against IED-enabled warfare and asymmetric conflicts. This could be accomplished by providing a host of unmanned payloads which to date have utilized primarily manned approaches. This reduces economy-of-scale issues besieging the DOD in this fight. Conceptually, this chapter proposes that UAVs are simultaneously a threat as well as an opportunity to reduce the effectiveness of this type of warfare. Using UAS systems to our advantage might render IED-focused warfare to the back pages of history, but requires breaking a lot of paradigms that we, as a country, and DOD do not typically deal well with. A basic understanding of history shows us that we typically do not figure out how to use an innovation in warfare for about 20 years or more. The tank and airplane are perfect examples of this. The airplane was seen as a reconnaissance platform not as a strike platform. This is what I refer to as the "flash to bang" concept. To date, my current observation of the understanding of how to use these platforms indicates we have not broken the code on how to truly take advantage of UAS systems with respect to C-IED and asymmetric warfare.

Part of the concern is that we continue to approach the problems in environments like Iraq, Syria, Afghanistan or half a dozen other like scenarios through the same organizational approach we did when we started in 2001. We are still using the same formations; we have not really changed our organizational structure, and we continue to believe it is working. We are no closer to solving those sets of problems than we were when we started this endeavor. This should force some serious reflection and additional assessment that asks where the threats from an asymmetric warfare perspective are, and in general, a holistic larger-picture threat. This then ought to drive a central question, which is: Are our actions achieving what we intended for them to accomplish (mission/objective accomplishment)? One of the observations I have had throughout this entire experience is that if we can take away the high ground enabling us to reduce the enemy's freedom of action and maneuver, why in the world have we not tried to do so. This chapter addresses how we might achieve that.

Procedural flaws and alternative theories to this problem are present. At various times throughout this war, there have been attempts to figure out how to reduce the effectiveness of the adversary's IED campaign. The amount of effort, resources, and money spent attempting to reduce IEDs when juxtaposed against the results defies any degree of logic given the lack of substantive results attained, to date. The IED is the current concept or weapon empowering the advancement of asymmetric warfare. IED-enabled asymmetric warfare approaches enable weaker actors to engage superior actors and win. Obviously, if we do not solve this, then this is a clear threat to the traditional nation-state international order. As a perfect example: If this problem almost brought the United States, to its knees then what will it do to those nation-states that do not have the resources, manpower, and technology that we do? In an emerging world of ungoverned space, asymmetric warfare threats, criminal networks, and hybrid threats create significant stability concerns.

Further to the development of a cost-efficient unmanned aerial adaptation to both tactics and payloads, one of the challenges faced throughout these conflicts is providing a cost-efficient alternative to the concepts of persistent surveillance, interdiction, positive identification (PID), and network disruption. The amount of money, technology, and platforms that have been thrown at this problem is so grandiose that it defies description. Attempts at utilizing coherent change detection, electronic attack, joint fires, signals intelligence (SIGINT), measures and signatures intelligence (MASINT), tracking, tagging, and locating (TTL) are just a few of the approaches that have been attempted through predominantly manned applications. While there are intelligence, surveillance, and reconnaissance (ISR) platforms, which are unmanned, most of the force and capabilities arrayed against this problem set are manned.

An Alternative Approach: Go Airborne and Unmanned

I recommend a radical departure from the conventional mindset previously utilized to attack this problem set. There has always been a perceived need to utilize manned platforms because of the perceived need to conduct PID and ensure that we maintained an adequate "decide function" inside existing targeting cycles associated with joint and service doctrine. We assume this cannot be done by an unmanned approach. UAVs with the right sensor payload to include coherent change detection, electronic attack, and geolocation functions could potentially render existing adversary TTPs untenable. Coupling this type of an unmanned "Chinese menu" of alternating payloads with re-configurable platforms based on threat conditions enables a robust interdiction function. UAV enhancements to ongoing TTPs as well as research and development guided by the right tactics could level the playing field and render adversary IED campaigns ineffective.

IED and UAV Threat Convergence

Simultaneous opportunity and threat are emerging in convergence with unmanned technology. Specifically, UAVs offer opposing approaches to utilization of this emerging technology. It is both a threat and an opportunity to use this technology to provide persistent stare capability. We are examining the potential convergence of IED and UAV issues. Caroline Rees provides an article discussing the Pentagon's shift toward greater utilization of spy planes and airborne sensors. This effort increased the efficiency of C-IED efforts in Afghanistan.[1] She discusses the percentages of increased found rates for differing types of operations and the measurable impact the airborne sensors have had in their brief time on the battlefield. A notable statistic in her article is that for the first time in five years, IEDs account for less than half of our KIA deaths. Of the two systems that the article describes—Desert Owl and Copperhead—only one is manned. Noteworthy in this construct is that an airborne approach created an increased operational capability for friendly forces, potentially reversing a problematic trend, namely, that IEDs created significant issues for years. While exact percentages for the capability were not specified, it is obvious that these techniques offer a potential solution to longstanding tactical threats.

Mark Pomerleau in a 2015 article detailed how the army is addressing an emerging threat of UAVs being utilized as IEDs.[2] The army is adapting the C-RAM antimissile system for use against small UAVs in response to UAV being uses as IEDs to attack our troops and FOBs. Key leaders in the army appear concerned over these types of potential uses of UAVs as IEDs and are investing into countering this potential threat. Additionally, this article points out that radioactive material was used on a UAS device in Japan in a similar attack profile. This is one of the major concerns I pointed out over many years and Chapter 10, "21st-Century Blitzkrieg," written in 2009, points out these types of attacks were a huge vulnerability, creating a significant threat. The C-Ram was originally a modified navy close-in weapons system (CIWS) and modified for use in Iraq and Afghanistan to defeat incoming rockets, artillery, and mortars. Another use of that weapon is shooting down UAVs. In fact, shooting down UAVs is much easier than incoming rockets, artillery, or mortars. It is possible that this may change but currently, that is not the case. This chapter points out an obviously disturbing proliferation trend, noting that in 1999, there were 20 UAV system types and 800 aircraft and 11 years later, there were 200 system types and 10,000 unmanned aircraft.[3] In 2024, there were 791,597 drones registered.[4] Clearly, this trend comes with its own internal threat because of the massive proliferation creating significant challenges for law-enforcement and airspace management.

With these types of platforms being easily available and relatively cheap, it is much easier for the enemy to mass these platforms toward asymmetric attacks. Essentially, this capability provides a TTP not previously present to offensively attack U.S. forces rather than waiting until troops are in an IED-enabled engagement area. The critical change here is this TTP enables offensive vice passive tactics. Heather Clark discusses how Sandia Labs is transferring mini synthetic aperture radar (Mini SAR) to the army to assist in the C-IED fight.[5] Copperhead, which is a Mini SAR system mounted on a UAV detects disturbances in the earth through what is called coherent change detection (CCD). CCD detects disturbances in the earth in fine detail. Sandia is a leader in the development of SAR. SAR utilizes microwave reflection, which results in a fine resolution image allowing for comparison of before and after images leading to discerning obvious changes. The ability to mount this on a UAV at the size necessary to conduct and transmit the processing was key to making this approach worthwhile. This is another example of an unmanned approach enabling friendly forces' ability to know when the enemy has taken actions to insert IEDs on the battlefield. This is an example of placing a payload on a UAV to enable or reduce the enemy's ability to use IEDs.

Platform Payloads

Reconfigurable snap-on, snap-off payloads enable an airborne 24/7 strike and reconnaissance capability. Securing critical key terrain in this fight, namely the airspace above the area of operations, is vital. Examining readily available systems provides a basic start point to complete the task of degrading the adversary's freedom of maneuver and action. In any platform analysis, it is first necessary to go back to the basic system requirements. Earlier, I offered insights on using UAVs with various payloads to conduct counter-IED missions. This necessitates analyzing what types of payloads might be required for use in a counter-IED configuration. It is essential to dig a bit deeper in analyzing the nature of basic counter-IED missions. The counter-IED fight characteristics are likely not defined by major combat operations but instead an asymmetric tactic used by our adversaries to attack friendly forces, without theoretically becoming decisively engaged. This is not major maneuver warfare where big armies or military forces are attacking large formations; it is instead a series of endless irregular or guerilla types of attacks, in protracted conflict.

Consequently, these conflicts will be typical missions like counterinsurgency, foreign internal defense, or unconventional warfare. This is not to say that IEDs cannot be used in a major conflict, as witnessed, for example, in the Ukrainian conflict; it is instead that we expect a predominance of IED attacks during the end of Phase III (Decisive Operations) or beginning of Phase IV (Stabilization) of a joint operation.* We are more likely to see air superiority or dominance in this portion of the conflict followed by IEDs. Given this assumption, the platforms, which could provide the capabilities desired for execution of counter-IED operations would fly in scenarios where there is no threat of being shot down where we have air superiority/dominance.

Given the above assumptions, these platforms are flying in a no-threat or limited-threat scenario; the platforms providing counter-IED payloads are not limited by factors like survivability, low radar cross-sections, stealth, or carrying onboard self-protection. Instead, these platforms are free to focus on ensuring they have redundant communications and enough load-carrying capability to focus on the counter-IED payloads they would carry. The following capabilities or requirements are most desirable for conducting counter-IED missions:

1. Coherent change detection and measures and signals intelligence (MASINT).
2. SIGINT terminal guidance or electronic attack close target reconnaissance.
3. Electro-optical, TV, and infrared.
4. Unintended radiated emissions (MASINT).
5. Armed strike (Hellfire, or other kinetic strike capability).
6. Electronic warfare (EA, ES, EP).
7. Spectral analysis to find IED chemical traces.
8. Tracking, tagging, locating (TTL) and traditional ISR.

Platforms should ideally have an ability to have a reconfigurable bay, allowing the platform to simply swap out payloads, reducing requirements for multiple variants. Given all the above, the next step in any research or comparison process is to examine the existing platforms that are already in service.

In determining what platform would be most ideal, the typical governing factors that any logical approach would dictate would be to figure out what the overall decision criteria for guiding the desired effect. If the goal were to have more speed,

---

* In joint operations, Phase III is decisive operations and where the majority of decisive combat operations occur. It is not to say that in any situation, an operation can move from being in stability operations back into major combat operations but typically once stability operations start, the overall nature of the campaign does not move back into decisive operations. In COIN, FID, or UW, you can simultaneously be in decisive operations in one sector while being in stability operations in others. In major combat operations the likelihood of being in decisive operations and stability operations simultaneously is fairly low and unlikely. In the case of this example IEDs are predominantly an asymmetric technique that is unlikely to show up in decisive operations within Phase III.

then the fastest platform would win out; if the goal were to have the largest payload capability, then the platform with the most weight-carrying capability would win out, but this presumes that the approach only recommends one platform. Ideally, an integrated approach focuses on utilizing existing platforms for what they are best suited for and not one size fits all, although that would be logistically more supportable because it reduces maintenance costs, as well as reducing additional programs of record. In this case, these platforms already exist, but a smart approach would be to use these existing platforms and some additional lighter reconnaissance variants, which have much smaller payloads (Sentinel, Raven, etc.) for a combined-arms approach. That approach would utilize less-expensive, lighter-weight platforms for additional ISR while using the larger payload-carrying devices for strike reconnaissance requiring much heavier boxes and armaments. Obviously, the more multifunction approaches the platform might possess, the more likely the operator on the ground (the forward operator who this capability is supporting, not the driver sitting at some remote location) can reconfigure the platform to meet the operational requirements on the ground. For the lack of a better term this provides a host of theoretical "counter-IED air force" capabilities available to the ground force commander.

As stated, the operating assumption in this approach is that the proposal focuses on a low-threat COIN or FID environment where friendly forces have established air superiority. Thus, having set the foundation for understanding the requirement, the discussion moves toward how to best approach the strike and reconnaissance payloads for whatever platforms are chosen. It is important to note that the platform in this type of scenario (COIN, FID) should be built to achieve the following: (1) Long station time, (2) Large payload capacity, and (3) Interchangeability (defined as the ability to rapidly swap out payload systems). Traditionally, these platforms have carried armaments that are predominantly laser-guided bombs or some type of missile like Hellfire. The problem with this approach is that it focuses on a single engagement with a small circular error because of ongoing fears of collateral damage. While it is still important to maintain that capability, the problem has always been that this capability provides typically a single strike opportunity. This is not a balanced approach with strike. A better approach is to provide a more robust engagement approach which might also carry more traditional fire-support capabilities like 7.62mm mini gun, MK-77 fuel air explosive (napalm like), more 2.75-inch folding fin rocket configurations, and 20 or 40mm cannon configurations. These are not as precise as the laser-guided and GPS-guided weapons kits that are attached to current platforms. Alternately, they provide significantly greater loiter and engagement times, so it is probably a mix of the current platforms with additional configurations as suggested which achieves the optimal COIN and FID approach. This is the essence of flexibility that allows ground unit commanders to configure their organic platforms to the support requirements necessary to defeat insurgents, hybrid forces, and irregular and asymmetric threats. This will not be an easy task because the traditional communities that have established the current approach don't do well with change.

Conversely, the additions to the reconnaissance capabilities are easy in comparison. The true effect we are trying to achieve in this approach is an easily reconfigurable payload that allows multiple approaches to finding and fixing IED network nodes. This approach focuses on providing the airborne capabilities that detect homemade explosive (HME) trace elements, electronic signatures, phones, computers, blasting caps, and other elements that assist in the construction of IEDs. To be clear, it might be possible with the bigger platforms to carry multiple payloads, which enable IED precursor identification. In this capacity, this is the start of a term commonly referred to as "police work." There is no magic bullet in this approach; it simply provides a better opportunity to focus collection efforts on likely areas where IEDs are potentially being made. The common analogy I have used extensively is this would be fishing with a better fish finder.

This approach provides maximum situational awareness with the existing communications suites already present, while allowing ground forces to task-organize and attack IED network nodes and simultaneously conduct ISR. Additionally, reconfigurable payloads allow the platform to conduct strike and ISR simultaneously or in teams, dependent upon the platforms being utilized. Why do we not push as much of this capability down to the guy on the ground fighting this fight? Someone, please tell me that's a bad idea because it isn't. Unfortunately, because of service politics and executive agency, you will never see that because the United States Air Force is the executive agent for that. I have offered solutions to this by letting guys on the ground use this stuff to get them off the line while simultaneously getting better support from forces who actually understand what the ground guy needs. That's just a no brainer. It will never happen. Why? Institutional paralysis. Can't think outside the box, threatens my rice bowl.

Recommendation: Utilize all available platforms in the available suite of UAVs. If one was forced into a singular choice of only one platform, then the decision criteria would change to the following requirements: (1) higher inventory, (2) capable of carrying both sensors and armaments, and (3) cost. In a singular choice, the most desirable platform would be the Predator version because it is cheaper, still holds a decent load—there are more of them—and it has both ISR and strike capability.

Airborne Applications Are Game-Changers

Throughout the conflicts in Iraq, Afghanistan, and other spots where IEDs are prevalent, one of the biggest challenges faced is that friendly forces simply do not have enough ISR, or strike capability to effectively monitor their battlespace. When the vast majority of IEDs are emplaced on existing roads or what are referred to as "lines of communication" (LOCs), then monitoring those LOCs with persistent ISR, if enabled, becomes a game-changing approach to how to deal with the problem. Put another way, what has always been problematic in the C-IED fight is the ability to maintain constant ISR in areas with friendly forces traffic. UAS platforms bring down the cost level to something manageable while also allowing an unmanned continuous strike capability. Add to this MASINT capabilities to find and fix areas where homemade explosives are being made, and you can start to reduce the networks and support zones that support IED networks. In the past, the cost and numbers of platforms reduced the ability of the military to enable manned 24-hour coverage. UAS platforms are almost made for a low-intensity conflict where friendly forces have complete air dominance. If anything, this drives insurgents to attempt to overcome the decisive advantage that a persistent ISR and strike capability offers. More concerning is that the same technology can be used for asymmetric warfare. UAS platforms can attack inside traditional nation-states' airspace because the nature of UAS platforms management is so problematic.

Recommended Force Structure

First and foremost, there is no existing doctrine for pushing UAVs or UAS platforms down to battalion- or brigade-sized units. Smaller UAS platforms like the RQ-7 Raven or the RQ-11 Raven are not present in brigade-sized units. For the record, neither of these platforms would support these types of operations, nor does Major Scott Masson's UAVs in Brigade Combat Teams (BCTs) thesis from the naval post-graduate school in Monterey address this problem.

The revolutionary approach in this proposal goes far above placing an operational reconnaissance UAV inside a BCT. This proposal is radical in that it removes the air force out of the equation and recommends that these platforms be pushed down in sufficient numbers to enable organic operations for each brigade with potentially a reserve or additional resources at a division (or equivalent USMC organization). While airspace still requires deconfliction through the service component designated as the producer of the air tasking order (ATO), that airspace deconfliction can be accomplished through the Air Liaison Officer (ALO) and their Air Support Operations Squadron (ASOS) elements assigned to brigade. The key to this concept is figuring out a basis of issue. To do that, any rational planner would look back at previous combat after-action reports and determine how many networks and supply routes went through their operating sector to begin to determine what kind of coverage would be required. Immediately, both strike and reconnaissance platforms should be paired as a bare minimum but if the units were able to achieve wider-angle surveillance (wide-angle stare) then those ratios might go down. In a normal BCT, there are three maneuver battalions, one artillery battalion and a series of combat-enabler companies (engineers, air defense, medical, transportation, and quartermaster assets). Typically, rotary-wing aviation units are maintained at a divisional level and are not pushed down to a BCT permanently. Consequently, the requirement probably centers on a total of four battalions and some requirement for convoy movement, potentially creating a requirement for a fifth battalion.

Personal experience in combat for almost eight years in Iraq and Afghanistan has shown first that a country like Iraq with its built-up areas requires more capability. On average two to four targeted areas of interest (TAIs) plus at least one to three supply routes exist in a BCT sector. Assuming worst-case scenario, that requires constant coverage of at least seven areas by a strike and reconnaissance platform team. More than likely, in addition to those seven areas, each maneuver battalion would require two to three additional platforms to conduct additional operations. That makes a total of nearly 20 strike and reconnaissance platforms per BCT. This may seem excessive, but this is a departure from previously standardized procedures. Over time, this would be adjusted by actual combat observations and terrain analysis, which would dictate a standardized basis of issue for each BCT. Finally, a note about cost: it may seem significantly expensive to resource a BCT with 20 strike and reconnaissance teams, but two factors immediately impact this over the long haul. First is the idea that over time, the requirement not to fly manned platforms saves significant amounts of money because manned platforms are significantly more expensive in cost per flight hour. Second, what is the cost of losing additional soldiers in training hours, the cost of their life insurance, and the cost to the mission when it would take significantly less time to achieve mission success with these assets? Although the cost is high up front, over time, the approach is a more cost-efficient strategy.

UAV Weapons

One of the most dangerous applications of UAS platforms is that they can be used inside the traditional airspace systems of countries like the United States to asymmetrically attack our infrastructure. The National Airspace System (NAS) is not prepared for the massive influx of unmanned platforms that are coming, if no drastic change occurs. We're on a glide path toward disaster by opening gigantic vulnerabilities to our infrastructure. There is no current policing function that can effectively interdict these threats if massive numbers of UAS platforms are allowed into the airspace without having a regulatory and police arm. UAS platforms could potentially deliver explosives, chemicals, biological agents, or dozens of other threats we have not even thought of yet. Once inside the United States, a cunning adversary could launch swarms of these drones with electronic warfare capabilities that could place existing aircraft at risk; they could also be uploaded with explosives to attack fuel storage areas and critical infrastructure. The country is simply not ready for this technology, and as it stands, the glide path we are on is a recipe for disaster. We must prepare for the worst-case scenario by realizing this technology represents a viable threat while simultaneously utilizing the same technology for altering the C-IED fight where our troops are conducting counterinsurgency, foreign internal defense missions, and facing irregular and asymmetric threats.

The underlying tenants of this construct are that UAS platforms provide both opportunity and risk, and that if properly utilized and controlled, UAS platforms provide an excellent vehicle to attack current asymmetric and irregular warfare challenges. We spend inordinate amounts of resources flying manned platforms in support of ongoing combat deployments in areas like Afghanistan, Iraq, Syria, and other places where American troops are deployed in support of the Global War on Terror. The nature of unmanned platforms provides a unique opportunity, where we have air dominance, to overwhelm the enemy's ability to wage war against us, while simultaneously saving money. Unfortunately, that same opportunity platform is a threat to our own national security inside the United States if not regulated, policed, and potentially interdicted when operating domestically. The threat of unmanned systems being utilized as weapons is both real and potentially uncontrollable if not properly restrained. There are no sky cops or UAV police. Is hijacking an airliner a bigger threat than UAVs being used to attack infrastructure in the United States? You will sense some anger and frustration in some of my observations, and a lot of cynicism. USAF dudes are wigging out because they sit in an air-conditioned CONEX flying a drone halfway around the world and have to watch some guy bleed out. Are you kidding me? Sorry, but the crowd I grew up in would be doing "cheetah flips" knowing that I took out bad guys and I wouldn't have one ounce of remorse. Call me callous or insensitive but the thought of this type of issue doesn't bother me one bit.

At a strategic level, I have said throughout this book and repeatedly to anyone who will listen, we are in two simultaneous conflicts, one hot (Global War on Terror), while the other is competition with China and Russia. So, every dollar I spend on these ongoing operations is a dollar I am not spending increasing our capabilities or building additional combat capabilities. UAS platforms are a game-changer regarding delivering capability that saves money over the long term and delivers solid defeat capability to our forces in the C-IED fight. This capability in a low-intensity conflict, UW, FID, and COIN environment provides a significant overmatch capability. We have to deal with the ongoing reality of the jihadist threat, but we also need to prepare for a peer or near-peer threat. At extended distances, with a complex anti-access area denial problem, UAVs and unmanned capabilities in multiple domains present additional dilemmas for adversaries. I do not know if a war with China is coming but it might if we do not take it seriously and check Chinese expansion in the South China Sea and the Pacific Rim. Rommel once said, "The more you sweat in peace, the less you bleed in war." That could not be truer and if we do not prepare for this fight, we will certainly see it, and it might not work out the way we would want it to.

Statistically Zero Enforcement of UAS Activity

The rapid influx of UAS into the NAS has been astronomical. The projections are even worse, with anticipation of tenfold growth of the sector by 2025 and add another $82 billion of revenue to the economy, and those estimates may be conservative.[6] In 2016, the Office of Science and Technology Policy announced steps to incorporate safe integration and innovative adaptation of UAS systems into the NAS. These efforts focused on several lines of effort. The main effort included investment of $35 million for research funding in the National Science Foundation to figure out how to best expedite design, control, and applications of UAS platforms. Key components to this were inspection safety, infrastructure development, and monitoring. Additional efforts are focused on how to best utilize these platforms for disaster response, improve government processes, and reduce privacy issues caused by rapid proliferation.[7] In late 2017, the Deputy Administrator of the FAA Daniel Elwell briefed the House Transportation and Infrastructure Committee on UAS integration efforts. The overall intent with regard to UAS systems is to integrate manned and unmanned systems by using the same air traffic management systems and occupying the same airspace.[8] Adding to the complexity of a tenfold increase in UAS systems into the NAS is the ongoing effort to bring on line the Next Generation Air Transportation System typically referred to as "NextGen." NextGen provides the FAA a supposed significant improvement over the existing system in place. NextGen makes uses of satellite-enabled navigation approaches to speed up and improve the process. In doing so, it supposedly provides greater accuracy, allowing controllers to see the exact location of the aircraft and all the other similarly enabled aircraft. Unfortunately, a 2014 FAA Inspector General report raises serious concerns over the FAA's ability to deliver on NextGen promises.[9] One of the foundational elements of this system is Automatic Dependent Surveillance-Broadcast and the FAA mandates compliance by January 1, 2020.[10] All aircraft operating in controlled airspace must be equipped with this capability by the 2020 date. This system also has already been shown to be hacked and consequently, the entire enterprise is suspect given an asymmetric threat of potential rogue UAS systems and an integration mechanism that is not even close to completion.[11] Simply put, the FAA is not on track to achieve this in any capacity, and one is forced to ask how in the world they could even attempt to integrate a tenfold increase of UAS systems with no current enforcement arm. There is no visible enforcement arm in the FAA and the expectation that all of this is synchronized and effective stretches any modicum of credibility. The problem is simple and straightforward: the FAA and greater law enforcement pay minimal attention to UAS regulations and enforcement of existing regulations. This creates significant vulnerabilities in the NAS and to the population, infrastructure, and economy. Left untreated, this problem will eventually lead to catastrophic disaster brought on by rogue actors or through accidents through irresponsible procedures and oversight by the FAA.

There is no effective regulatory arm or organization in the FAA. In simple terms, what organization conducts safety inspections, routine traffic stops, or interdicts violators of regulatory policies? If that organization is the FAA, then a reasonable presumption would exist that there would be a substantial number of citations issued by the FAA against UAS users. The entire system inside the United States appears to operate on the honor system. Thus, the refined premise is that there is no enforcement arm regulating UAS use of the NAS. Therefore, the comparison of UAS system citations with citations inside the large truck and busing industry provides an ideal comparison for comparison and contrast. As a percentage of overall traffic in this industry, there are verifiable amounts of citations issued and tracked in the Federal Motor Carriers Safety Administration.[12] If the numbers are similar in both sectors, then that would constitute supporting the null hypothesis associated with this study.

Observations, Identification of Gaps, Seams, and Vulnerabilities

The first obvious gap is that there is effectively no law-enforcement arm that regulates these activities. UAS systems currently present a significant threat to our infrastructure through both safety concerns and rogue use by adversarial actors. At the user level, one concern is that there is no requirement for a photo ID or address to get a license for operating a UAS system. This creates obvious opportunities for criminals, terrorists, or rogue actors to buy up multiple systems, which could eventually be used as a mass infrastructure attack in the United States. More importantly, the critical concept that should be considered in any asymmetric attack is that all this is limited to the imagination of the attacker. One of the worst types of attacks could be placing chemical or biological agents into something like the water supply. With complete candor, the author is continually surprised that our adversaries have not figured this vulnerability out yet. As the FBI Director Christopher Wray said, "It is not if, but when" and thus it is just a matter of time before our adversaries figure out how to do these types of things.[13]

Within the maintenance realm, the current approach the FAA is taking makes little sense. If one contrasts programs out there for fixed-wing and rotary-wing systems to maintenance requirements in the UAS world, a rationally minded person questions the entire approach. There is no Continuing Analysis and Surveillance System (CASS), crew resource management (CRM), line operations safety assessments (LOSA), production, planning and Control (PPC), quality control (QC), or quality assurance (QA) in the overall system. All the responsibility is placed on an individual that almost typically lacks the systemic prerequisite knowledge to even come close to the requirements for existing systems in place with traditional fixed-wing platforms. The registration requirement differences between systems are significant. An individual can buy multiple systems with one registration number and no requirement exists to produce identification or a physical address. This should be a concern to any law-enforcement intelligence apparatus and creates opportunities for rogue, criminal, or terrorist use. The specificity in the system for fixed wing is robust while in the UAS system it is almost non-existent. Bringing the UAS system up to the same level of scrutiny as well as increasing the knowledge requirements to operate UAS platforms would significantly reduce these gaps and issues.

The So What

The FAA must take control of this situation and the sooner they do it, the safer we will all be. This encompasses establishing a regulatory arm, authority to stop these incidents, stiff penalties, and the tools to do so. To do that, the FAA and the government will more than likely need to reallocate resources. In a zero-growth environment maybe there are some efficiencies that might be obtained through combining disparate portions of this problem set under one greater construct which would include TSA, air traffic controller, air marshals, and the remainder of the FAA. An immediate comment would be that we are spending billions of dollars on the TSA infrastructure every year on a threat that is probably unlikely to occur given that the situation has changed and that the likelihood of hijackers ever succeeding again is astronomically low. When I say this in other circles, people often ask what I mean. No plane in the United States will ever likely be hijacked again because the passengers and crew would rise up and take the plane back because they have been conditioned to realize that if they don't, they are going to die in a suicide crash of the airplane while being used as a weapon. In fact, one can argue that the plane that crashed in the fields of Pennsylvania on 9/11 was exactly that type of realization where the passengers and crew rose up to take back the plane. It just won't happen again in the United States unless the population becomes significantly more subservient and that's highly unlikely given the stakes. So because of the above realization, we appear to be spending a lot of money on a scenario that is highly unlikely to even occur again. Could some of those funds be reallocated so solve some of this problem as one potential course of action? The answer is maybe but it would be worth exploring.

The FAA needs to establish standards that encompass maintenance, airspace control, and technology and enable fail-safe operations. Allowing operators to take a simple test with no basic understanding of air procedures and register a UAV/UAS platform does not equate to what the system should require. Instead, what NCATT has offered as a baseline for conducting maintenance on a UAS system should be the standard or something like it. The entire system is a huge accident waiting to happen. The FAA must immediately institute changes that make it more difficult to purchase, register, and operate a UAS. Beyond that, the government must take steps to establish a responsible law-enforcement arm for the safe conduct of UAS operations. All UAS platforms must include the ability to recognize what type of airspace they are in, using sense and avoid technology, and an even safer approach would include an FAA fail-safe override capability. A final set of recommendations is that all UAS systems should be configured with a sense-and-avoid capability as well as software that could allow the FAA or government to take over the platform to remove it from airspace they should not be in.

The FAA needs to take a serious look at the UAS training, certification, and licensing process to address some of the shortfalls recommended in this chapter. The FAA must also establish an intelligence and enforcement arm that can do background checks on potential students and operators to assist in eliminating rouge actors before they potentially act. In the case of enforcement, this is also a major concern that needs to be rectified to protect the homeland and our infrastructure. The government should not wait till we have another 9/11 to act. Roles and responsibilities should be articulated now to establish procedures, capabilities, and approaches to eliminate the threats described in this book. As a closing thought on how vulnerable we are, a cunning adversary, once inside the United States, could launch swarms of these drones with electronic warfare capabilities that could place existing aircraft at risk; they could also be uploaded with explosives to attack fuel storage areas, and critical infrastructure. The country is simply not ready for this technology without some meaningful change.

The aim of this section is to show that the FAA and for that matter law enforcement in general is not regulating the use of UAS systems. The methodology used to show this is both quantitative and qualitative comparisons. In the quantitative case, the null hypothesis provides that if law enforcement is regulating the UAS in the NAS, then the interdiction rate for UAS systems would be like the large truck and bus industry. In fact, it is not, it is not even close. The percentage difference is 2,343 times greater in the large truck and bus industry than the UAS enterprise. The Chi Square comparison also reinforced this because the 0.05 percent interval required an X stat of roughly 3.4 and the Chi Square computation was nearly 15,000. In simple terms, both figures reinforce that the UAS system is completely unregulated and that the null hypothesis can clearly be rejected.

From a qualitative comparison, the requirements for licensing, registration, and maintenance are so drastically different that it defies common sense. One system requires months of training and certification to operate in whether one is a pilot, maintenance technician, or even an air traffic controller, while the other requires a written test equivalent to a driver's license exam and no basic aviation knowledge or airmanship. In almost brutal terms, the FAA has placed the entire general aviation training, air traffic control, maintenance, and certification process on an individual. For obvious reasons this creates multiple threat streams that must be eliminated. Eventually through negligence, or overt acts of terrorism, our infrastructure or population will be attacked. There is no regulation in the system that is a gigantic accident waiting to happen.

I briefly referenced this before but this is a mathematical proof approach to showing that we are broken on how we deal with UAVs in this country and as I keep pointing out, no one will ever hijack a plane in this country again and succeed, because the passengers and crew will rise up and overpower the hijackers; it just won't happen but yet we spend $8.8 billion a year on a threat that isn't relevant anymore. These resources would be better served being repurposed to creating an interdiction and enforcement arm associated with UAS issues in the National Airspace System. I have also briefly discussed that unmanned capabilities, not just UAS systems, are something that we aren't properly focused on. Where does it make sense to invest in these capabilities in terms of great power competition and how do we defend against these same types of issues? At the time I wrote this, I was trying to make a point that we are woefully prepared to deal with this threat. Nothing has changed. It's not a matter of if, it's a matter of when. Now, here is where hope springs eternal, because maybe we can make the logical leap to find out where we can use this rather than do what we so often do—react to innovation. I continue to point out that we are one of the primary initiators of unconventional or guerilla warfare. The reason we defeated the British in our Revolutionary War was because we fought that way, and not the way the British wanted us to. We stressed their supply lines, we fought in ways they hadn't been exposed to, and we finally arrived at a point where we had their backs to the wall at Yorktown, and that's when the French showed up to block their withdrawal. We have been spoiled for too long and we need to reembrace these concepts and apply them once again.

Utilizing Crew Resource Management Approaches in the IED Fight

There may be additional value in utilizing crew resource management (CRM) techniques inside the asymmetric warfare realm, specifically, the C-IED fight. CRM provides a previously unutilized approach, potentially providing additional value in training soldiers and troops operating in IED environments. Focus on the use of CRM techniques and methodology to train ground vehicular crews in CRM IED training methodologies assists in combating where most of our casualties occur. Disproportionately, IEDs kill, maim, or injure our troops while operating vehicles. This analysis focuses on the potential incorporation of CRM techniques and principles into an area where the suggested approach has not been previously considered for C-IED TTP. Essentially, for the lack of a better explanation, this chapter examines the potential value that an approach that has arguably contributed to the reduction of aviation accidents, might also yield similar results in reducing crew error regarding military forces and crews operating in C-IED environments. An innovation which could assist is aviation crew-centric training applied to ground force-related crew-operated processes, requiring small crews, typically two to five personnel, operating in IED environments focusing on C-IED operations, strategy, and TTP.

The most glaring example of this is the mine-resistant ambush-protected vehicle. We spend billions of dollars developing and then fielding the MRAP, so the enemy just adds more bombs to an IED engagement and destroys the vehicle. Now if you're driving around in that MRAP, you probably think it's a pretty good idea because it gives you better capability and capacity to survive that event, but it misses the greater point—there must be a better approach to this than simply spending billions of dollars to offset a $500-dollar problem. Instead, the aim here is to zero in on one portion of this problem by examining how using CRM as a potential-crew served approach might bring better results in this ongoing dilemma and set of IED challenges. Well trained crews do better than poorly trained crews whether it's a tank, an artillery weapon system, a plane, or a machine gun.

Crew Resource Management Applications

The previous information in this chapter sets up the intellectual underpinnings of this argument and enables the forthcoming premise of this chapter. Combat vehicular platforms (trucks, HMMMVs, Strykers, tanks, personnel carriers, etc.) and their crews could benefit from the undertaking of IED-focused CRM training. C-IED training focuses on three primary lines of effort, which consist of: (1) Attack the Network, (2) Defeat the Device, and (3) Train the Force. CRM training would focus primarily in the Train the Force line of effort on vehicle crews and how they operate. Just like a crew on an airplane, a vehicle crew must function as a team. The greater aviation community has benefited by utilizing CRM, but no effort has been made by the land forces community (Army, Marine Corps, and Navy Special Warfare) to incorporate a similar type of approach for conducting ground mobility operations in an IED environment.

Any approach that reduces or ultimately removes human error from standard operating procedures during operations is likely to increase an organization's efficiency. In this case, the premise of this chapter suggests that ground mobility operational crews might also benefit from the same type of training that aircrews received with modifications to C-IED environments. Within the Train the Force line of effort there is no mention or even an inkling of considering how the crews work together as a crew, which seems almost impractical yet that is exactly where the Department of Defense is at. Any approach that enhances or improves the communication of members of any crew, their aptitudes, physical conditioning, how the crew functions as a team, and their understanding of the operating environment would surely improve their survivability as it relates to the C-IED threats they face. The factors just listed comprise what the CRM approach would call crew performance input factors.

Most military vehicles are typically equipped with some form of crew-served weapon whether it is the main gun on an Abrams tank, or the 25mm cannon on a Bradley fighting vehicle. The crews that operate these vehicles are required to go through gunnery qualification tables and qualify on the crew-served weapons that are associated with these vehicles. Despite the obvious correlation to a similar requirement, there is no requirement in the train-up cycle for crews to qualify as a crew and function as a crew as aviation-trained crews do in CRM training. The contrast of this approach seems illogical. The number of times we shoot our main guns when conducting ground vehicular movement pales in comparison to the amount of time required to survive in IED environments. Increased situational awareness, when moving between points on the battlefield increases survivability. It seems so obvious that when examining this threat, there should be equal if not greater time devoted to dealing with the IED threat. As a result, if that logic resonates, the CRM approach clearly increases crew situational awareness, crew formation, communication skills, team decision process, and overall team situational awareness toward the mission and assigned responsibilities.

Coupled with an ability to utilize virtual and constructive training devices, there is no reason that crews could not practice in trainers much like an airplane simulator by taking light direction and ranging (LIDAR) data and recreating the exact environments they are going to potentially be operating in before ever arriving in theater. The technology exists on the open market with many of the companies that manufacture games like *Call of Duty*, *HALO*, *Spec Ops*, or half a dozen other game variations. Taking this one step further, utilizing existing map data from applications like LIDAR and other geographic mapping techniques would allow our troops to be significantly more prepared than they are now. The most dangerous period is when units arrive in theater and start conducting operations. Historically, this is when our troops are the most vulnerable and when units incur the most casualties. Coupling this capability with the ability to merge existing IED strike reports (obviously at a classified level) into the same software would provide the virtual reps and sets as well as familiarization for deploying troops, providing enhanced situational awareness. The final portion of this problem is not something that falls into the CRM model but only makes sense. Our leaders need to start focusing on long-term fights; units that have deployed three, four, and five times do not deploy back to the same location, often deploying to a different location each time. Simply put, this is stupid. We need to assign sectors of responsibility for 10 years and resource units to maintain their own rotations so that we develop familiarity and relationships in the areas. CRM also applies to the introduction of Artificial Intelligence and Machine Learning and Human AI/ML teaming.

Human Factors Issues

There are two distinct factors that impact the significance of this issue. The first is the obvious situation that the country found itself in with 17 years of persistent conflict with no end in sight. The IED issue is significant and therefore any strategy or capability that reduces the casualties inflicted upon U.S. forces is a positive step. The secondary significant and primary effort in this analysis is examining these issues from a human factor perspective. The critical factor in any UAV or UAS platform-centric approach is the fact that multiple platforms will be up and operating simultaneously across a unit's battlespace. The implications of this approach stand out immediately. The United States Air Force (USAF) was already having problems with morale, stress, and fatigue in their UAS/RPV community. In fact, National Public Radio, on "All Things Considered" provided a piece that detailed the impact these operations were having on their UAV crews. One of their chief complaints was that the UAV operator goes from being in combat (mentally) and witnessing the horrors of war live to being at home in a matter of minutes, depending on how far they live from base.[14] This can obviously create multiple levels of stress from different areas of life. Long hours, changing schedules, the horrors of warfare, uneasy transitions between work and civilian lives as well as feeling isolated are all contributors to stress and fatigue. A normal fighter pilot flies approximately 250 hours a year while the normal UAS crew operates 900 hours a year.[15] The obvious fix that solves multiple issues in this is utilizing ground forces to do this as a break from the front line.

As stated previously, one of the most effective ways to integrate operations is to ensure that units have air or ground personnel embedded in their respective functions. What that means is that units that provide air support have ground personnel to assist them in what the maneuver unit is doing while the maneuver unit has air personnel in their formation to assist them in the process of providing advice on the best use of air assets. A completely out-of-the-box approach that would solve several problems is to take ground personnel and train them on the use of UAS platforms and embed them in these units, which increases the total amount of personnel available for the system and thus reducing man hours and shifts. It also provides a ground operator a break, and as Anderson points out, some of the personnel who have the easiest time adjusting to the psychological stressors associated with this have prior "on ground" experience with these same problem sets. Finally, the convergence that occurs from ensuring that ground maneuver units and the UAV operators have the same level of understanding cannot be overemphasized. This creates synergy, achieves inherent coordination, and provides needed rest and recuperation from the front lines all in a self-contained approach.

Train infantry and special operations soldiers to also operate these platforms on a rotational basis. This is an out-of-the-box solution that might also provide other ancillary benefits unseen. Fire support officers and fire support soldiers might also offer another solution since many of them are already trained to call for fire, some are event-qualified joint terminal air controllers (JTACs) and have many of the same targeting and collateral damage estimate (CDE) training. There is convergence in this field, which offers potential alternatives. With the advent of an automated landing and takeoff capability this might have been previously unrealistic but now with these capabilities, it makes even more sense.[16] Any of those options would reduce the workload on existing operators. Exploring the rotational approach might also offer both the ground maneuver unit and the UAV operator crew additional insights into how to improve operations and enhance a combined-arms, maneuver-warfare approach. This would undoubtedly have to be tested and adjusted but any time an organization can put operators from both the air and on the ground in the same room it can lead to nothing but enhanced capability. It seems an ideal match to rotate people through a training regimen to support ground units with ground personnel increasing the total number of operators, sensor operators, or analysts while giving those same personnel a break from deploying forward. Obviously, the use of contractors to fill these positions might also provide some sort of relief although there are legal obstacles associated with a contractor launching kinetic strike operations from a UAV. There might be some potential in this construct to allow contractors to operate the non-kinetic strike platforms.

Increase the use of ROC drills, rehearsals, LNOs, air ground teams, and pre-deployment training maximizing the use of gaming and LIDAR. The goal in all this is to increase situational awareness and compress the gap that always occurs in combat for the first 90 days where troops are most vulnerable and get killed or wounded until they reach a better understanding of the terrain on which they are operating. The following is a brief list of options that are available to increase the knowledge, situational awareness, and understanding of the entire team before deploying to combat.

1. Gaming with LIDAR support and computer simulations that prepare crews before they ever arrive in theater.
2. Fusing IED strikes into those gaming scenarios that include IED strikes, cache finds, IED factory locations, and IED cleared and found locations.
3. While deployed, increasing the use of ground LNOs attached to the UAS units, and UAS LNOs attached to ground units.
4. Establishing habitual relationships prior to deployment and maintaining those relationships increases the ability of units to function at the highest levels. This enables each arm to be familiar with their respective capabilities while increasing their understanding of the fires, targeting, and commander's intent portions of operations. The role of the UAS platform in the C-IED strategy is to deny, degrade, collect, and destroy when positive identification or rules of engagement permit.

More than anything, what has been missing in this equation is what can be best described as an air–ground–team concept. This concept extends to multiple approaches in a greater approach. First, establishing ground and air liaison officers to increase understanding and coordination makes perfect sense. Knowing what to look for from the air or on the ground is enhanced when the unit that is being supported has a liaison officer (LNO) or a ground liaison officer (GLO). This is customary practice inside of maneuver units at brigade and battalion level in special operations. As discussed previously, one potential solution to the lack of personnel and extended work hours is rotating troops. Concurrent to all this and it cannot be overstated enough is that we need to do more rehearsals of concept (ROC) or ROC drills. There is an old saying in the Ranger Regiment and USSOCOM community. "The C plus plan rehearsed seven times is infinitely better than the A plus plan never rehearsed." This means that the people providing support to the ground troops have run through multiple rehearsals prior to executing a particular operation or are so infinitely familiar with the terrains, the troops, and the mission that they understand inherently what the commander's intent for the operation is. That is not the case currently and this more than anything would go some way to a greater return on investment while also fostering a greater team construct which might also reduce the feeling of isolation exhibited by UAS crews. A final thought on mitigating this problem is really a subset of the comment about rehearsals and LNOs. To truly gain SA on the ground one is fighting on, both the air and ground elements should be infinitely familiar with where they are operating.

Conclusion

The underlying premise of this chapter is that at some point the DOD will move to establish an airborne 24/7 UAS C-IED approach because it provides technological overmatch against our current adversaries and their use of asymmetric IED techniques. For this to work we must find a way to train, develop, and maintain a significantly greater number of UAS pilots, sensor operators, and analysts. It is not beyond achieving but it will require a notable change in how the problem is attacked. I listed several distinct approaches to achieve this. Recent technological advances have enabled the concept of "Going Airborne All the Time" to negate existing IED networks and TTP used in irregular and asymmetric adversary strategies. The U.S. was in Afghanistan from 2001–2021 (where we solved nothing), in Iraq from 2003–2021 (with the remaining 2,500 troops due to leave in 2025), the Philippines and the Horn of Africa since 2002, and with an involvement in Syria and potentially the Ukraine. Of course, as of 2024, the major conflagration is in the Levant and the Red Sea (Yemen), with some American troops now in Israel. Iran beckons. Given that as a backdrop for perpetual conflict, traditional approaches have not worked as evidenced by the fact that we are still spending blood and treasure in these areas and have not established stability, in part because we have not overcome IED-enabled asymmetric warfare.

We have laid the intellectual framework for understanding how IEDs are the greatest killer on the battlefield, and what the characteristics are of IEDs, as well as how irregular and asymmetric warfare impact this fight. The emergence of UAS platforms and UAVs provides a unique opportunity to negate IED-enabled asymmetric warfare as an effective adversary approach. This chapter went further to make an attempt at defining what strike and reconnaissance platform requirements are best suited for this fight while pointing out that the most advantageous approach to this problem is to ensure that any platforms we develop have both flexibility and balance. As a result of this examination, it is clear that the DOD should push these capabilities down to the combat user (the BCT) while simultaneously dramatically increasing the total number of platforms available to the BCT, establishing a standardized basis of issue. In conclusion, the current approach has not achieved victory and makes no appearance of drastically changing the status quo any time in the foreseeable future, therefore this approach, while it may seem radical in its nature, provides an opportunity to achieve more effective operations, reduces costs, and save lives.

When I brought in an airborne strike capability in northern Iraq to target the two worst TAIs in the country, it worked. It didn't work the way I wanted it to, but it worked for reasons that I didn't think about when I did it, being more focused on the kinetic end of it, but it still achieved the effect I was attempting to achieve. It was in fact a precursor to what I have offered here as one of the primary ways to severely hamper the enemy's freedom of action and maneuver by going airborne 24/7 and doing this differently than we have to date. It didn't happen but it should have and if we find ourselves in this type of scenario again, that's a way to assist in solving this problem. Quite honestly, it will be our own ROE that gets in the way of this problem, to which my answer is, you don't create an omelet without cracking a few eggs. Keep sight of the objective not the problems on the way there. This was about getting after the enemy. It still is.

CHAPTER 10

21st-Century Blitzkrieg: Fires and Effects Integration Prisms

As discussed in the introduction, this book is primarily about IEDs and secondarily about suggesting that there is a better way to attack the emerging fires and effects integration issues that have challenged the army for the last 20 years. Everyone arrives at a problem through their own lens, and I arrived at this lens through an almost unique set of personal experiences. I enlisted in 1984 in 19th Special Forces Group, as an infantryman and was later commissioned in 1986 as an infantry officer. I played football in college and was not academically aligned, which is to say that I was commissioned before I graduated from school and was still playing football until I got injured and had a partial tear of my ACL. I also participated in an external evaluation which included isolation, insertion, and training guerillas in an exercise during that same timeframe which is the equivalent of the active-duty qualification and the Robin Sage portion of the course. I was commissioned in 1986. Because of being academically non-aligned, I was later rebranched as an artillery officer despite already having been awarded an infantry military occupation specialty, which at the time I wasn't overly excited about. As it turned out, later, I was grateful and appreciative for receiving that experience and it has enormously helped shape a lot of how I view these problem sets. The ability to see problems from both a maneuver and fires perspective is critical.

From my experience and prism, I determined that the two most effective military occupational specialties (MOSs) that can deal with IEDs are artillery officers with significant amounts of fire support time and special forces officers. Additionally, infantry officers who have spent a lot of time in special operations formations are also adept at understanding targeting, dealing with and attacking networks, and then ultimately destroying networks. The observation in all this is that there is a better way to do this. What does that mean? It means that the existing fires integration model currently being utilized today is outdated for the capabilities that are in the inventory. I personally focused on putting all fires (kinetic and non-kinetic) under one commander, director, or process wherever anyone would listen or let me do it this way. I am still convinced that this approach is far superior to any other approach. I am also ambivalent about what you call it, but that having done it for four different Combatant Commander- (COCOM0-) level exercises where all fires worked under one director, the Joint Staff J7/JFCOM evaluators in each and every exercise designated that approach as best practice. Comments were, "Wow, what are you guys doing? We have never seen anything else like that." Despite that universal observation we still haven't done a damn thing with this; it should have driven a wholesale examination of how we are approaching this problem, but the fires community is stuck in an outdated paradigm. The only logical approach in this is to change how we are doing all this and attempt to refocus our doctrine for future fights which require constant and effective integration. The model we use currently only produces that by pure luck or occasionally by placing the right person in the job with the right skills and background. That is not the way we should approach this problem from a DOTMLPF perspective, instead we should aim that the system creates an acceptable norm rather than trying to find that needle in a haystack.

So, in examining this problem set, I determined a basic problem statement.[*] How do we reinvigorate a 21st-century fires and DOTMLPF development process which enables rapid and continuous integration against peer or near-peer adversaries?

In this discussion the debate has centered on how we transition from a process or approach that at best has produced episodic integration rather than rapid and continuous integration?[1] Several senior leaders have brought up the need to move away from episodic integration to a better end state which is akin to rapid and continuous integration, especially in a near-pear/peer fight. Expanding on that discussion, one way of looking at this problem is that artillery, aviation, and air defense artillery deliver "support by fire." Those capabilities provided are a fires delivery mechanism, just like a joint close air support platform or a naval gunfire platform delivering either Tomahawk Land Attack Missiles (TLAM) or traditional naval gunfire. One can extend this same concept to mortars, rockets, rotary-wing CAS, AC-130, nontraditional fires platforms, and the non-kinetic side which includes special technical operations (STOs), space, cyber, and inform/influence activities and should include the operational security (OPSEC) and military deception (MILDEC)

---

[*] In four separate exercises, in two combatant commands, I put fires under one director, commander, or system and each and every time the Joint Forces Command evaluators designated what we were doing as best practice. That included two *Terminal Fury*, one *Talisman Saber*, and one *Austere Challenge* exercises. One would think that after two of these designations that we would have seen change but four for four is beyond even what I thought was possible given the nature of using differing personnel and accounting for variances in results yet that is exactly what was achieved. The author believes that there is a better and more efficient way to achieve these types of results and compasses true military revolution enabling U.S. military dominance. Unfortunately, to date, these changes have not even been considered. As an example, the U.S. Army's Artillery School clings to old methods and paradigms. They have not realized the nature of how fires has changed and so they are rapidly making themselves obsolete.

processes and then think about adding in unmanned air, surface, and subsurface strike capabilities. Delivery is a science (support by fire). Fire-support integration or fires is an art. The true warfighting task is the integration and synchronization of those fires with the maneuver plan, not the task of delivery. Additionally, there is no requirement that a soldier needs to be an artillery officer (13A MOS) to do this and in fact, the path to success for most artillery officers is not through fire support but time on the guns. Special operations forces (SOF) fires community time rarely produces flag officers, yet these officers are probably the most efficient and deadly practitioners of this art. To expand on this construct, we already have 13F-enlisted MOS and noncommissioned officers (NCOs), we have targeting warrants, therefore why wouldn't we extend that to create full-time commissioned officers?

My personal observation: I believe the model proposed here produces better-trained, more lethal officers and formations capable of providing rapid and continuous integration instead of episodic integration. This is for several reasons, which include increased experience, specific focus, more capable officers, better staff synergy approaches, and an insurance policy not often thought about. Additionally, the current DOTMLPF model does not reward the officers who go to recurring hard SOF, joint, or conventional fires billets.[2] Success is through Fire Direction Officer (FDO), Executive Officer (XO), Battery Command, Operations Officer (S3), and Battalion and Brigade XO time, not fires time. If we build an alternative model that allows officers to serve and be promoted solely as fires officers under a Fires MOS this creates significant expertise in a rapidly expanding field. Doing this will create a better officer who is better at fires than anything produced in the current method. In truth, the current model contributes to the episodic integration phenomenon that has been so problematic. Instead, the model that I am suggesting here actually creates a systemic development process enabling rapid and continuous integration.

This method also offers something that most people often do not understand. In a typical battle-rhythm/critical-path approach, the more any organization moves toward the fires model proposed in this discussion, the more it requires less coordination, staff interaction, and meetings to execute operations because it creates integration by default. Personally, this is one of the major contributing factors that led to this model succeeding in those four previous geographic COCOM exercises previously mentioned.[3] This model turns faster, tighter, and with higher situational awareness (some would call this decision superiority). The move since about 2007 has been to desegregate these functions with fires being separate from information operations (IO) and military information support operations (MISO), electronic warfare (EW), cyber, and STO, space, military deception (MILDEC) and operational security (OPSEC) being all separate stovepipes under differing staff directorates. To simply achieve a marginal degree of synchronization, the number of meetings becomes exponential vis-à-vis what could be synchronization by default with significantly fewer battle-rhythm events.† Compare the current approach to making all this work under one director, commander, or process that has people who are experts in most of the kinetic delivery mechanisms while familiarizing themselves over time with what I would refer to as emerging fires capabilities (space, STO, cyber). The fact that these activities must all be coordinated through the fires and targeting processes enables true synergy, run by full-time experts, whose sole purpose from ideally the rank of captain forward, is to integrate, synchronize, and execute fires in support of maneuver.

In a peer/near-peer fight, the discussion in the point above about rapid and continuous integration is exacerbated because the model I proposed turns faster and creates decision superiority with less work. It is also reinforced by the likelihood that our communications will be severely degraded. In simple terms, the ability to fight without communications utilizing our understanding of commander's intent is better served with a true fires expert rather than an episodic fires officer who occasionally does fires when they are not spending time ensuring they are competitive by doing delivery-related artillery jobs.

Finally, I will offer that this is an insurance policy. Delivery of fires is a science. The five requirements for accurate predicted fire require accurate (1) firing unit location, (2) weapon and ammunition info, (3) target location and size, (4) meteorological data, and (5) computational procedures.[4] That's science. The art of fire support takes years to develop. In a world where our forces might be required to expand rapidly, as we did in World War II, we can teach gunnery/delivery to formations and personnel in a couple of months. The art of fires requires years to master. If you have a cadre of fires experts, you can teach them gunnery and delivery as you expand from 7 Division Artillery (DIVARTY) or fires brigades to 70 of the same formations. What you cannot build overnight is capable fires integrators to support 70 divisions.

As an aside, one of the biggest ongoing problems inside the counter-IED effort inside the inter-agency (IA) and the military is that we admire the problem a lot but don't do much about it. Someone or some entity must get punched in the face at the end of all this work, or there needs to be a good reason why they don't.

---

† One of the most notable impacts on disaggregating the concept of information operations (IO) was that it took what was five disparate concepts and placed them under one director at the brigade and higher levels in the U.S. Army. In about 2007, Fort Leavenworth began a move to put MILDEC back into the Plans Directorate and OPSEC back under the G3 Current Operations. This move was a disaster, and in fact some of greatest victories in the Global War on Terror were undertaken by IO practitioners. In the opinion of the author, the army made a huge mistake and has gone sideways since 2007 when these efforts were initialized. In fact, in the opinion of the author, the army has completely dropped the ball on what was a viable and effective concept and abandoned it for a complete unrealistic approach which is not rooted in how organizations effectively conduct operations. The proposals in this chapter are far superior to any model that the Army currently has or could conceivably undertake.

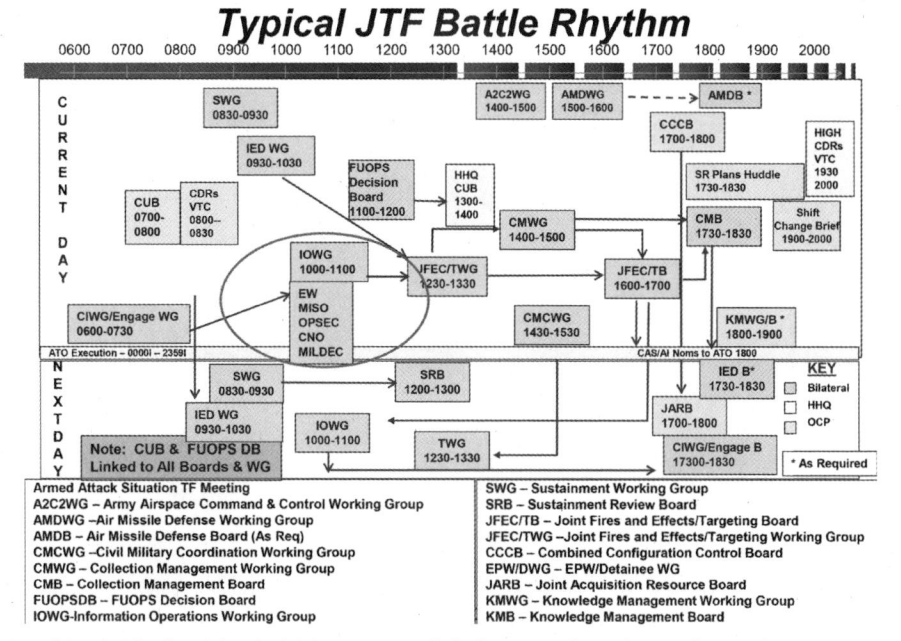

21ST-CENTURY BLITZKRIEG: FIRES AND EFFECTS INTEGRATION PRISMS • 181

Typical JTF Battle Rhythm

Typical Battle Rhythm. The ideal COA is to put all the kinetic and non-kinetic fires under one construct of all domain fires. (M. D. Matter)

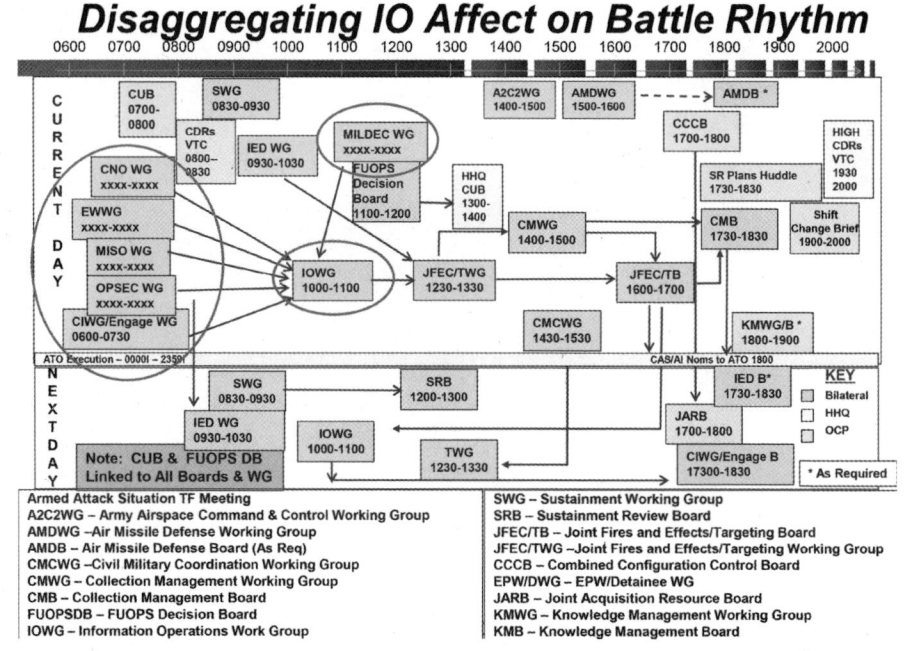

Disaggregating IO Affect on Battle Rhythm

Typical Battle Rhythm. This is an example of a battle rhythm where all kinetic and non-kinetic fires haven't been placed under an all-domain fires construct, and this clearly creates exponential interactions. (M. D. Matter)

182 • HARD BROKE

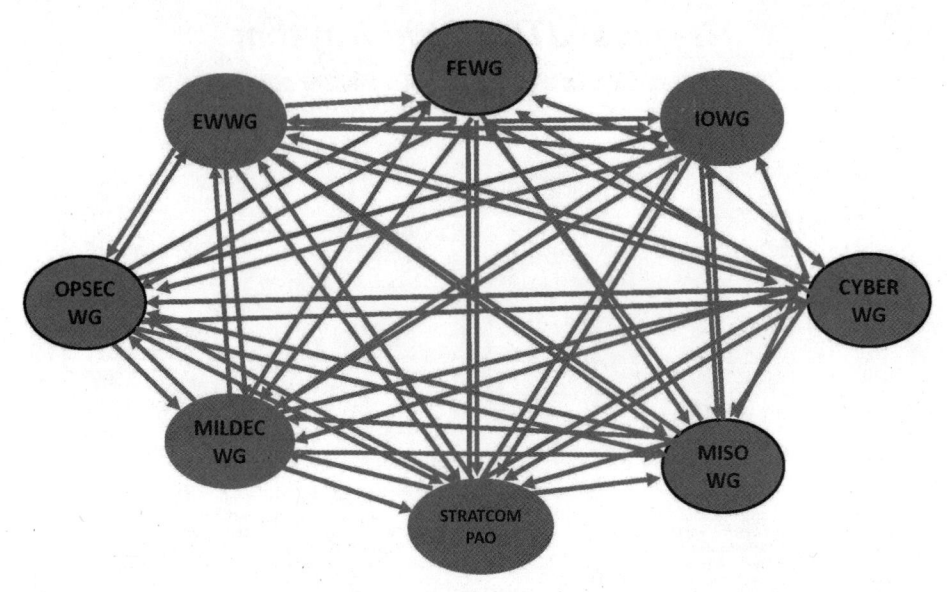

This diagram shows exactly why the all-domain fires COA works better than individual stovepipes. The above diagram demonstrates the exponential work created and how each work group (WG) adds the requirement for that WG to go to all the other WGs and the other WGs to come to the new one. It's a bad choice and works much better when it is under one directorate or commander. (M. D. Matter)

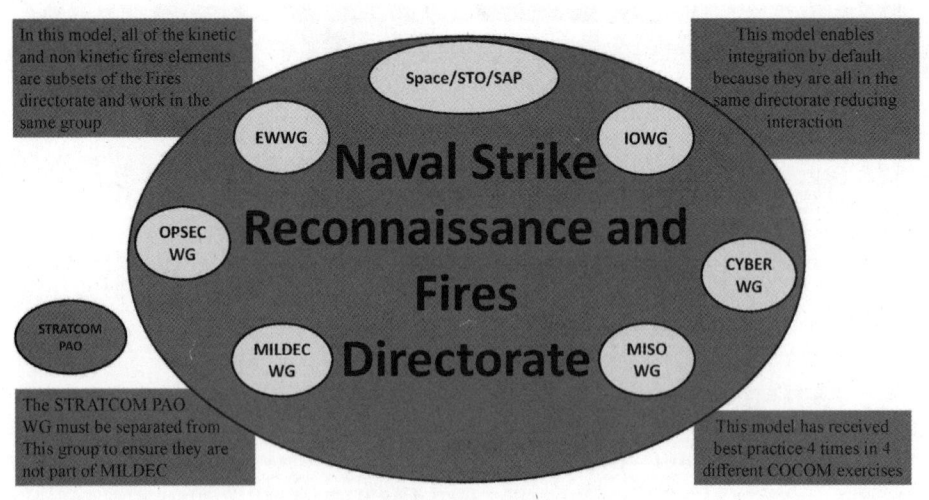

This is the alternative to the previous diagram and creates significantly less work and meetings and provides greater situational awareness for group members. (M. D. Matter)

Believe it or not, often that doesn't happen, and we admire the problem rather than taking action to reduce the problem. As I started out this chapter, we all arrive at a problem through our own lens and mine was guided by having spent significant time in infantry, special forces, artillery, special operations, and special mission units. As such, I was influenced by some great officers and noncommissioned officers that I am proud to have served with, that helped me in understanding these issues.

The Way Ahead to Integrated Full-Spectrum Fires

Despite the downsizing of the Department of Defense and continued minimal growth guidelines, this chapter aimed to conceptualize a more efficient and better way to conduct full spectrum fires and effects processes than currently exist. Over the last few years, the services have developed various new capabilities and functions, which fit into a greater fires and effects functionality, yet has failed to truly address the revolutionary change in how we conduct warfare. At first, artillery was once truly "the king of battle" but has decayed into a shell of what it once was. The true revolutionary nature of how we conduct warfare is the holistic integration of both kinetic and non-kinetic fires. When conducted through that construct, the result is far superior to the previously established methods. I have personally driven this method in four different COCOM-level exercises with four different unique problem sets and achieved best practice on four different occasions (a designation by the joint force evaluators) and each time was asked: How in the world are you accomplishing this? In contrast, the artillery community as an institution has placed minimal importance on the true warfighting task of fires and effects integration, choosing instead to focus on the delivery side of the equation. The path to success in the artillery branch in either the Army or Marine Corps, was through time on the "guns" vice time delivering fire support for maneuver formations. Yet, the pointy edge of the spear is fires and effects integration, not delivery and in a peer-on-peer or near-peer fight, this will make the difference between victory or defeat. The force that can integrate long-range and all-domain fires to arrive at the right time and place (mass) or sequentially to maximize destruction of enemy formations on land or sea will win the next fight.

As we continue to downsize the Department of Defense, or remain stagnant, we are afforded an opportunity to fix what is currently wrong with our doctrine and approach. We can do more with less and by putting all kinetic and non-kinetic fires, effects, information operations, cyber, special technical operations, and electronic warfare under one concept. Currently they are all essentially various forms of fire support but are disparate, unsynchronized, and stovepiped. There is absolutely no doubt that there is a much better approach to all of this. The most obvious and best course is to separate the fires delivery process from the fire support and integration processes. Furthermore, given the nature of what the modern battlefield requires, it only makes sense and is more efficient in its approach. Finally, in a zero-growth environment, this achieves more with less (a true win-win).

How to Build a 21st-Century Fires Capability

For a long time, I struggled with how to address this problem because I always saw myself as a fires integrator whether I was doing the kinetic or non-kinetic aspects of this problem. Additionally, some of the skill sets I picked up in the special mission world led me to come to significantly different conclusions than most of the rest of the army writ large. As an added note that I will discuss later about integrated effects, we were so close, and we blew it.

For the most part, IO is fires, and the way we use it in the special operations world, it is one of the biggest killers on the battlefield if not the biggest killer on the battlefield. Find and fix was developed by my unit, and I was at ground zero for this fight. I wrote most if not all the operational needs statements which developed and perfected these capabilities but have slowly watched the "big army" try to get this back under their control. Instead of actually learning the critical lessons we took away, they actually went backwards and from what I have seen recently haven't made much progress in fixing any of this.

First and foremost, what we need to create is an assess branch, at the O3 level, to create what I will refer to as "fires officers" who command, integrate, synchronize and execute fires and effects for the rest of their military careers. If I had been offered this at the captain level vice being an artillery battery commander, I wouldn't have even thought twice about it and would have jumped at this. Delivery of cannon and rocket fires is not the same task as the integration of all kinetic and non-kinetic fires. Honestly, the delivery of fires is support by fire, not "fire support." Air defense artillery, attack aviation, and artillery are "supporting arms," which provide support by fire. Fire support and the integration of that fire support or "effects" is the true master warfighter task. It takes years of experience to master this art. Delivery of projectiles is science, not an art. We already have 13F-enlisted soldiers and targeting warrant officers. What we need to complete the process is a permanent fires officer or something akin to it. These soldiers would be trained in the following core competencies:

1. Qualified and current joint terminal air controller delivering all types of kinetic fires to include mortars, rockets, artillery, naval gunfire, rotary-wing CAS, joint precision strike platform, and can plan joint fires for TLAM, MST, NSM, and PRISM strikes. Integrate all kinetic fires with maneuver.
2. EW coordinator who is trained to integrate, deconflict, manage, and execute EW.
3. Offensive cyber operations through CYBERCOM representatives and oversight through the targeting process.
4. Tracking, tagging, and locating (TTL).
5. Special technical operations (STO).

Transition to Network Warfare Paradigm

INTEL
ES
INTEL SPT to C/EM Warfare
INTEL SPT to BA
CNE (NSA)
Human Terrain Analysis
Crony Analysis
TTL (Intel Overnight)
CI

PROTECTION
OPSEC
CI

FIRES
Physical Destruction (PD)

CYBER EM WARFARE C-EM)
Electronic Attack (EA)
Electronic Attack Close Target Recce (EA CT)
CNA/CND RA/CNO
Space Negation/STO
Electronic Protect/CREW (EP)
TRWO (Medium) VAUVIA
Enterprise Development (CNOVEW)

MISSION COMMAND
Inform and Influence Activities (IA)
MISO
Engagement
STRAT COMMS
MBPD
PA
CA

MANUEVER & MOVEMENT
MILDEC
Engagement
Support to Mission Command

SUSTAINMENT

HUMAN NW — NETWORK WARFARE — TECH NW
RELATED / ENABLED / CORE

MISO
PD / CYBER / EW / STO / SPACE NEG / TTL / IIA
INT SPT / OPSEC / CI
MILDEC / CNE
CND
CA / PA
TRWI
EP
MSPD/SC ENGAGE

CONFLICT INTENSITY

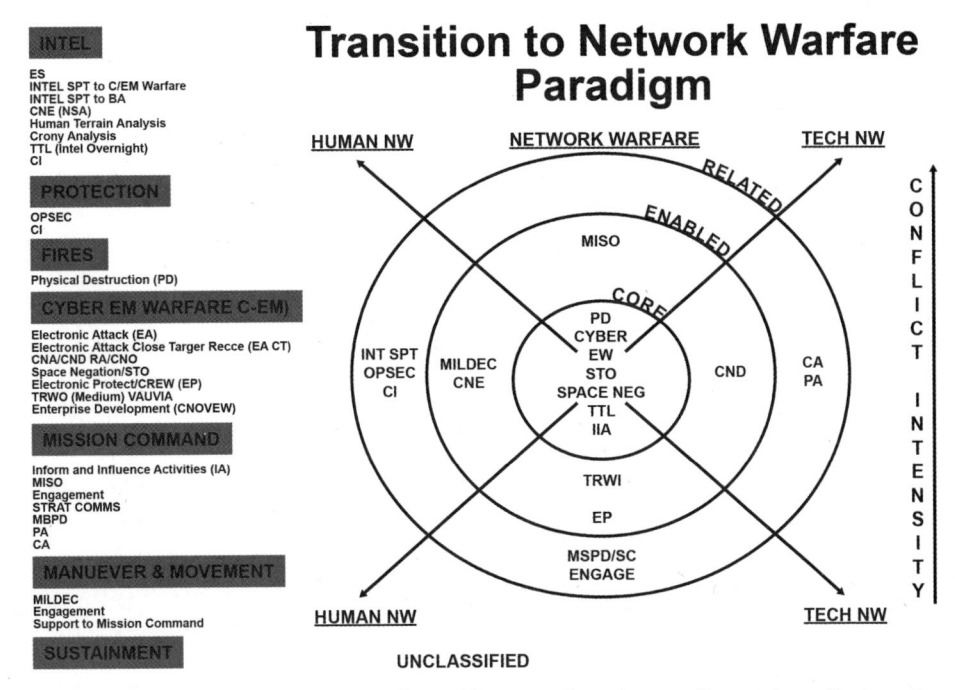

HUMAN NW — TECH NW

UNCLASSIFIED

A way of looking at Network Centric Warfare and kinetic and non-kinetic effects with conflict intensity. (M. D. Matter)

6. How to integrate, deconflict, and execute influence and inform (non-kinetic influence/inform operations) with existing maneuver operations which include PAO, MISO, key leader engagements, and deception.
7. Ownership of the targeting operations process (D3A or F3EA).
8. Counter-IED targeting and effects.
9. Offensive and defensive space capabilities.

Creating a dedicated branch of officers who do nothing but integrate, synchronize, and execute fires and effects creates gates for the necessary training, enabling the ability to effectively manage and oversee the complex 21st-century requirements associated with delivering full-spectrum effects.

Data Points

If you can integrate, synchronize and execute attack helicopters, mortars, artillery, naval gunfire, and close air support with maneuver and do it well, it isn't that much more of a stretch to add electronic warfare, cyber, STO, PSYOP, IO, OPSEC, MILDEC, as well as integrate SAP and space capabilities. If you are like me, you start to wonder if the brass just missed the entire target when they did the functionality analysis for these types of capabilities.

IO as another form of fires. I expressed my frustration to my former DIVARTY commander over where the artillery branch was headed while assigned to 18th Airborne Corps FSE after he made a by-name request. IO was really part of fires although predominantly non-lethal fires and clearly these capabilities converged. As it turned out, almost every time I showed up to a new job, I was put back in charge of the fires portions of most of the units I was assigned to. Even when I wasn't leading fires, I was often so deeply involved in the fires/effects process the overall impact was the same. Over the last 20 years of my career, I was involved in one portion or another of the fires/effects process although in many instances I was completely immersed in every aspect of the process. I was more amazed to see no greater effort at synchronization for the army as a whole. This exposed the initial reality that we weren't maximizing the disparate efforts of fires, IO or related activities. Clearly, there was greater value to synchronized complementary approaches rather than continuing uncoordinated piecemeal efforts.

No one knew what IO or EW were doing, and we certainly weren't aware of any OPSEC, MILDEC, or coordinated efforts of all these capabilities across the unit. I started asking myself if there wasn't a better way to approach this. A natural extension is to synchronize MISO, EW, IO, OPSEC, CNO, and any IO-related physical destruction missions as part of the original C2W construct. As discussed, none of this was synchronized—there were elements doing whatever they wanted all over the place with no integration. The bottom line was that it just didn't occur, nor were there any attempts to bring these elements together for greater synergy. To put it mildly, no one had a freaking idea what was going on. It was ignorance, it was turf battles, it was cultural, and the answer is simple: put it all under one construct of fires and separate fires from the artillery.

We are no closer to rapid and continuous integration. One is forced to conclude by deduction that no one has ever taken that role seriously, with little progress in corralling all these disparate constructs. "Full spectrum fires" including IO provides a much better approach to it all than each element operating independently. We need to move closer to expanding nontraditional fire support to coordinated full-spectrum operations. Furthermore, it requires similar levels of coordination with maneuver and traditional indirect and joint fires. This requires painstaking detail and optimally requires training in these skill sets but doesn't require you to be an expert at everything. Instead, a decent understanding of each capability and ensuring it is synchronized through one overarching process is probably the most effective way to achieve this. On the other hand, attempting to coordinate capabilities with minimal or limited experience typically limits the effectiveness of the plan. When possible, planners with experience in both lethal and non-lethal fires produced better products than attempts to synchronize efforts by untrained or partially trained personnel.

Returning to Fort Bragg to an Elite Special Mission Unit, three members of my unit stood up a new organization. One of the most interesting investments we made focused on a form of close target reconnaissance. We were plank owners in the development of Electronic Attack Close Target Reconnaissance (EA CTR) and Computer Network Attack Operational Preparation of the Battlespace (CNA OPB). For obvious reasons I cannot expand into this approach, but it's been decisive on the battlefield. We were part of multiple groundbreaking operations that have been the biggest killer on the battlefield. We missed a critical HVT by minutes in April of 2004, during Fallujah I. I unilaterally dropped 300,000 leaflets with the HVT's face and tip line numbers to drive him to an exploitable device that we could geolocate him on. We missed him by five to 10 minutes. Our forces passed him as we were entering the area near Fallujah. This was another breakthrough moment. I truly started to see the "21st-century blitzkrieg" potential. I always questioned why we didn't put a JDAM on the HVT's location when we found him, and I told my boss that that night. The lesson learned that day was that while we had found and fixed him, we didn't finish him. Their early warning network was too good. Prior to that day, our goal was to capture him for intelligence value. We learned our best bet was to kill him. That was confirmation for me that this all belonged under one directorate, commander, or primary staff officer. The ability to turn faster than the enemy was enormous. Within the J3 the potential for full spectrum fires reduced overall "flash to bang" time. Obviously, between fires and my troop, the J3 possessed independent find, fix, and finish capability, which is truly revolutionary.

One of the target sets I worked against was foreign fighters. One of the crazier episodes allowed me to go home for approximately four weeks in 2004. My immediate boss, the unit deputy, gave me advice at the time. telling me to just leave. I told him I would try to bring the replacement up to speed since he had been here for a month or less. What a waste of effort that was. He was a special forces officer working at the CIA and buddies with the unit commander. I asked him to ensure that the electronic attack platform I requested got into the fight. He said sure, and then didn't do a damn thing, instead focusing on things he was more comfortable with. Returning four weeks later, nothing had been done. I got off the plane and didn't sleep for three days because things were so damn jacked up. The platform hadn't flown once and there were discussions about sending the asset home. Within several days I scheduled an operational test over Baghdad. There were skeptics afraid of frequency fratricide and one contemporary, another artillery officer who was working at our higher headquarters, actually said this to me. "Matt, isn't that thing going to fry our comms." After laughing out loud and recomposing myself I said, "Brother, if we had something like that don't you think we would be flying the fuck out of that thing?" at which point everyone else in the room laughed. I said I got it, I will fly on this thing, run the operational test, and I will show everyone that this thing doesn't mess up our comms.

Traditional approaches like decide detect, deliver, assess (D3A), over time were replaced by thought-provoking models like find, fix, finish that later became find, fix, finish, exploit, assess (F3EA) and what some called the "unblinking eye." Personally speaking, I don't think we ever got to the "unblinking eye" as discussed by General Stanley McChrystal in his article, "It Takes a Network to Defeat a Network." Truth be told, I think we stumbled into that, as I had a front-row seat to that development and subsequent modifications. It honestly doesn't matter what you call the process if you have a process and everyone else is operating on the same terms of reference. The more important aspect of this entire problem set is attacking the adversary's center of gravity while protecting your own. As part of a special mission unit task force, we were tasked with reducing foreign fighters and hunting down the Al-Qaeda in Iraq leadership. My observation was that we were very good at this but ultimately, the enemy evolved to a point where even when we took out their leadership, they simply adapted and continued to drive on. We were losing and probably losing the war of ideas going on in this discussion.

Enemy IED engagements and associated propaganda assisted recruiting and financing that in turn swelled the ranks of our primary target set, namely foreign fighters. I made that same argument when I explained why I forced the electronic attack platform operational test on CJTF-7. At this point it is important to understand that this effort went back to early December 2003, when I constructed and validated requirements for offensive electronic attack capability for both the task force and CJTF-7. The capability arrived mid-to-late February 2004. As I detailed in the previous paragraph, I got a break and after having been there for the better part of eight months on and off (I did get three short breaks). I enlisted the help of the MNF-I Strategic Communications Director BG Mark Kimmit (an artilleryman) to arrange a meeting with the Effects Coordinator, BG Richard Formica (also an artilleryman). Prior to this meeting CJTF-7 elements were dead set against using this platform for communications jamming or offensive electronic attack missions. BG Kimmit called BG Formica, requesting a meeting for me. I met BG Formica at Al Faw Palace and explained our request. I explained the capabilities of the aircraft and how we wanted to use it to isolate enemy communications and create problems for IED networks. Reluctant to utilize the platform, he asked me if it was possible for the platform to potentially kill some of our own personnel. I said yes, but it was highly unlikely because we could deconflict operations and maneuver. He was still skeptical, at which point I said, "Sir, while it is theoretically possible that you could kill some of our own personnel by using this platform, *failure* to use this platform will result in killing our own personnel." He looked at me a bit funny and said, "I don't understand what you are saying." I expanded that it amounted to the difference between aimed fire (waiting till troops were in the kill zone) and erratic fire (arbitrary explosions) and that I would opt for erratic fire over aimed fire any day of the week. At that point, I believe I broke through, and I got buy-in to start using the asset. I flew down to Talil to ensure the asset went up and flew on the initial mission, returning to Baghdad the next day. On that first mission we were able to prove there was no electromagnetic interference with internal communications while registering seven observed explosions in operating parameters and range of the platform. In simple terms, the thing worked, it had observable metrics, and we didn't mess up any friendly units' ability to communicate.

IED threats and TTL became one of the functions that just fell on me as being a unique capability in my organization. To return to the central theme of all this, I found increasing value in understanding multiple capabilities and gained knowledge on emerging capabilities of the F3EA approach. I was even more convinced that this fell into the fires model, making analogies between electronic attack capabilities that were delivering lethal effects and TTL capabilities that assisted in our ability to find and fix targets. One was fires while the other was potentially reconnaissance that enabled fires solutions or kill/capture operations. The EA platform flew for most of the conflict and contributed greatly to reducing IED effects against soldiers, sailors, airman, and Marines.

Being at ground zero for developing EA CTR capability in coordination with USAINSCOM G3 IO Combat Developments was enlightening.[‡] Most of this capability is still classified but is the biggest killer on the battlefield. The army intelligence community, after 30 years of atrophy, wanted this capability back despite the fact that it was a small group of operators that rebuilt it. Our actions even made the NSA uncomfortable. They modified a United States Signal Intelligence Directive attempting to prevent our personnel from utilizing these platforms to kill or capture enemy personnel. It remains a disingenuous argument which borders on being grossly irresponsible for the simple reason that the target set we were using this capability against was responsible for untold numbers of friendly casualties and deaths. I start to get punchy and frustrated because they were worried about their perceived "rice bowl" and American soldiers were dying while people are telling me we can't do this! I distinctly remember having a "Come to Jesus" meeting in June 2004, in our compound and telling them, "You can take over this mission tomorrow. I don't care who operates the capability as long as they operate it, and it continues to run. I am not waiting a single day because I am using it to kill or capture bad people. Get your people out here or get out of my way. I am also taking it Airborne.

[‡] The intelligence community calls this capability SIGINT Terminal Guidance. It isn't. There is no SIGINT database created. It is similar to an EA 6B or EA 18 flying EW missions. If the target emanates too long, then the plane sends a HARM missile back at the radar, homing in and locking on to the frequency it is emanating from and destroying it. There is no difference in this construct. Instead of a plane flying it is a box or platform that finds the emanation and then we direct a maneuver element to its location. Depending on the positive identification required and the rules of engagement it is just as easy to direct a precision strike with a JDAM or some other ordnance to destroy the target.

You can be an obstruction or get on board." Believe it or not, these folks, actually attempted to sabotage our combat tests! I still have a tough time with that concept when it comes to the potential loss of American soldiers' lives and folks are purposely low-balling combat tests to ensure that a capability remains in a certain field rather than getting on board to kill the enemy. I didn't listen to them and figured out that they were intentionally attempting to sandbag the whole thing. I am limited in this construct to address the specifics that are involved but here is how I would characterize this approach. First, while there is no universal axiom that applies to this business, you take savvy ground guys and you make them smart on technology, you incorporate full spectrum approaches to attack problems to prepare the battlespace, facilitate operations, and then ultimately execute operations.

We did the same thing for building computer network operations into a working fires capability. It's fires, just a 21st-century version, and should be treated as such. We developed actual deliverables and capability used in combat, resulting in multiple kill/capture missions. My personnel developed these capabilities, and I wrote most of the initial concept of operations (CONOPs) to include the interagency deconfliction and collaboration processes ensuring rapid target engagement and action. Any theoretical targeting approach requires simultaneous law enforcement (Title 18), intelligence gathering (Title 50), and military authorities (Title 10) and necessitates every attempt to compress requirements without losing time. Our own laws prevent effective and timely engagements, and we developed work around solutions to solve these problems. I wrote the CONOPs ensuring time was not lost. That's what this chapter is about; it's about full-spectrum fires, turning faster than your adversary, 21st-century blitzkrieg.

Sometimes you can't make this shit up, you just can't. I am often amused by all the adversity and stupidity that I faced in these endeavors and the institutional resistance that we faced. By May of 2005, I developed an operational needs statement (ONS) for the ongoing EA CTR capability I had worked so hard on previously. Known as ISIS, it was a helicopter- and airborne-mounted RCIED detonation capability as well as a find and fix capability against multiple adversary command and control capabilities, I wrote the ONS for these, I got them in front of my boss, the two-star, and I got them into the system; it consisted of a man, train and equip request supporting the entire package. Within 30 days of arrival, we had killed or captured 30 HVTs. This was an increase in magnitude of ten times or more than the normal number of HVTs. If it had been up to MNC-I G2 who appeared was representing the NSA, and not the army, we would have never seen that equipment. This capability was decisive in combat, it broke the enemy's back in our sector.

In August 2005, I attended the first tracking, tagging, and locating (TTL) meeting for the conventional force structure, at Camp Pendleton, California. The outcome resulted in my unit receiving the first 10 TTL classes in Germany bringing TTL into the regular army. Because of where I had worked previously, I knew all about this capability. I received the first 10 classes and even took my guys out of theater into Germany for two weeks of training and returned with kit and capabilities that I provided to other units to include 4th ID, 1st Armored, and even 3rd Ranger Battalion. This had huge impacts on the fight in multiple sectors. So much so that this drove the precursor of the Joint IED Defeat Organization (on the Army Staff) to immediately fund this. Specifically, the Deputy Director for Operations and Intelligence, Joint Improvised Explosive Device Defeat Task Force, then BG Dan Allyn, saw what we did in Iraq, and funded this for the rest of the army.

Another example is the way we approached the EW problem that we were walking into. EW is fires, it's a different kind of fires but it's still fires and defensive EW when used in the C-IED fight is a form of electronic attack. I took approximately 15 of my folks who constituted the core of the Electronic Warfare Coordination Cell to Randolph Air Force Base in San Antonio and went through a modified EW coordinator course and used it to build all the requirements for the problems in Iraq. This approach ultimately produced what became the baseline EW document adopted by MNC-I about eight months later. We coordinated to have the EW coordinator's course taught and modified the culmination exercise to a ground-centric event producing the EW annex for MND-N for the IED threat environment. That product became the EW annex for all of Iraq.

Having previously participated in bringing the electronic attack platforms into the fight, I was acutely aware of their flight patterns. Returning a year later, I was shocked to find it flying exactly the same block times. From an operational security approach this was extremely puzzling, and honestly stupid. The enemy may not understand our capabilities but eventually they figure out that when they place IEDs during that time frame, bad things happen. I immediately requested changes for block times. On the second day of daylight burns operating in our sector, the Golden Mosque in Samarra blew up. Using the same metrics for providing "effects credit" for unexplained IED explosions, the platform received credit for the "Golden Mosque." All this is speculation. We will never know since no investigation followed. That was a mistake. We knew the enemy used mosques as IED factories because we wouldn't enter them. We know the aircraft was flying in our area, within range, and emanating electrons. I ran into the CG in the hallway that morning, and he had a big smile on his face. He said, "Matt, you blew up the Mosque." Again, we will never know. One theory was we got an initial detonation off a wing housing all kinds of explosives leading to multiple sympathetic detonations. I know that the official explanation of six men setting explosives and subduing all the guards in the amount of time allocated was highly unlikely. Put another way, I question the official story, and the timeline associated with it.

During the first week of October 2006, I stopped in Fort Leavenworth, Kansas discussing our recent deployment with the CAC proponent. I spent four to five hours on the porch of the proponent director relaying the lessons learned from our deployment. I learned the proponent had brought in a retired brigadier and general colonel to assist in studying where all this IO stuff should go to. I don't remember the overall conversation specifics, but I recall telling them they were headed the wrong direction. I suggested they should reorganize along a fires or network warfare construct. I expressed deep concern over the direction they were heading. The proponent LTC's comment was, "Matt you are probably five to ten years ahead of everyone."

It appeared they were not interested in what the 101st had learned over their last year in combat.§ I reported to USPACOM, convinced that we needed a different approach consolidating IO and fires into a holistic capability. Fate has an interesting way of impacting things and once again fate intervened. I arrived in Hawaii to find out that I was no longer the Deputy J39 at USPACOM and instead the Fires and IO director at Standing Joint Force Headquarters (SJFHQ) at USPACOM, an operational deployable unit.

Fusion and Integrated Effects

There is a better way to do this. I saw many similarities between IO and fires efforts although they utilized different channels. It obviously required deconfliction through the operations synchronization process. After multiple deployments I realized the critical role that IO and effects played at all levels of our operations. My journey through various fires and IO positions ultimately led to the formulation of an alternative construct and probably why I always ended up doing both the Fires and IO jobs simultaneously. In 1996, the army created FM 100-6 (Information Operations). That document listed Command and Control Warfare (C2W) as one of the elements of IO. 100-6 listed the following critical data: C2W, Civil Affairs (CA), and Public Affairs (PA) are the three operations the army currently uses to gain and maintain information dominance and effective C2. The manual went on to state that C2W is the warfighting application of information warfare in military operations. The aim of C2W is to influence, deny information to, degrade or destroy adversary C2 capabilities while protecting C2 capabilities against such actions. C2W is composed of two major branches: (1) Command and Control-attack and (2) Command and Control-protect. At that time, the core capabilities that supported this construct

---

§ As stated earlier, the 101st returned in September and October of 2006. We were not contacted about any IO study. It is regrettable but we weren't even aware this study was undertaken until after the fact. After careful consideration I came to the conclusion that they did really poor staff work of they deliberately did not want to hear what we had to say because it ran counter to their narrative and desire to make changes to army doctrine. Our experiences in Iraq lead seasoned combat leaders to arrive at *different* conclusions than they came up with. It was unfortunate that the 101st was not contacted about their newly learned lessons from OIF and apply those through a potential capabilities based assessment led by BG Wass de Czege's experience and historical appreciation. We would have very much appreciated being part of that study.

were (1) physical destruction, (2) PSYOP, (3) electronic warfare, (4) OPSEC, and (5) MILDEC. If I could take us back in time, it would be to this definition because what has emerged since 2007 is almost complete madness. If you were attempting to purposely fail at integrating fires and effects, the course of action the army chose to go with is what you would choose. I tried relentlessly to get people to understand the madness of the choices that have been made and I would hazard to guess that I am probably one of the most deployed officers in the army, even till this day with something to the effect of 93 months of combat operations after 9/11, being in the Pentagon on 9/11, and having had multiple deployments before 9/11.

By 2003 Field Manual 3-13 existed, followed in 2006 by the Joint Publication 3-13 (Information Operations) that replaced the 1996 construct of IO with the following definitions:

> FM 3-13: Information operations is the employment of the core capabilities of electronic warfare, computer network operations, psychological operations, military deception, and operations security, in concert with specified supporting and related capabilities, to affect or defend information and information systems, and to influence decision making.[5]
>
> JP 3-13: Information operations (IO) are described as the integrated employment of electronic warfare (EW), computer network operations (CNO), psychological operations PSYOP), military deception (MILDEC), and operations security (OPSEC), in concert with specified supporting and related capabilities, to influence, disrupt, corrupt, or usurp adversarial human and automated decision making while protecting our own.[6]

The existing FM 3-13 (2003) construct met operational commanders' requirements and provided trained articulate forces to the field able to support both army and joint forces. Both the 1996 version and the 2003 version of IO more accurately depict desired effects and completely resembled a fires construct. The older definitions provide a better path for synchronizing the disparate elements of IO while proposed future versions or disaggregating approaches limit coordinated synergy. Creating more stovepipes between PSYOP, OPSEC, MILDEC, CNO, EW, and IO reduces efficiencies while increasing friction during operations. Previously, IO provided a single integrated concept in which OPSEC, MILDEC, EW, CNO, and MISO were integrated into an overarching IO plan. In essence what used to be done by one directorate (G7) is now farmed out to the G3 (OPSEC and EW), G5 (MILDEC), MISO (G7) and a yet-to-be-determined lead directorate for cyber. This fails in creating greater synergy. In fact, it likely increases the likelihood of fratricide and uncoordinated stovepiped activities. In fact, in all this madness, I suggested that we ought to put this all under fires. To add insult to injury, every time I have ever been involved in doing the military decision-making process approach to this debate, the Fires COA comes out superior every single time. Putting all these elements either under fires or ensuring that these differing capabilities synchronize through the fires and effects process reduces meetings, increases situational awareness, and creates the ability to turn faster in B2C2WG processes. As I continue to preach this approach it's madness that we haven't moved to this approach. I will say it again and again, four separate exercises in two distinctly different COCOMs, and each and every time it was designated best practice. Might be worth looking into.

Reexamining the 1996 definition and the concept of physical destruction provides both a linkage and potential solution to many of the problems created by changing definitions. Differences between the 1996 version and the 2003 version of IO focused largely on semantics. In 1996 kinetic action was a core element and primary means to achieve any desired effect designed to achieve C2W approaches. By 2003, physical destruction became a related activity, but most practitioners understood physical destruction was always a legitimate approach to achieve any end state. Thus, returning to an approach including physical destruction always made sense. IO is combat arms and almost certainly should be a subset of fires. It is operations. IO practitioners are operators. It is a holistic full-spectrum approach to attacking the adversary or achieving the commander's objectives. Removing the mumbo jumbo that is out there, fires and IO brings to bear lethal, non-lethal fires, and full-spectrum, combined-arms approaches to shape the battlefield by destroying, denying, degrading, deceiving or defeating adversaries by using core, related, and supporting capabilities. I have difficulty with concepts viewed as black and white. A common euphemism references this kind of thinking: when every problem looks like a nail, every solution looks like a hammer. That is the level of thinking we are talking about that led to the conundrum we are currently facing. The proponent at Fort Leavenworth was presented with an obvious course of action including a solid MDMP showing decisively to move to a fires approach, yet continued moving toward irrelevancy. The proponent discarded a concept that worked and destroyed any synergy and successes gained from those efforts. I am not suggesting there weren't things requiring adjustment. I advocated existing approaches didn't go far enough and should move toward a full-time fires and effects officer (separate MOS).

Fire support became so complicated, requiring such extensive knowledge we needed to establish a separate MOS for officers. There is no guarantee that when an individual arrives as the Division ECOORD/FSCOORD, he has the requisite knowledge, experience, and background to synchronize the division fight. IO officers with an infantry, armor, or DS artillery background are more likely to succeed as a DIV ECOORD/FSCOORD than a former artillery BN CDR or FIRES BDE CDR who did not have the right fires developmental assignments. As we move forward into the 21st century we are struggling to find what the mission of the field artillery is. I suggest the following: (1) Sooner or later we will find ourselves in a significant mid- to high-intensity conflict with peer/near-peer competitors and we will require traditional cannon and rocket fires units in substantial numbers. Current force structure does not address that requirement. (2) We can teach fires experts to become gunnery experts more easily than we can teach gunnery experts to become fire support experts. The alternative is reckless. Every division should have an O6 CSL select fires brigade (fire support). No guns. The fires brigade that we know today is really a cannon or rocket brigade.

Decision Criteria

- Reduced staff requirements, coordination, and meetings (less is better).
- Natural alignment of capability to function (fires, combined arms, staff).
- Billet realignment (less restructuring is better).
- Unity of effort.
- Potential for fratricide (synergy) (less is better).
- Institutionalized army structure. Proposed "fires" construct schoolhouse versus individual additional skill identifier (ASI) training across multiple venues.
- Implementation structure (fire support coordination network vice disparate staff officers/NCOs working individual actions). Existing network vice individual effort.

Fires, IO, and Effects Courses of Action

Course of action development, comparison, and analysis.
There were two COAs which were alternatives to the proponent's COA.

- **COA 1:** Everyone becomes a fires MOS (13F like) MOS. Fires consist of kinetic fires (FSOs), JTAC, EW, PSYOP, CNO, PA, Face-to-face engagement planners (IO), CA, OPSEC, MILDEC, STO, and TTL.
- **COA 2:** Partial conversion to fires MOS (FSOs). EW officers, CNO officers, IO, STO, and TTL officers become a fires MOS. The PA, PSYOP, CA, OPSEC, MILDEC personnel retain their MOS but work for the lethal/non-lethal fires officer, the lethal/non-lethal FSCOORD.
- **COA 3:** This is the Proponent COA: No MOS. IO is broken up. Information engagement equals PA, PSYOP, Stratcoms, and engagements. That is IO. EW and CNO go to fires. OPSEC goes to the G3. MILDEC goes to the G5.

COA Comparison (Higher is Better)

DEC CRITERIA	COA 1	COA 2	Proponent COA (3)
Reduced staff requirements, coordination, and meetings (less is better)	3	2	1
Natural alignment of capability to function (EW, CNO, TTL, STO to fires, while not forcing a function like OPSEC to fires)	2	3	1
Billet realignment (change where needed, but less change is better)	1	3	2
Unity of effort and command. One element in charge of IO versus multiple staff sections	2.5	2.5	1
Potential for fratricide between elements of IO and maneuver operations/fires (less is better)	2.5	2.5	1
Institutional army structure. Proposed fires construct. Schoolhouse vice disparate efforts, within reason	2	3	1
Implementation structure (existing network vice individual efforts)	2.5	2.5	1
Total	15.5	18.5	8

Conclusion

Defining this problem, it is glaringly apparent that both COA 1 and COA 2 are far superior to the proposed proponent COA. The number of work groups and additional meetings required to get to the bare level of equal synchronization and coordination are exponential. Each element you add requires an additional set of meetings with each other element. When it was under one leader or commander, it was synchronized by default. An even smarter approach is to align it all under fires because it reduces the number of meetings required to achieve the same or greater synergy. I question the proponent's methodology, and I have proven this in combat.

A holistic Fires MOS with people doing nothing but coordinating all lethal and non-lethal fires as well as related activities with existing maneuver plans are much more in tune with the entire F3EA construct than any of the crazy schemes disaggregating IO that send various portions to the G2, G3, G5, and other stovepiped staff elements.

Merge 13 series-coded fire support billets with IO and EW series billets, as a new MOS under a fires center (integration). Create one schoolhouse and MOS responsible for integration of all fires and effects. Create fires units (fire support/effects) at the O3/O5/O6 level in which command is coded multifunctional effects, like multifunctional logistics or air support operation squadrons. This enables integrated full-spectrum effects process from the platoon all the way to the corps with an already existent manpower, communication infrastructure, weapons, and vehicles. This enables the forward observer (FO) at platoon level to be completely integrated through echelon to the corps or army level formations with elements at every maneuver formation level. Presently this does not exist. The proposed method enables deconfliction, synchronization, and unity of effort all in accordance with the commander's intent.

In the shrinking defense budget atmosphere we operate in, this is an insurance policy which enables the army to respond to peer or near-peer national threats requiring sudden and rapid expansion to field traditional cannon and rocket artillery formations. It takes years to develop the experience necessary to effectively integrate, synchronize, deconflict, and execute full-spectrum fires and effects. When we make the modifications associated with this approach, we enable what I will call a 21st-century blitzkrieg approach, enabling our forces to turn faster than our adversaries and this creates military advantage over our adversaries. Utilizing one process, instead of multiple processes, under one director/commander enables increased or greater decision superiority through a top-to-bottom-linked and networked process which by the very nature of the changes will increase our ability to deliver lethal and non-lethal coordinated effects.

Examining this through a nonparochial lens and looking at the commonality of tasks associated with this greater problem set, it is clear we need to make a change in how we are approaching this problem. The integration of full-spectrum fires and

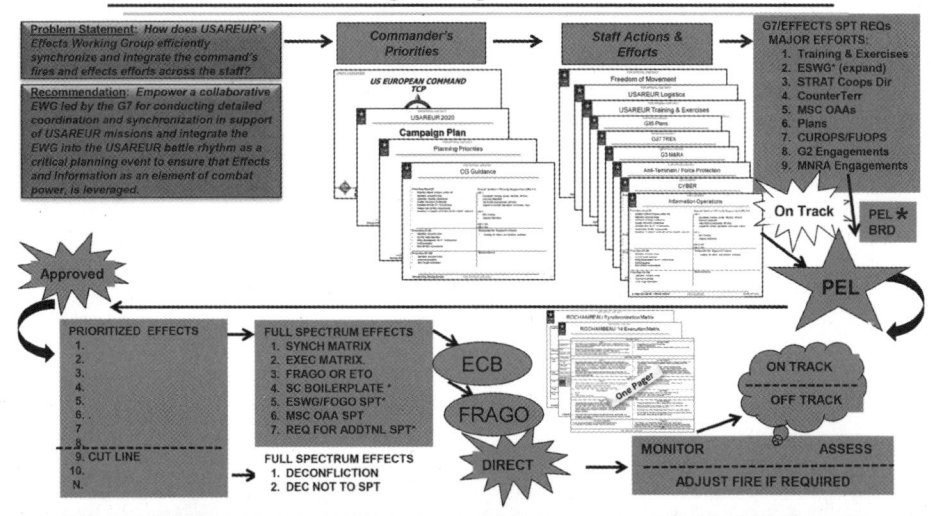

21ST-CENTURY BLITZKRIEG: FIRES AND EFFECTS INTEGRATION PRISMS • 197

Targeting and Effects Prioritization Process and levels of effort. (M. D. Matter)

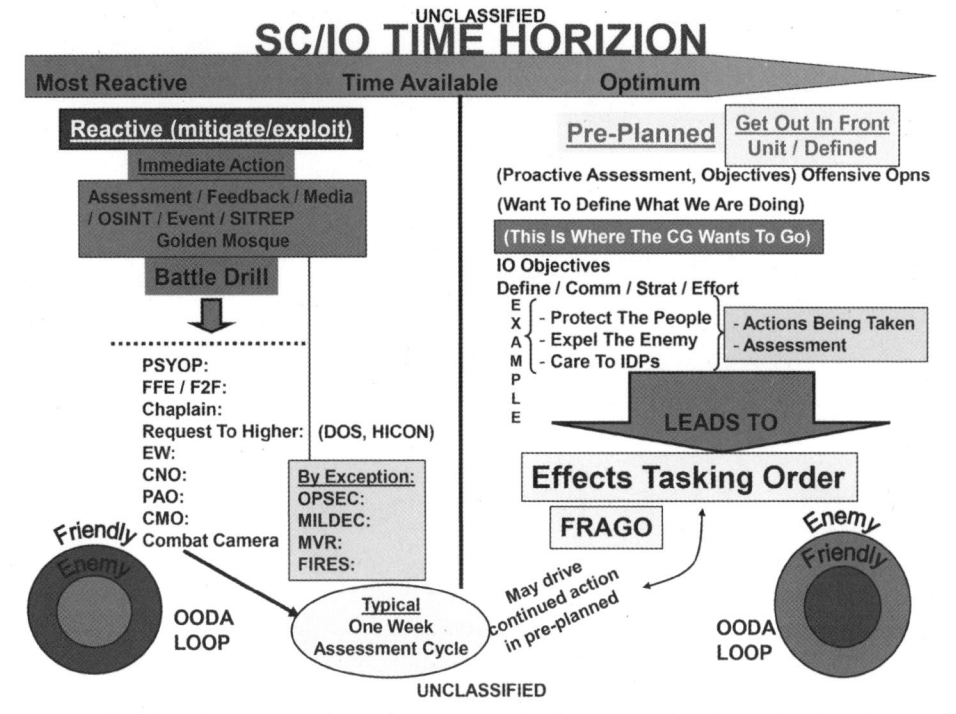

A way of breaking down OODA loop advantages and disadvantages and understanding how Strategic Communications and Information Operations fit in to timeline horizons and where friendly forces have advantages and conversely when the adversary has the advantage. (M. D. Matter)

effects has arrived at a level of complexity where we need to change our doctrine and how we train people to achieve these tasks. The ability to turn faster is a decisive advantage in the world we operate in today. Putting all types of fires under one commander who directs the integration of all fires, kinetic, and non-kinetic, in conjunction with the existing maneuver plan provides a decisive advantage. It is essentially the principle of massing at the critical time and place on the battlefield to achieve the desired end state. Whatever military does this best during the next major war will likely win.

CHAPTER 11

Great Power Competition: Relevant Lessons from the Past

War is a deadly business, and the institutions charged with conducting war must study history to learn from it. An unfortunate reality is most militaries plan to fight the "last" war and not the one looming on the horizon. Historically, the United States has had mixed to terrible results in the opening months of many conflicts.[1] At Pearl Harbor, we were lucky. The Japanese only struck the capital ships in the harbor, failing to strike the dry docks and fuel storage facilities. Those two actions could have crippled the Pacific Fleet for a year. We often suffer from what H. R. McMaster calls "strategic narcissism," creating a narrow view of what our enemies are doing.[2] Understanding our peer and near-peer adversaries' capabilities is a critical task we must master. Events leading to the "surprise" attack on Pearl Harbor were avoidable. Our failure to view the Japanese Empire as an enemy peer and treat them accordingly manifested itself at Pearl Harbor. A 1941 strategist or planner would be looking through a soda straw when comparing the 1941 intelligence and information to that of 2021. History treats ruthlessly those who fail to adapt. The Japanese fleet of a carrier strike force required synchronization of only two primary delivery systems. Three, if submarines are accounted for. As we emerged from a 20-year conflict in the Middle East, the warfighting institutions have filled their ranks with seasoned overseas contingency operations (OCO) experts; lost is the capable strategist, planner, and practitioner of major combat operations (MCO) against peer threats. China and Russia are now referred to as great power competition (GPC). A war with either or both these nations requires significant doctrinal adjustments, especially in the Pacific.

A naval-centric fight in the 21st century demands the overhaul of strategy and a review of the challenges associated with a sophisticated enemy. The U.S. military must return to the basic principles of war and concepts embodied within to prevail in this potential fight. Over the last 75 years, the navy has been a supporting component in joint warfare, not the supported component. World War II was the last conflict where the maritime component was the supported component in MCO. Clearly, in the Pacific, the navy must return to the organization for combat and structure like World War II. Ultimately, any potential GPC fight in the Pacific is by definition a "war at sea." The four primary principles of war that apply to this problem frame are, simplicity, mass, unity of command (effort), and maneuver (with a focus on speed). To win that war, we must mass at the time and place required. This requires a combination of speed, mass, simplicity and unity of effort, enabling decisive action. The simplest way of framing this problem shows that mass by itself is ineffectual if not done at the right time and place, while maneuvering to strike (through speed and stealth) is inadequate if it lacks the punch to deliver a decisive blow. Simultaneously, the processes to achieve these combined effects must be simple, easily understood, and repeatable. In laymen's terms, it is combined-arms warfare at sea, with the ability to bring to bear long-range precision surface fires, long-range precision air strike, surface strike, underwater strike capabilities, space, cyber, electronic warfare, special technical operations, and strategic communications in a synergistic approach faster than our adversary. This is not an easy undertaking for multiple reasons that are the focus of this chapter.

First and foremost, the navy has no dedicated personnel who are fires experts and integrators.* There is no fires organization, training, or doctrine that currently exists for the following reasons. The navy has not been in a situation where the maritime component was the supported component over the last 75 years. Consequently, there was no need to have trained fires personnel in the navy to conduct maritime fires for a war at sea. Instead, the navy provided strike support to other components through naval aviation, surface warfare strike (Tomahawk Land Attack Missiles), and sub-surface capabilities as supporting efforts to either the air component or land component. This did not require internal fires officers to coordinate and execute those fires, they came from other services, not the navy. The USMC and U.S. Army have fires personnel who are trained fires officers and they come from their respective artillery communities in both services, but using these personnel as a substitute adds challenges. Most artillery officers are unfamiliar with navy capabilities, limitations, and constraints. In addition, many artillery officers lack substantial fire support time for reasons that exacerbate this problem and contribute to the existing problem construct.

---

* A fires officer is really a fire support officer that integrates indirect fire, direct fire, and maneuver. Typically, in the past, this involved integrating maneuver and the organic direct fire weapons systems with artillery, mortars, close air support, electronic warfare, and attack helicopter support. Over the last 20 years, additional capabilities have been added to the kitbag of potential effects that require close integration and synchronization to maximize their impact and these can include cyber, special technical operations, spectrum attack capabilities which can include electronic warfare, information operations, influence operations, space capabilities, OPSEC and military deception. Because of the growth of the responsibility of integrating these effects the complexity has reached a point where it's almost certainly arrives at a dedicated full time military occupational series.

Ideally, nesting both task and purpose back into this obvious requirement we must make every effort to develop officers and systems that provide rapid and continuous effective fire support to formations. At best, we might be able to deliver episodic success from the existing structure, and this is due primarily to a lack of repetitive fires assignments in the artillery communities. Why? The uncomfortable reality is that the artillery community in both the USMC and the army have rarely rewarded repetitive fires assignments. Put another way, "Want to be a general officer, more gun time, less fires time." Fires is an art and it takes years to develop expertise. Gunnery is a science and can be taught in two months. While an extreme comparison, it is provided in the context that gunnery is a science and fire support is an art. The deadliest practitioners of this art are inside special operations, primarily the Rangers and special mission units. For years, there have been suggestions emanating from these communities that fires should be separated from the delivery function by creating a permanent fires officer rather than one who does both fire support and leads cannon and rocket delivery formations. This chapter will not explore that construct any deeper but offers that the complexity and importance of these tasks is so difficult that it potentially warrants a military occupational specialty of its own for officers, not just enlisted, and warrant officers. These fires officers and their enlisted soldiers, sailors, airmen, and Marines are vital in the fight envisioned. The side that does this better will be the one that wins any potential fight at sea. In simple terms, the side that can mass at the critical time and place in that war at sea and turn faster than the adversary will be the side that is victorious.

Problem Statement

Define the concept of maritime fires and how it fits into the construct of great power competition, and once defined, develop the doctrine, organization, training, material, personnel, facilities and policy (DOTMLPF-P) for the execution of maritime fires for a Joint Maritime Force Component Commander (JFMCC)-led fight. How do we facilitate synchronization, alignment, execution, and deconfliction to achieve speed, mass, simplicity, and unity of effort? Solving this problem requires three primary lines of effort.

Three Lines of Effort

In any effort aimed at problem solving, it is typically best practice to frame the problem that one is attempting to solve. In this capacity, there are three primary lines of effort requiring examination. The first is an organizational approach to fix the gaps and seams that exist to execute maritime fires in GPC. Immediately, the navy must man the required billets, establish a simple but effective command and control mechanism that allows friendly forces to mass fires faster than our adversaries and be thoroughly familiar with the tasks required to execute this construct. The tasks are commonly referred to as a mission essential task list (METL). Once there are trained people in these billets who know what they are supposed to do, and how to do it, then practice it over and over to find the gaps and the seams in that process. Ideally, all efforts at this should be built into scenarios so that this organizational approach can succeed with minimal communications and act off commander's intent.

The second line of effort is resourcing. As stated earlier, every dollar spent on OCO is a dollar not spent on GPC. This is not a world of unlimited resources and consequently requires prioritizing what the navy spends its resources on. This should go without saying but every effort must be made to avoid allocating resources against capabilities or functions that do not support GPC above and beyond what is minimally necessary to support ongoing OCO requirements. Again, a simple way of looking at this problem is if the navy is going to war in GPC, then it will do so with subs, SEALS, and strike groups, and the logistics that support those formations. It should not take a black swan event for this problem-solving rationality to set in. An ounce of prevention is better than a pound of cure and in this case the current approach is woefully short in that applied rationality. Any proposed cuts in the navy's budget should be weighed against these emerging requirements and the lion's share of those resources should go to elements which would deploy to this type of fight. A final point on that construct, if the Department of Defense national leadership is focused on some attempt to achieve cost savings, there are more creative solutions that achieve those cost savings. Simply put, one does not cut what one might need to go to war with in a GPC scenario.

The third line of effort is threat representation and investment in our training ranges. Rommel said that, "Sweat saves blood, blood saves lives, brains saves both."[3] This is another of those truths of warfare that never changes. To train properly and win in this fight the navy must train against the most current threat. It is referred to as "what right looks like." To train to high-end combat scenarios associated with GPC, the navy requires threat representative ranges with the most up-to-date modern threat representative adversary systems, and this standard applies to any other service faced with the same issues. It is true that significant investment in virtual and constructive capabilities assists in validating these concepts but anyone who has ever deployed and seen shots fired in anger will tell you that you must validate whatever tactics, techniques, and procedures you develop. If you don't, you eventually kill your own people. This means threat representation, airspace, and enough maneuver space to execute end-to-end validation.

Logistics

A humble suggestion from a warfighter ... in this politically charged atmosphere and budgetary quagmire focused on infrastructure, the DOD might be better served if the country stood up long-dormant defense industrial base capabilities focusing on critical ammunition and fuel resupply chains and supporting delivery capabilities. This improves the supply chain infrastructure while simultaneously increasing our available defense stockpiles and capabilities. Returning to the concept of problem framing, how long does a GPC type of fight last? One cannot go "Winchester" in this fight.[4] Our forces will win with what we have if they have enough of it and the navy adapts the organizational structure to deliver all-domain fires rapidly, continuously, and precisely at the time and place of choice. In addition, existing theater security cooperation efforts should focus on building capability and infrastructure, which enables and facilitates rapid and distributed delivery constructs supporting various predictable scenarios. These types of efforts create opportunities for multiple axis of advance and strike support options while improving the logistical infrastructure and provide solid, good-paying jobs for American workers.

Create Multiple Dilemmas for Our Adversaries

Returning to the concept of using historical examples which apply to potential GPC scenarios is critical in how to approach this problem. Prior to World War II, the French built a supposedly impenetrable defensive system, the Maginot Line. The German Army in May 1940, facing the combined forces of the French and the British, did not attack that impenetrable defense, but instead went around it through the Ardennes Forest and in in doing so, routed the Allied forces. While this example is not the same situation as GPC, the concept is as relevant today as it was then. Why fight the way the enemy wants you to? Create multiple dilemmas from multiple avenues, controlling the timing, tempo, and pace of the fight to create asymmetric advantages and remove the enemy's ability to find and fix our forces using friendly movement and joint fires. This elongates and extends the battlefield. Then, at the place and time of our choosing deliver decisive blows through the massing of joint precision all-domain fires capabilities from space, cyber, air, surface, and sub-surface domains directed at adversarial centers of gravity and their associated critical vulnerabilities. To reinvigorate these capabilities, the following actions are recommended.

Recommendations
1. Develop and resource DOTMLPF-P requirements to enable a navy joint fires architecture.
2. Resource submarine forces, SEALs, and strike groups and their enablers. This is what the navy will fight GPC with.
3. Provide threat representative ranges for our naval aviators, special operators and submariners to train on.
4. Recapitalize, stand up, and modernize the defense industrial base that provides critical commodities to support great power competition.
5. Create a rapid equipping function shortening support to the fleet.

Conclusion

The DOD must change the glide path that it is on. We must learn from previous failures and avoid repeating these mistakes, especially in the current GPC construct. The nation is headed for another epic first battle disaster if nothing changes. The current geopolitical environment is unforgiving, and we cannot afford failure in the opening rounds of any future fight. There are solutions to these problems, but they require action. We cannot continue to admire these problems; it requires action and resources. In taking action, nothing says more about the American way of war than the Doolittle Raid in the emerging months of World War II. The American ingenuity and creativity displayed by coming up with new ways and means to destroy the enemy is epitomized by flying B-25s off carriers to strike at the heart of Japan. There is a need to return to the concepts of our past and focus on how we mass effects in support of GPC. In the spirit of that concept, the ability to mass joint and combined fires faster than our adversaries will be the innovation that provides the devastating blows that win any potential future fight.

Author's Comments on Institutional Paralysis

This chapter was late to this book. This chapter was written and submitted to Proceedings as an attempt to get people to think about this problem set and start making changes. I wrote this at almost my six-year mark as the Chief of Staff at NAWDC at Naval Air Station Fallon, in Fallon Nevada. I no longer work for the army; I retired in late 2015. Hope springs eternal and for what it's worth, maybe the institution will start to change. The navy knows it's broken on this subject and is taking action (slowly). I contrast that with the army as an institution that knows things have changed, working yet continued down the same path, attempting to drive square pegs into round holes. The recommendations in this chapter are the best hope for fixing these problems.

CHAPTER 12

End-to-End Kill-Chain Convergence

This book really represents a chronological journey through some of the most difficult problem sets which the DoD has faced over the last 30 years. At the same time, emerging problems like Great Power Competition continue to present themselves and are an even greater threat to our national interests. This chapter grew out of these events and offers a unique opportunity to resolve long-standing and challenging problems afflicting the defense community. Recent developments and convergence of traditionally disparate warfighting functions offer the opportunity for innovation. The previous two chapters established the foundation for understanding how to create decisive advantages by creating personnel and developing processes enabling multi-domain fires capability. Chapter 10 provided conceptual arguments for advancing a singular fires specialty separating fire support from gunnery because the art of fire support has become so complicated, requiring personnel dedicated solely to integrate, synchronize, coordinate, and execute fires. Great power competition and the advancement of A2AD/C2D2E adversary capabilities forces professional military leaders to rethink existing paradigms. Traditional models create episodic success at best. The recommended model guarantees significant advancement toward continuous excellence.

Immediately, to the uninformed, traditional models of synchronizing fires to the maneuver plan demands reevaluation and examination. While there will be times that we retain that model, the pacing threat forces a wholesale change to that model. For most of the last century, if not the last two, we developed fire support plans to enable combined-arms warfare approaches supporting maneuver objectives and maneuver-focused warfare. This was done to seize key terrain or defeat an adversary through the application of combined-arms warfare. Recent operations focused fires on supporting the joint force land component, joint forces air component, or joint special operations component as the supported component. Developments in the Indo-Pacific region require returning the navy to designation as the supported component. As Great power competition in the Pacific emerged, reexamining relationships became critical. New paradigms require maneuver to facilitate long-range fires, applying multi-domain fires as defeat mechanisms. Coordinated combined-arms warfare, from seabed to space, enables the critical warfighting function of multi-domain fires. Recent developments in Ukraine demonstrate the navy strike and all-domain fires training produces disproportionate effects relative to their footprint. Conceptually, shortening the find and fix functions in any kill chain enables increased speed and massing capabilities. Navy strike and all-domain fires personnel bring knowledge, capabilities, and understanding that facilitates compressing target identification and prosecution timelines. Having served in the National Mission Force when the concept of the unblinking eye was developed, I see similar opportunities to create military advantage.[1]

Prior to employment as a civilian in what was formerly Naval Air Strike Warfare Center, I didn't envision solutions to these problems potentially present in the navy. Opportunistically, that's exactly where we are. GPC in the Pacific forces institutional leadership to examine this problem. They must realize they don't have personnel trained to integrate, synchronize, deconflict, and execute full-spectrum multi-domain fires. Consequently, the institution must adapt to deal with this requirement. Navy strike and all-domain fires success provides a departure point to compress these kill chains in an even tighter OODA loop by training the same personnel as maritime fires professionals.[2] Simply making an investment in the left side kill chain isn't enough—the navy must develop the right side. The problem statement follows:

> ## Problem Statement
>
> Define maritime fires, naval strike, and maritime ISR and how those concepts fit into the construct of great power Competition (GPC).
>
> Why? Simple. In GPC, in INDOCPACOM, the U.S. Navy is the supported component and the Navy must have personnel to lead this fight (Naval Strike, MISR and Maritime Fires).[3]

Leading this fight requires personnel that can integrate, synchronize, and execute long-range precision surface fires, long-range precision air strike, surface strike, and underwater strike capabilities, space, cyber, electronic warfare, special technical operations, SOF, IO, strategic communications, and sensor task management. Accomplishing this requires merging aspects of traditionally disparate warfighting functions that include fires, information, and intelligence that focuses on surveillance and reconnaissance. This is not an easy task and requires integration, synchronization, and execution of close air support, air interdiction, cannons, rockets, mortars, long-range precision fires, Tomahawk, Maritime Strike Tomahawk, PriSM, Nemesis, naval gunfire, attack helicopters, naval strike missile, cyber, STO, EW, space, TTL, IO, Stratcom, engagement, MISO, OPSEC, MILDEC, and potentially manned and unmanned capabilities designated for strike warfare, and sensor tasking and management.

There are currently seven warfighting functions in joint doctrine. They are intelligence, movement and maneuver, fires, information, protection, sustainment, and command and control.[4] Creating personnel that master three of these warfighting functions (fires, information, and intelligence, surveillance, and reconnaissance) enables speed and mass. Highly proficient practitioners of these concepts enable advanced operational art empowering simultaneity and depth. This GPC paradigm shift suggests fire support and sensor task management functions are critical. Previous conflicts synchronized these functions to maneuver tasks and GPC demands conducting movement and maneuver to find, fix and destroy adversaries at extended distances with all-domain fires. This is combined-arms warfare in all-domains to destroy adversary formations utilizing joint all-domain fires as the defeat mechanism. Joint Publication 5-0 defines a decisive point as a geographical place, specific key event, critical factor, or function that, when acted upon, allows commanders to gain a marked advantage over an adversary or contribute materially to achieving success (e.g., creating a desired effect, achieving an objective).[5] The ability to maintain key terrain (defined as key sea lines of communication or terrain) or mass joint multi-domain fires faster and more accurately at a time and place of our choosing creates decisive military advantage. Logically, the side that retains key terrain as well as the ability to mass faster and more accurately at the critical time and place than the other side will win.

Facts Bearing on This Problem
1. No Navy Maritime Fires MOS.
2. Navy not supported component since WWII in major combat operations.
3. Navy maritime fires doctrine does not exist. No equivalent of JP 3-09 (In draft).
4. No DOTMLPF-P designation for U.S. navy maritime fires (In draft).
5. NAWDC is executive agent for joint close air support and strike.
6. NAWDC's U.S. Navy Joint Fires Executive Steering Committee representative.
7. Strike warfare and IW represent mostly all lethal and non-lethal fires. OPSEC and MILDEC are considered part of Joint Information Operations (JP-3-13).
8. GPC INDOPACOM problem set is the greatest challenge for U.S. Navy. In CENTCOM and EUCOM JFACC or JFLCC are likely the supported component. JFMCC provides air sorties and TLAM to ATO or support to JFLCC. Same with non-lethal functions.
9. NAWDC stood up Maritime ISR (MISR) WTI and is only training for MISR WTI.[6]
10. NAWDC and NIWDC are WDCs with a vast majority of capabilities in maritime fires problem set. NAWDC (JCAS, Strike, HAVOC, Seawolf, TLAM, MISR) and CAEWWS (Integration and Airborne Tactical C2). NIWDC focuses on cyber, space, and navy IW functions.

11. GPC requires operational level of war solutions focusing on operational fires and sensor tasking and management. This is essentially end-to-end kill-chain execution or left-side kill-chain sensor tasking and management to right-side kill-chain execution and finish.

Assumptions Bearing on Problem
1. Maritime fires and MISR architecture requires personnel down to echelon IV (potentially V) as well as at echelon III- and II-level MOCs.
2. The nature of GPC and volume of potential fires requires decentralization with maritime staff, MISR, fires and IW capability down to echelon IV, potentially Echelon V.
3. Joint forces will operate in an A2AD/C2C2E and comms denied environments.
4. GPC shifts paradigm from fires in support of maneuver to maneuver to conduct fires in a war at sea.
5. Decentralization enables operational design constructs consistent with critical principles of war (mass, maneuver through speed, simplicity, and unity of effort).
6. Within the navy CSG/ESG formations must be capable of synchronizing all-domain fires, MISR, and command and control. This requires synchronization, coordination, deconfliction, and execution of joint and combined multi-domain fires and sensor and tasking management supporting COCOM objectives.
7. GPC navy maritime fires architecture requires a short-term bridging strategy as well as a long-term construct that assigns DOTMLPF-P responsibilities. Existing manning approaches do not adequately address these requirements. Solutions should encompass a multi-component approach. Naval special warfare requires no additional maritime fires personnel.
8. Minimal or zero growth in the Navy and Maritime Fires Executive Agency should align with existing strike and IW capabilities.
9. Repetitive maritime fires assignments create the required expertise and is better than single one-time assignments. This suggests we should create a MOS, Warfare Designator, ASI or AQD that permanently assigns maritime fires personnel to maritime fires billets as well as MISR billets.

Recommended Decision Criteria
Principles to fix the problem. Ideally future decision criteria in determining executive agency and training venues.
1. Long-term solutions should aim to create organic navy capability.
2. Ideally, cheaper solutions are better than more expensive ones.
3. Attempt to align maritime fires, MISR, and joint all-domain fires navy capabilities with how the navy has traditionally done strike warfare and IW if possible. Avoid drastic change unless requirement dictates change.

4. Speed to fleet is better. Faster to the fleet is better.
5. Should align against emerging JROC joint construct for fires and existing warfighting functions.
6. Doctrinally aligned with Joint Warfare with JFMCC acting as supported component in a worst-case scenario.
7. Use existing infrastructure and training relationships to reduce cost and increase speed to fleet.

Initial Requirements

1. The navy requires dedicated fires experts and integrators
2. Define navy strike and all-domain fires requirements: Definition: The synchronization, coordination and execution of close air support, air interdiction, cannons, rockets, mortars, long-range precision fires, Tomahawk, Maritime Strike Tomahawk, PriSM, Nemesis, naval gunfire, attack helicopters, naval strike missile, cyber, STO, EW, space, TTL, IO, Stratcom, engagement, MISO, OPSEC, MILDEC, and manned and unmanned capabilities designated for strike warfare ISO JFMCC objectives, and sensor tasking and management oversight. The MISR and Naval Fires Officer require different training pipelines but do have some common core elements.
3. Assign executive agency: primary stakeholders are strike and information warfare.
   a. Short term: Immediate expeditionary needs.
   b. Fight tonight: Establish model manager, initial navy strike and all-domain fires training.
   c. Long-term construct:
      i. Military Occupational Specialty or Warfare Designator requirement (active and reserve).
      ii. Agency.
      iii. DOTMLPF-P.

GPC problem frame suggests the critical warfighting function is fires, whether lethal or non-lethal. Most lethal and non-lethal fires reside under two primary WDCs in the navy. Most of the navy's conventional strike capability is located at the Naval Strike Training command. It includes a TLAM department, Strike, Naval Special Warfare (NSW) JTAC training. It is essentially a navy strike and all-domain fires find-and-fix focused effort enabling first operational recce through aviation WTI departments facilitating end-to-end kill-chain completion. This enables the oversight of nearly all Find, fix, and finish portions of the kill chain (F2T2EA).[7] Information warfare capabilities reside at NIWDC and include cyber, space, and IO functions. Integrated Training Facility/Advanced Training Environments offer a unique venue facilitating end-to-end kill-chain execution utilizing strike and IW supporting critical exercises and readiness. Emerging capability enabled by LVC linked to distributed nodes provides recurring training scenarios for echelon II and III MOCs and other WDCs driving all warfighting and warfare tactics development.

End-to-End Kill-Web Lines of Operation (LOO)

LOO 1: Individual Training

To enable the model envisioned here, we must train personnel to perform both left-side sensor tasking management and right-side integration and execution tasks. Achieving this requires proficiency in current operations, future operations, plans, and dynamic targeting. Inside these four functions we must build leaders who understand B2C2WG, joint and combined operational planning, and nested navy strike and all-domain fires responsibilities.

Training

Create core baseline training for both sensor task management, reconnaissance, and maritime fires allowing end-to-end kill-web practitioners to serve on either the left side or right side of these kill-chain execution models. To maximize the value of this

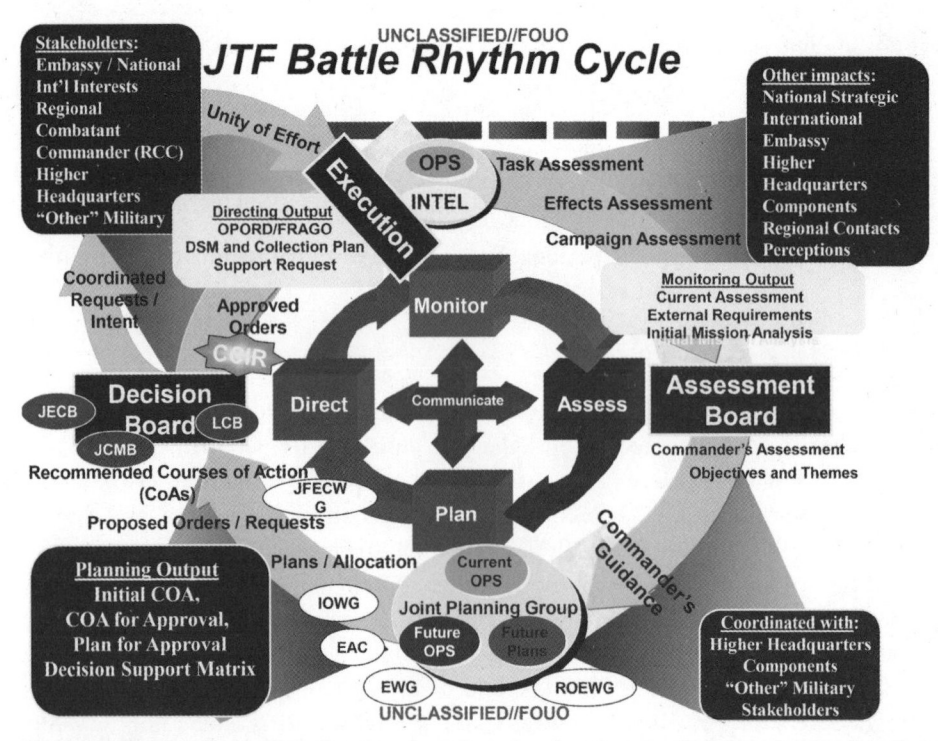

JTF Battle Rhythm Cycle adjusted to show how the various boards and cells fit into the overall cyclical battle rhythm. (M.D. Matter)

proposal we must create a full-time permanent military occupational series career path. This supports a continuous excellence model vice episodic success.

1. Core level training: Entry level.
   a. Navy strike and all-domain fires senor task management and operational reconnaissance):
   b. All-domain fires capabilities and integration.
2. Core processes.
3. CUOPS, FUOPS, plans, dynamic targeting (B2C2WG).
4. Advanced military education/centers of gravity.

Collective Staff Training

This is essentially a mission essential task list (METL). These are tasks we must execute in high-end combat operations and require an analysis into critical fire support and navy strike and all-domain fires tasks at each echelon, their relationship to each other, and how each operates with adjacent and higher echelons. For clarity, that problem frame is a communication-denied environment where execution is decentralized in an A2AD/C2DE environment requiring echelons to organically conduct full-spectrum all-domain fires internally.

Tactical METL Tasks: Fires and Maritime Reconnaissance

1. Employ joint fire support.
2. Employ joint fire support and synchronize the joint all-domain fire support system.
3. Sustain joint fire support system and the all-domain fire support system.
4. Manage ISR.
5. Manage intelligence collection.
6. task-organize fire support Assets to support scheme of fires/maneuver by main and supporting efforts.
7. Position assigned fires assets enabling the massing of joint all-domain fires assets.
8. Facilitate rapid end-to-end kill-web senor tasking, management, and fires execution to mass all-domain fires against threat contingencies (most likely, most dangerous).
9. Conduct deliberate and dynamic targeting in a C2D2E.
10. Coordinate precision engagement counter-countermeasure operations.

Operational METL Tasks: Fires and Maritime Reconnaissance

1. Employ joint fire support.
2. Employ joint fire support and synchronize the joint all-domain fire support system.
3. Sustain joint fire support system and the all-domain fire support system.
4. Manage ISR.

5. Manage intelligence collection.
6. Task-organize fire support assets to support scheme of fires/maneuver by main and supporting efforts.
7. Position assigned fires assets enabling the massing of joint all-domain fires assets.
8. Facilitate rapid end-to-end kill-web senor tasking, management, and fires execution to mass all-domain fires against threat contingencies (most likely, most dangerous).
9. Conduct deliberate and dynamic targeting in a C2D2E.
10. Coordinate precision engagement counter-countermeasure operations.
11. Facilitate joint all-domain fires systems weapons replacement operations (WSRO).

Strategic METL Tasks: Fires and Maritime Reconnaissance
1. Deploy joint all-domain fires forces.
2. Employ joint all-domain fires.
3. Sustain joint all-domain fire support system.
4. Provide command and control of joint all-domain fires forces.
5. Coordinate protection for joint all-domain fires force and command and control.
6. Establish force requirements for joint all-domain fires forces.
7. Perform military engagement, strategic communication, and inform and influence operations.

LOO 2. Personnel

Total billets required for both navy strike and all-domain fires enabling end-to-end kill-web execution by echelon.

1. Fires.
2. Navy strike and all-domain fires.
3. Surveillance and Reconnaissance.
4. Echelon:
   a. Echelon IV: CSG/ESG/MEU/MEB.
   b. Echelon III: MOC.
   c. Echelon II: MOC.

Objective: The immediate goal should focus on providing as many trained personnel in the shortest amount of time. Five primary courses of action exist:

1. Resource with navy personnel.
2. Resource with GS Navy personnel.

3. Resource with contractors.
4. Resource with other DOD personnel.
5. COAs 1-4 combined.
6. No change.

COA 5 is optimal because it rapidly integrates personnel with extensive fires experience while simultaneously creating longer-term continuity by developing internal navy capability, GS personal redundancy, and facilitating institutional memory at training institutions. This COA is the most expensive.

Theater Air Control System / Army Air-Ground System

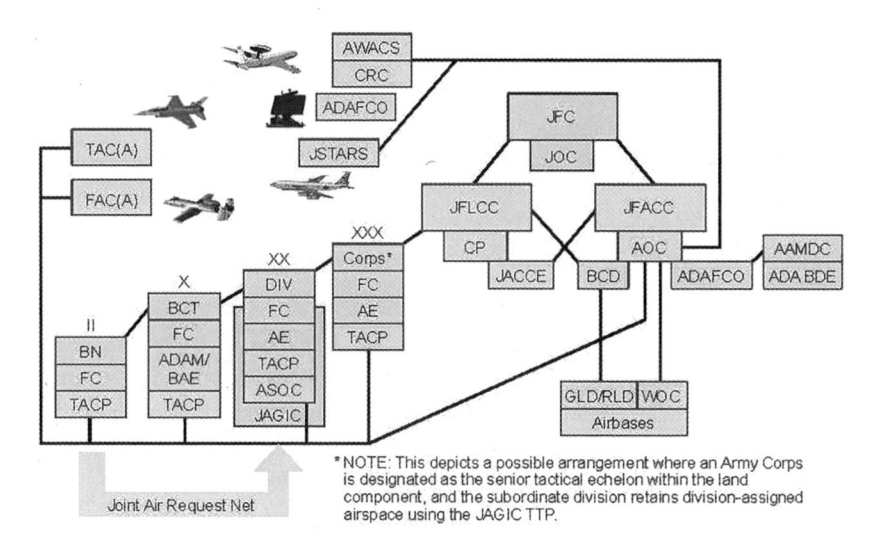

*NOTE: This depicts a possible arrangement where an Army Corps is designated as the senior tactical echelon within the land component, and the subordinate division retains division-assigned airspace using the JAGIC TTP.

Legend

AAMDC	Army air and missile defense commander	FAC(A)	forward air controller (airborne)
ADA BDE	air defense artillery brigade	FC	fires cell
ADAFCO	air defense artillery fire control operations	GLD	ground liaison detachment
ADAM/BAE	air defense airspace management/brigade aviation element	JACCE	joint air component coordination element
		JAGIC	joint air ground integration center
AE	airspace element	JFACC	joint force air component commander
AOC	air operations center	JFC	joint force commander
ASOC	air support operations center	JFLCC	joint force land component commander
AWACS	Airborne Warning and Control System	JOC	joint operations center
BCD	battlefield coordination detachment	JSTARS	Joint Surveillance Target Attack Radar System
BCT	brigade combat team	RLD	reconnaissance liaison detachment
BN	battalion	TAC(A)	tactical air coordinator (airborne)
CP	command post	TACP	tactical air control party
CRC	control and reporting center	TTP	tactics, techniques, and procedures
DIV	division	WOC	wing operations center

TACS/AAGS. (Command and Control of Joint Air Operations, Joint Publication 3-30)

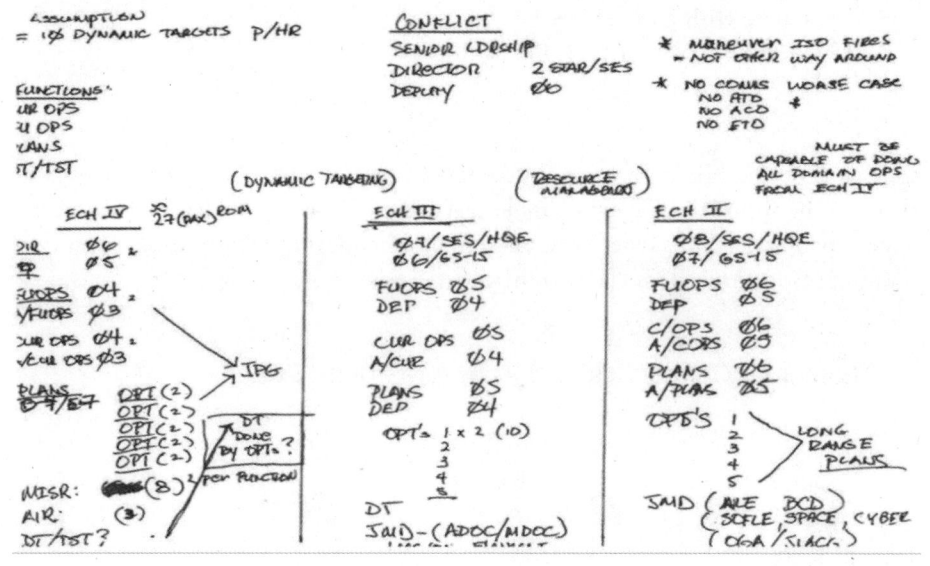

Bar napkin discussion which resulted in the next three slides, attempting to properly man the MFEC/JIFEC requirements to execute end-to-end kill web/chain all-domain fires from the MOCs or CSG/ESG.

MFEC/JIFEC ECH II

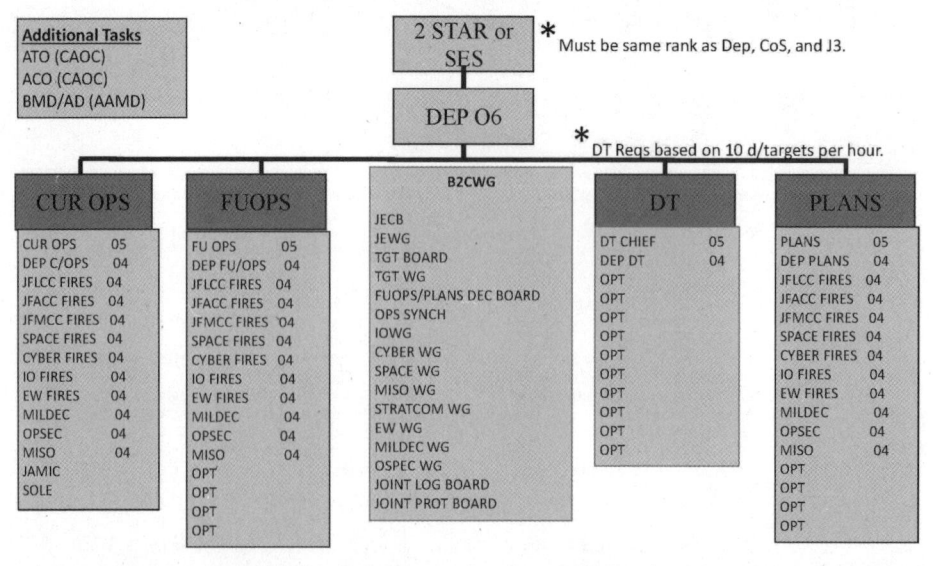

Echelon II MFEC recommended manning approach to cover B2C2WG and four primary functions of Current OPS, Future OPS, Plans, and Dynamic Targeting to include rank structure. (M. D. Matter)

END-TO-END KILL-CHAIN CONVERGENCE • 215

MFEC/JIFEC ECH III

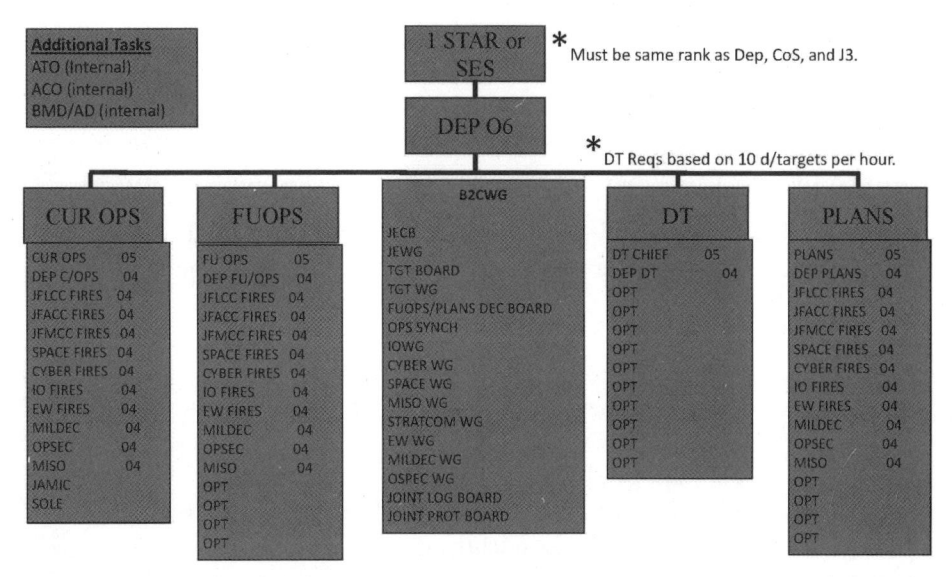

Additional Tasks
ATO (Internal)
ACO (internal)
BMD/AD (internal)

1 STAR or SES
* Must be same rank as Dep, CoS, and J3.

DEP O6

* DT Reqs based on 10 d/targets per hour.

CUR OPS		FUOPS		B2CWG	DT		PLANS	
CUR OPS	05	FU OPS	05	JECB	DT CHIEF	05	PLANS	05
DEP C/OPS	04	DEP FU/OPS	04	JEWG	DEP DT	04	DEP PLANS	04
JFLCC FIRES	04	JFLCC FIRES	04	TGT BOARD	OPT		JFLCC FIRES	04
JFACC FIRES	04	JFACC FIRES	04	TGT WG	OPT		JFACC FIRES	04
JFMCC FIRES	04	JFMCC FIRES	04	FUOPS/PLANS DEC BOARD	OPT		JFMCC FIRES	04
SPACE FIRES	04	SPACE FIRES	04	OPS SYNCH	OPT		SPACE FIRES	04
CYBER FIRES	04	CYBER FIRES	04	IOWG	OPT		CYBER FIRES	04
IO FIRES	04	IO FIRES	04	CYBER WG	OPT		IO FIRES	04
EW FIRES	04	EW FIRES	04	SPACE WG	OPT		EW FIRES	04
MILDEC	04	MILDEC	04	MISO WG	OPT		MILDEC	04
OPSEC	04	OPSEC	04	STRATCOM WG	OPT		OPSEC	04
MISO	04	MISO	04	EW WG	OPT		MISO	04
JAMIC		OPT		MILDEC WG			OPT	
SOLE		OPT		OSPEC WG			OPT	
		OPT		JOINT LOG BOARD			OPT	
		OPT		JOINT PROT BOARD			OPT	

Echelon III MFEC recommended manning approach to cover B2C2WG and four primary functions of Current OPS, Future OPS, Plans, and Dynamic Targeting to include rank structure. (M. D. Matter)

MFEC/JIFEC ECH IV

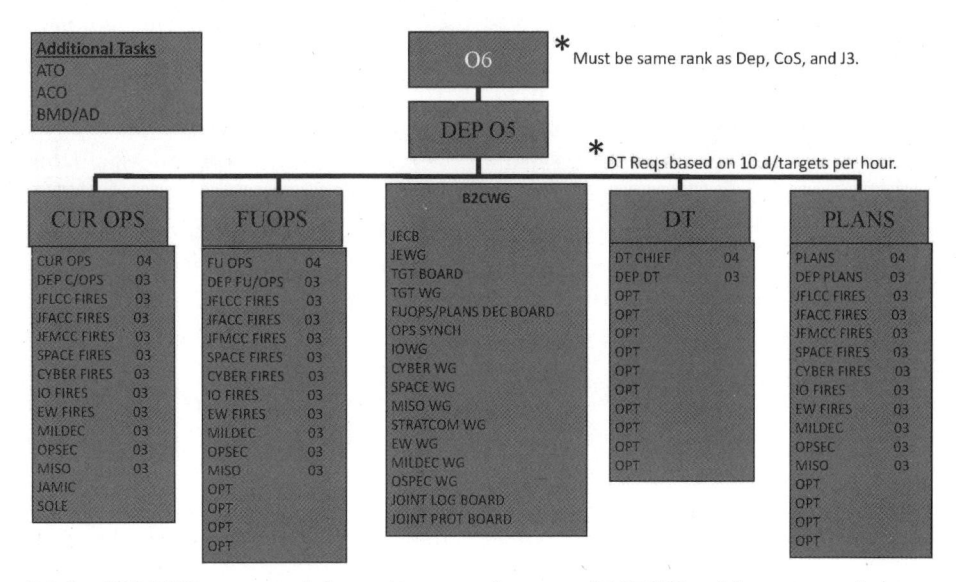

Additional Tasks
ATO
ACO
BMD/AD

O6
* Must be same rank as Dep, CoS, and J3.

DEP O5

* DT Reqs based on 10 d/targets per hour.

CUR OPS		FUOPS		B2CWG	DT		PLANS	
CUR OPS	04	FU OPS	04	JECB	DT CHIEF	04	PLANS	04
DEP C/OPS	03	DEP FU/OPS	03	JEWG	DEP DT	03	DEP PLANS	03
JFLCC FIRES	03	JFLCC FIRES	03	TGT BOARD	OPT		JFLCC FIRES	03
JFACC FIRES	03	JFACC FIRES	03	TGT WG	OPT		JFACC FIRES	03
JFMCC FIRES	03	JFMCC FIRES	03	FUOPS/PLANS DEC BOARD	OPT		JFMCC FIRES	03
SPACE FIRES	03	SPACE FIRES	03	OPS SYNCH	OPT		SPACE FIRES	03
CYBER FIRES	03	CYBER FIRES	03	IOWG	OPT		CYBER FIRES	03
IO FIRES	03	IO FIRES	03	CYBER WG	OPT		IO FIRES	03
EW FIRES	03	EW FIRES	03	SPACE WG	OPT		EW FIRES	03
MILDEC	03	MILDEC	03	MISO WG	OPT		MILDEC	03
OPSEC	03	OPSEC	03	STRATCOM WG	OPT		OPSEC	03
MISO	03	MISO	03	EW WG	OPT		MISO	03
JAMIC		OPT		MILDEC WG			OPT	
SOLE		OPT		OSPEC WG			OPT	
		OPT		JOINT LOG BOARD			OPT	
		OPT		JOINT PROT BOARD			OPT	

Echelon IV MFEC recommended manning approach to cover B2C2WG and four primary functions of Current OPS, Future OPS, Plans, and Dynamic Targeting to include rank structure. (M. D. Matter)

LOO 3: Navy Strike and All-domain Fires Systems

These are the systems and battle management aids that enable rapid and continuous end-to-end kill-chain execution. We must standardize system requirements and establish digital interoperability up and down echelons. Further discussion on this requires higher classification.

Understanding the Operating Environment (Problem Framing)

This requires understanding the assumptive operating environment our forces will operate in in GPC. This utilizes logic and deductive reasoning for sequential decision points (DP).

DP 1: Is the navy supported or supporting? We believe the navy is supported. Thus, the JFMCC is the supported component for execution of GPC high-end combat operations. The primary elements in this fight are submarines, SEALs, and strike groups, and the logistics that support them. Key and decisive is our ability to synchronize the joint and combined fight.

DP 2: Command and control. Submarines will not lead the joint or combined fight. They will likely operate independently or as a subordinate component. NSW will not lead this fight providing support to conventional task forces. There may be exceptions when their assigned operational tasks rise to the main effort rather than supporting. Instead, I believe the central components of this fight will be navy or Marine task forces task-organized, based on task and purpose as well as geography. There may be times when a CSG/ESG is organically task-organized with SOF, Joint all-domain fires elements snapped on to them and other enablers. This approach could also enable an MEF unit to have a CSG and other joint capabilities attached to it. This concept is like the way that World War II was task-organized in the Pacific where Admiral Halsey and General MacArthur each had their own assigned service component forces. Admiral Halsey had his own army and air corps and MacArthur had his own navy and Marine Corps assets. Unity of effort as an underlying principle suggests this is the best way forward. Ideally, Echelon II MOC (4 Star), Echelon III MOC (3 Star), and Echelon IV CSG/ESG components can operate independently and conduct joint all-domain fires. This requires units and personnel to conduct end-to-end kill-web operations inclusive of navy strike and all-domain fires tasks without reachback.

DP 3: Do we fight as individual service components or as a unified task force? We see COA 1 as the most optimal for this type of fight. It creates unity of effort and reduces the need for B2C2WG meetings to synchronize and execute operations.

DP 4: Span of control/operational graphics: This is where operational art is utilized. The application of creative imagination by commanders and staff, supported by their skill, knowledge, and experience to design strategies, campaigns, and other major operations and organize and employ military forces.[8] In this scenario, subordinate

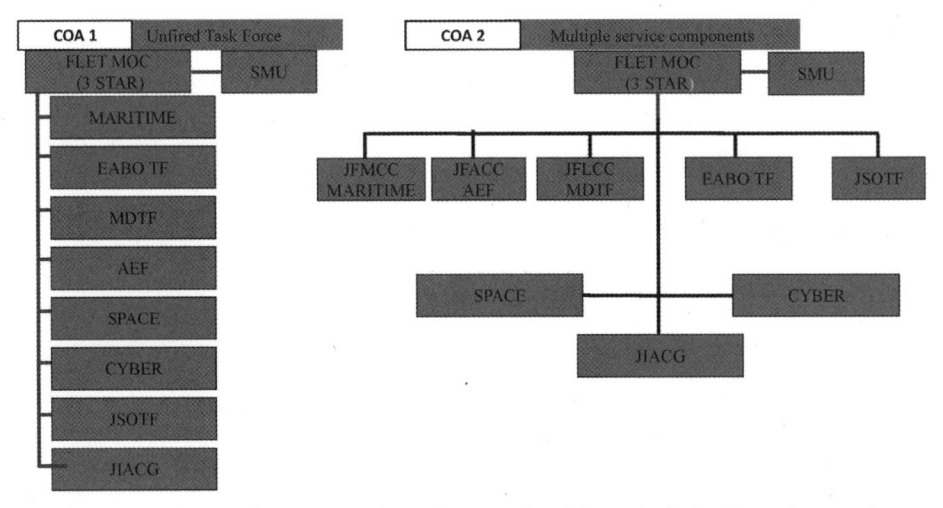

An examination of two different approaches to Command and Control of subordinate forces in theater. If you are after unity of command and effort, then you go with COA 1. You can still decentralize execution in COA 1, but COA 2 creates disaggregation of effort and is in the author's opinion less effective especially in GPC. (M. D. Matter)

forces must focus on adversary centers of gravity. They must have the operational reach to strike the critical capabilities in these centers of gravity while ensuring there is adequate simultaneity and depth across the AOR. This ensures the ability to mass joint all-domain fires quicker and more accurately at the desired time and place of our choosing.

DP 5: Centralized/decentralized. In any GPC scenario, mission-type orders, commander's intent, and initiative to achieve desired effects is critical to success and victory. The only way to process a fight of this potential magnitude is through a decentralized approach. The sheer volume of potential actions precludes executing this type of warfare from a centralized approach.

DP 6: Communications/no communications. Prudent planners approach this decision point by framing the problem. If we can execute our actions in communications-denied environments and we are blessed with the ability to communicate routinely, then things are great. If on the other hand, we assume we have communications and cannot communicate then we are in a world of hurt. Better to prepare for the worst-case scenario and be pleasantly surprised than rely on wishful thinking and be overcome by an inability to communicate. Our actions must be capable of being executed in communications denied environments using last known data, commander's intent, and initiative.

DP 7: Assign relevant tasks and purpose to subordinate units (deny, degrade, defeat, destroy, or neutralize). What are equivalent naval tasks, sea control/denial, what is key terrain in this that provides decisive military advantage?

Factors to Consider in Addition to Assigning Relevant Tasks

Mass, maneuver (through speed and processes), unity of command/effort, simplicity, and economy of force. We cannot overemphasize that we must not go Winchester in this fight. We cannot run out of ammunition halfway through this fight.

Additional factors to consider:

- Mutually supporting positions/positioning.
- Processes. Rehearsals of concept. Battle drills. Permission/authorities. B2C2WGs.
- Agility/depth.
- AI/ML applications.
- Digital interoperability.
- Defense in depth/redundancy.
- Graphic control measures that support decentralized independent operations.
- Size, composition, and capabilities of adversary. Locations, ranges, sustainment.
- JIPOE/MCOO/IPB. Slow go/no go/chokepoints.
- Most Dangerous/Most likely COAs with Red Team participation.
- Key/decisive terrain.
- Key/essential tasks and processes. Example, key/essential fire support tasks.

Command and Control, Executive Agency, and Center of Excellence Designation

An emerging unique opportunity exists to capitalize on the convergence of these problems. The navy should create a holistic end-to-end kill-chain execution capability by creating maritime surveillance, reconnaissance and fires personnel (navy strike and all-domain fires). The navy's former Strike and Air Warfare Center model is an ideal model to accomplish this by expanding existing into a wholistic sensor task management, kill web, and navy strike and an all-domain fires construct.

Rationale

Primarily, the problem we face is fires based. The two chapters "21st-Century Blitzkrieg" and "Lessons from the Past" provide clear rationale for this approach. Ideally, the navy should return to the original construct and change NAWDC back to Naval Strike and Air Warfare Center which would be a subset of navy strike and all-domain fires. All strike is fires but not all fires is strike. At present, NAWDC conducts WTI training for MISR, which culminates with a left-side kill-chain exercise called *Resolute Hunter*. They also have a TLAM department that certifies other TLAM sections. NAWDC has the navy's only joint terminal air controller course and conducts all Carrier Air Wing targeting training. NAWDC runs Air Wing

Fallon which trains the Carrier Air Wing prior to deployment as part of the navy's Optimized Fleet Response Plan (OFRP). Additionally, they should create a joint planning element which would support the development of concepts in support of service component and COCOM GPC focused plans. NAS Fallon possesses a robust range complex that is capable of being linked to the Nevada Test and Training Range (Nellis), the Utah Test and Training Range, and the Southern California Offshore Range (SCORE). The combination of these ranges enables training at the required distances for modern major combat operations challenges. Completing the entire kinetic and non-kinetic fires structure can be accomplished by establishing non-kinetic or non-lethal fires detachments at NAS Fallon while simultaneously standing up a joint IO range node to leverage any exquisite parts of that portfolio. All the above is exacerbated when one considers the impact of our magazine depths and critical munitions availability. Simply put, there is no better course of action that makes sense and meets both cost and timeline constraints for the navy.

A final critical observation in all this is we are taking too long to fix this. Some might say we continue to admire the problem rather than taking action to correct the capability gaps. A recurring theme is we are living in the construct labeled "institutional paralysis." A natural skeptic at this point, even if by some set of miracles, the institution can correct itself and start training people to execute the functions required to execute full spectrum multi-domain fires and effects to an acceptable level, the force must advance beyond basic levels of proficiency. That requires enabling these systems to be able to talk to each other, which is no small task. We need to work through those requirements for both permissive and non-permissive environments, which stress the importance of a contested spectrum and denied or limited communications. Unfortunately, we have yet to acknowledge the rationale laid out in this chapter and the previous two, creating optimal solutions. In simple terms, we haven't re-prioritized one body or spent one dollar to fix this set of issues. The following recommendations provide a baseline for correcting the current situation and ideally provide a start point to create a decisive military advantage enabling mass, speed, and unity of effort in a GPC fight.

Recommendations

1. Expand navy strike and all-domain fires production to create more capability enabling 24/7 manning from echelon IV through echelon II.
2. Stand up navy strike and all-domain fires production or merge fires with the navy's existing MISR WTI (only personnel currently available in the Navy). This creates officers that excel in end-to-end kill-chain compression.
3. Establish a navy strike and all-domain fires career field with two subfields creating an end-to-end kill-chain execution process with both the left side and the right side of the kill chain being addressed.

4. Stand up a navy strike and all-domain fires command for the navy. Collocate this capability at NAS Fallon where the navy already has JCAS, TLAM, MISR and enables the potential for a comprehensive end-to-end kill-chain center of excellence.
5. Request and assign non-kinetic detachments, enabling navy non-kinetic fires, space, cyber, IO, and that has STO/SAP representation. This should also include manned and unmanned emerging strike capabilities.
6. Stand up a navy strike and all-domain fires reserve element at NAS Fallon. This would be a reserve unit that can train and keep personnel for many years that is inclusive of primarily navy strike and all-domain fires expertise creating a bench of reserve personnel.
7. Take full advantage of joint processes that already exist by utilizing the Joint Fires ESC *Bold Quest* exercise series linking digital interoperability to enable a joint and combined multi-domain massing capability.
8. Continue to drive increased lethality.

Increased Lethality

Process Improvement
End to end KC improvement
B2C2WG/JPG understanding

Personnel Improvement
WTI Improvement
Advanced Skills

Weapons Improvement
Strike WIP
HG Salvo Table
New WPNS
ONS
Unmanned

Aircraft Capability Improvement
5th Gen integration
Air Wing of the Future

Increased Lethality

General Objective: Win in GPC

How Much? = X

Initial Goal: Where do we want to go?

Long term Goal: ?

Operational Support Improvement

Dual use (ports, repair, ammo, gas
Theater Security Cooperation

JADOCs
MTC-X/A
AFATADs
Digital Interoperability

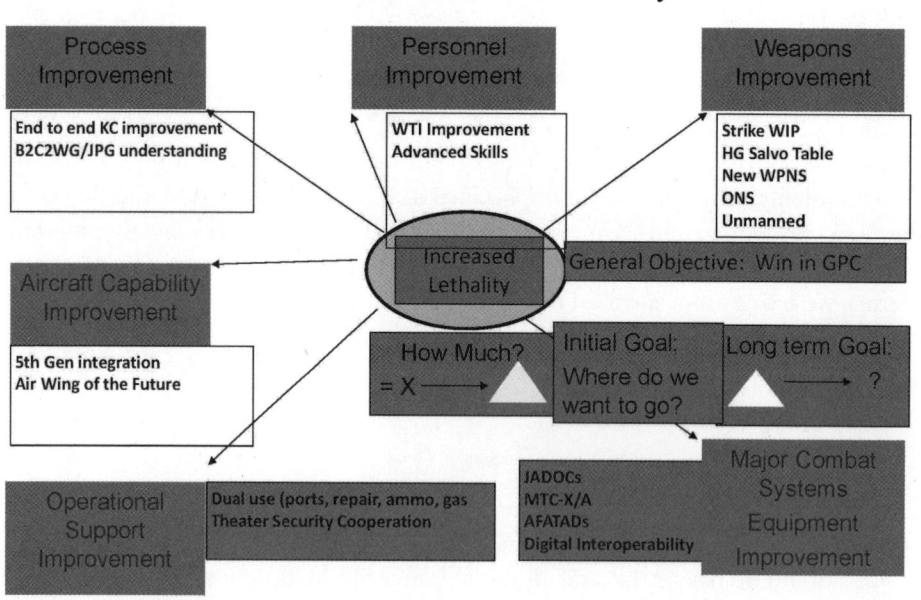

Major Combat Systems Equipment Improvement

A synopsis of different ways to improve lethality through different means and then measure that to enable weapons, process, personnel, support and combat systems. (M. D. Matter)

Conclusion

My immediate comment is if you see something wrong, speak out, respectfully, but speak out. Many of us in Iraq knew we were doing some really stupid things and headed in the wrong direction. It took General Petraeus being brought back during the surge (February 2007–mid-2008) who went and pulled in a lot of "out-of-the-box thinkers" to save ourselves from ourselves.

We, the DOD writ large, have lost the warrior spirit and we need to get it back. True candor is absent.

Trying to recreate the United States in Iraq or Afghanistan was a waste of time and blood and resources. Ask the simple question of what were we really trying to accomplish in this area of the world? Did we really think we, the United States, were going to succeed in that endeavor, or did we fool ourselves into actually believing that? Ask yourself whether we were really after creating democracies in that part of the world. Be careful what you ask for, if it does not turn out the way you want or the second- and third-order effects result in civil war or upheaval. Might we have been better off in Afghanistan by enabling existing tribal warlords and paying them to keep the peace while keeping Al-Qaeda out? What I do know, if you are going to go down the road of nation-building but don't address the underlying causes of conflict or the root cause of the existing problems, you are being completely unrealistic. You can't do nation-building without solving religious tolerance, women's rights, and education issues in that part of the world without first changing the underlying belief system which rejects that approach. In other words, you are pissing into the wind, and it is all a complete waste of time, resources, and lives, and collapses the minute you pull out. I used to ask where the Iraqi Marshall Plan was and how were we going to get rid of the zero-sum game mentality that exists in that part of the world. If you have ever been in northern Iraq, it reminds me of the San Joaquin Valley in California. With modern irrigation, they could feed the entire Middle East, and create a surplus agricultural economic base. I am not saying this by itself will change the entire nature of the problem, after all 2,000 years of zero-sum game politics by itself is hard enough to change. If there is enough to go around, then when you are in a different sect or tribe, and someone else is successful, you do not lose something because there is enough to go around. We blew it on this one. We should have gone with water, irrigation, and created an agricultural base rather than trying to reinforce existing oil infrastructure. Remove the root cause of the problem, do not exacerbate it. Democracy in and of itself doesn't solve a thing if those who have power use it to oppress those who don't.

So, what was the desired end state in all of this? Did we want a democratic Iraq, or did we want an Iraq that might not have been democratic but that was friendly to the United States, and served as a regional counterbalance to Shia Iran? Knowing that there are more Shia than Sunni in Iraq as it was defined, the minute our leadership chose to go down the path of Iraqi nation-building and create a democracy where it did not previously exist, we were doomed to failure. If we were looking for a friendly ally to assist in countering Iran, then adopting the democratic approach was unwise. On the other hand, if you are attempting to create a democracy and hope that they will figure it out, then you probably have unrealistic expectations. Honestly, I am not sure we ever knew what we were doing regarding this discussion. From all observations, our approach was either misguided or simply unrealistic. Thus, when you look at the Sons of Iraq approach, you must ask yourself, what the effect was that we were trying to achieve in the context of the given situation. If we are doing nation building, and you are going with the Shia in charge, then arming Sunni militias seems irresponsible if the goal is creating long-term stability. It may, in fact, lead to an eventual civil war. Conversely, if you are trying to defeat the insurgency, then you do what is necessary to get there, because it is the greater of the two evils. In essence, you are getting rid of the insurgency at the expense of a potential civil war because you have empowered the Sunni minority but haven't solved the potential long-term root cause discussion of Sunni concerns over perceived Shia abuses, realizing that is exactly what the Sunni did for most of the history of Iraq. Yes, by now, one may realize this was an extremely complex problem. Therefore, as I started out this observation, what was it that we were really trying to achieve? Maybe the rest of the world is not ready for our form of democracy, and we need to take an appetite suppressant when starting out on these missions. Did we need to get rid of Saddam Hussein? I don't know. I, like most good planners, could make the case for or against that course of action. As an army officer, I was not paid to determine policy; I was paid to execute it. What I can say is that at the point you decided to take out Saddam, then you needed to have a solid plan for what you were trying to achieve. I do not think establishing an Arab democracy was ever realistic or consistent with what we were trying to achieve.

This brings up an important point, which is often missed in how we arrived at some of the problems we ended up dealing with. There was never capitulation early in the war. What we potentially could have achieved once we rid the Iraqis of Saddam, followed by a capitulation and then empowering a friendly Ba'ath Party member was probably more consistent with realism than any other potential option. None of these options occurred, so in my opinion we were chasing a pipedream. You could not have democracy in Iraq and have expected Iraqi Shia to be confrontational to Iran. The decision to purge Ba'ath members in Iraq in 2003/4 was monumentally stupid.

For a military banking on the Iraqi military as the constabulary force for stabilization operations once you DeBa'athify, ultimately driving Sunni military officers or Ba'ath Party members to resist.

Returning to the original discussion on strategic communication, the glaring issue that I saw throughout this fight was the U.S. unwillingness to address the nature of Islam being hijacked by extremists. That was a critical issue in the war. It may even have been the central issue in the fight, but we did not address it at all, namely addressing the issue of distorting Islam. Part of that discussion focuses on the fact that Islam never had a reformation, and that we ought to be attempting to promote moderate Islamic interpretations rather than completely ceding the information environment to the enemy.

At the time, I said the Russians were not going anywhere, and they wanted to be a player on the big stage again, but they were not the Soviet Union. When the wall came down, the game changed. We needed to be cognizant of their perceived positions, to find ways to cooperate on joint interests to enable discussion on points of contention. We needed to reexamine what our approach was. In this retired colonel's opinion, our national leadership blew it with Ukraine then and we allowed Sweden and Finland to join NATO. I can't imagine anything more threatening to the Russians than having three neighboring or adjacent countries joining an alliance that was formed to combat the former Soviet Union and the Warsaw Pact. It would be the moral equivalent of Mexico, Canada, and the Bahamas joining the Warsaw Pact during the height of the Cold War.

There has been a long conflict between Ukraine and Russia dating back several hundred years.[1] Finland has also had its share of conflict with the Soviets. Any attempt at bringing Ukraine into NATO was universally going to be opposed by the Russians and this would be exacerbated by the inclusion of Sweden and Finland. This isn't exactly a recipe for stability. If you are a Russian and Ukraine, Sweden, and Finland are joining NATO, that prism does not look like a friendly approach, and appears as continued encirclement. The Russians are now back in the Middle East because U.S. foreign policy has been rooted in disaster for more than a decade. As an officer in the army, had I used the Obama/Clinton record, I would have been fired for incompetence. Make no mistake, the Bush administration had its share of screw-ups too, but the level of incompetence that existed in the Obama years is beyond comparison. I would instantly trade where we were at in 2009 when Obama took over to where we were at in 2017, when he gave it up. In 2009, Iraq was stable, so was Afghanistan, Syria wasn't in a civil war, Libya wasn't ungoverned space, Egypt hadn't been overthrown (not once, but twice), IS (Islamic State) didn't exist, Turkey, a long-time NATO ally, wasn't bordering on becoming an Islamic dictatorship, China wasn't building islands in the South China Sea, the Philippines wasn't giving us the middle finger, there weren't Islamic extremist terrorist attacks across Western Europe and in the United States, and the Russians weren't in the Crimea and the Middle East.

The Russians must be dealt with from strength and not idealism. Find the win-win with the Russians, then open dialogue on issues that you do not agree with. To add insult to injury, adding the Biden debacles in foreign policy and we may be in the early stages of World War III because we have hot conflicts in Ukraine, as well as Israel dealing with Iran and Lebanon. We have driven the Russians toward the Chinese and although the Russians aren't the threat they once were, when you potentially combine their capabilities with the Chinese, that becomes exceptionally concerning. A smarter approach is to reconcile with the Russians and find a way to drive a wedge between China and Russia which might not be that difficult if we hadn't blown all the above. Economically, Russia's national interest will always be focused financially, economically, and socially toward Western Europe. It's always a better approach to attempt to find the win-win.

Understand the fight you are in and the nature of the problems we face today. If you are in an IED fight in a counterinsurgency or similar environment, then take back the offensive and do not cede the initiative to the enemy. That is what we have been doing for most of the last 20 years. Get off the FOB. Take away access to the border and sanctuary. Take away the enemy's ability to receive supplies from outside the country. Attack the support zones through a multitude of means but understand the term "tactical patience" and go after critical components or entities in the network. Most, if not all this simply did not occur; I didn't see any holistic grand strategy. Technology offers both a solution and a threat to these problems and you must be prepared for both. The government has not put the necessary thought into dealing with the problems.

The last three chapters of this book focused on GPC and institutional paralysis and provided a plethora of changes that needed to occur to ultimately avoid a rerun of Pearl Harbor. The glide slope we are on will produce another military disaster without any meaningful change. Chapter 10 focused on recommendations which would enable a professional fires integration force that would give a decisive advantage in any future military conflict with a peer competitor by providing personnel that can turn faster and run processes that enable speed and mass from diverse locations across wide areas enabling agility, depth, and simultaneity. In GPC the side that masses all-domain fires at the critical place and time will have a distinct advantage. The model proposed in Chapter 10 creates fires officers who do nothing but fires for the rest of their career once they assess into the fires integration field. Consequently, as discussed in that chapter, we want to create rapid and continuous excellence while avoiding episodic mediocrity.

Unmanned systems are here to stay, and in my opinion we aren't doing enough to incorporate them into GPC and all-domain fires. This book focused on enabling a persistent unmanned solution to both strike and IEDs that was brought on by the asymmetric warfare challenges we faced in Iraq and Afghanistan and various other parts of the Middle East and Southwest Asia. That problem set has now morphed into an even greater problem that is just as much of a challenge in GPC and may in fact be even greater. Extended distances and A2AD/C2D2E create similar opportunities and challenges which we must embrace and master. A perfect example of this is that, from a maritime perspective, we should be embracing as a minimum four distinct roles within the UAS role and those are Reconnaissance, Strike, Fuel, and Communications, enabling long-range strike from both the Air perspective as well as an all-domain fires perspective. Unfortunately, we have not invested any meaningful manpower or resources in those capabilities. This is a huge mistake and must be rectified whether it's solely unmanned or manned unmanned teaming.

Chapter 11 discussed relevant lessons from the past that apply to GPC and focuses the reader on establishing and resourcing DOTMLPF-P requirements enabling a Navy joint fires architecture. The simple truth is we aren't moving fast enough and if I were king for the day I would create a new warfare designator inside the Navy and create Navy Strike and All-Domain Fires squadrons and bring in Army and Marine Fires Officers to providing a bridging solution within the Navy until the Navy could stand up its own internal maritime fires training pipeline and personnel. This will take at least 7 to 10 years and is well outside the potential window of dealing with the existing pacing threat we face. To approach this from a parochial lens is military malpractice and stinks of an inability to think critically.

A further recognition that GPC is a maritime fight reminiscent of the fight in the Pacific in World War II. We must focus on what the Navy will fight with, which will be subs, SEALs, and strike groups and the resources that support these capabilities while simultaneously enabling these formations with joint all-domain fires. Restating the obvious, to train our forces to do these things requires threat representative ranges designed to replicate scale, speed and what we will actually face when we send forces into harm's way. Finally, in order to provide our forces with the most up-to-date equipment we must scrap our current procurement process and timelines. We need to turn to industry to reestablish and modernize our defense's industrial pace that turns at the speed of relevancy and provides enough ammunition and lethality to win the day.

The final chapter on end-to-end kill-chain compression is my latest attempt at fixing a broken system. We are on a glide slope to military disaster and failure. Chapter 12 and the recommendations within that chapter, if actioned, will go a long way in rectifying the issues we face. We are in a paradigm shift where long-range land-based precision munitions can out-stick our Naval Forces and the days of parking a CSG 300 miles off an adversary's coast are over. To get the CSG in requires setting conditions which enable that and that's really the battle we are in; where in order to potentially deter aggression and support our allies we have to relearn how to fight with long-range fires and we may be in fact at a point where we need to do combined arms warfare at sea with multiple capabilities and all-domain fires systems to achieve victory. The recommendations in this final chapter enable the processes, people, training, and digital interoperability required to succeed.

APPENDIX A

C-IED White Paper

Executive Summary

The purpose of this document, written March–May 2007 during the surge, was to provide a framework and methodology to decisively defeat insurgent and terrorist forces who utilize improvised explosive devices (IEDs) against the United States and Coalition Forces in Iraq and by extension anywhere that U.S. Forces are required to deploy in an extended Global War on Terror (GWOT) conflict. Additionally, in this document there are several critical decisions on the question of best way to approach "how to" defeat and or destroy the IED network in Iraq. Insurgent or terrorist success with IEDs in Iraq will certainly proliferate in other areas of the world and challenge the traditional state actor paradigm if the United States fails at effectively defeating this current threat. The examination of these crucial debates is critical to a greater understanding of the tools which are available to commanders in Iraq and how to most effectively engage and defeat the enemy given the nature of warfare that we face.

This document is provided as a "start point." There is no foolproof solution. This is a "thinking man's game" and requires constant assessment and adjustment. Updating TTPs and strategy is critical to success. The aim of this document is to empower our troops and leaders with the information and approach for success in combat. Defeating the enemy's primary engagement system enables long-term victory while saving American and Coalition lives. Reducing the overall casualty rates provides our leadership more time to achieve stability in Iraq, ultimately furthering our national interests.

The current security environment in Iraq, characterized by a recurring and systemic use of IEDs, is single handedly killing more American soldiers than any of the other approaches combined, yet we have done little to address the TTP to aggressively counter this ongoing trend. This paper will attempt to provide a suggested way ahead, codify the current situation, and provide a set of recommended solutions to initially disrupt and ultimately defeat the enemy's IED effort.

This paper was written to change the way we were organizing for combat to fight this fight. I was then and am still an advocate of creating a mobile C-IED strike force rather than attempting to provide traditional formations with IED capabilities. To be clear it's not an either-or approach, or more aptly binary. Instead, the more complicated and offensive capabilities lend themselves to specialization while defensive capabilities need to be pushed to all forces. As far back as this paper, I started formulating a belief that there were better ways to approach this problem than the way that we were.

Structural Framework

Philosophically, an IED is designed to be a standoff engagement system, initiated through some type of remote control, which allows the initiating force to disengage rapidly and escape detection by friendly forces. This type of attack allows the enemy to asymmetrically overcome firepower and disadvantages that are inherent in an insurgent force. The insurgent does not want to become decisively engaged. Direct engagement usually results in being killed or captured by Coalition forces. IEDs serve another purpose by decreasing Coalition forces' freedom of action and increasing the insurgents' ability to move around the battlefield at significantly lower risk. The key to defeating or disrupting the concept of IEDs is understanding the development cycle, employment cycle, and vulnerabilities that are intrinsic in the IED system.

Counter-IED Approaches

There are six primary approaches to conducting counter-IED operations that apply equally to command-detonated, victim-operated, or radio-frequency-controlled IEDs.

1. Offensive electronic attack (EA): This methodology works against RCIEDs. It is not a silver bullet. Instead, the use of airborne electronic platforms (AEPs) combined with changing the operational patterns of AEP use could have a disrupting effect upon the enemy. We have established a recurring pattern with this capability. We do not utilize this asset during the middle of the day. Changing the times of this asset would potentially cause increased detonations during the setup of RCIEDs.
2. Defensive electronic attack: The use of warlock and IED jammers provides local convoy protection to prevent radio frequency signals from getting to the IED by conducting reactive jamming. This works only if the device is on and if you are in the effective jamming to signal ratio.
3. Tactics: This paper will devote an entire section to potential tactical approaches which increase the effectiveness of our current counter-IED campaign. Unconventional approaches to this problem increase the likelihood of success

while failure to modify established procedures and operational patterns decreases our effectiveness.
4. Import control methodology (police work): This concept is like the approach used by the inner agency in dealing with nuclear weapons proliferation or sensitive technology export controls that we do not want to fall into the hands of our adversaries. The goal of this approach is to limit the critical components which enable the construction, manufacture, and employment of IEDs. Examples of this include but are not limited to: key fob alarms, washing machine timers, blasting caps, high-power cordless phones, hobby boxes, PIR sensors, detonation cord, explosives, and ordnance. By reducing the availability of components available to the insurgent, we will be able to see a corresponding reduction of IEDs. This approach requires assistance from the State Department, Other Government Agencies (OGA), Law Enforcement, Department of Treasury, the Iraqi DBE, and the Threat Intelligence Financial Unit. The overall aim of this approach is to reduce the availability of the available components for IEDs while also disrupting the manufacturing cycle, and the logistical and monetary sources which fuel the IED cycle.
5. Information operations (perception operations): This approach is often the least used and often forgotten aspect of the counter-IED fight. The use of "face-to-face" spheres of influence (SOI) engagements, Psychological Operations, Deception, OPSEC, and civil-military operations to address the conditions that allow the insurgents to emplace them is typically not synchronized or orchestrated in a manner that assists the overall kinetic fight to eliminate the IEDs, the IED-emplacement team, and the cells that manufacture them.
6. Emerging technologies: The use of cameras in a deception and baited ambush role has had recent success in Mosul. This is just one example of ways to deny terrain or give the impression that you are denying terrain while providing some form of overwatch that enables Coalition forces to draw insurgents into areas where they can be engaged. Real-time coherent change-detection radar can alert ground forces to the potential placement of IEDs by noting change between an established baseline and a corresponding change. This technology combined with potential existing technology that can detect unintended radiated emissions of electronic equipment provides the opportunity to detect the triggerman and the IED before the system is engaged against Coalition forces. Other examples include defeat of passive infrared devices through the use of the electromagnetic spectrum. Tracking, tagging, and locating operations can expand the division and brigade capabilities to conduct unconventional information-gathering operations and can assist units in potentially identifying IED-manufacturing cells, financiers, moneymaking operations, cache sites, and many other options that will potentially arise as situations evolve.

Combined-Arms Approach

Few could argue that approaches to date have failed to achieve the desired results or impact that we would like to have on the enemy's IED campaign. This is likely attributed to the fact that we have and continue to use many of these high-demand, low-density assets in independent stovepiped operations, which fail to achieve the synergy of a combined-arms approach. We know where the enemy will typically present himself and we have a substantial understanding of how he employs the capability, but we are currently unable to make a significant impact against his operations. If we could portray all the task force movements and operations on a given day, and visualize them as one continuous ongoing operation, the enemy uses dead space (in time) and an existing early warning network (likely GSM phone networks) to place IEDs along the MSRs and frequented avenues of approach. Despite the knowledge of this problem and knowledge of the enemy's tactics we have failed to effectively disrupt his IED campaign. Why is this happening? This is directly attributable to our failure to integrate the available assets that we have into a single synchronized operation designed to find, fix, and destroy IED-emplacement teams, their manufacturing cells, and the support networks that go with them. There are other factors that contribute to this problem. One of the consistent arguments that I hear is that this is a "brigade problem." That is partially true and at the same time considerably false. Yes, it is a brigade problem, but part of the problem is the brigade. Within the 101st Airborne Division, to date, the BCTs have yet to fully embrace this action and probably see this as something that is happening in their battlespace that has to be deconflicted with other ongoing operations and at the same time they have shown very little or no propensity to attach combat-multiplier assets such as air weapons teams, close air support (CAS), snipers, or dedicated ISR to this problem. What kills more American soldiers than anything else on the battlefield? The very simple and straightforward answer is IEDs. It is the enemy's weapon of choice. Yet we allocate minimal combat power and assets to address this problem. Again, we know exactly where the enemy is going to emplace IEDs (MSRs, ASRs, and frequented routes), we have substantial knowledge of his TTPs, and yet we have limited to minimal success against the system prior to emplacement. One of the primary aims of this document is to investigate why we are having minimal effects on this target set, examine the benefits of a division-centric approach vice a brigade-centric approach, and move to a holistic full-spectrum approach, that will increase our lethality against IEDs.

Mobile Counter-IED Strike Force

This debate centers around whether we should be enabling the brigades to conduct this operation or whether this should be a division-run operation. The debate in our headquarters had centered on whether it might not be better to create a special C-IED strike force and use the inkblot method to destroy networks. The theory centers around creating expertise in a particular area and by doing so, the theory extends that as long as you can destroy networks faster than they can regenerate, then you will ultimately defeat the insurgency and adversary networks because you can destroy them faster than they can reappear and once you arrive at a point where you can protect the population from the insurgents, then the population will turn them in. The nature of the operation almost requires or demands that the division-run the prioritization, resource allocation, and employment of a counter-IED combined-arms task force. This task force should have organic to its composition, rifle platoon(s), scouts, or pathfinders, snipers, dedicated ISR (or first priority of EAD/EAC ISR), overhead SIGINT collection, dedicated EA assets, EA/ES close target reconnaissance assets, attack weapons teams, access to joint fires (CAS), JTAC-qualified personnel, persistent electronic intrusion camera kits, and rotary-wing lift assets. Once this force is assembled, it should work together on a habitual basis and move to where the division's priorities are. In very simple terms, utilize the inkblot method of stamping out hot spots in our AOR. Thus, the highest-density IED area would be the very first target that we dedicated this force to attack. In essence, we would have a mobile counter-IED strike force. This mobile counter-IED strike force would have the ability to be moved around the battlefield to defeat or destroy high-density IED engagement zones. Possibilities to achieve economy of force and deception are enhanced after the successful employment of these types of operations. Following successful employment, we could bring in cameras and continue to do routine clearance operations that would likely be left unchallenged and the TTPs of the enemy reseeding after our clearance would be significantly reduced for fear of mobile-counter IED strike force response operations. The threat of kinetic operations following employment of this asset makes face-to-face engagements and PSYOP much more effective because it is perceived completely differently than when we fail to address this recurring problem. This force could be assembled from either the current division reserve or 555th Engineer Brigade or a combination of both. Ultimately, the goal of this approach is to create one combined-arms unit that is solely responsible for prosecuting mobile counter-IED strike force operations.

An alternative to the above course of action is to attach the assets to the BCT to attack this problem. This seems to be a less favorable course of action for several reasons. First and foremost, the BCT would be sourcing the maneuver forces organically which would take them away from their current existing missions. Additionally, it is likely that this force would be of an ad-hoc nature. Most of the assets would have little familiarity with regards to working with each other and would be less likely to develop effective CONOPS. The first COA would be a force dedicated solely to the elimination of IEDs and develop SOPs and CONOPS rapidly and efficiently vice the second force, which would have greater difficulty achieving similar effects. It is also probable that the first force would have significantly more success than the second given the nature of unfamiliarity of the second force in conducting mobile counter-IED strike force operations, as well as only doing them on an occasional or part-time basis. Finally, by conducting operations in the division-centric mobile counter-IED strike force mode, we relieve the brigade commander of the responsibility to dedicate command and control assets for these operations. Simply put, the task force shows up and comes as a complete package and works for the brigade commander in his battlespace and leaves when they have completed the mission.

Conducting Mobile Counter-IED Strike Force Operations

Earlier in this paper, we addressed the six primary methods for conducting counter-IED operations. The intent for this section is to provide a set of concepts that will provide potential options for the mobile counter-IED strike force or BCTs operating independent counter-IED operations. The concepts are provided as start points to enable unconventional approaches to solving the overall IED problem.

1. Sniper interdiction: This provides back-end sniper coverage of routes being cleared or provides overwatch of assets that deny the insurgent opportunity to emplace IEDs. An example of this is providing sniper teams to overwatch cameras on critical areas or recurring areas where the enemy places IEDs.
2. Attack weapons team (AWT): This rotary-wing capability can be used to screen forward of clearing elements as well as the flanks, looking for triggermen. Given the recent targeting of the RG-31 and Buffaloes, this would enhance the survivability of both these high-demand, low-density assets. Finally, this asset can be held in a standoff laager area anywhere from 4–8 kilometers off the clearing element's path, in both daylight and nighttime operations to provide back-end ISR and precision fires assets.
3. Joint terminal air controller/enlisted terminal air controller (JTAC/ETAC)-equipped full-motion video (FMV) capability: There are multiple options that could be utilized with this asset. JTAC/ETACs could be attached to snipers to provide a link to enable joint fires or inserted separately into a hide site to watch areas from a designated observation post (OP).
4. RAID/tethered balloons: This asset could be provided with greater optical enhancements and a laser range finder and designator to provide immediate targeting information or pass coordinates to a multitude of fires platforms. It is best suited for operations near the FOB and can be moved around to cover problem areas near the FOBs.
5. Airborne forward air controller (ABN FAC): CATCH ops have shown that close air support (CAS) from the CAS stack can be used to provide responsive

joint fires when we can get PID of insurgents emplacing IEDs. An interesting option from this concept is to move our CAS stack-holding areas to locations where we believe activity will likely occur through predictive analysis tools like Crystal software.
6. Airborne jamming platform in support of (ISO) jamming early warning network: As we transition to some form of deliberate counter-IED operations, we should provide whatever task force is conducting this operation, a dedicated electronic attack platform. To some extent, this may in fact give us the capability to jam the enemy's initial early warning network and potentially expose another node that we are currently unaware of. If the early warning network is only one level deep, then we may achieve success simply jamming the network and thereby preventing potential reseeding operations. As the concept of operations (CONOPS) go to second- and third-order reactions by the enemy, it may be necessary to do preemptive jamming and simultaneous cueing to develop SIGINT on the secondary and tertiary early warning nodes.
7. Airborne SIGINT platform to collect on the early warning network: This can be provided by a host of systems and is really an effect that we are looking for. As we initiate these operations, the very nature of the operation itself will generate SIGINT, and we should be poised to collect as much as possible. This in turn could lead to greater fidelity on financiers, manufacturing sites, caches, and varied support for the IED employment cycle.
8. Airborne surveillance & target attack radar platform (ASTARP) support: An ASTARP can provide real-time, back-end coverage and provide forensic examination of post-blast VBIEDs and IED events if they are on station and have a complete field of view for event post analysis.
9. Flash traffic control points (TCPs) with electronic attack/electronic support (EA/ES) close target reconnaissance (CTR) capabilities with overhead SIGINT collection: This can provide a significant amount of targeting information provided we have the tactical patience to do the analysis and collection necessary to identify higher-value targets. We can use this technique to expose early warning networks and force HVTs to carry exploitable devices, which provide friendly forces the capability to geolocate these devices. In a worst-case scenario, this technique can significantly reduce the freedom of movement of HVTs and key enablers. As part of a greater mobile counter-IED strike force, we can use maneuver flash TCPs to block in emplacement teams once they have started to reseed areas just cleared.
10. Camera emplacement with interdiction capability (snipers, CAS, AWT): Use of these devices can enhance economy-of-force missions and can confuse the insurgents about what areas have active mobile counter-IED strike force operations and those that do not. Use of these devices is enhanced by publicizing their arrival, conducting face-to-face engagements with key leaders, and an

active PSYOP campaign to warn local citizens of the dangers of approaching these devices. The devices should also have clearly visible warning signs. They should be emplaced in areas that are difficult to get to and reduce the likelihood of innocent bystanders being engaged for chance contact.

11. Persistent electronic intrusion (camera kits covering significant areas) 20 miles by 5 miles: These can be further used to deny significant amounts of terrain to insurgents who are part of the IED cycle. When they are used as part of a greater mobile counter-IED strike force, they can instill confusion, instill fear, incite apprehension, and encourage insurgents to attempt to take action against the devices themselves, and they can provide targeting information for kinetic strikes and counter-IED operations. This capability is limited to the imagination.

12. Daylight airborne electronic platform burns: This capability when utilized with constant shuffling of our operational patterns and changing our combat logistics patrol (CLP) movement times can wreak significant havoc with the emplacement portion of the IED cycle. Routinely moving this capability will significantly impact certain sets of IED devices and as improvements for new devices become available, this capability can cause reluctance on the enemy to emplace IEDs or move completely from certain devices, ultimately reducing the total number of IEDs being used.

13. Air interdiction support: If this asset can be scheduled in conjunction with Combined Joint Special Operations Task Force (CJSOTF) or Other Coalition Forces Iraq (OCFI), this asset can cause significant pain for the insurgent because of the platforms it has on it. With a precision direct-fire 105mm capability and the ISR assets available, this would be an ideal platform to cover areas where we believe the insurgents are planting IEDs. This asset provides an even greater capability to cause severe impact on nighttime insurgent operations because of the distances that the asset can engage from with minimal signature.

14. Aerial or ground unintended radiated emissions support: This asset could theoretically provide a standalone capability and would be brought in as part of other Coalition forces or task forces. It remains to be seen if it can be integrated into a standalone suite with a coherent change-detection radar. We will see what this system can do as we undertake training on this capability in Idaho or Arizona (April 2006).

15. Coherent change-detection radar (highlighter): Provides real-time coherent change detection, which as a standalone system can assist with the identification of IEDs and caches. Combining highlighter with emerging technologies like unintended radiated emissions, we could develop a capability that could be able to find remotely controlled IEDS (RCIEDs) and their respective triggermen prior to the initiation of the device (April 2006).

16. Aerial or ground digital receiver technology (DRT) support. This capability provides both ground and air electronic support and electronic attack (ES/EA) functions that are typically provided by echelons above division assets. The box provides significant increase in capability over existing ES/EA close target reconnaissance capabilities (Gossamer). This technology will enable a helicopter-borne remotely piloted vehicle-type capability for the division (April 2006).
17. CMO and PRT economic incentives: This is often viewed as a carrot-and-stick approach. This provides a community a carrot for "cleaning their own house." This can be a very effective way to reduce or cease IED activity provided the threat of the hammer is equally as effective. Commanders and Department of State officials need to make joint efforts at reducing the opportunity for insurgents to offer incentives that outweigh economic investment and peace. Information operations planners, PSYOP, civil affairs, and key leaders must synchronize efforts to deliver effective messages and themes that delineate that investment comes with security.
18. Soft information operations (IO): PSYOP, IO, and face-to-face engagements delivered to key tribal and religious leaders, which emphasize the benefits of cooperation. Contrasting the damage to areas that have not cooperated like Fallujah and Ramadi vice Irbil or Sulaymaniyah reinforces that choosing to cooperate with insurgents brings consequences. Using Iraqi Army and Iraqi security forces support enhances this concept. Finally, when there is a credible threat to bring down the hammer with an element, which would contain the combat power and robust enablers like those previously suggested in the mobile counter-IED strike force, it enhances all the soft IO efforts.
19. Minority enfranchisement: Minorities feeling threatened by the changing situation (e.g., Sunni) provide a pool of available recruits for insurgent IED efforts. Providing representation, alleviating fears of reprisal, sharing the resources of all Iraqis, and increasing employment strip away the arguments and monetary incentives that insurgent and terrorist groups can offer. Every effort should be made to provide inclusion as exposed exclusion. Inclusion eliminates sources of manpower and sanctuary for insurgents.

Way Ahead

Where do we go from here? Clearly, we need to do more than we are currently doing. Placing the additional burden of requiring units to conduct existing steady-state combat operations and patrols as well as operations of the magnitude suggested in this paper may in fact be a "bridge too far." Creating one or two mobile counter-IED strike forces across the division with 555th MEB, Pathfinder, and division troops would create an additional capability that would relieve BCTs of this task. Creating a mobile counter-IED strike force would enable the division to weight the main effort as well as defeat or destroy recurring high-density IED engagement zones. Over time, this will significantly decrease the effectiveness of the enemy's IED campaign, reduce friendly casualties, and increase our freedom of movement.

APPENDIX B

Optimized Fires Brigade

Recommended structural approach to this problem: The following represents a basic modified table of organization and elements MTOE for personnel for placing all this under a fires approach and is the fastest way to achieve increased synergy across the lethal and non-lethal effects enterprise.

Fires Brigades

consist of the following:
FIRES BRIGADE: (COL CMD)
HHB
    Specialized requirements (Cav, Avn, Pthfdr, etc.)
    4 fires bns (1 per BCT)
    Fires sqdn: 1 per maneuver BCT
        Traditional fires
        Tactical PSYOP company
        EW company
    Crew OIC and support structure
    TTL OIC/NCOIC section/support structure (tracking, tagging, locating)
    DIV PAO (LTC) and traditional PAO support structure
    DIV targeting element/DFSCOORD
    1st IOC land/LIWA FST like capability
    DIV STO element
    ASOS/joint fires observers/planners (NGF, AC-130, TLAM)
    Non-traditional fires (PMESII/SOSA) focused
    MILDEC planner(s)
    OSINT section
    Face-to-face engagements section/crony analysis: non-lethal targeting
    CAT-B
    Cultural experts

FIRES BN/SQDN: (LTC CMD)
HHB/HHS
    3 fires battery/troop (1 x IN/AR BN) 13F structure (FSNCO/FO/RTO)
    Traditional fires
    Tactical PSYOP support element (TPE)
    EW detachment
    Crew Element
    TTL OIC/NCOIC
    BCT PAO/PANCO
    Bn non-lethal targeting warrant/section
    Bn lethal targeting warrant/section
    ALO
    STO officer/NCO (read on)
    CAT-A
    Cultural experts

FIRES BATTERY/TROOP: (CPT CMD)
    Traditional fires
    FSO/FSNCO per company
    FO/RTO per plt
Tactical PSYOP team
EW team (part of the EW detachment which supports the BCT) Min 3–5 boxes/capability at BCT level (might be 6–10). Crew/EW capability to conduct counter-IED EW/TTL capability

For officers this becomes an accession MOS. You do not have to be an artillery officer to become a "fires officer." Obviously, gates would have to be established along the way to ensure that by the time a fires officer became an LTC he would have experience in most if not all the elements of fires. This is a combat-arms MOS. This officer is skilled in all aspects of fires.

    There would be specialized units to support the SMUs, the 75th Ranger Regiment, SOCOM, and Special Forces Groups.

    There is also a need to send officers to advanced civil schooling (international relations) among other things, and likely EW and CNO advanced degree subjects as well.

    The concept of effects already exists although it has been largely rejected by the army. Example: Maneuver and logistics achieve effects. It is more accurately described as lethal and non-lethal fires. This causes a doctrinal disconnect.

    Gunnery, and more specifically artillery, is one portion of a greater joint fires system. It includes close air support, naval gunfire, STO, attack helicopters, electronic warfare, air-launched Cruise missiles (CALCMs), sub- and surface-launched Cruise missiles (TLAM/CALCM), and special operations fires platforms (AC-130, AH- 6G, DAP, Predator). This process works through the targeting process, using decide, detect, deliver, assess (D3A) or as in SOCOM where they use find, fix, finish, exploit, and assess (F3EA). Ultimately you use a joint/combined effects process that produces a C/JIPTL and executes joint and organic fires through an effects tasking order and air tasking order.

Currently many of our FSOs do not even possess JTAC/JFAC qualifications. They need JFCC, LFTACP, JTAC qualifications. STO is primarily in the intel/space and IO realm. EW is operations and must be deconflicted through the fires/effects/targeting process. In the army for most of the last 35 years EW has been broken. In the navy, USMC, and air force, EW is an operations function. EW = EA, EP, ES. ES is SIGINT.

It becomes obvious that the FSO does not have a monopoly on the fires system. In fact, currently the FSO is not even the resident expert in most of these systems. I suggest that we, as an army, need to remedy that problem. If all this falls under a single fires system (COA 1 or COA 2) and we align these capabilities under one fires construct (COA 1 or COA 2), then we will get better at this. It may hurt at first, but I contend that we will rise to the challenge and produce officers, warrant officers, and NCOs that are truly masters of these difficult concepts.

Electronic attack close target reconnaissance (EA CTR) is the biggest killer on the battlefield. The army has lost the ability to do EW. We are broken. There was a recommended fix to all this back in 2005. Randolph AFB teaches the joint EW course at San Antonio, approximately 124 days of instruction. The recommendation was to create an army EW course that covered all the theory applications which were important and physics requirements which guide the underpinnings of EW but none of the aircraft specific requirements (self-protect, navigation, etc.). CAC developed a POI to address many of these requirements but the whole effort stalled. Within that construct, I doubt very seriously that anyone has thought about some of the second- and third-order effects of standing up a robust EW branch in the army. Will we move to air platforms (UAV, helo, A-10, EA-6B) while simultaneously adding emerging technologies like tracking, tagging, and locating (TTL) to those same platforms? The modern battlefield can be electronically mapped and when the ROE catches up, we will be able to target and conduct direct and indirect fires on to these types of targets.

A quick synopsis: CNO: Part of a 21st-century electronic warfare capability (non-lethal fires). STO: (lethal/non-lethal fires). PSYOP (non-lethal fires). The reserve PSYOP already belongs to FORSCOM. Only the active-duty element belongs to USASOC. This does not pass the "common sense" test. Beyond that, the entire requirement for all of it to be airborne should be aligned against support requirements rather than all of it to be airborne for the sake of being an airborne capability.

I question the logic of any approach that wants to create five to six more work groups where one previously existed and worked effectively. That is the moral equivalent of getting rid of the company, battalion, and brigade model and replacing it with some new concept that added in six more coordinating requirements between the brigade, battalion, and the company.

Endnotes

Chapter 1

1. Eric Schmitt, "Iraq-Bound Troops Confront Rumsfeld Over Lack of Armor." *The New York Times* December 8, 2004. www.nytimes.com/2004/12/08/international/middleeast/iraqbound-troops-confront-rumsfeld-over-lack-of.html.
2. There are two main authorities for terrorism designations of groups and individuals. Groups can be designated as *Foreign Terrorist Organizations* under the Immigration and Nationality Act. Under Executive Order (E.O.) 13224, a wider range of entities, including terrorist groups, individuals acting as part of a terrorist organization, and other entities such as financiers and front companies, can be designated as *Specially Designated Global Terrorists* (SDGTs).

Chapter 2

1. Sun Tzu, *The Art of War*. New York: Buccaneer Books, 1976.
2. Kenneth F. McKenzie, *The Revenge of the Melians: Asymmetric Threats & the Next QDR*. April 2007. www.ndu.edu/inss/McNair/mcnair62/toc.html.
3. Harry Summers, *On Strategy: A Critical Analysis of the Vietnam War*. Monterey: Presidio Press, 1982.
4. Helen Chapin Metz, *Algeria a Country Study: Area Handbook Series*. Washington, D.C.: Library of Congress, Field Research Division, 1994.
5. Ibid.
6. Ibid.
7. Douglas Porch, *The French Foreign Legion*. New York: Harper Collins Publishers, 1991.
8. Ibid.
9. Ibid.
10. Ibid.
11. Ibid.
12. Ibid.
13. Ibid.
14. Ibid.
15. Ibid.
16. Helen Chapin Metz, *Algeria a Country Study: Area Handbook Series*. Washington, D.C.: Library of Congress, Field Research Division, 1994.
17. Jonathan R. White, *Terrorism and Homeland Security*, Fifth Edition. Belmont, CA: Thomson Wadsworth, 2006, p. 190.
18. Ibid., p. 192.
19. Trita Parsi, "It's Not Just About Hezbollah." April 2007. www.atimes.com/atimes/Middle_East/HG20Ak03.html.

20. General consensus of senior leaders in OIF V-VII, Multi-National Corps-Iraq, Multiple Briefings, September 05–October 06, Iraq.
21. Russell F. Weigley, *The American Way of War: A History of United States Military Strategy and Policy*, First Edition. New York: Macmillan Publishing Co. Inc., 1973.

Chapter 3

1. I wrote most of this in early 2007, after being called back to Iraq, to be the Commander MNF-I's personal Counter-IED advisor. There was no understanding throughout the force on how to deal with this problem. I was and to some degree and still am an advocate of creating some type of mobile counter-IED strike force-enabling specialization.
2. Rick Atkinson. The Single Most Effective Weapon Against Our Deployed Forces. *The Washington Post*, 2007. www.washingtonpost.com/wp-srv/world/specials/leftofboom/index.html.
3. "IEDs: The Poor Man's Artillery," *The Week*, January 8, 2015. https://theweek.com/articles/508637/ieds-poor-mans-artillery. General Meigs also visited MND-N when then LTC Matter had already brought this up in 2005 and 2006 during his multiple tours in Iraq.
4. While stated earlier in this book, there is no doubt that the enemy perceived the U.S. national will as a weakness. Having left Lebanon and Somalia without having achieved U.S. objectives, it is fairly easy to see how the enemy would have come to that perception.
5. James Dunnigan, "IED Characteristics." www.strategypage.com/dls/articles2005/20053108.asp.
6. Michael Carden, "IED class improves Soldiers' safety." Army News Service. www.globalsecurity.org/military/library/news/2005/03/mil-050307-arnews01.htm.
7. Globalsecurity, "Improvised Explosive Devices (IEDs)/Booby Traps IED Overview." www.globalsecurity.org/military/intro/ied.htm.
8. Ibid.
9. Joe Strange, *Centers of Gravity & Critical Vulnerabilities: Building on the Clausewitzian Foundation So That We Can All Speak the Same Language*. Quantico, VA: Marine Corps University, 1996.
10. United States Army, John F. Kennedy Special Warfare Center and School, *Political Military Analysis Handbook*, 2003. This manual details out 16 different political military factors which also impact understanding the operational area and environment that forces could be operating in.
11. LTC (Ret.) Antulio Echevarria, *Clausewitz's Center of Gravity: Changing our Warfighting Doctrine Again*. Carlisle Barracks, PA: Strategic Studies Institute, 2002. www.clausewitz.com/readings/Echevarria/gravity.pdf.
12. Ibid.
13. Rick Atkinson. "The Single Most Effective Weapon Against Our Deployed Forces." *The Washington Post*, 2007. www.washingtonpost.com/wp-srv/world/specials/leftofboom/index.html.
14. Tony Capaccio, "More U.S. Troops Die in Iraq Bombings Even as Armoring Improves." *Bloomberg*, 2007. www.bloomberg.com/apps/news?pid=10000103&sid=aftH7bcepI8I&refer=us.
15. H. John Poole, *Tactics of the Crescent Moon: Militant Muslim Combat Methods*. Emerald Isle, NC: Posterity Press, 2004. This is an important concept to note that while the Arabs are awful at conventional force-on-force battles and wars, they appear to be exceptional when fighting asymmetric or guerilla campaigns. This was also consistent with my earlier comment on the global security comparison between Arabs and Vietnamese.
16. Robert D. Steele, *Studies in Asymmetry the New Craft of Intelligence: Achieving Asymmetric Advantage in the Face of Nontraditional Threats*. Carlisle Barracks, PA: Strategic Studies Institute, 2002.
17. Ike Skelton, "America's Frontier Wars: Lessons for Asymmetric Conflicts," *Military Review* September–October 2001. Fort Leavenworth: Combined Arms Center, 2001.

18. DK Matai, The World beyond 11th September: Focus on Asymmetric Warfare. 1 Whitehall, RTC: Keynote Speech, October 22, 2001. www.mi2g.com/cgi/mi2g/reports/speeches/221001.pdf.
19. Charles E. Heller & William A. Stofft, *America's First Battles, 1776–1965*. Lawrence, KS: University Press of Kansas, 1986.
20. Bernard B. Fall, *Street Without Joy*. New York: Schocken Books, 1964.
21. Department of the Army, Pamphlet 20-243. Historical Study: German Antiguerrilla Operations in the Balkans (1941–1944). Washington, D.C., Government Printing Office, 1954.
22. Mao Tse Tung, *On Guerilla Warfare*. 1937. www.marxists.org/reference/archive/mao/works/1937/guerrilla-warfare/.
23. T. E. Lawrence, *Seven Pillars of Wisdom*. New York: Doubleday, 1926.
24. Jonathan R. White, *Terrorism and Homeland Security*, Fifth Edition. Belmont: Thompson Wadsworth, 2006.
25. H. John Poole, 2004.
26. Ahmed S. Hashim, MEI Perspective: The Sunni Insurgency In Iraq, 2003. https://conference.brtrc.com/CamelConference/resources/Sunni_Insurgency_in_Iraq.pdf.
27. Sandra Mackey, *The Reckoning: Iraq and the Legacy of Saddam Hussein*. New York: W. W. Norton & Company Inc., 2003.
28. John L. Esposito, *What Everyone Needs to Know About Islam*. New York: Oxford University Press, 2002.
29. Rohan Gunarata, Suicide Terrorism: A Global Threat, 2000. www.pbs.org/frontlineworld/stories/srilanka/globalthreat.html and Inside Al Qaeda Global Network of Terror. New York: Berkley Books, 2003.
30. Ahmed Rashid, *Taliban: Militant Islam, Oil, and Fundamentalism in Central Asia*. New York: Yale Nota Bene Books, 2001.
31. Dictionary.com, Definition of "Asymmetric Warfare," 2007. www.dictionary.com/browse/asymmetrical-warfare.
32. Kenneth F. McKenzie, The Revenge of the Melians: Asymmetric Threats & the Next QDR. April 2007, www.ndu.edu/inss/McNair62/toc.html.
33. John A. Nagl, *Counterinsurgency Lessons from Malaya and Vietnam: Learning to Eat Soup with a Knife*. Westport, CT: Praeger, 2002.
34. John L. Esposito, *What Everyone Needs to Know About Islam*. New York: Oxford University Press, 2002.
35. Ibid.
36. Jonathan R. White, *Terrorism and Homeland Security*, Fifth Edition. Belmont: Thompson Wadsworth, 2006.
37. Bruce Hoffman, *Holy Terror: The Implications of Religious Terrorism*. Rand, 1993.
38. Rick Atkinson, "The Single Most Effective Weapon Against Our Deployed Forces." *The Washington Post*, 2007. www.washingtonpost.com/wp-srv/world/specials/leftofboom/index.html.
39. James E. Szepesy, The Strategic Corporal and the Emerging Battlefield: The Nexus Between the USMC's Three Block War: Concept and Network Centric Warfare, 2005. http://fletcher.tufts.edu/research/2005/Szepesy.pdf.
40. Sun Tzu, *The Art of War*. New York: Buccaneer Books, 1976.
41. Gareth Porter, "POLITICS: U.S. Military Ignored Evidence of Iraqi-Made EFPs," October 25, 2007. www.ipsnews.net/2007/10/politics-us-military-ignored-evidence-of-iraqi-made-efps/.
42. John A. Nagl & Jonathan White in their respective texts provide opinions that when examined statistically, most irregular warfare movements do not succeed. This is statistically true and relevant to this discussion in terms planning on worst case scenario. It is also critical to the premise in this chapter that IED enabled asymmetric warfare potentially changes this equation.

43. Roger Trinquier, *A French View of Counterinsurgency*. London: Pall Mall Press, 1961.
44. John A. Nagl, *Counterinsurgency Lessons from Malaya and Vietnam: Learning to Eat Soup with a Knife*. Westport, CT: Praeger, 2002.
45. Utilizing the concept of a reverse center of gravity study as espoused by Dr. Strange, one of the primary center-of-gravity elements is the support and national will of the U.S. population. Thus, casualties become the critical vulnerability which links back to that center of gravity.
46. Rick Atkinson. The Single Most Effective Weapon Against Our Deployed Forces. *The Washington Post*, 2007. www.washingtonpost.com/wp-srv/world/specials/leftofboom/index.html.
47. Ibid.
48. Mao Tse Tung, *On Guerilla Warfare*. 1937. www.marxists.org/reference/archive/mao/works/1937/guerrilla-warfare/.
49. George S. Patton, Paul, S. Harkins & Beatrice Banning Ayer Patton, *War as I Knew It*. Boston: Houghton Mifflin Co., 1947.
50. Richard Halloran, "Strategic Communication." *Parameters*, Autumn 2007. www.carlisle.army.mil/usawc/Parameters/07autumn/halloran.htm.
51. Russell F. Weigley, *The American Way of War: A History of United States Military Strategy and Policy*. New York: Macmillan Publishing Co. Inc., 1973.
52. The Manhattan Project had approximately 40 laboratories and factories and involved nearly 200,000 people. https//manhatttanprojectmegsar.weebly.com/people-involved.html.

Chapter 4

1. This chapter and the next chapter arose from an exercise to define the root causes of resistance by using both the Center of Gravity (COG) theory and the methodology taught at United States Army John F. Kennedy Special Warfare Center (JFKSWC) to understand a particular area, by focusing on what are referred to political military factors.
2. Paul Melshen, The JUSMAG in the Philippines, 1947–55: Lessons Learned from a Successful Counterinsurgency Campaign, *Low Intensity Conflict & Law Enforcement*, Vol. 6, No. 1, Summer 1997. London: Frank Cass, 1997.
3. Paul Melshen, Joint Forces Staff College, Low Intensity Conflict, Insurgency & Counterinsurgency Warfare: Theory, Case Studies & Applications Lectures, October 2009.
4. Eric Shinseki, General, U.S. Army, Army Chief of Staff brief to Senate Armed Services Committee, February 25, 2003.
5. This was written tongue in cheek while taking an elective at Joint and Combined Warfighting School and a portion of this chapter was written as a paper for that class. Dr. Melshen was the instructor for this class and this was in a sense having a bit of fun with my instructor for that class, to see if he got a kick out of reading that. Sarcasm is often misunderstood when conducting it during an exercise like this but it was well received. The instructor got a laugh out of it.
6. Paul Melshen, Joint Forces Staff College, Low Intensity Conflict, Insurgency & Counterinsurgency Warfare: Theory, Case Studies & Applications Lectures on the Mau Mau Insurgency, October 2009.
7. "Fulda Gap is Key Point in NATO Defense Against Soviet Forces," *Los Angeles Times*, March 1, 1987. www.latimes.com/archives/la-xpm-1987-03-01-mn-6926-story.html. This was always the conventional scenario that NATO and U.S. forces anticipated where the Soviet Union would attack through.
8. Paul Melshen, Joint Forces Staff College, Low Intensity Conflict, Insurgency & Counterinsurgency Warfare: Theory, Case Studies & Applications Lectures and class materials, Malaysia case study, October 2009.

9. Micheal Hastings, "The Runaway General: The profile that brought down McChrystal" was what appeared to be the cause for the relief of General McChrystal. www.rollingstone.com/politics/politics-news/the-runaway-general-the-profile-that-brought-down-mcchrystal-192609/, 2009. I just don't see a bit of sarcasm or callousness as rising to the same level of the insubordination of MacArthur in Korea and consequently question the decision to relieve McChrystal. On the other hand, I grew up in this community between having served in 19th Special Forces Group while at Colorado State and then later the Rangers and Elite Special Mission Units. You develop pretty thick skin when working in places like that and consequently don't get offended at much when it comes to levity. Better to be able to laugh at bad situations than freak out over stupidity.
10. James Holmes, "Unorthodox and Chaotic: How America Should Fight Wars: 'A serious problem in planning against American doctrine is that the Americans do not read their manuals,'" *The Diplomat*, September 27, 2017. https://thediplomat.com/2013/09/unorthodox-and-chaotic-how-america-should-fight-wars.

Chapter 6

1. Joe Strange, *Centers of Gravity & Critical Vulnerabilities: Building on the Clausewitzian Foundation So That We Can All Speak the Same Language.* Quantico, VA: Marine Corps University, 1996.
2. Ibid.
3. Ibid.
4. Ibid.
5. Ibid.

Chapter 8

1. Defense Threat Reduction Agency, Joint Improvised-Threat Defeat Organization (JIDO), *History*, 2018. www.jieddo.mil/history.htm.
2. Defense Threat Reduction Agency (DTRA), *History*. 2018. www.dtra.mil/Mission/.
3. Ibid.
4. Ibid.
5. Jonathan R. White, *Terrorism and Homeland Security*, Fifth Edition, Belmont: Thompson Wadsworth, 2006.
6. Matthew Engel, "Scorned General's Tactics Proved Right," *The Guardian*. March 29, 2003. www.theguardian.com/world/2003/mar/29/iraq.usa.
7. Department of Defense (DOD), Joint Publication 3-0., Operations, 2017. www.dtic.mil/doctrine/new_pubs/jp3_0.pdf.
8. Cherish M. Zinn, "Consequences of Iraqi De-Baathification," *Cornell International Affairs Review*, 2016. www.inquiriesjournal.com/articles/1415/consequences-of-iraqi-de-baathification.
9. Department of Defense (DOD), Joint Publication 3-0., Operations, 2017. www.dtic.mil/doctrine/new_pubs/jp3_0.pdf.
10. Any decent planner knows that assumptions replace facts in the absence of known information. When the decision to DeBa'athify occurred, the assumption that we could use the Iraqi Army as a constabulary force was no longer valid, and that assumption was replaced with factual information that rendered the existing force structure inadequate for the task it was being assigned. This should have triggered massive deployments to stand up more stabilization forces in Iraq. Honestly, it should have been done prior to the announcement and the forces should have ideally

been on the ground prepared to take over the mission prior to ever embarking on any type of DeBa'athification approach.
11. J. Ismay, "The Most Lethal Weapons Americans Faced in Iraq." *The New York Times*, October 18, 2013. https://atwar.blogs.nytimes.com/2013/10/18/the-most-lethal-weapon-americans-faced-in-iraq/.
12. It was touch and go for a while. I had personal conversations with the Commander of MNF-I regarding the total number of KIA in Iraq because I was brought back to work specifically on that problem. I think we all realized that we couldn't sustain 127 KIA a month and that we knew that when we increased the operational tempo and put forces outside the FOB, that initially KIA and casualties would go up but over the long haul it went down and eventually to five, and then one day it was zero.
13. Tom Varden, "UAVs Help to Mitigate IED Threat in Afghanistan." *Unmanned System News*, July 17, 2012. www.unmannedsystemstechnology.com/2012/07/uavs-help-to-mitigate-ied-threat-in-afghanistan/.
14. Mathew D. Matter, *Unmanned Aerial Vehicles and Improvised Explosive Devices, Asymmetric Warfare, and the Impacts of this Technology.* Embry Riddle Aeronautical University, 2018.
15. Mark Pomerleau, "Army addressing an emerging threat: Drones as IEDs." *Defense System*, 2015. https://defensesystems.com/articles/2015/07/10/army-drones-as-ieds-defense.aspx.
16. Heather Clark, "IED detector developed by Sandia Labs being transferred to Army," 2014. https://share-ng.sandia.gov/news/resources/news_releases/copperhead_army.
17. Daniel McCoy, "FAA forecast: Slow general aviation growth, drone explosion." *Wichita Business Journal*, 2017. www.bizjournals.com/wichita/news/2017/03/22/faa-forecast-slow-general-aviation-growth-drone.html.
18. Kris Osborn, "The U.S. Army is Now Under Attack by Enemy Drones," *The National Interest*, October 23, 2017. http://nationalinterest.org/blog/the-buzz/the-us-army-now-under-attack-by-enemy-drones-22858.
19. Natalie Johnson, "FBI Warns Terrorists Groups Could Soon Launch Drone Attack Against U.S.," *Freebeacon*, 2017. http://freebeacon.com/national-security/fbi-director-warns-terrorist-groups-soon-launch-drone-attack-u-s/.
20. Robert K. Ackerman, "Unmanned Systems the New Weapon for Terrorists," 2017. https://www.globenewswire.com/news-release/2017/07/13/1044193/0/en/Unmanned-Systems-the-New-Weapon-for-Terrorists.html.
21. Daniel McCoy, "FAA forecast: Slow general aviation growth, drone explosion." *Wichita Business Journal*, 2017. www.bizjournals.com/wichita/news/2017/03/22/faa-forecast-slow-general-aviation-growth-drone.html.
22. United States Department of Transportation Federal Aviation Administration (FAA), How NextGen Works, 2018. www.faa.gov/nextgen/how_nextgen_works/.
23. Dante Alighieri, *The Divine Comedy: The Vision of Purgatory*, 1321. www.gutenberg.org/files/8800/8800-h/files/8795/8795-h/8795-h.htm.
24. Douglas Waller, How the OSS Shaped the CIA and American Special OPS, 2015. https://warontherocks.com/2015/09/how-the-oss-shaped-the-cia-and-american-special-ops/.
25. Russell F. Weigley, *The American Way of War: A History of United States Military Strategy and Policy*, First Edition. New York: Macmillan Publishing Co. Inc., 1973.

Chapter 9

1. Caroline Rees, "UAVs Help to Mitigate IED Threat in Afghanistan." *Unmanned System News*, July 17, 2012. www.unmannedsystemstechnology.com/2012/07/uavs-help-to-mitigate-ied-threat-in-afghanistan/.

ENDNOTES • 247

2. Mark Pomerleau, "Army addressing an emerging threat: Drones as IEDs." *Defense System*, 2015. https://defensesystems.com/articles/2015/07/10/army-drones-as-ieds-defense.aspx.
3. Ibid.
4. Federal Aviation Administration, Drones by the Numbers (as of 10/1/24), https://www.faa.gov/node/54496.
5. Heather Clark, "IED detector developed by Sandia Labs being transferred to Army," 2014. https://share-ng.sandia.gov/news/resources/news_releases/copperhead_army.
6. Daniel McCoy, "FAA forecast: Slow general aviation growth, drone explosion." *Wichita Business Journal*, 2017. www.bizjournals.com/wichita/news/2017/03/22/faa-forecast-slow-general-aviation-growth-drone.html.
7. The White House, FACT SHEET: New Commitments to Accelerate the Safe Integration of Unmanned Aircraft Systems, 2016, https://obamawhitehouse.archives.gov/the-press-office/2016/08/02/fact-sheet-new-commitments-accelerate-safe-integration-unmanned-aircraft.
8. United States Department of Transportation, Federal Aviation Administration (FAA), Statement by Ellwell, D. Unmanned Aircraft Systems Integration: Emerging Uses in A Changing National Airspace, 2017. www.transportation.gov/content/unmanned-aircraft-systems-integration-emerging-uses-changing-national-airspace.
9. Elizabeth A. Tennyson, "Watchdog Report Highlights Problems with NextGen mandate: AOPA Seeks Cost-Effective, Flexible Solutions," September 25, 2014. www.aopa.org/news-and-media/all-news/2014/september/25/watchdog-report-highlights-problems-with-nextgen-mandate.
10. United States Department of Transportation Federal Aviation Administration (FAA), Automatic Dependent Surveillance Broadcast (ADS-B), 2019. www.faa.gov/nextgen/programs/adsb/.
11. Darlene Storm, "Curious Hackers Inject Ghost Airplanes into Radar, Track Celebrities," 2012. www.computerworld.com/article/2472455/cybercrime-hacking/curious-hackers-inject-ghost-airplanes-into-radar--track-celebrities--flights.html.
12. United States Department of Transportation, Federal Motor Carrier Safety Administration (FMCSA), Analysis and Information Online: Crash Statistics, Large Trucks and Buses, Driver Citations Issue, 2019. https://ai.fmcsa.dot.gov/CrashStatistics/rptDriver.aspx?rpt=DCIC.
13. *Mercury News*, "Editorial: Coming soon—a weaponized drone terrorist attack near you, unless we act," 2017. www.mercurynews.com/2017/10/14/editorial-coming-soon-a-weaponized-drone-terrorist-attack-near-you-unless-we-act/.
14. Sarah Mccamon, "The Warfare May Be Remote But The Trauma Is Real," April 24, 2017. www.npr.org/2017/04/24/525413427/for-drone-pilots-warfare-may-be-remote-but-the-trauma-is-real.
15. W. J. Hennigan, "Air Force struggles to add drone pilots and address fatigue and stress," *Los Angeles Times*, November 9, 2015. www.latimes.com/nation/la-na-drone-pilot-crisis-20151109-story.html.
16. A. Butler, "In Reversal, USAF Plans Automatic Takeoff and Landings, For Reapers," *Aviation Week*, July 23, 2015. hcttp://aviationweek.com/defense/reversal-usaf-plans-automatic-takeoffs-landings-reapers.

Chapter 10

1. Joint Fires Executive Steering Committee Annual Conference briefing from General Stephen Townsend, February 2019, Virginia Beach.
2. DOTMLPF is an acronym used in the military for Doctrine, Organization, Training, Material, Personnel, and Facilities.
3. The geographical combatant commanders are referred to COCOMs and this comprised the five 4-star commands which include U.S. Africa Command (AFRICOM), U.S. Central Command (CENTCOM) U.S. European Command (EUCOM), U.S Indonesia and Pacific Command (INDOPACOM), and U.S. Southern Command (SOUTCOM).

4. United States Army, Field Manual 6-40, Manual Cannon Gunnery, Tactics, Techniques, and Procedures. https://usacac.army.mil/sites/default/files/misc/doctrine/CDG/cdg_resources/manuals/fm/fm6_40.pdf.
5. United States Army, Field Manual 3-13 Information Operations (2003), 2003. www.globalsecurity.org/military/library/policy/army/fm/3-13/fm3-13.pdf.
6. Department of Defense, Joint Publication 3-13 Information Operations (2006), 2006. www.globalsecurity.org/intell/library/policy/dod/joint/jp3_13_2006.pdf.

Chapter 11

1. Heller, Charles E. & William A. Stofft, *America's First Battles, 1776–1965*. Lawrence, KS: University Press of Kansas, 1986, p. 338.
2. H. R. McMaster, *Battle Grounds: The Fight to Defend the Free World*. New York: Harper Collins Publishers, 2020, p. 127.
3. Erwin Rommel, *Infantry Attacks*. Provo, UT: Athena Press, 1979.
4. The concept known as "Winchester" is fighter pilot terminology for being out of weapons. In the context of GPC, once hostilities break out it would be exceptionally bad to not have the required weapons to prosecute this fight to conclusion.

Chapter 12

1. Stanley McChrystal, "It Takes a Network." *Foreign Policy*, February 21, 2011. https://foreignpolicy.com/2011/02/21/it-takes-a-network/.
2. OODA LOOP.
3. Make More Maritime ISR Weapons and Tactics Instructors | Proceedings, July 2023 Vol. 149/7/1,445 (usni.org); www.usni.org/magazines/proceedings/2023/july/make-more-maritime-isr-weapons-and-tactics-instructors.
4. Joint Publication 3-0, Joint Operations. https://irp.fas.org/doddir/dod/jp3_0.pdf.
5. Joint Publication 5-0., Joint Planning. https://irp.fas.org/doddir/dod/jp5_0.pdf.
6. Make More Maritime ISR Weapons and Tactics Instructors | Proceedings, July 2023 Vol. 149/7/1,445 (usni.org); www.usni.org/magazines/proceedings/2023/july/make-more-maritime-isr-weapons-and-tactics-instructors
7. F2T2EA.
8. Joint Publication 3-0, Joint Operations. https://irp.fas.org/doddir/dod/jp3_0.pdf.

Conclusion

1. Serhy Yekelchyk. "The Ukrainian Crisis: In Russia's Long Shadow," *Origins: Current Events in Historical Perspective*. Ohio State University, Vol. 7, Spring 2014. http://origins.osu.edu/article/ukrainian-crisis-russias-long-shadow.

Bibliography

Ackerman, Robert, K., "Unmanned Systems the New Weapon for Terrorists," July 13, 2017. https://www.globenewswire.com/news-release/2017/07/13/1044193/0/en/Unmanned-Systems-the-New-Weapon-for-Terrorists.html.

Alighieri, Dante, The Divine Comedy: The Vision of Purgatory, 1321. https://www.gutenberg.org/cache/epub/8795/pg8795-images.html.

Air Force Association (AFA), "Air Force vs Army Concepts for UAV employment." http://secure.afa.org/grl/UAV_CONOPS.pdf.

Allen, Thad, ADM (USCG). "Friend or Foe? Tough to Tell." *Proceedings*. October 2008. https://www.usni.org/magazines/proceedings/2008/october/friend-or-foe-tough-tell.

American Fuel and Petrochemical Manufacturers, "Unmanned Aircraft Systems (UAS) Toolkit," 2018. https://www.icao.int/Newsroom/Pages/icao-launches-unmanned-aircraft-systems-toolkit.aspx.

American Society for Testing and Materials, The History of ASTM International, https://www.astm.org/about/125th-anniversary/astm-timeline.html.

Anderson, Brian, "The Drone Doctors," July 17, 2015. Vice. https://www.vice.com/en/article/the-drone-doctors/.

Atkinson, Rick, "Left of Boom: The Struggle to Defeat Roadside Bombs." *The Washington Post*, November 8, 2007. https://www.washingtonpost.com/wp-srv/world/specials/leftofboom/index.html.

Author unknown, Crew Resource Management, 2017, https://skybrary.aero/articles/crew-resource-management-crm.

Author unknown, "U.S. Intelligence Support to Find, Fix, Finish Operations," Zone d'Intérêt. June 10, 2015. http://zonedinteret.blogspot.com/2015/10/us-intelligence-support-to-find-fix.html.

Avihai, Hillel. "Aviation Security: The Human Eye vs. Detection Technology." International Institute for Counter-Terrorism, 2009. https://ict.org.il/aviation-security-the-human-eye-vs-detection-technology/.

Bamberger, Robert L. & Lawrence Kumins. "Oil and Gas: Supply Issue after Katrina." Congressional Research Service RS22233, September 6, 2005.

Blinkinsop, S., Matter, M., & Richard, C., "The 21st Century Maginot Line: The United States government's failure to grasp the implications of the Improvised Explosive Device: Another 9/11 … it's closer than you think!" 2009. Joint Forces Staff College.

Butler, A., "In Reversal, USAF Plans Automatic Takeoff and Landings, For Reapers," July 23, 2015. *Aviation Week*. http://aviationweek.com/defense/reversal-usaf-plans-automatic-takeoffs-landings-reapers.

Capaccio, Tony, "More U.S. Troops Die in Iraq Bombings Even as Armoring Improves," *Bloomberg*, October 13, 2005. www.bloomberg.com/apps/news?pid=10000103&sid=aftH7bcepI8I&refer=us.

Carden, Michael J. SGT, "IED awareness class." *DVIDS*, April 1, 2005. https://www.dvidshub.net/news/1467/ied-awareness-class.

Chatterjee, Pratap, "A Chilling New Post-Traumatic Stress Disorder: Why Drone Pilots are Quitting in Record Numbers," *Salon*, March 6, 2015. www.salon.com/2015/03/06/a_chilling_new_post_traumatic_stress_disorder_why_drone_pilots_are_quitting_in_record_numbers_partner/.

Clark, Heather, "IED detector developed by Sandia Labs being transferred to Army," https://news-releases.sandia.gov/copperhead_army/#:~:text=Sandia%27s%20Copperhead%20%E2%80%94%20a%20highly%20modified,Sandia%20senior%20manager%20Jim%20Hudgens.

Clausewitz, Carl von, *On War*, Germany: Von Kriege, 1832.

Collins, John M., *Military Strategy: Principles, Practices, and Historical Perspectives*. Dulles, VA: Brasseys Inc., 2002.

Commercial Vehicle Safety Alliance (CVSA), CVSA Releases 2018 Operation Safe Driver Week Results," September 18, 2018. https://www.cvsa.org/news/2018-osd-week-results/.

Defense Threat Reduction Agency, Joint Improvised-Threat Defeat Organization (JIDO), (n.d.). *History*. https://www.dvidshub.net/news/169850/joint-improvised-threat-defeat-agency-established-new-mission-set.

Defense Threat Reduction Agency (DTRA), (n.d.). *History*. www.dtra.mil/Mission/ (accessed May 11, 2018).

Department of the Army, Pamphlet 20-243, *Historical Study: German Antiguerrilla Operations in the Balkans (1941–1944)*. Washington, D.C.: Government Printing Office, 1954.

Department of Defense (DOD), Joint Publication 3-0, Operations, 2017. https://www.moore.army.mil/mssp/security%20topics/Potential%20Adversaries/content/pdf/JP%203-0.pdf.

Dunnigan, James, IED Characteristics, 2005. www.strategypage.com/dls/articles2005/20053108.asp.

Duudu, P., "Unmanned and unmatched: the world's deadliest drones." *Army Technology*, January 19, 2016. www.army-technology.com/features/featurethe-worlds-top-military-drones-4785852/.

Echevarria, Antulio, *Clausewitz's Center of Gravity: Changing Our Warfighting Doctrine Again*. Carlisle, PA: Strategic Studies Institute, U.S. Army War College, 2002.

Engel, Matthew, "Scorned General's Tactics Proved Right," *The Guardian*. March 29, 2003. www.theguardian.com/world/2003/mar/29/iraq.usa.

Esposito, John L., *What Everyone Needs to Know About Islam*. New York: Oxford University Press, 2002.

European Defence Agency (EDA), "EDA programme launched to improve IED Detection." January 12, 2017. www.eda.europa.eu/info-hub/press-centre/latest-news/2017/01/12/eda-programme-launched-to-improve-ied-detection.

Fall, Bernard B., *Street Without Joy*. New York: Schocken Books, 1964.

Globalsecurity, Improvised Explosive Devices (IEDs)/Booby Traps: IED Overview, 2007. www.globalsecurity.org/military/intro/ied.htm.

Gunaratna, Rohan, *Inside Al Qaeda: Global Network of Terror*. New York: Berkley Books, 2003.

Gunaratna, Rohan, "Suicide Terrorism: A Global Threat," 2000. www.pbs.org/frontlineworld/stories/srilanka/globalthreat.html.

Halloran, Richard, Strategic Communication. From Parameters, Autumn 2007. https://press.armywarcollege.edu/parameters/vol37/iss3/18/.

Handel, Michael I., *Masters of War: Classic Strategic Thought*, Third Edition. London: Frank Cass Publishers, 2001.

Hardison, Chaitra. et al., Stress and Dissatisfaction in the Air Force's Remotely Piloted Aircraft Community: Focus Group Findings. Santa Monica, CA: RAND Corporation, 2017. www.rand.org/content/dam/rand/pubs/research_reports/RR1700/RR1756/RAND_RR1756.pdf.

Hashim, Ahmed S., MEI Perspective: The Sunni Insurgency in Iraq, 2003. https://conference.brtrc.com/CamelConference/resources/Sunni_Insurgency_in_Iraq.pdf.

Heavy Duty Trucking (HDT), "2019 CVSA Safe Driver Week Focuses on Speeding," April 30, 2019. www.truckinginfo.com/330850/2019-cvsa-safe-driver-week-focuses-on-speeding.

Heller, Charles E. & Stofft, William A., *America's First Battles, 1776–1965*, Lawrence, KS: University Press of Kansas, 1986.

Hennigan, W. J., "Air Force struggles to add drone pilots and address fatigue and stress," *Los Angeles Times*, November 9, 2015. www.latimes.com/nation/la-na-drone-pilot-crisis-20151109-story.html.

Hoffman, Bruce, *Holy Terror: The Implications of Religious Terrorism*. Santa Monica, CA: RAND Corporation, 1993.

Holmes, James, "Unorthodox and Chaotic: How America Should Fight Wars: 'A serious problem in planning against American doctrine is that the Americans do not read their manuals,'" *The Diplomat*, September 23, 2017. https://thediplomat.com/2013/09/unorthodox-and-chaotic-how-america-should-fight-wars/.

Ismay, John, "The Most Lethal Weapons Americans Faced in Iraq." *The New York Times*, October 18, 2013. https://atwar.blogs.nytimes.com/2013/10/18/the-most-lethal-weapon-americans-faced-in-iraq/.

Jenkins, Darryl & Bijan Vasigh, *The Economic Impact of Unmanned Aircraft Systems Integration in the United States*. Arlington, VA: The Association for Unmanned Vehicle Systems International (AUVSI), 2013.

Johnson, Natalie, "FBI Warns Terrorists Groups Could Soon Launch Drone Attack Against U.S." *The Washington Free Beacon*, September 28, 2017. http://freebeacon.com/national-security/fbi-director-warns-terrorist-groups-soon-launch-drone-attack-u-s/.

Joint Fires Executive Steering Committee Annual Conference briefing from General Stephen Townsend, February 2019, Virginia Beach.

Joyner, James, "Kerry on Iraq: Wrong War, Wrong Place, Wrong Time," *Outside the Beltway*. https://outsidethebeltway.com/kerry_on_iraq_wrong_war_wrong_place_wrong_time/.

Kagan, Julia, "What Is Hawala? Money Transfer Without Money Movement," *Investopedia*, December 2017, 2023. www.investopedia.com/terms/h/hawala.asp.

Kanki, B., Helmerich R., & Anca, J., *Crew Resource Management*. San Diego, CA: Academic Press, 2010.

Karl, Jonathon, "Surface-to-Air Missile Downed U.S. Chopper in Iraq." *ABC World News*, January 17, 2006. http://abcnews.go.com/WNT/International/story?id=1515168 (accessed October 22, 2009).

Lal, Rollie, Jackson, Brian A., Chalk, Peter, Ali, Farhana & Rosenau, William, The MIPT Terrorism Annual Report, 2006, MIPT. www.tkb.org/documents/Downloads/2006-MIPT-Terrorism-Annual.pdf.

Lawrence, T. E., *Seven Pillars of Wisdom*. New York: Doubleday, 1926.

Liddell Hart, B. H., *Strategy*. London: Faber & Faber, 1954.

Locke, R., Fatigue Management in the Airline Industry: Pilot Fatigue, 2014. https://www.linkedin.com/pulse/20141022033120-86096902-fatigue-management-in-the-airline-industry.

Los Angeles Times, "Fulda Gap is Key Point in NATO Defense Against Soviet Forces," March 1, 1987. www.latimes.com/archives/la-xpm-1987-03-01-mn-6926-story.html.

Lowe, Christian, New Source: Counter IED Plus Up in the 'Stans. Defense Tech. www.defensetech.org/archives/005001.html (accessed October 16, 2009).

Mackey, Sandra, *The Reckoning: Iraq and the Legacy of Saddam Hussein*, New York: W. W. Norton & Company Inc., 2003.

Mao Tse-Tung, M., *On Guerilla Warfare*, 1937. www.marxists.org/reference/archive/mao/works/1937/guerrilla-warfare/.

Masson, S., Unmanned Aerial Vehicle Use in Army Brigade Combat Teams: Increasing Effectiveness Across the Spectrum of Conflict, 2006. https://core.ac.uk/download/pdf/36696195.pdf.

Matai, DK. The World Beyond 11th September: Focus on Asymmetric Warfare. 1 Whitehall, RTC: Keynote Speech, October 22, 2001. http://www.mi2g.com/cgi/mi2g/reports/speeches/221001.pdf.

Matter, M., Unmanned Aerial Vehicles and Improvised Explosive Devices, Asymmetric Warfare, and the Impacts of this Technology, Embry Riddle Aeronautical University, 2018.

McCammon, Sarah, "The Warfare May Be Remote but The Trauma Is Real," *NPR*. April 24, 2017. www.npr.org/2017/04/24/525413427/for-drone-pilots-warfare-may-be-remote-but-the-trauma-is-real.

McCoy, Daniel, "FAA forecast: Slow general aviation growth, drone explosion." *Wichita Business Journal*, March 22, 2017. www.bizjournals.com/wichita/news/2017/03/22/faa-forecast-slow-general-aviation-growth-drone.html.

McKenzie, Kenneth, The Revenge of the Melians: Asymmetric Threats & the Next QDR. April 2007. https://apps.dtic.mil/sti/tr/pdf/ADA421982.pdf.

Melshen, Paul, Joint Forces Staff College, Low Intensity Conflict, Insurgency & Counterinsurgency Warfare: Theory, Case Studies & Applications Lectures, October 2009.

Melshen, Paul, Joint Forces Staff College, Low Intensity Conflict, Insurgency & Counterinsurgency Warfare: Theory, Case Studies & Applications Lectures and class materials, Malaysia case study, October 2009.

Melshen, Paul, Joint Forces Staff College, Low Intensity Conflict, Insurgency & Counterinsurgency Warfare: Theory, Case Studies & Applications Lectures on the Mau Mau Insurgency, October 2009.

Melshen, Paul, "The JUSMAG in the Philippines, 1947–55: Lessons Learned from a Successful Counterinsurgency Campaign," *Low Intensity Conflict & Law Enforcement*, Vol. 6, No. 1, Summer 1997. London: Frank Cass, 1997.

Mercer, Charles, *Legion of Strangers: A Vivid History of a Unique Military Tradition—The French Foreign Legion*, New York: Holt, Reinhart, & Winston, 1964.

Mercury News, "Editorial: Coming soon—a weaponized drone terrorist attack near you, unless we act." *The Mercury News*, October 14, 2017. www.mercurynews.com/2017/10/14/editorial-coming-soon-a-weaponized-drone-terrorist-attack-near-you-unless-we-act/.

Metz, Helen Chapin, *Algeria a Country Study: Area Handbook Series*, Washington, D.C. Library of Congress, Field Research Division, 1994.

Mola, Roger, "Do Drones Get Vertigo, Too?", *Smithsonian Magazine*, July 13, 2008. www.airspacemag.com/flight-today/do-drones-get-vertigo-too-1029847/.

Nagl, John A., *Counterinsurgency Lessons from Malaya and Vietnam: Learning to Eat Soup with a Knife*. Westport, CT: Praeger, 2002.

O'Neil, Bard E., *Insurgency and Terrorism: Inside Modern Revolutionary Warfare*. New York: Brassey's Inc., 1990.

Osborn, Kris, "The U.S. Army is Now Under Attack by Enemy Drone," *The National Interest*. October 23, 2017. http://nationalinterest.org/blog/the-buzz/the-us-army-now-under-attack-by-enemy-drones-22858.

Parsi, Trita, "It's Not Just About Hezbollah." April 2007. www.atimes.com/atimes/Middle_East/HG20Ak03.html.

Pekoske, David, "TSA Administrator, remarks to House Homeland Security Appropriations Committee," Transportation Security Administration. April 2, 2019. www.tsa.gov/news/testimony/2019/04/02/examining-presidents-fy-2020-budget-request-transportation-security.

Pelkofski, John, CAPT (USN), "al Qaedea's Maritime Campaign." *Proceedings*. December 2005. www.wbbinc.com/articles/200512_pelkofski_alqaedas.pdf (accessed November 3, 2009).

Pomerleau, Mark, Army addressing an emerging threat: Drones as IEDs. *Defense Systems*, 2015. https://www.defenseone.com/defense-systems/2015/07/army-addressing-an-emerging-threat-drones-as-ieds/191129/?oref=d1-homepage-noscript-river.

Poole, H. John, *Tactics of the Crescent Moon: Militant Muslim Combat Methods*, Emerald Isle, NC: Posterity Press, 2004.

Porch, Douglas, *The French Foreign Legion*. New York: Harper Collins Publishers, 1991.

Porter, Gareth, "POLITICS: U.S. Military Ignored Evidence of Iraqi-Made EFPs." *Inter Press Service News Agency*. October 25, 2007. www.ipsnews.net/2007/10/politics-us-military-ignored-evidence-of-iraqi-made-efps/.

Rashid, Ahmed, *Taliban: Militant Islam, Oil, and Fundamentalism in Central Asia*. New Haven, CT: Yale University Press, 2001.

Rees, Caroline, "LDS Unveils Drone-Based Explosive Detector Sensor." *Unmanned System News*, November 15, 2016. www.unmannedsystemstechnology.com/2016/11/lds-unveils-drone-based-explosive-detection-sensor/.

Rees, Caroline, "UAVs Help to Mitigate IED Threat in Afghanistan." *Unmanned System News*, July 17, 2012. www.unmannedsystemstechnology.com/2012/07/uavs-help-to-mitigate-ied-threat-in-afghanistan/.

Robinson, S., "Unmanned 'river drones' could be used for IED detection, port security." *Stars and Stripes*, August 13, 2011. www.stripes.com/news/unmanned-river-drones-could-be-used-for-ied-detection-port-security-1.151058.

Rosen, Stephen P., *Innovation and the Modern Military: Winning the Next War*, Ithaca, NY: Cornell University, 1991.

Schmitt, Eric. "Iraq-Bound Troops Confront Rumsfeld Over Lack of Armor." *The New York Times*. December 8, 2004. www.nytimes.com/2004/12/08/international/middleeast/iraqbound-troops-confront-rumsfeld-over-lack-of.html.

Schogol, Jeff, "Air Force moves to reduce stress on drone pilot." *Air Force Times*. May 20, 2015. www.airforcetimes.com/news/your-air-force/2015/05/20/air-force-moves-to-reduce-stress-on-drone-pilots/.

Shachtman, Noah, CSI vs. IEDs: Inside Baghdad's Forensic Bomb Squad, 2007. https://www.airforcetimes.com/news/your-air-force/2015/05/20/air-force-moves-to-reduce-stress-on-drone-pilots/#:~:text=The%20Air%20Force%20is%20looking,65%2C%20a%20service%20spokesman%20said.

Shinseki, Eric, General, U.S. Army, Army Chief of Staff brief to Senate Armed Services Committee, February 25, 2003.

Skelton, Congressman Ike, "America's Frontier Wars: Lessons for Asymmetric Conflicts," *Military Review*, September–October 2001, Fort Leavenworth: Combined Arms Center, 2001. https://www.armyupress.army.mil/Portals/7/military-review/Archives/English/MilitaryReview_20140831_art016.pdf

Steele, Robert, D., *Studies in Asymmetry the New Craft of Intelligence: Achieving Asymmetric Advantage in the Face of Nontraditional Threats*. Carlisle Barracks, PA: U.S. Army War College Strategic Studies Institute. 2002.

Storm, Darlene, "Curious Hackers Inject Ghost Airplanes into Radar, Track Celebrities." *Computerworld*. August 1, 2012. www.computerworld.com/article/2472455/cybercrime-hacking/curious-hackers-inject-ghost-airplanes-into-radar--track-celebrities--flights.html.

Strange, Joe, *Centers of Gravity & Critical Vulnerabilities: Building on the Clausewitzian Foundation So That We Can All Speak the Same Language*. Quantico, VA: Marine Corps University Foundation, 1996.

Summers, Harry, *On Strategy: A Critical Analysis of the Vietnam War*. Monterey, CA: Presidio Press, 1982.

Sun Tzu, *The Art of War*. New York: Buccaneer Books, 1976.

Szepesy, James E., The Strategic Corporal and the Emerging Battlefield: The Nexus Between the USMC's Three Block War: Concept and Network Centric Warfare, 2005. https://dl.tufts.edu/pdfviewer/qv33s771j/8336hc616.

Tennyson, E., "Watchdog Report Highlights Problems with NextGen mandate: AOPA Seeks Cost-Effective, flexible solutions." *AOPA*. September 25, 2014. www.aopa.org/news-and-media/all-news/2014/september/25/watchdog-report-highlights-problems-with-nextgen-mandate.

Trinquier, Roger, *A French View of Counterinsurgency*. London: Pall Mall Press, 1961.

The Joint Chiefs of Staff, Joint Publication 1-02 *The Department of Defense Dictionary of Military and Associated Terms*, April 12, 2001, as amended through August 19, 2009.

The White House, "FACT SHEET: New Commitments to Accelerate the Safe Integration of Unmanned Aircraft Systems," 2016. https://obamawhitehouse.archives.gov/the-press-office/2016/08/02/fact-sheet-new-commitments-accelerate-safe-integration-unmanned-aircraft.

United Kingdom Home Office. "International Terrorism: The United Kingdom's Science and Technology Strategy for Countering International Terrorism." UK Home Office, 2009. https://assets.publishing.service.gov.uk/media/5a795e6e40f0b642860d784c/science-and-technology-strategy.pdf.

United States Air Force, "MQ-1B PREDATOR Fact Sheet," 2012. www.webcitation.org/66id-KJIvU?url=www.af.mil/information/factsheets/factsheet.asp?fsID=122.

United States Air Force, "MQ-9 REAPER Fact Sheet," 2015. www.af.mil/About-Us/Fact-Sheets/Display/Article/104470/mq-9-reaper/.

United States Air Force, "RQ-4 GLOBAL HAWK Fact Sheet," 2013. www.af.mil/About-Us/Fact-Sheets/Display/Article/104516/rq-4-global-hawk/.

United States Army Field Manual 100-5: Operations. https://www.bits.de/NRANEU/others/amd-us-archive/fm100-5%2893%29.pdf

United States Army John F. Kennedy Special Warfare Center, *Special Operations and International Studies Political Military Analysis Handbook*, Fort Bragg, NC: John F. Kennedy Special Warfare and School: Regional Studies Course, 2003.

United States Army, Training Circular 3-09.81 Manual Cannon Gunnery, https://armypubs.army.mil/epubs/DR_pubs/DR_a/pdf/web/tc3_09x81.pdf.

United States Department of Homeland Security. Homeland Infrastructure Threat & Risk Analysis Center. *Strategic Sector Assessment: U.S. Aviation (May 2006)*. Released on January 29, 2007 in accordance with Freedom of Information Act request. Washington, D.C., 2006.

United States Department of Transportation Federal Aviation Administration (FAA), Aircraft Registry: Register an Aircraft, 2018. www.faa.gov/licenses_certificates/aircraft_certification/aircraft_registry/register_aircraft/.

United States Department of Transportation, Federal Aviation Administration (FAA), Airworthiness Certification of Unmanned Aircraft Systems and Optionally Piloted Aircraft, Order 8130.43B, 2011. www.faa.gov/documentLibrary/media/Order/8130.34B.pdf.

United States Department of Transportation Federal Aviation Administration (FAA), Automatic Dependent Surveillance Broadcast (ADS-B), 2019. https://www.govinfo.gov/content/pkg/FR-2019-07-18/pdf/2019-15248.pdfUnited States Department of Transportation, Federal Aviation Administration (FAA), Become a Pilot, 2013. www.faa.gov/pilots/become/.

United States Department of Transportation Federal Aviation Administration (FAA), "FAA Drone Registry Tops One Million." January 10, 2018. www.transportation.gov/briefing-room/faa-drone-registry-tops-one-million.

United States Department of Transportation Federal Aviation Administration (FAA), NextGen Implementation Plan, 2018. https://www.faa.gov/sites/faa.gov/files/2022-06/NextGen_Implementation_Plan_2018-19%20(1).pdf/.

United States Department of Transportation Federal Aviation Administration (FAA), Let's Talk About the FAA Drone Registration FAQs, 2018. https://drone-registration.net/drone-registration-faqs/?msclkid=3493ed252d3c112e99edb00861bdef2f&utm_source=bing&utm_medium=cpc&utm_campaign=Drone%20Registraton%20NEW&utm_term=%2Bregister%20%2Buav&utm_content=Drone%20Registration.

United States Department of Transportation, Federal Aviation Administration (FAA), Statement by Ellwell, D. Unmanned Aircraft Systems Integration: Emerging Uses in A Changing National Airspace, 2017 https://transportation.house.gov/uploadedfiles/2017-11-29_-_elwell_testimony.pdf

United States Department of Transportation, Federal Aviation Administration (FAA), Summary of Small Unmanned Aircraft Rule (Part 107), 2016. https://b4udrone.us/faa-part-107-proposed-regulations/#:~:text=No%20operations%20are%20allowed%20in,with%20the%20required%20ATC%20permission.&text=No%20person%20may%20act%20as,No%20careless%20or%20

reckless%20operations.United States Department of Transportation, Federal Aviation Administration (FAA), UAS Sightings Report. 2019, www.faa.gov/uas/resources/public_records/uas_sightings_report/.

United States Department of Transportation, Federal Aviation Administration (FAA), UAV Preflight Checklist, https://www.faa.gov/forms/index.cfm/go/document.information/documentid/1027892.

United States Department of Transportation, Federal Motor Carrier Safety Administration (FMCSA), Analysis and Information Online: Crash Statistics, Large Trucks and Buses, Driver Citations Issue, 2019. https://www.fmcsa.dot.gov/safety/data-and-statistics/large-truck-and-bus-crash-facts-2019.

United States Department of Transportation, Federal Motor Carrier Safety Administration (FMCSA), Pocket Guide to Large Truck and Bus Statistics, 2018. www.fmcsa.dot.gov/sites/fmcsa.dot.gov/files/docs/safety/data-and-statistics/413361/fmcsa-pocket-guide-2018-final-508-compliant-1.pdf.

United States Navy, "MQ-8 FIRE SCOUT Fact Sheet," 2009. https://www.esd.whs.mil/Portals/54/Documents/FOID/Reading%20Room/Selected_Acquisition_Reports/FY_2019_SARS/20-F-0568_DOC_60_MQ-8_Fire_Scout_SAR_Dec_2019_Full.pdf.

Waller, Douglas, "How the OSS Shaped the CIA and American Special OPS." *War on the Rocks*. September 30, 2015. https://warontherocks.com/2015/09/how-the-oss-shaped-the-cia-and-american-special-ops/.

Weigley, Russell F., *The American Way of War: A History of United States Military Strategy and Policy*. New York: Macmillan Publishing Co. Inc., 1973.

White, Jonathan R., *Terrorism and Homeland Security*, Fifth Edition. Belmont, CA: Thomson Wadsworth, 2006.

Yekelchyk, Serhy, "The Ukrainian Crisis: In Russia's Long Shadow," *Origins: Current Events in Historical Perspective*, Ohio State University, Vol. 7, Spring 2014. http://origins.osu.edu/article/ukrainian-crisis-russias-long-shadow.

Zinn, Cherish M., "Consequences of Iraqi De-Baathification," *Cornell International Affairs Review*, Vol. 9, No. 2, 2016. www.inquiriesjournal.com/articles/1415/consequences-of-iraqi-de-baathification.